THE JAMES BOND BEDSIDE COMPANION

Ian Lancaster Fleming. May 28, 1908–August 12, 1964. (Photo by Douglas Glass.)

□ The □
JAMES BOND
Bedside Companion

by RAYMOND BENSON

WITH AN INTRODUCTION BY
ERNEST L. CUNEO

DODD, MEAD & COMPANY □ NEW YORK

Library of Congress Cataloging in Publication Data

Benson, Raymond, 1955–
  The James Bond bedside companion.

  Bibliography: p.
  Includes index.
  1. Fleming, Ian, 1908–1964—Characters—James Bond. 2. Bond, James (Fictitious character) 3. James Bond films—History and criticism. 4. Spy stories, English—History and criticism. 5. Fleming, Ian, 1908–1964—Film adaptations. I. Title.
PR6056.L4Z58 1984   823′.914   84-4111
ISBN 0-396-08383-8
ISBN 0-396-08384-6 (pbk.)

Grateful acknowledgment is made to the following:

Quoted selections from CASINO ROYALE by Ian Fleming reprinted by permission. © Copyright 1953 by Glidrose Productions, Ltd. Copyright © renewed.

Quoted selections from LIVE AND LET DIE by Ian Fleming reprinted by permission. © Copyright 1954 by Glidrose Productions, Ltd.

Quoted selections from MOONRAKER by Ian Fleming reprinted with permission of Macmillan Publishing Co., Inc. © Copyright 1955 by Glidrose Productions, Ltd.

Quoted selections from DIAMONDS ARE FOREVER by Ian Fleming reprinted with permission of Macmillan Publishing Co., Inc. © Copyright 1956 by Glidrose Productions, Ltd.

Quoted selections from FROM RUSSIA, WITH LOVE by Ian Fleming reprinted with permission of Macmillan Publishing Co., Inc. © Copyright 1957 by Glidrose Productions, Ltd.

Quoted selections from DOCTOR NO by Ian Fleming reprinted with permission of Macmillan Publishing Co., Inc. © Copyright 1958 by Glidrose Productions, Ltd.

Quoted selections from GOLDFINGER by Ian Fleming reprinted with permission of Macmillan Publishing Co., Inc. © Copyright 1959 by Glidrose Productions, Ltd.

Quoted selections from FOR YOUR EYES ONLY by Ian Fleming reprinted with permission of Viking Penguin Inc. © Copyright 1959, 1960 by Glidrose Productions, Ltd.

Quoted selections from THUNDERBALL by Ian Fleming reprinted with permission of Viking Penguin Inc. © Copyright 1961 by Glidrose Productions, Ltd.

Quoted selections from THE SPY WHO LOVED ME by Ian Fleming reprinted with permission of Viking Penguin Inc. © Copyright 1962 by Glidrose Productions, Ltd.

Quoted selections from ON HER MAJESTY'S SECRET SERVICE by Ian Fleming reprinted by arrangement with The New American Library, Inc., New York, New York. © Copyright 1963 by Glidrose Productions, Ltd.

Quoted selections from YOU ONLY LIVE TWICE by Ian Fleming reprinted by arrangement with The New American Library, Inc., New York, New York. © Copyright 1964 by Glidrose Productions, Ltd.

Quoted selections from THE MAN WITH THE GOLDEN GUN by Ian Fleming reprinted by arrangement with The New American Library, Inc.,

New York, New York. © Copyright 1965 by Glidrose Productions, Ltd.

Quoted selections from OCTOPUSSY by Ian Fleming reprinted by arrangement with The New American Library, Inc., New York, New York. © Copyright 1962, 1963 by Ian Fleming and © Copyright 1965 by the Literary Executors of Ian Fleming deceased.

Quoted selections from COLONEL SUN by Robert Markham reprinted with permission of Glidrose Publications, Ltd. © Copyright 1968 by Glidrose Productions, Ltd.

Quoted selections from THRILLING CITIES by Ian Fleming reprinted with permission of Glidrose Publications, Ltd. © Copyright 1964 by Glidrose Productions, Ltd.

Quoted selections from LICENSE RENEWED by John Gardner reprinted with permission of The Putnam Publishing Group. © Copyright 1981 by Glidrose Publications, Ltd.

Quoted selections from FOR SPECIAL SERVICES by John Gardner reprinted with permission of The Putnam Publishing Group. © Copyright 1982 by Glidrose Publications, Ltd.

Quoted selections from ICEBREAKER by John Gardner reprinted with permission of The Putnam Publishing Group. © Copyright 1983 by Glidrose Publications, Ltd.

Quoted selections from THE JAMES BOND DOSSIER by Kingsley Amis reprinted with permission of Jonathan Cape, Ltd. © Copyright 1965 by Kingsley Amis.

Quoted selections from THE LIFE OF IAN FLEMING by John Pearson reprinted with permission of Jonathan Cape, Ltd. © Copyright 1966 by John Pearson and R. C. & C. (Authors), Ltd.

Quoted selections from THE NOËL COWARD DIARIES edited by Graham Payn and Sheridan Morley reprinted with permission of George Weidenfeld & Nicolson, Ltd. and Little, Brown and Co. © Copyright 1982 by Graham Payn.

Quoted selections from JAMES BOND IN THE CINEMA by John Brosnan reprinted by permission of A. S. Barnes & Co., Inc. © Copyright 1981 by A. S. Barnes & Co., Inc.

Quoted selection from "007's Oriental Eyefuls" by Roald Dahl reprinted by permission of Playboy Magazine. © Copyright 1967 by Roald Dahl.

Quoted selections from Bondage Magazine reprinted by permission. © Copyright 1979, 1980, 1981 by the James Bond 007 Fan Club.

The James Bond Bedside Companion
was written in memory of Ian Lancaster Fleming,
for whom the world was not enough.
It is dedicated to my father
(who made the mistake of taking me to *see Goldfinger* when I was nine),
and to my English "aunt," who made much of this possible.

Contents

☐
ACKNOWLEDGMENTS

Among the many people who have helped shape this book, I must first thank those on the business side: Patricia Berens, Peter Janson-Smith, Norman Kurz, Ruth Pollack, Maryann Richichi, Eric Roper, Haydee Santiago, Miriam Spaulding, Cynthia Vartan, Victoria Woods, and Lydia Zelaya.

For certain photographic material, I owe gratitude to John Bianchi, Fred Cantey, Paul Dantuono, Morris L. Hallowell III, Pamela Cunningham Hampton, Giorgio Levi, Marna Libbey, Bob McGee, Steven Jay Rubin, Pete Sansone, Richard Schenkman, Rick Sylvester, Michael Van Blaricum, the Lilly Library of Indiana University, and especially Mary Slater.

A great deal of appreciation goes to Kingsley Amis, Clare Blanshard, John Brosnan, Ivar Bryce, Josephine Bryce, Naomi Burton, Iain Campbell, Lady Mary Clive, Kenneth Corden, Violet Cummings, Ernest Cuneo, John Gardner, Robert Harling, Al Hart, Kevin McClory, Fionn Morgan, and John Pearson.

Finally, on a personal basis, I must thank George Almond, Andy East, Janet Kroll, Doug McGrath, Kenneth Siegel, Richard Schenkman and the James Bond 007 Fan Club, everyone at Technimetrics, Inc. (for their tolerance), my supportive parents, and all my friends who have been behind the project, especially James Goodner and Stuart Howard, whose encouragement, enthusiasm, and advice I couldn't have done without.

The author and publisher wish to express their deep gratitude to Glidrose Publications, Ltd. for permission to use quoted material from the James Bond novels.

INTRODUCTION

Ian Fleming was of the twentieth century and indeed, his creation, James Bond, who emerged full blown from his imagination as a Greek God from the brow of Zeus, may be one of the twentieth century's landmarks. The twentieth century marked the conflux of divergent forces, and a number of these forces converged within Ian Fleming. Typical of twentieth-century artists, Ian Fleming was many people, and indeed, some of the most pointed anecdotes of the century can be applied to him. Thus, in a debate with George Bernard Shaw, Graham Wallas read two contrary opinions by Shaw, adding sarcastically, "I suggest that on different occasions, Mr. Shaw speaks like two different people!" "What?" screamed the red-headed Irishman leaping from his seat. "Only two?!"

Ian Fleming was the warmest kind of friend, a man of ready laughter, and a great companion (everything James Bond is not!). Fleming was really quite simple to understand, but only within the complex class structure of the British civilization into the upper stratum of which he was born. He was not English; he was a Scot by his father's line, only third generation in a class structure which reserves its highest accolades for the peerage. Ian was not a peer of the realm nor were any members of his family. He was the second son of a second son. This explains much of Ian Fleming's basic drive. One night at the White House, President Franklin D. Roosevelt, no admirer of the British caste system,

questioned Prime Minister Winston Churchill about the rule of primogeniture, whereby the first-born gets everything and the others nothing. "Mr. President," Churchill said, ". . . in Great Britain, the first son gets all and thus keeps the family capital intact. The other children, witnessing and indeed sharing in the benefits, though not the ownership of the good things of life, are determined to acquire them for themselves, to go out and dig for it. In the digging out of their fortunes, they lay the foundations of our empire." (Having made his point, Churchill grandly added, with his captivating twinkle, "Moreover, the first son, being heavily endowed, marries not for money, but for beauty, which, Mr. President, accounts for my good looks!") This, it seemed to me, was the basic drive of Ian Fleming: money. He was brought up on the good things the British privileged class counts as its birthright, and actually, he was never without them as long as he lived.

Fleming was regarded by many as sombre. It is a wonder he was able to smile at all. His father was killed during the First World War when Ian was nine. His brother Michael was killed in action in World War II as were many of his Eton friends. Thus, by the time he was thirty-seven, his life had been deeply affected by the two worst wars in the history of the United Kingdom. Fleming saw that though victor in both wars, the British Empire was dying of its wounds, suffering a hemorrhage of its capital as well as its blood. The effect on him was something akin to the gloom Nelson might have felt at Trafalgar had he been forced to watch his fleet defeated. Fleming felt it deeply. Furthermore, his personal fortunes were closely tied to the fate of his country. He desperately wanted to make money, big money, in the style of the banking house of Fleming founded by his grandfather. But, when the chips were down, he was as certainly Etonian as a West Pointer is a West Pointer: he sought no fate better than that of his country; he was more deeply troubled about England's future than his own.

Kierkegaard made a profound impression on Fleming, and to a certain considerable extent, his own life experience paralleled Kierkegaard's. One aphorism of Kierkegaard's had particular application to both Ian and his wife: "Rather well hanged, than ill-wed."

There were four things of which Solomon himself said he knew nothing and one of them was "the way of a man with a maid." Ian was an experienced man when he met Anne. She was twice married before, when, née Anne Charteris, she was widowed as Lady O'Neill when Lord O'Neill was killed in action in Italy. She then married Lord Rothermere, one of Great Britain's press lords, and divorced him to marry Ian. In all human affairs, luck is an intangible factor. From an objective standpoint, luck is without blame. By almost any count, the Flemings' marriage was ill-fated from the first. There is evidence that Anne and Ian did not drift apart; they tore each other apart instead.

Both moved in top-drawer Mayfair: Maugham, Coward, and the satellite world of heartless literati. The Flemings, particularly Anne, were very close to Prime Minister Eden, much as the American jet set was close to President Kennedy. It was a fast, slippery track. It is worth mentioning that both Prime Minister Eden and President Kennedy came a cropper on it, as did Fleming, his son Caspar, and eventually Anne. However, it would be fatuous to suggest there was any causal relationship. All one can do is note that whatever his literary existence, James Bond appears as an evil talisman in the very real lives of people in his periphery. Eden's illness and his fleeing to Fleming's place, Goldeneye, has an overtone of *Appointment in Samara*. Jack Kennedy, professing his preference for James Bond, certainly imitated him to a degree no President had even remotely approached before. President Kennedy's death duel with Cuba's Castro has James Bond overtones.

I had thought I knew Ian Fleming thoroughly, in and out. Thus, I was surprised, and a trifle miffed with Ian, when I read John Pearson's book on Fleming. I was amazed to learn that Fleming had not graduated from either Eton or Sandhurst, which he certainly permitted and even encouraged me to believe. In fact, he even told me that on graduation from Sandhurst, he had selected the Black Watch as his regiment. I was also under the impression he left the Foreign Service for journalism. Actually, he had not; he never belonged to it. I was annoyed also, because his broken nose led me to believe that he had taken terrific physical punishment during his athletic years. I assumed his broken nose was acquired in amateur boxing or one of the collision sports. Once, however, when we playfully squared off, I perceived that he hadn't the slightest notion of the conventional boxing stance. "Egads," I said to him, "no wonder you've got a busted nose!" There is a certain intrinsic knowledge gained from physical damage which can only be learned by experience, which most civilians never learn, and never have to. Those who do experience it form a sort of freemasonry, a brotherhood, as it were, of those who have been badly hit, knocked unconscious, and managed to come back to life. This group was called by an appellation of the Old Frontier: "Fighting Men." I assumed that Fleming was a Fighting Man. Fighter he was, but a Fighting Man he was not: he was a very badly wounded civilian, both in life and in love. He lived a hard emotional life, because unlike Fighting Men, he never emotionally accepted death—especially of his ideal love.

It is my belief and experience that most British and American boys receive a terrible emotional mauling in their first love affair because of the chivalry and Boy Scout ideals with which they are indoctrinated shortly after they can read: the Knights of Old, King Arthur, Sir Galahad. It seemed to me that Fleming was too badly wounded in his first love to talk about it. But I sensed there was some lissome, ivory-skinned girl with blue-black hair—for this is what he considered to be the ultimate type of beauty—off in some fir-clad hills in the idyllic Alpine snowlands, who was the cause of his deep wound. It seems to me that James Bond embodies Ian's revenge for the terrible hurt; Bond tumbles them into bed, leaves them with the memory of a savage ravishment which, ye gods, leaves them pining for Bond and forever bereft without him. This, of course, is the exact opposite of the ethereal "pure" love of the adolescent English and American boy. I think it is possible that Ian carried the image of the ideal damsel throughout his life, and found his adult ideal in Anne; that Anne was the ideal superwoman, the super-sophisticate, the toast of Mayfair, and the

Madame de Stael of statesmanship and empires. This society is a twentieth-century version of *Vanity Fair*. It is dangerous, a maelstrom of descending disaster, and Anne and Ian got into its swirl when they were both old enough to know better. I suppose it is more accurate to say, she was already caught in it and he jumped in after her.

There is one thing, I think, that marks Ian's *modus operandi*: he mastered whatever he undertook. He was a first-class journalist, a magnificent administrator, a most excellent wordsmith, a writer who created his opposite, an upper-class knave, in Bond, an elegant cad, an amoral bastard, who performed every kind of crime, and with Ian's final, wry revenge on his class— of all things—in the service of Their Britannic Majesties! What a bitter twist!

Gresham's Law of the Twentieth Century is applicable to fields far wider than economics. Like bad currency, bad literature is driving out the good. If this be so, Ian Fleming's James Bond certainly gave the Gresham's Law of Literature a grand shove into the spotlight. Ian Fleming knew exactly what he was trying to do. Not the slightest presumption of innocence attaches to either his effort or the character of James Bond. His objective was the making of money. It made him a lot, but, ironically, not nearly as much as it made for others after his death. James Bond is no Sherlock Holmes, but as long as sexual fantasy exists (and it

has existed from the Pompeiean friezes through *Fanny Hill*), James Bond will live on as a Popeye the Sailorman, a combination of the supermale and the Little Jack Horner of the Intelligence Services, who from here to eternity, will stick in his thumb and pull out a plum and say what a smart boy am I. Actually, in even the flaming character of Bond it can be seen that Ian Fleming was a great wordsmith and most excellent writer.

It so stunned me to find out that Ian hadn't graduated from Eton and Sandhurst, that I examined the pattern of his departures. There was a curious twist: he did not drop out until he had met the challenge. He had mastered the course but refused to cross the finish line. Having demonstrated he could win, he threw in his hand. That's what he probably did with his life: at the end, in pain, tired, and disillusioned, he said, "The hell with it, it's a bore. I've proven I can play the hand, I've won the pot—and now you can keep it." James Bond, who, in the novels, is often stricken with the malady of ennui, would probably have done the same thing had he been a real person. After all, what could be more ridiculous than a seventy-five-year-old James Bond?

Ernest L. Cuneo
Washington, D.C.

AUTHOR'S NOTE

Primary reference sources for Parts One and Two were John Pearson's *The Life of Ian Fleming* and personal interviews conducted with several of Fleming's close friends and associates. Parts Three and Four draw from the novels. There is an abundance of quoted material from the books; hopefully, these "clips" will serve as a collection of memorable passages—"The Best of Bond," so to speak. Primary reference sources for Part Five were John Brosnan's *James Bond in the Cinema,* Steven Jay Rubin's *The James Bond Films, Bondage* Magazine (published by the James Bond 007 Fan Club),

and, of course, the films themselves. Finally, much trivia and information throughout the book was contributed by members of the James Bond 007 Fan Club and other Bond fans around the world.

To avoid confusion, all James Bond book titles and other books by Ian Fleming mentioned in the text are shown in small caps (GOLDFINGER), and all film and other book titles are italicized (*Goldfinger*).

□ ONE □
The James Bond Phenomenon

An early publicity shot of Ian Fleming, circa 1954. (Photo courtesy of owner.)

THE FIFTIES

The James Bond phenomenon began one sunny morning in Jamaica as Ian Fleming pondered what to name the hero of a novel he was writing. Fleming said that he wanted "the dullest name he could find," and he discovered it on his coffee table. One of his favorite books, *Birds of the West Indies,* was written by an ornithologist named James Bond. Promptly christening his hero, Fleming began the novel which would change the direction of British spy literature.

It was January 1952. Ian Fleming was Foreign Manager for Kemsley Newspapers, the huge organization which owned the London *Sunday Times* and dozens of other newspapers throughout Britain. He had accepted the job in 1945 with the special condition that he be allowed two months paid vacation per year. Since the war, Fleming had spent those two months every year at his retreat in Oracabessa, Jamaica. The three-bedroom house was called "Goldeneye," which he had named after one of his favorite American novels, Carson McCullers' *Reflections in a Golden Eye.* "Goldeneye" was also a code name for a wartime operation conceived and led by Fleming while he was Assistant to the Director of Naval Intelligence. (A personality sketch and detailed account of Fleming's life prior to 1952 appears in Part Two.)

This particular January, Ian Fleming's mind was on a number of matters; of most importance was his upcoming marriage to Anne Rothermere, whose divorce from Lord Esmond Rothermere was to be announced on February 8. Fleming had been a confirmed bachelor all his life. There are several possible explanations for his decision to write his first novel, but the reason he gave was to relieve his mind from "the shock of getting married at the age of forty-three." Another reason could be that he was simply tired of being "Peter Fleming's younger brother." Though Ian Fleming was a journalist, he had never written anything longer than an article for the *Sunday Times.* Peter Fleming was already a well respected author, and up to this point, Ian Fleming had avoided competing with him.

For whatever reason, Fleming needed a distraction. It was Anne who suggested he write something to amuse himself. The atmosphere at Goldeneye provided the perfect conditions. Amuse himself is precisely what he did. The book that Ian Fleming wrote in 1952 was CASINO ROYALE, the first adventure featuring a secret agent named James Bond.

At Goldeneye, Fleming initiated his standard operating procedure for writing the Bond books. Each day he rose about 7:30 a.m. and swam in his private cove. After returning for breakfast, his favorite meal of the day, he relaxed until 10:00 a.m. Then he would begin to type, using folio paper (forty-four lines to a

Goldeneye, Oracabessa, Jamaica. Ian Fleming built his winter retreat in 1945 and spent every January and February there until his death in 1964. (Photo by Mary Slater.)

full page, double-spaced). (Sometimes the paper would slip in the typewriter on the last line, invariably causing the row of words to slope down to the right.) Fleming composed at the typewriter as he worked. He finished around noon, after which he would sun himself or go snorkeling among the coral. After an afternoon nap, Fleming resumed work at the typewriter for about an hour. A day's work produced about 2,000 words. Next came supper, and afterwards, perhaps a relaxing visit from an island neighbor (such as Noël Coward). The next day the entire routine would be repeated, and so on, until the 70 to 80,000 words were on paper. Fleming never looked back at what he'd written. He emphasized that it was important to keep the plot *moving,* and by dashing through the first draft in this way, he created the "sweeping" quality of the James Bond novels. Only when he stopped over in New York or returned to England would he look over his manuscript and revise, polish, and embellish. Using a ballpoint pen, he corrected words and passages. Sometimes he added inserts written in longhand on pieces of personal stationery. During the following months, he would add the rich detail associated with the Bond books, title the chapters, and finally turn in the finished manuscript to his publishers, Jonathan Cape, Ltd., in the fall.

Unlike the rest of his novels, CASINO ROYALE was written entirely from Fleming's own personal experiences and imagination. For instance, Fleming used his impressions of the casinos at Le Touquet and Deauville in Northern France for the background of Royale-les-Eaux. The camera-bomb trick, in which two hit men are blown up by their own bomb, was used by the Russians in an assassination attempt on von Papen in Ankara during World War II. In this particular instance, all the detail Fleming needed was already in his head. The only corrections that were required dealt with grammar, word choice, and spelling. (He had spelled Bond's gun "Biretta" instead of "Beretta.") The CASINO ROYALE manuscript was 238 pages long.

When the novel was completed, it was time to return home. But before they left Jamaica, Anne Rothermere became Mrs. Ian Fleming in Port Maria's town hall on March 24. Noël Coward and his secretary were witnesses.

Fleming kept his book a secret for the first few weeks after returning to England. There was the job at Kemsley House to attend to, and he had just accepted a tempting proposition. His lifelong friend, Ivar Bryce, and perhaps his closest American friend, Ernest Cuneo, had recently acquired the North American Newspaper Alliance. While Fleming was stopping over at Bryce's

country home in Vermont, Cuneo and Bryce offered him the position of European vice president. Never one to be idle, Fleming agreed to it and found time to perform his functions for Kemsley House as well as for NANA.

On May 12, Fleming was back in England again, and was having lunch with his old friend, poet/novelist William Plomer. Fleming had known Plomer since the thirties when he wrote him a fan letter. Plomer also happened to be a reader for the prestigious publishing house, Jonathan Cape, Ltd. During their conversation, Fleming asked Plomer a curious question. "How does one get cigarette smoke out of a woman once you've got it in?" Fleming went on to explain that the word "exhale" somehow did not describe the act properly. Plomer realized that Fleming had been writing a book. He implored Fleming to show it to him, and a month later, the author gave Plomer the manuscript of CASINO ROYALE to read. Fleming was very humble about the entire matter and acted as if he was ashamed of what he'd written.

But Fleming knew he had tapped something within himself by writing the book. It had been a shot of adrenalin, and now nothing could stop him. He was suddenly excited by the prospect of becoming a thriller writer and following in the footsteps of authors he admired: Raymond Chandler, Eric Ambler, Georges Simenon, among others. On May 17, a month before he gave Plomer his manuscript, an enthusiastic and confident Fleming ordered a gold-plated typewriter from the Royal Typewriter Company in New York. Ivar Bryce brought it over on his next trip to England. In jest, Fleming wrote to Kemsley House's New York representative that since he was unsure what type of paper should be used in a golden typewriter, he was ordering his "personal goatherds in Morocco" to manufacture a thousand "sheets of vellum." These would then be sent to Cartier to be "studded with diamonds." He went on to say that if this did not signify that he was a "writer of distinction," then perhaps he could use his "own blood as ink" to round off the picture! It is fitting that Ian Fleming completed his first novel on a golden typewriter. By purchasing it, he demonstrated his belief in himself as a novelist.

After reading CASINO ROYALE, William Plomer promptly passed it to Cape's other reader, Daniel George. Both Plomer and George were extremely impressed with the novel; they strongly recommended its publication to Jonathan Cape. Cape had also known Fleming since the thirties, and had published some of Peter Fleming's works. The verdict was that CASINO

Ian Fleming and the desk at which he wrote all of the James Bond novels. Behind him is a treasured collection of Vienna Riding School paintings. (Photo by Mary Slater.)

The original dust jacket cover from the first British edition of CASINO ROYALE, published by Jonathan Cape, Ltd. in 1953. Ian Fleming devised the cover himself. (Photo courtesy of Lilly Library, Indiana University, Bloomington, Indiana. Reprinted by permission of Jonathan Cape, Ltd.)

Productions, and Fleming became a director. Glidrose became the "James Bond Company" and was the owner of the copyright to the novels. During the last months of 1952, the Flemings bought a beautiful Regency house in Victoria Square. The year was one of fresh starts for Ian Fleming: he had a new wife; a new son; the prospect of a new career with his friends Bryce and Cuneo; a new house; and a new life ahead of him as the creator of James Bond.

In January of 1953, Ian and Anne Fleming flew to New York, then took the Silver Meteor to St. Petersburg, Florida. Fleming wanted to research a worm factory located there for his next book. From Tampa, the couple flew to Jamaica, where Ian Fleming wrote the second James Bond novel, provisionally titled THE UNDERTAKER'S WIND. It was changed to LIVE AND LET DIE, and the book contained locations in New York, Florida, and Jamaica.

The original manuscript for LIVE AND LET DIE went through many changes and revisions. One paragraph that was deleted was at the end of the novel after Solitaire's line, "What about my back?" Fleming had Bond reach his hand down Solitaire's pajama top and tell her that her back must get well soon because she'll never know when she may need it! Also, in the original manuscript, Felix Leiter does not survive the shark attack and is dead when Bond finds him in their Florida hotel. Naomi Burton, Fleming's American agent with Curtis Brown, Ltd., later protested the killing of such a fine character, and, perhaps at her insistence, Fleming eventually allowed Leiter to live. Instead of having both arms, a leg, most of his stomach, and part of his face missing, Leiter just lost one arm, half a leg, and received minor face lacerations.

After leaving Jamaica with the first draft of a novel, Fleming sometimes allowed select friends other than William Plomer to read the non-revised version. Clare Blanshard, who had been a close friend of his since their days in Naval Intelligence during World War II and was now the New York representative for Kemsley Newspapers, read LIVE AND LET DIE in one night, and at Fleming's request, made a list of comments. Fleming also managed to persuade Ms. Blanshard to research barracuda teeth for him at the New York Public Library.

On April 13, 1953, CASINO ROYALE was published. The first printing amounted to 4,750 copies, and was sold out by May. Today copies are extremely rare and are worth hundreds of dollars apiece. There was a

ROYALE would be published if revisions were made. Fleming set to work immediately, and by the end of August, the final manuscript was submitted to Plomer.

Coincidentally, Anne Fleming gave birth that same August to a son, Caspar Robert, and Ian Fleming, to his own surprise, was enjoying marriage and fatherhood. And in October of 1952, Jonathan Cape accepted CASINO ROYALE for publication in April of the following year. Contracts were signed, and a series of James Bond novels was projected. With the lucrative forecast of fame and fortune and the responsibilities of supporting a family in front of him, Fleming bought a company to ease the tax burdens he was likely to assume as a successful novelist. It was called Glidrose second printing in May of 1953, and a third in May of 1954. The original jacket was devised by Fleming himself, and consisted of nine "bleeding" hearts on a grey background with the words CASINO ROYALE in gold and an inscription, "a whisper of love, a whisper of hate," in the middle of the pattern of hearts. The jacket was later re-designed by Pat Marriott.

The fact that CASINO ROYALE was published by Jonathan Cape, who hadn't really delved into the suspense genre before, gave the book a certain prestige and when the reviews came out, Fleming had a critical winner. The *Times Literary Supplement* said that "Mr. Ian Fleming's first novel is an extremely engaging affair," and that he might become the best new thriller writer since Eric Ambler." R. D. Charques in the *Spectator* said, ". . . lively, most ingenious in detail, on the surface as tough as they are made and charmingly well-bred beneath, nicely written and except for a too ingeniously sadistic bout of brutality—very entertaining reading."

Many of Fleming's friends liked it as well. Somerset Maugham and Paul Gallico both praised the work, and suddenly he was being compared to Peter Cheyney and others. The royalties from the book didn't amount to as much as he'd hoped, but Fleming looked forward to the prospect of an American sale. That spring, Fleming became a client of Curtis Brown, Ltd. in New York. His agent, Naomi Burton, was struck by the card game in the story, which she felt was "frightfully excitingly written." She offered the book to three publishers, Doubleday, Norton, and Knopf, all of whom rejected it.

While CASINO ROYALE was making the rounds with American publishers, Ian and Anne traveled to the South of France in April on behalf of Kemsley House to observe Jacques Cousteau salvaging a Graeco-Roman galley. Buried treasure fascinated Fleming, and indeed, the plot of LIVE AND LET DIE had to do with a pirate hoard of seventeenth-century gold coins. Three articles Fleming wrote on the Cousteau expedition for the *Sunday Times* show his mastery of describing the underwater world. The Cousteau experience no doubt gave Fleming a great deal of the detail he needed to fill out LIVE AND LET DIE.

When Fleming returned to New York in May, Naomi Burton introduced him to Al Hart at Macmillan Publishing Co. Hart read CASINO ROYALE and was struck by its "sheer readability." Macmillan made an offer, and the novel was scheduled for early 1954. Al Hart edited the first six Bond novels in America, and became

a good friend and drinking companion to Fleming whenever he was in New York. By the end of 1953, the James Bond snowball was beginning to grow.

The beginning of 1954 found Ian and Anne traveling again to Jamaica for their two months leave. Ian arrived with a temperature and flu, but nevertheless began writing the third Bond opus, MOONRAKER. He apparently had some trouble naming this one, for he alternated between two working titles, MONDAYS ARE HELL and HELL IS HERE. MOONRAKER was a much lower-key story than the previous two, and Fleming had doubts about it. In jest, he wrote to Clare Blanshard in New York that he wasn't sure about the book yet because there "was no sex in the first 30,000 words!" The ending to the novel underwent many changes. The first draft featured Gala Brand (the heroine) taking a month's leave in France with Bond, after they both receive the Queen's award of the George Cross. One revision featured only Gala receiving the award, with the two of them still running away together. A further revision found Gala opting to remain in England to marry a "Peter Bruce." In the final version, Gala is engaged to "Detective Inspector Vivian," and Fleming, for once, did not end his story with a girl in James Bond's arms.

On March 23, CASINO ROYALE was published in the United States by Macmillan. The book went virtually

The author takes a look at the first American edition of his first novel, CASINO ROYALE. (Photo by Maurey Garber.)

unnoticed. Actually, Ian Fleming had little success in America until 1961, when President Kennedy stated that he was a James Bond fan. In the fifties, Fleming was successful primarily in England, where James Bond had a sizable following. But even the British were slow to catch on, and it wasn't until two or three years later that the books began selling at a rate sufficient to make the literary world sit up and take notice.

Save for a few noted exceptions, the U.S. reviews for CASINO ROYALE were not particularly flattering. Anthony Boucher, in the *New York Times Book Review,* began what became long-standing complaints against Fleming by saying that the writer "pads the book out to novel length, leading to an ending which surprises no one but Bond himself." But on the positive side, Boucher credited the author for the gambling sequence:

Mr. Fleming, in a style suggesting a more literate version of Cheyney's "Dark" series, manages to make baccarat completely clear even to one who's never played it and produces as exciting a gambling sequence as I've ever read.

Sergeant Cuff, in *Saturday Review,* stated that CASINO ROYALE was a "fine thriller by a new hand." *Time* said that "Author Fleming keeps his incidents and characters spinning through their paces like juggling balls."

However, the real problem was not the reviews, but the sales. The first edition of CASINO ROYALE came and went in America, and James Bond was off to a disappointing start.

On April 8, 1954, LIVE AND LET DIE was published by Jonathan Cape in the United Kingdom. The attractive jacket was scarlet with the title in large yellow letters. On the spine was an Edward IV gold rose noble coin. The jacket was again designed by Fleming. LIVE AND LET DIE received very good reviews in England. The *Times Literary Supplement* stated that "Mr. Ian Fleming is without a doubt the most interesting recent recruit among thriller-writers." It went on to say that Fleming's second novel "fully maintains the promise of his first book," and that he wrote "wincingly well." *Time & Tide* said the book was "a snorter—from first word to last." The book was an immediate bestseller, and today this first edition, too, is both valuable and difficult to find.

By June of 1954, the British edition of CASINO ROYALE had sold over 8,000 copies. In the United States, despite poor sales of a mere 4,000 copies, Popular Library bought paperback rights to the book and published it under the title, YOU ASKED FOR IT. Apparently, it was thought that American readers wouldn't know how to pronounce "Royale."

LIVE AND LET DIE sold out its 7,500 first printing, and was reprinted. It was around this time that film companies and producers began to be interested in James Bond. Sir Alexander Korda asked to see an advance copy of LIVE AND LET DIE, but later returned it. Then the Columbia Broadcasting System offered Fleming $1,000 to do a one-hour television adaptation of CASINO ROYALE. The deal was made through Curtis Brown in New York, and James Bond would make a "live" debut in America that October.

Fleming then began thinking about his next novel, which was to deal with diamond smuggling. Fleming never hesitated to enlist the help of experts in their fields for background material to his books. In this instance, he contacted an old Etonian friend, Philip Brownrigg, a senior executive of De Beers, one of the largest and wealthiest diamond merchants in the world. Brownrigg arranged for Fleming to visit the London Diamond Club to observe the cutting, polishing, and trading of stones. Brownrigg also introduced Fleming to Sir Percy Sillitoe, head of the Diamond Corporation's security organization created especially to combat illicit diamond trade. Sillitoe was a former head of M.I. 5, the cover title given to British Security Service (which is responsible for counterespionage). Of course, Fleming and Sillitoe took to each other immediately, and the two men worked together again a couple of years later on the story of Sillitoe's organization itself.

In July, Fleming flew to New York to attend to Kemsley business, as well as meet with Ivar Bryce and Ernest Cuneo about NANA. They stayed at the Bryces' home, Black Hole Hollow Farm in Vermont, which is not too far from the racetrack in Saratoga Springs, New York. Because Josephine Bryce had horses running, the group paid a visit to Saratoga, an experience that promptly went into DIAMONDS ARE FOREVER. It was here also that Fleming met William Woodward, Jr., a handsome millionaire who owned the famous race horse, Nashua. Woodward was the owner as well of the "Studillac" car which Fleming appropriated for Felix Leiter in his fourth novel. The Studillac was a mixed breed, a Studebaker body with a Cadillac engine, and could reach a speed of 85 m.p.h. in a matter of seconds! The Bryces remember that once when Fleming and Josephine were speeding down a country road in the Studillac, they were stopped and arrested by the highway patrol. Fortunately, the local sheriff happened to have recently read a James Bond novel and let Fleming off the hook. A few months later, William Woodward was shot by his own wife in a tragic accident; she mistook him for a burglar. DIAMONDS ARE FOREVER was dedicated to Ivar Bryce, Cuneo, and Woodward.

After the visit to Saratoga, Fleming and Cuneo decided to take a cross-country trip together. Fleming had never seen the Midwest or California, so the pair took off on the Twentieth Century Limited to Chicago. Cuneo fondly remembers that the train was already pulling into Albany before Fleming had finished instructing the steward how he wanted his martinis mixed!

In Chicago, much to Cuneo's chagrin, Fleming was intent on seeing the location of the St. Valentine's Day Massacre. Cuneo convinced him first to visit the Art Institute of Chicago, which contains some of the great Impressionist masterpieces of the world. Fleming was entranced, and when Cuneo ribbed him about the fact that it was nice to find this much "culture" on the "great American prairie," Fleming grandly declared that the pictures had no right being in Chicago! The

two men's relationship, remembers Cuneo, was one of constantly "guying" each other.

The pair took the Superchief to Los Angeles, and Cuneo again remembers that they were halfway to Iowa before the stewards had absorbed *their* instructions on how to make Ian's martinis. Because Cuneo was a friend of Errett Cord, a chief stockholder in the Santa Fe Railroad, the men gained access to the engine room. During the ride, Fleming questioned the engineer and his assistant on everything from the block-signal system to something called the "dead man control." Fleming was particularly interested in railroads, and his novels frequently contained scenes taking place on trains.

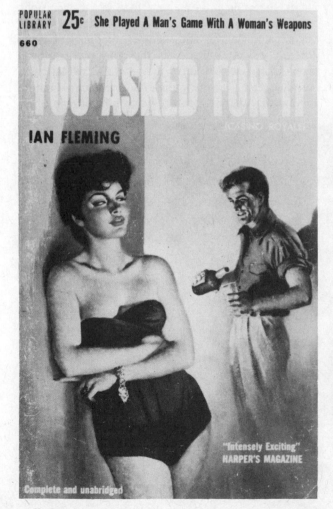

Front and back covers of the first American paperback edition of CASINO ROYALE, published in 1955. (© Copyright 1955 by Popular Library. Photo courtesy of collection of Michael Van Blaricum.)

In Los Angeles, Fleming was in heaven when he and Cuneo visited the Los Angeles Police Intelligence Headquarters. Cuneo introduced Ian and himself to Captain James Hamilton, explaining that Fleming had the "usual distorted view" all Englishmen have of America. "They believe, you know, our country is laced by organized gangs of racketeers, of tremendous wealth, and of enormous influence." The captain, to Cuneo's amazement, replied, "Don't *you?*" The captain proceeded to conduct an animated conversation with Fleming about the criminal world. He took out charts and showed the author the Mafia organizations, its discipline, and how it works. Los Angeles' detective work had been reduced to what Cuneo calls a "business machine fineness." A detective at the scene of a fresh crime could telephone the details to his office, where the information was punched on a card and run through a machine. The computer matched specific details of the crime with particulars of other cases. In this way, the detectives determined if there was a similar pattern between the new case and earlier ones. Fleming scribbled down notes on a handy pad that he carried with him at all times. Cuneo was bored by the proceedings, but Fleming was fascinated.

From Los Angeles, Fleming and Cuneo went to Las Vegas, a perfect locale for James Bond. They had hardly stepped off the plane when Fleming called to Cuneo with a "yelp of delight." He had found a coin machine from which, for a quarter, one could inhale pure oxygen for a couple of minutes. "This," Cuneo said to him, "ought to tell you all you want to know about the joint."

The pair stayed at the Sands, and went to the blackjack tables even before going to their rooms. There, Fleming met Jack Entratta, the owner of the hotel, who moved them into a better suite and offered the use of the private barbershop. Entratta and Fleming had lengthy conversations about gambling statistics and methods of cheating. The entire security system of the hotel was explained to Fleming, and he relished every word.

One evening, Cuneo told him that they would beat every joint in Las Vegas. "We started out at the Sands. I bet one dollar—one thin chip in a game of blackjack. I won $1.00. 'One down,' I said, 'We leave.' We called over a girl, took a shot of champagne, and off we went. We did the same at the Sahara, the Old Frontier, right down the strip. One buck ahead and a one buck bet, we quit, took a sip, and went on to the next joint. Whether it was the liquor or my grim intent to beat every joint, I do not know. But literally, we laughed ourselves sick. One buck ahead and we quit—grandly announcing we had beaten the house to everyone's

Barry Nelson was the first actor to portray James Bond in a one-hour television version of CASINO ROYALE on CBS' Climax Mystery Theater program in 1954. The kinescope, long forgotten and missing for years, was recently found in Chicago by film historian Jim Schoenberger. The program was "unveiled" again at a gathering in Los Angeles. Here, Nelson is interviewed by Steven Jay Rubin, author of The James Bond Films. (Photo courtesy of Steven Jay Rubin.)

amazement, took a drink and whisked out, as if there were another notch on our guns. We ended way out at Steamboat Springs, about 4:00 a.m. We went out there because we wanted no possible questioning either in our minds or anybody else's that we beat every house in Las Vegas."

Fleming used much of the material from his cross-country trip in DIAMONDS ARE FOREVER. He even named a character in the book, a Las Vegas cab driver, "Ernest Cureo." He later sent Cuneo a plain gold money-clip inscribed, "To Ernie—my guide on a trip to the Angels and back. 007."

For Fleming the final important event in 1954 was the TV showing of CASINO ROYALE in America on October 21. Presented by William Lundigan on his "Climax Mystery Theater" series (an anthology of suspense stories), the live broadcast was directed by Bretaigne Windust, adapted by Charles Bennett, and starred Barry Nelson as James Bond. Peter Lorre was cast as Le Chiffre and Linda Christian portrayed "Valerie Mathis." The basic plot of the novel was somewhat adhered to, with one major change: James Bond was portrayed as an American, and it was Felix Leiter who was British! One amusing incident took place during the live broadcast due to a technical error. After Le Chiffre's "death," the camera remained on Peter Lorre until he stood up and began to walk toward his dressing room! The presentation went, for the most part, unnoticed, and was soon forgotten. Clare Blanshard wrote Fleming a critique of the television show. She states that she "tore it to shreds," but Fleming later told her that he laughed at her comments until the tears ran down his cheeks.

In early January 1955, LIVE AND LET DIE was published in the United States by Macmillan. Again, the critics did nothing to increase Fleming's success. Anthony Boucher wrote that the "high spots are all effectively described . . . but the narrative is loose and jerky . . ." There *were* a few publications that caught on early, such as the *Springfield Republican*. Its reviewer wrote, "The narrative moves at a headlong pace, there is sheer terror enough for a month of comic books, and a climax that is truly exciting. Don't read it unless your nerves are in pretty good shape." But the book sold hardly better than its predecessor.

The American editions of Fleming's books rarely differ from their British counterparts. It is interesting to note, however, one specific change that was made in LIVE AND LET DIE. The title of Chapter Five was changed from "Nigger Heaven" to "Seventh Avenue" for obvious reasons.

In January and February of 1955, Ian Fleming wrote DIAMONDS ARE FOREVER at Goldeneye. The original manuscript, 183 pages long, went through a few changes as well. The most important one, perhaps, was that the two Spangled Mob killers were originally named Wint and Gore. One of Anne Fleming's cousins was familiarly known as "Boofy" Gore and he had objected to the use of the name. Fleming reportedly apologized and changed the name Gore to Kidd.

In March, film producer Gregory Ratoff offered to buy the film rights to CASINO ROYALE for $6,000. At this point, perhaps Fleming was a little discouraged over James Bond's poor performance. He was disappointed in the American sales, though there was still a small, but appreciative, English audience. Fleming sold the rights and promptly bought a Thunderbird. Ratoff died before he ever did anything with the property, and his widow sold it to producer/agent Charles K. Feldman. Feldman eventually made the film, as discussed later.

In April 1955, MOONRAKER was published by Jonathan Cape. The jacket, designed by Kenneth Lewis from suggestions by the author, featured an orange, white, and yellow "flame" pattern. This time, the reviews were mixed. MOONRAKER was a little different from the previous two novels, concentrating more on character than plot. The *Times* called it a "disappointment," and *The Spectator*'s John Metcalf called it "not one of Mr. Fleming's best" and said it was "further marred by a series of improbabilities." But the book received favorable reviews from *The New Statesman,* the *Daily Telegraph,* and the *Observer.* A few weeks later, when the book was published in the United States, there was a similar reaction. Anthony Boucher wrote in the *New York Times:* "I don't know anyone who writes about gambling more vividly than Fleming and I only wish the other parts of his books lived up to their gambling sequences." But Karl Brown in *Library Journal* highly recommended the book, saying that "Fleming tells his story with both ease and grace, making the cloak and dagger episodes most plausible . . ." When the book was published in paperback by Perma Books in the United States a year later, the title was curiously changed to TOO HOT TO HANDLE. This rare paperback edition is significant because it is the only English-language Bond novel that was "Americanized." Throughout the book, all British idioms were changed to American ones, for example, "lift" to "elevator," "knave of hearts" to "jack of hearts," "zebra" to "pedestrian crossing." There were also significant paragraph deletions, particularly descriptions of Eng-

An explosive mixture of gambling, danger, sex, chills and murder!

TOO HOT TO HANDLE
(MOONRAKER)

by
IAN FLEMING
Author of LIVE AND LET DIE, a writer whom the Associated Press calls "super-special...with blows below the belt the way Mickey Spillane delivers them!"

The first American paperback edition of MOONRAKER, published in 1956. Both front and back covers are shown. (© Copyright 1956 by Perma Books, Inc. Photo courtesy of collection of Michael Van Blaricum.)

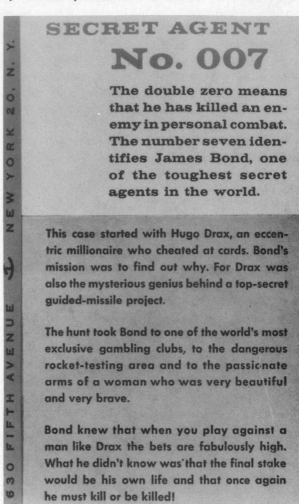

SECRET AGENT
No. 007

The double zero means that he has killed an enemy in personal combat. The number seven identifies James Bond, one of the toughest secret agents in the world.

This case started with Hugo Drax, an eccentric millionaire who cheated at cards. Bond's mission was to find out why. For Drax was also the mysterious genius behind a top-secret guided-missile project.

The hunt took Bond to one of the world's most exclusive gambling clubs, to the dangerous rocket-testing area and to the passionate arms of a woman who was very beautiful and very brave.

Bond knew that when you play against a man like Drax the bets are fabulously high. What he didn't know was that the final stake would be his own life and that once again he must kill or be killed!

lish customs or history. Fleming also added certain explanations in the form of footnotes, such as the value of the English pound in American money at the time.

In June, something happened that lifted Fleming's spirits. He had recently become friends with Raymond Chandler, and Fleming had given the writer copies of the Bond novels to read. Chandler liked Fleming's work, and offered to endorse one of the books for the benefit of Fleming's publishers. As a result, Chandler commented on LIVE AND LET DIE, saying that "Ian Fleming is probably the most forceful and driving writer of what I suppose still must be called thrillers in England." Chandler's praise greatly encouraged Fleming. When Ian Hunter, representing the Rank Organization, offered to buy film rights to MOONRAKER, Fleming asked for £10,000, which was a little over three times what was paid for CASINO ROYALE. The Rank Organization sat with the property until the spring of 1959, when Fleming bought it back.

In July, Fleming heard through his friend at Scotland Yard, Sir Ronald Howe, that an Interpol conference was being held in Istanbul. It was arranged for Fleming to attend the conference as a journalist, and in September, he journeyed with Howe to that famed city in Turkey. The trip provided experiences which went into his next book, FROM RUSSIA, WITH LOVE. In Istanbul, Fleming met an Oxford-educated shipowner named Nazim Kalkavan, who gave the author an inside view of the city. Kalkavan became the model for the character of Darko Kerim, the head of the Secret Service station in Turkey. From Istanbul, Fleming took the Simplon-Orient Express to Paris, finding it to be less romantic than he had envisioned. From there he rejoined his family at their house at St. Margaret's Bay, near Dover.

That autumn, CASINO ROYALE was published in England in paperback by Pan Books, Ltd. But Ian Fleming was tiring of James Bond, and felt that he was running out of ideas. So for his next novel, he decided to try something different and began to think about how, on the advice of Raymond Chandler, to elevate the literary merits of the Bond books.

In January and February of 1956, Ian Fleming labored with what might have been James Bond's swan song. In the front of his own copy of FROM RUSSIA, WITH LOVE, he wrote that he "took great trouble" over this particular novel. It is clearly one of the author's best. The original manuscript, 228 pages long, was heavily corrected. At the end of Chapter Nine, in which Rosa Klebb attempts to seduce Tatiana Romanova in her office/apartment, Tatiana does *not* run out of the room in a panic. Instead, the chapter ends as Klebb sits on the sofa and gestures for Tatiana to sit beside her, saying they should become better acquainted! And the final scene is altered, as Bond is *not* kicked by the poisoned blade in Rosa Klebb's shoe. Instead, he succeeds in pinning the woman down with a chair. After she is taken away by Mathis' men, Bond tells Mathis he has a date with the "most beautiful woman in SMERSH" (Tatiana). Therefore, it was after Fleming returned from Goldeneye that he decided to "kill" Bond at the end of the book.

About the time he was finishing the manuscript of his fifth novel, Fleming received a telegram invitation from Ivar Bryce to join Dr. Robert C. Murphy (American Museum of Natural History), Arthur Vernay (Bahamas Flamingo Protection Society), and Bryce in the first scientific expedition since 1916 to a flamingo colony on the island of Inagua. He couldn't resist such an invitation, and on March 15, he flew with the party to the small island in the Bahamas. The men lived in tents and roughed it as Fleming gathered material for what would be his next James Bond adventure. Inagua became the model for Dr. No's island fortress, Crab Key, and the marsh buggy on which the party rode was the germ for the "dragon" tank. It was pure adventure for Fleming.

The party stayed part of the time at the house of a family called Ericson—three brothers who were virtually "The Lords of Inagua." Inagua had a small population of about 1,000, and the Ericsons employed them all in their salt works, salt being the family's (and island's) only export. The Ericsons were originally from Boston, two brothers graduates of Harvard, the other having done graduate work at MIT. The two Audubon wardens who guided the party around the island were Bahamian brothers, Jim and Sam Nixon. The center of activity on Inagua was Matthewtown, which consisted of a few fairly solid shacks and one communal store. Fleming wrote about his experience for the *Sunday Times*. Just before dawn on the first day, the group rode out in the buggy to the flamingo colony. Fleming, Bryce, and Dr. Murphy sat in garden chairs placed on a platform of the truck. Dr. Murphy wrote in his journal that as they rode through the hot wind, "stinging particles" began hurting their faces. The truck was moving

The Inagua expedition party of 1956. Left to right: Ian Fleming, Ivar Bryce, Sam Nixon, Arthur Vernay, and Jim Nixon. Inagua served as the model for Crab Key Island in DOCTOR NO. (Photo by Dr. Robert C. Murphy, courtesy of American Philosophical Society.)

through a swarm of tiny flies. Jim Nixon warned them that if one got in an eye, it would "burn like fire." The threesome immediately donned sunglasses. Arriving at the flamingo colony, Fleming wrote that everywhere one looked there was nothing but pink. He began to appreciate even more the purpose of the expedition. The group had a good laugh as the marsh buggy rode over swarms of "wonderfully grotesque land crabs" that had been brought by the rain. Although Jim Nixon did his best to avoid hitting them, invariably one would "explode with a *plop*" under a wheel. Eventually, the party, organized by Dr. Murphy, made an approximate count of the flamingoes on the island. Fleming reported that the final estimate was 15,000; but if hurricanes (the season concurred with the mating season) happened to miss the island that year, another 5,000 would be added.

Fleming also reported that a very aged fisherman lived on the island. Two or three times each year, he would go to the local bank, which was the commissioner's office, and lay on the table a "neat pile of Spanish doubloons of the sixteenth century." After the old man received his pound notes in exchange for the treasure, he would leave as discreetly as possible. The old man died the year Fleming visited the island, and no one had ever discovered where the fisherman was getting his gold coins. Fleming presumed that perhaps Inagua held something else besides salt and flamingoes.

It is easy to see how Ian Fleming could embellish an exciting but tame adventure such as this into the background of a James Bond story. In DOCTOR NO, the flamingoes became spoonbills as Bond travels to a mysterious island to investigate an Audubon Society complaint. Fleming imaginatively turned Inagua into the dreadful island of Crab Key.

On April 4, 1956, Jonathan Cape published DIAMONDS ARE FOREVER, and the *Daily Express* bought the serial rights to the novel. The jacket was the first to be designed by Pat Marriott, who would later revise some of the earlier jackets. DIAMONDS ARE FOREVER featured the neck and shoulders of a girl in a V-neck dress, painted in orange, pink, and black. Around her neck is a pearl-shaped diamond pendant.

Most critics lauded Fleming's writing style and descriptive passages, but complained that the dialogue and characters were weak. The *Birmingham Post*, however, called it "the best thriller of the season," and Raymond Chandler particularly praised Fleming's descriptions of America. It was around this time that through Eric Ambler, Fleming was introduced to literary agent

Peter Janson-Smith. Fleming was disappointed with James Bond's performance in the international market, and Ambler suggested that the author meet his agent. Janson-Smith was successful in obtaining a Dutch publisher for the existing Bond novels on the very first day of working for Fleming. From then on the agent handled all of the author's literary negotiations for the world (excluding the United States), being appointed to the board of directors of Glidrose in 1964. He is still a director.

Also around this time, Fleming visited a health clinic called Enton Hall. His sciatica was bothering him, and the ten-day treatment not only helped that but revitalized him. He would one day use the experience in a Bond adventure called THUNDERBALL. But Fleming didn't take his doctor's advice upon returning from the clinic. Told to cut down his intake of alcohol and tobacco, Fleming showed only minute signs of cooperation. Already, his doctor wrote, Fleming's heart was going.

During this period of ill health, Fleming became disenchanted with James Bond again. He wrote to Raymond Chandler on April 27 that he personally didn't think very highly of his own books, and should perhaps take them more seriously. On May 1, Chandler replied that Fleming didn't do himself justice with Bond, and should try something of higher quality. Chandler admitted to feeling that CASINO ROYALE was still Fleming's best book. On June 22, Fleming replied, saying that he was weary with Bond and it wasn't easy guiding the character through his "tricks" in FROM RUSSIA, WITH LOVE, which he was still revising at the time. It was probably during these few weeks that Fleming decided to have Rosa Klebb kick Bond with a poison-tipped shoe at the end of the novel, leaving the reader to wonder if the secret agent was dead or not. Fleming may have wanted to do away with Bond altogether, killing him with a jarring, cynical ending. Or he might have done it with tongue in cheek, knowing full well that a resurrection was indeed possible and it would be great fun to pull such a joke on his readers. Indeed, when one fan wrote to him after the novel was published, Fleming replied, saying not to worry; if and when Bond "goes," he will do it with a "bang."

In May of 1956, a curious friendship began between Fleming and a gun expert and writer, Geoffrey Boothroyd. Boothroyd wrote to Fleming out of the blue, first explaining how much he liked the Bond books. But then he went on to complain about Bond's use of a .25 Beretta, saying that in reality it was a "lady's gun, and not a really nice lady at that." He suggested that

Bond be armed with a revolver, in particular, a Smith and Wesson .38 Centennial Airweight. Boothroyd then described his own model, which had a barrel sawed-off to 2-3/4 inches and a cutaway trigger guard for quicker shooting. He went on to suggest a Smith and Wesson .357 Magnum for long-range work, and a Berns-Martin triple-draw holster instead of Bond's chamois shoulder holster.

Fleming welcomed the criticism and suggestions, and throughout the summer of 1956, he corresponded with Boothroyd, who lived in Glasgow. Several types of guns were discussed, and Fleming was delighted at having an entirely new source for the kind of detail he loved to write into the Bond books. What he finally did was create a character called "Major Boothroyd," the Armourer, who, on M's orders, recommends that James Bond change his guns. This happens at the beginning of DOCTOR NO, after Bond has recovered from Rosa Klebb's near-lethal kick. Bond is armed with Fleming's preference, a Walther PPK in a Berns-Martin triple-draw holster, and a Smith & Wesson .38 Centennial Airweight for long-range. But Fleming must have mixed up his notes—a Berns-Martin triple-draw holster is made only for revolvers and a Walther PPK would slip out. And it was the .357 Magnum that was for long range, not the .38 Centennial model. Fleming jokingly passed the letters of complaint as to accuracy he received on to the expert from that day forward.

Boothroyd's services came in handy again when the jacket for FROM RUSSIA, WITH LOVE was devised that summer. Fleming wanted a *trompe l'oeil* style painting, and Cape hired the excellent artist, Richard Chopping. Fleming asked Boothroyd to lend him his Smith & Wesson with the sawed-off barrel so that Chopping could use it for a model. Boothroyd sent the gun, and Fleming delivered it to the painter's studio in Essex. About that time, a multiple murder took place in Glasgow, which would later become known as "the Burnside Murders." The bullets recovered from the three corpses were .38 caliber. Boothroyd, whose Smith & Wesson was registered, was visited by the police. He worriedly explained that Fleming had the gun in London and a few hours later, Fleming himself was visited by Scotland Yard. Not wanting the police to disturb the artist at work, Fleming produced his correspondence with Boothroyd and explained the situation. The police granted Fleming's request to allow Chopping to keep the gun until the painting was finished. As it happened, Chopping finished the painting the next day and promptly returned the gun. Needless to say, Boothroyd's revolver was not the murder weapon.

In June, Ivar Bryce sold his share of NANA, as he and Ernest Cuneo were planning to acquire some independent American television stations. Fleming was invited to join them. The project was eventually dropped, but Fleming continued his interests in American television when NBC producer Henry Morgenthau III approached him about collaborating on a series provisionally called "Commander Jamaica." It was to be an adventure series filmed in the Caribbean. Fleming worked on a script, which featured a character named James Gunn. The plot involved Gunn investigating an island fortress in the Caribbean where a group of criminals were believed to be deflecting missiles from Cape Canaveral from their course. The project fell apart, but Fleming later used the basic plot for DOCTOR NO.

In October, DIAMONDS ARE FOREVER came out in America. Anthony Boucher was kinder this time, saying that Fleming's "handling of America and Americans is well above the British average; as before he writes excellently about gambling; and he contrives picturesque incidents and a moderately believable love story." But Boucher went on to say that the "narrative is loose-jointed and weakly resolved . . ." In America the works of Ian Fleming were still enjoyed by only a small group.

But in November an event occurred that placed Ian Fleming's name more prominently in the press. The Prime Minister, Sir Anthony Eden, was suffering from severe exhaustion; on the advice of his doctors, he was looking for a spot to enjoy a "restful holiday." It was most likely Lady Eden, an old friend of Anne Fleming and godmother to Caspar Fleming, who suggested Goldeneye, and Fleming was eventually approached on the matter by the Secretary of State for Colonial Affairs, Mr. Alan Lennox-Boyd. On November 24, Goldeneye received its distinguished guests, but the Edens did not enjoy the peace and quiet they expected. The governor of Jamaica at the time had inspected Goldeneye and had decided that it did not befit a Prime Minister. As a result, additional servants were called into the house, despite the protests of Violet the cook. A telephone was installed, and the area was provided police protection. Anthony Eden's "private" visit was anything but private. Goldeneye was beseiged by reporters who caused Fleming some embarrassment when the *Evening Standard* revealed that Goldeneye had rat trouble. But the Prime Minister seemed to enjoy his stay anyway, and wrote to Fleming later saying so.

After Eden's visit, the sales of Fleming's books rose.

The publicity in a way foreshadowed the publicity and increased sales that resulted when another political figure, President Kennedy, in 1961, said that FROM RUSSIA, WITH LOVE was one of his ten favorite books. Late in the fall of 1956, the *Daily Express* bought the serial rights to the yet unpublished novel, and the James Bond snowball began to increase in speed and size.

The January-February stint in 1957 produced DOCTOR NO; and an examination of the original manuscript suggests it was a much easier novel for Fleming to write than FROM RUSSIA, WITH LOVE. Two hundred and six pages long, it contained less revisions than its predecessors. The first chapter was originally titled ''The Quick, Neat Job,'' rather than ''Hear You Loud and Clear,'' and Honey's last line was changed from ''Do what I tell you,'' to ''Do as you're told.''

That spring, against the advice of his friend and reader William Plomer, Fleming sold the rights for the *Daily Express* to turn James Bond into a cartoon strip. For £1,500 a novel, Fleming went for the deal, but kept a strong hand in approval of the strip for publication. CASINO ROYALE was the first book to be featured, followed by LIVE AND LET DIE, DIAMONDS ARE FOREVER, and others. The cartoon strip was enormously successful and managed, as well, to retain a level of quality faithful to Fleming's writing.

April brought another opportunity for adventure. Sir Percy Sillitoe, former head of the International Diamond Security Organization, decided to have a book written about the organization's efforts in combating illicit diamond trade. He commissioned one of his own men, an English solicitor named John Collard, to write the story. The piece that Collard wrote was shown to Denis Hamilton at the *Sunday Times,* who was impressed but thought it could use some flair. Hamilton, of course, knew Ian Fleming, and arranged for the two men to meet. A series of articles for the *Sunday Times* concerning diamond smuggling was the result, all told to Fleming by Collard (who was using a pseudonym of John Blaize).

Fleming flew to Tangier to meet Collard, and the two men spent two weeks in a hotel room fleshing out the manuscript. The articles involved the IDSO's solving of several smuggling cases. Fleming's talents as a thriller writer added that extra touch of drama to the facts which made the articles a success.

The British and American editions of FROM RUSSIA, WITH LOVE were published within weeks of each other that spring. It was an immediate success, and Richard Chopping's jacket design received special attention.

Featuring Geoffrey Boothroyd's Smith & Wesson with the sawed-off barrel and a rose, the jacket won several prizes. Chopping would design the jackets for all but one of the remaining Bond books. FROM RUSSIA, WITH LOVE received tremendous critical support as well. The *London Times* called it ''Mr. Fleming's tautest, most exciting and most brilliant tale.'' Anthony Hartley in *Spectator* said that ''Mr. Ian Fleming's latest thriller will be another shot in the arm for addicts . . .'' In America, James Sandoe of the *New York Herald Tribune Book Review* wrote that it was ''the best thriller we have had since whatever you may admire most of the admirable Ambler.'' Only Anthony Boucher of the *New York Times* was not enthusiastic, referring to it as ''a half-

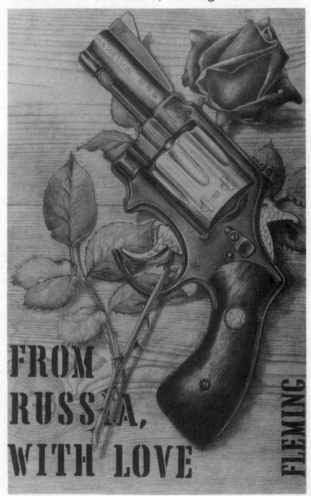

Richard Chopping's award-winning dust jacket cover to FROM RUSSIA, WITH LOVE, published by Jonathan Cape, Ltd. in 1957. (Photo courtesy of Lilly Library, Indiana University, Bloomington, Indiana. Reprinted by permission of Jonathan Cape, Ltd.)

guinea dreadful.'' FROM RUSSIA, WITH LOVE, though, is easily one of Fleming's best novels, and is still cited today as a favorite among fans.

That summer, Fleming was invited to compete in the Bowmaker Professional-Amateur golf tournament at the Berkshire Golf Club. He had loved golf most of his life, and was an avid player. He partnered the three-time Open champion Peter Thomson at the tournament, and was pleased with his performance. Fleming also frequented the Royal St. George's golf course at Sandwich, an exclusive club whose members included royalty. It was from here that Fleming pulled the background for the famous golf match between James Bond and Auric Goldfinger, that he would use in his next novel.

The diamond smuggling articles ran in the *Sunday Times* that autumn. They were published in book form by Jonathan Cape in November under the title THE DIAMOND SMUGGLERS. Fleming said that he personally felt it was a good story until all the possible libelous material was cut out. There had nearly been an injunction brought against him and the *Times* by De Beers. The book received mixed reviews on both sides of the Atlantic. Most critics lauded Fleming's skill with words, but found the book ''sketchy.'' Nevertheless, it proved to Ian Fleming that he could write something besides James Bond. And with the sales of his books beginning to skyrocket, Ian Fleming found that the Bond phenomenon was now snowballing on its own— he no longer had to push it himself.

GOLDFINGER was written at Goldeneye in January-February in 1958. This is the longest of the Bond novels, with an original typescript of 270 pages. Its working title was THE RICHEST MAN IN THE WORLD, and the first draft was only moderately changed.

Ian Fleming suddenly became controversial that March when DOCTOR NO was published in England. The book was subjected to a vicious attack by Paul Johnson in the *New Statesman:*

The nastiest book I have ever read . . . By the time I was a third of the way through, I had to suppress my strong impulse to throw the thing away, and only continued reading because I realised that here was a social phenomenon of some importance . . . Fleming deliberately and systematically excites, and then satisfies the very worst instincts of his readers.

Bernard Bergonzi, in *Twentieth Century* magazine, also objected to the ''sex, snobbery, and sadism'' in the book. But Simon Raven in the *Spectator* defended the novel:

. . . Commander Fleming, by reason of his cool and analytical intelligence, his informed use of technical facts, his plausibility, sense of pace, brilliant descriptive powers and superb imagination, provides sheer entertainment such as I, who must read many novels, am seldom lucky to find.

The *Times Literary Supplement* noted that a lesser writer couldn't have pulled the story off. Controversy always helps, and DOCTOR NO began outselling the previous Bond novels.

The jacket, the last designed by Pat Marriott, featured a silhouette of Honeychile Rider standing among tropical plants on a brown background. It was the first novel to actually show Glidrose Productions as copyright holders as a result of the 1956 copyright act. DOCTOR NO was released in the United States in June. (In Britain the title was written DR NO, in the United States it was DOCTOR NO.) James Sandoe of the *New York Herald Tribune Book Review* said that it was ''. . . the most artfully bold, dizzyingly poised thriller of the decade. You'd much better read it than read about it.'' L. G. Offord of the *San Francisco Chronicle* said, ''This reviewer must admit that it strikes her as so wildly funny that it might almost be a leg-pull, and at the same time hair-raising in a loony way.'' True to form, Anthony Boucher continued his tirade against Fleming by saying, ''. . . it is 80,000 words long, with enough plot for 8,000 and enough originality for 800.''

In April 1958, Fleming flew to Bombay to investigate a treasure hunt in the Seychelles islands for a *Sunday Times* article. There, the French pirate Levasseur supposedly had hidden £120 million worth of gold and other booty. The treasure hunt turned out to be disappointing, but Fleming retained his impressions of the islands for the setting of a future James Bond short story entitled ''The Hildebrand Rarity.'' From there, Fleming flew to Rome to meet Anne, and the couple spent a holiday in Venice and the Lido peninsula, which provided the background for another short story, ''Risico.''

When Fleming returned to London, he discovered that CBS had made him a lucrative offer to write thirty-two James Bond episodes for television over the next two years. Fleming accepted the offer and began working on the first few outlines.

At about this time Fleming and his friend Ivar Bryce began talking about making a James Bond movie themselves. Bryce had recently gone into film production, and had formed a partnership, Xanadu Productions, with young writer/director Kevin McClory. McClory had been associate producer and foreign location director for *Around the World in Eighty Days,* and had also worked with director John Huston. He was at that time directing and producing a film called *The Boy and the Bridge,* which he had also co-scripted. Ivar Bryce had put up the money for the production.

McClory met Fleming in late winter of 1958. Bryce had asked Fleming to preview a rough cut of *The Boy and the Bridge* in his absence. Fleming liked the film very much, only complaining a bit about the sentimentality of the story. As he and McClory saw more of each other they began talking about a James Bond film. Bryce had given McClory some of Fleming's novels to read, and the writer/director, immediately grasping the cinematic potential of a character like James Bond, became excited about making a 007 picture after *The Boy and the Bridge* was completed. McClory, keen on oceanography, had written a screenplay to an underwater picture he had always planned to make someday. It followed that the Bahamas was suggested for a setting for the Bond film, especially since McClory knew the area well, and the production could also benefit from the Eady Subsidy Plan, which allowed the making of a film on a British base with American actors. It was finally agreed that Fleming and McClory would collaborate on a new story rather than adapt one of the author's existing novels. But these dreams of making the first James Bond film resulted in an unnecessary and catastrophic chapter in the lives of all parties concerned.

In January and February of 1959, Fleming took an easy route with his Bond effort, adapting to short stories four of the television outlines he had prepared for CBS. He added a fifth story which he had written the previous summer, and planned to turn in this anthology, provisionally titled THE ROUGH WITH THE SMOOTH, to Jonathan Cape that year. The original manuscript of "From a View to a Kill" was 23 pages. "For Your Eyes Only" originally titled "Man's Work," and later changed to "Death Leaves an Echo," was 34 pages. "Quantum of Solace," the story he had written after returning from the Seychelles, was 21 pages. "Risico" (originally spelled "Risiko") and "The Hildebrand Rarity" were both 31 pages. All were corrected only moderately. In "For Your Eyes Only," for example, the name of the slain Jamaican couple was Wilson, and halfway through the manuscript it was changed to Havelock. This collection, subtitled "Five Secret Occasions in the Life of James Bond," was ultimately published a year later as FOR YOUR EYES ONLY.

In March of that year, GOLDFINGER was published. Dedicated to Fleming's "gentle reader, William Plomer," the book featured another attractive jacket design by Richard Chopping—a picture of a skull with gold coins in its eye sockets and a red rose entwined in the teeth. The *Times* said: "A new Bond has emerged from these pages: an agent more relaxed, less promiscuous, less stagily muscular than of yore . . . the story, too, is more relaxed." Indeed, GOLDFINGER is the most introspective of all the Bond novels. In the United States, reviewers began to take notice. Even Anthony Boucher, this time, stated that "the whole preposterous fantasy strikes me as highly entertaining." And James Sandoe of the *New York Herald Tribune* called it a "superlative thriller from our foremost literary magician."

That spring Fleming made the decision to change both agents and publishers in the United States. He hadn't been happy with the way Curtis Brown, Ltd. handled his film rights, and wanted another agency with more Hollywood connections. Naomi Burton, his friend, agent, and reader, was also leaving the agency, so Fleming made the switch to Music Corporation of America. Phyllis Jackson represented the literary side of his work and Laurence Evans the film side. Evans immediately began working on film deals, and one of his first accomplishments was buying back the rights to MOONRAKER from the Rank Organization, which had done nothing with the property. His new American publisher was Viking Press.

Talks resumed about the production of the future James Bond film. *The Boy and the Bridge* had been selected as the official British entry to the Venice film festival, and eventually won several awards at other European festivals. Its premiere was set for July. With that promise of success, it looked as though a Bond film directed by McClory, and scripted by Fleming and McClory, would indeed be a lucrative undertaking. In May, during a weekend at Moyns Park, Bryce's home in Essex, followed by other meetings in McClory's home in London, Fleming, Bryce, McClory, and Ernest Cuneo came up with ideas for a story. It was basically a collaborative process. The first treatment featured the Russians as villains, but it was McClory who came up with the idea of using an international gang of terrorists, instead. This group was eventually called SPECTRE, the Special Executive for Counterintelligence, Terrorism, Revenge, and Extortion. Cuneo added the idea for a spectacular underwater battle at the story's climax. Over the coming months, the original outline changed and there were no fewer than ten outlines, treatments, and scripts. They had various titles, including *SPECTRE, James Bond of The Secret Service,* and *Longitude 78 West.* Henceforth, these treatments shall be collectively referred to as "The Film Scripts."

In July, when *The Boy and the Bridge* premiered, critical reaction was unfavorable, and as a result, the film did not do well at the box office. At this point, Fleming's excitement and hope for the Bond film must have begun to diminish. MCA was hinting that other production companies were interested in James Bond, and the CBS deal was still being worked out. Hubbell Robinson had made a $10,000 bid for a 90-minute TV "spectacular" of FROM RUSSIA, WITH LOVE, sponsored by the Ford Motor Co., with James Mason as Bond. (But this never came to pass.) There were, perhaps, other possibilities, and relations between Fleming and McClory began to cool. Nevertheless, on July 8, Fleming wrote to Bryce saying that in exchange for $50,000 worth of shares in "the new company," the company would have the right to make "the first full-length James Bond feature film." Fleming added that he would write a full suggested treatment which could be altered if the company wished, and that he would be on hand to provide "editorial and advisory services." In September, Fleming made the suggestion of bringing in another director, with McClory acting as producer. McClory suggested Hitchcock, but the director eventually declined the offer.

Another thing worrying Fleming was the cost factor. The projected James Bond film was going to be very expensive. Bryce had lost a fair amount of money on *The Boy and the Bridge,* and would need strong backing in order to finance the film. (According to Bryce, *The Boy and the Bridge* eventually recouped its costs.) Fleming had been advised by MCA that a more experienced director would attract the needed money from investors. By October, Fleming was spending less and less time with the project; screenwriting was not particularly his fancy, and he was becoming increasingly busy at the newspaper office. McClory, with

Fleming's approval, brought in another writer named Jack Whittingham to complete the screenplay.

Fleming was also preoccupied with changes at Kemsley House. Lord Kemsley had sold the newspapers to Roy Thomson, a Canadian, and Fleming was apprehensive he might not have the same freedom and opportunites for adventure he'd had in the past. He found, however, that his new situation at Thomson Newspapers would be just as favorable if not better. Thomson and the future *Sunday Times* editor, Denis Hamilton, asked Fleming to take a five-week trip around the world and record his impressions of several famous cities for a series of articles in the *Sunday Times.* They would later be reprinted in a book to be called THRILLING CITIES. Fleming had always filled the Bond novels with what could be called "travelogue material" which added to their exotic quality. Thus, at the end of October, 1959, Fleming began his world tour in Hong Kong. He covered Macao, Tokyo, Honolulu, Los Angeles, Las Vegas, Chicago, New York, Hamburg, Berlin, Vienna, Geneva, Naples, and Monte Carlo. In the New York article, he also included a brief short story entitled "007 in New York," which described James Bond's impressions of and feelings about New York.

In December, Fleming met with McClory and Whittingham for more script conferences about the James Bond film. Fleming was impressed with the work Whittingham and McClory had done, but still had reservations about the film's projected budget. Nevertheless, plans for the film continued. McClory and Whittingham sent the latest script, now called *Longitude 78 West,* to Fleming from the Bahamas. At this point, Fleming changed the title to *Thunderball.*

The fifties drew to a close. The Cold War was reaching a peak. Now more than ever before, the time was ripe for James Bond. In eight short years, Ian Fleming had created a character which would soon become internationally famous. His popularity in America was rising and Fleming felt that nothing could go wrong.

THE SIXTIES

The sixties is the decade with which James Bond is most closely associated. The films, debuting in 1962, brought Ian Fleming and James Bond into the lives of millions of people in almost every country in the world. The novels' sales rose rapidly as a result, and James Bond, by the middle of the decade, was big business. The James Bond "image" was appealing and the media were quick to catch on to the fact. *Playboy* magazine began serializing Fleming's novels very early in the decade, and later featured pictorial spreads from the films. (In many ways, the *Playboy* image was fed by James Bond and *vice versa*.) Millions of dollars were made by merchandisers of James Bond toys and novelties in the mid-sixties. "Bondmania," as it was called, reached a peak in 1966 and remained high throughout the decade. Many books and articles were written attempting to analyze the cult and why the phenomenon existed. Ian Fleming would actually be "studied" in university sociology and psychoanalytical courses. Parodies of the Bond books even began cropping up. The most notable of these were *Alligator* by I*n Fl*m*ng, published by the *Harvard Lampoon* (it was actually written by Michael K. Frith and Christopher B. Cerf), and Cyril Connolly's "Bond Strikes Camp," which appeared in the April 1963 issue of *London Magazine*. In this latter short story, Bond is forced to dress in drag to catch a Russian spy.

At the beginning of 1960, Ian Fleming may not have realized the tremendous scope with which his creation would become a cult figure. Kevin McClory, however, somehow sensed the James Bond potential. That January, McClory visited Fleming at Goldeneye in order to find out what was happening with the film project. As reported in John Pearson's biography of Fleming, Fleming told McClory he wanted to hand the screenplay to MCA with his and Bryce's joint recommendation for McClory to produce the film. But if a studio rejected the film on the basis of McClory as producer, then it was up to McClory to sell himself to the studio, back out, or go to court. McClory, feeling rejected and betrayed, left Goldeneye only hours after he had arrived. For Fleming, the film project

completely died in the next few months. But the Xanadu Productions experience would return to haunt him.

Ian Fleming's new novel that year, the ninth James Bond book, was THUNDERBALL, based on the screenplay, *Longitude 78 West*, that had been written by Kevin McClory, Jack Whittingham, and himself.

John Pearson suggested a possible reason for Fleming's not acknowledging the story's source. He was accustomed to using discarded film or TV scripts as bases for novels. DOCTOR NO was originally a film script written for producer Henry Morganthau III. Four of the short stories in FOR YOUR EYES ONLY were adapted from his television scripts. The consequences, however, were not revealed until THUNDERBALL was published a year later in the spring of 1961.

In March of 1960, Ian Fleming met an important fan of his books. Senator John Fitzgerald Kennedy was a good friend of Mrs. Marion "Oatsie" Leiter, with whom Fleming was well acquainted. Mrs. Leiter happened to be dining with the Kennedys on March 13 and Fleming had come by to see her in Washington on his way back from Jamaica. He had come to the city on the invitation of Henry Brandon, the *Sunday Times* correspondent there. While Mrs. Leiter and Fleming were driving through Georgetown, they saw the senator and his wife walking down a street. Mrs. Leiter stopped the car and asked if she could bring a visitor to dinner. When Kennedy learned that the visitor was Ian Fleming, he connected the name with James Bond and replied, "By all means." The men took to each other, and Fleming soon also came to know Robert Kennedy and Eunice Kennedy Shriver. In the future, Fleming sent them all signed copies of his books.

In April, FOR YOUR EYES ONLY was published. The jacket, again by Richard Chopping, featured an eye looking through a hole in an unpainted wooden door. The book received fair notices, and the story "Quantum of Solace" was compared to the work of Somerset Maugham. The *London Times* said, ". . . the Bond ambience is pervasive and there is lots of sunshine." Francis Iles in *Guardian* found the anthology better than the novels. But Christopher Pym (Kingsley Amis) in the *Spectator* complained that each new Bond adventure got less probable and more preposterous and was losing the "zing." The book was published in America by Viking Press in August. Fleming's kindest critic in the United States, James Sandoe, said that the book featured "urban savagery and mighty smooth tale-spinning." Anthony Boucher again praised Fleming's readable and "smooth" prose, but complained about the weakness of the stories.

In November, Fleming was invited to spend two weeks in Kuwait as a guest of the Kuwait Oil Company. He had been requested to write a book about the country's way of life and how the oil industry affected it. It was a condition of the deal that the book should have the approval of the oil company before publication. Fleming wrote the book with zest, because the adventurous past of the country naturally fascinated him. The book was called STATE OF EXCITEMENT—IMPRESSIONS OF KUWAIT. When it was finished, the Kuwait Oil Company approved the book but felt it was their duty to show the manuscript to the Kuwait Government. The sheikhs concerned didn't particularly take to some of Fleming's comments and criticisms referring to the country's history of pirating and bloodshed. They wanted to project a more "civilized" image to the world, and banned the publication of the book. As a result, the only bound copy belonged to Fleming. (It is now in the Lilly Library at Indiana University.)

In December, while Fleming was on holiday with Anne in the Swiss Alps, two men became involved with James Bond who would be responsible for the most successful film series of all time. Harry Saltzman, a Canadian producer who had just left his company, Woodfall Films, had taken an interest in the James Bond novels. In a dramatic coup, he secured a six-month option on all of the existing and future Fleming titles except for CASINO ROYALE, which had been sold to Gregory Ratoff in 1955 (and which his widow had sold to Charles K. Feldman). Little did he know that another producer, Albert R. Broccoli, had also become interested in the Fleming novels. This London-based New Yorker had been co-producer of Warwick Films, and had attempted to gain interest in the Bonds from Columbia Pictures as early as 1957. Broccoli did not meet Saltzman, however, until a few months later.

Ian Fleming experimented with the structure of his tenth James Bond book that January and February of 1961. THE SPY WHO LOVED ME was certainly an oddity in the series in that the story was told from the point of view of a female character. James Bond did not enter the tale until two-thirds into the book. The orig-inal manuscript was 113 pages, and few revisions were made. Being the shortest Bond novel, it is only fifteen chapters long.

On March 17, *Life* magazine published an article featuring a list of John F. Kennedy's favorite books. In ninth place was FROM RUSSIA, WITH LOVE by Ian Fleming. This literally made Bond in America overnight. From then on, Fleming was "in," and sales improved almost immediately. What was so striking about *Life*'s list of books was that the other nine books were mostly biographies of political leaders and sophisticated nonfiction. Fleming's book was the only one of its type on the list. It was good public relations for Kennedy as well—it showed that even a President can enjoy a little "sex, sadism, and snobbery."

That same month, Kevin McClory read an advance copy of THUNDERBALL. He found that Fleming had made no acknowledgement to him or Jack Whittingham for what was essentially a work of joint authorship. THUNDERBALL contained the plot that was created over the last two years. McClory and Whittingham immediately petitioned the high court for an injunction to hold up publication of the book, which was set for April. At the hearing on March 25, evidence was given that 32,000 copies of THUNDERBALL had already been shipped to booksellers, and a hefty amount of money had already been spent on advance publicity. The judge ruled that the book could be published, but that it in no way affected or slanted in either Fleming's or McClory's and Whittingham's favor the result of the trial. Unfortunately, it was two years before the case was resolved.

Regardless of legal problems, THUNDERBALL was certainly a success. Perhaps the publicity of the hearing helped sales. The book had another colorful Richard Chopping jacket featuring a skeletal hand and wrist with a knife sticking through the bones and into two playing cards. The *London Times* said, "Mr. Fleming's special magic lies in his power to impart sophistication to his mighty nonsense." Viking Press published THUNDERBALL in the United States, and it sold better than any of its predecessors. Anthony Boucher wrote: "As usual, Ian Fleming has less story to tell in 90,000 words than Buchan managed in 40,000; but THUNDERBALL is still an enjoyably extravagant adventure." L. G. Offord said the book was "just about as wild as ever, with a walloping climax."

The stress and tension from the snowballing of James Bond became too much for Fleming. On April 12, during a *Sunday Times* Tuesday conference, he had a major heart attack. That afternoon he was admitted to London Clinic, where he remained for a month. He was told by his doctor that he must cut down on his smoking and drinking and get plenty of rest. But how could the creator of James Bond exist without living life to the fullest? It simply wasn't possible. Fleming chose to disregard his doctors' orders after he left the clinic, confiding to his friends that he didn't intend to spend his life not being able to enjoy it.

While he was in the hospital, Fleming wrote a children's book called CHITTY-CHITTY-BANG-BANG about the adventures of an eccentric family who owned a magical car. The car was able to fly, sail, and catch crooks. It's entirely schoolboy fantasy stuff, but heightened by Fleming's knack for detail. It must have been good therapy for him to write the book. His own philosophy of life was planted in the words of Commander Pott, the father of the fictional household: "Never say 'no' to adventures. Always say 'yes,' otherwise you'll lead a very dull life."

That May, while Fleming was recuperating in France with Anne, Harry Saltzman's six-month option on the novels was about up. It was then that Saltzman was introduced, through the writer Wolf Mankowitz, to Albert R. Broccoli. Saltzman had the option, and Broccoli had the connections. They decided to form a partnership and created Eon Productions Ltd. "Cubby" Broccoli, as he is called by almost everyone who knows him, first offered the Bond film package to Columbia Pictures, who turned him down. Broccoli had several connections at United Artists, and on June 21, he and Saltzman met with UA executives to discuss the package. The London UA head, David Picker, a fan of the novels, highly recommended buying the package. Broccoli and Saltzman signed that very day for a six-picture deal. THUNDERBALL, surprisingly, was chosen as the first film.

Broccoli hired Richard Maibaum, a screenwriter with whom he had worked a few times before, to adapt the book, despite the fact that more than one screenplay by a group of writers existed already. Maibaum's first draft of the *Thunderball* screenplay followed the novel fairly closely, except that Blofeld's initial meeting with SPECTRE to discuss Plan Omega preceded the Shrublands sequence. When the screenplay was submitted to United Artists, it was rejected because the title was in litigation at the time. Broccoli and Saltzman had failed to secure the rights to the book because of McClory's injunction.

Therefore, DOCTOR NO was chosen as an alternate, and United Artists agreed to finance the film for $900,000. Maibaum immediately began working on the script, with the help of several other writers. Terence Young, another acquaintance of Broccoli from the Warwick days, was chosen to direct. That August, a talent search began for the actor who would play James Bond.

By October, the producers had their leading man. Sean Connery, a rugged, darkly handsome Scottish actor was chosen from over a thousand possibilities. He was signed to a picture-a-year deal until 1967. Connery didn't really match Fleming's description of James Bond. Bond wasn't necessarily Scottish, although Fleming made him so in his subsequent novels, and Connery lacked the "long, thin scar" on his right cheek and the "cold blue eyes." But he was quickly molded into a particular image that audiences seemed to like. Sean Connery's portrayal of James Bond became a cinematic landmark. One way in which he made the character his own was by giving Bond a sense of humor. Connery was responsible for many of the one-liners and asides which made the film Bond a more sardonic and wittier character than Fleming's secret agent.

The film world held a curious, but somehow alienating, fascination for Fleming. He didn't particularly care to become involved with the proceedings. The people weren't his sort. But he was excited by the fact that films were being made from his books. Although his first reaction to Sean Connery's casting was negative, once he saw how the actor looked in character, he changed his mind. Fleming gladly posed for publicity shots on the sets and with the actors. He enjoyed camping up his own image, but preferred to leave the filmmaking to Eon Productions.

Interestingly, in August of 1961 Fleming sent a "critique" of Hitchcock's *North by Northwest* to Ivan Bryce. He liked the film enormously but complained about the fact that the "master of suspense" tended to throw away the plot by adding touches of comedy. Preferring to "keep jokes at a minimum," Fleming hoped that the future James Bond films would be told with a "straight face" and a "desperate sense of urgency." He added that the kind of film he had in mind was Clouzot's *The Wages of Fear*. (Perhaps this is indicative of what he might have thought of the United Artists Bond films had he lived to see more than the first two.)

Early in 1962 *Dr. No* began production with locations in Jamaica, and Ian Fleming sat down at Goldeneye to write ON HER MAJESTY'S SECRET SERVICE.

The first time Fleming visited the set of *Dr. No,* Terence Young was in the middle of shooting the scene in which Honeychile Rider (Ursula Andress) was coming out of the water onto the beach where Bond was hiding. Young's shot was ruined by four people walking down the beach towards the area. Young screamed and waved for them to lie down. The four men hit the sand and the remainder of the scene was shot. Half an hour later, Young remembered the men on the beach and sent someone to look for them. The men turned out to be Fleming, Noël Coward, Stephen Spender, the poet, and Peter Quennell, the author and critic.

ON HER MAJESTY'S SECRET SERVICE is one of Fleming's best novels. Originally titled THE BELLES OF HELL, it was 196 pages long. The original manuscript contained several sections that were added later in England, including the technical descriptions of biological warfare and heraldry. For expertise on heraldry, Fleming contacted the Rouge Dragon at the College of Arms, Robin de la Lanne-Mirrlees. The Comte de la Lanne-Mirrlees researched the Bond family and created a special coat of arms for the character. To express his appreciation, Fleming dedicated the book to "Sable Basilisk Pursuivant" (the clever reference to a basilisk, a type of dragon, avoided giving the Comte unwanted publicity).

On February 4, 1962, the *Sunday Times* published in the first issue of the new color supplement a James Bond short story by Fleming entitled "The Living Daylights." The *Daily Express,* which had been serializing the novels and held the rights to the comic strip, was incensed about this, but Fleming managed to smooth things over once he got back to England.

THE SPY WHO LOVED ME was published in April, with a lovely Richard Chopping jacket picturing a Wilkinson dagger, red carnation, burnt paper and a burnt matchstick. On the title page, Fleming added a co-author under his own name: Vivienne Michel, the heroine of the story. In a preface to the American edition, Fleming stated that he found the manuscript on his desk at his office one day, spruced it up, and submitted it for publication. But he didn't pull anyone's leg. The world knew it was Ian Fleming's novel. The author was expecting mixed reviews for this one, and got them. In fact, Fleming was quite distressed at several violent attacks (one on television) for what some critics called the "pornographic" episodes of the heroine's early life before Bond enters the story. As a result, the book was banned in some countries, including the paperback

A slightly revised version of James Bond's coat of arms, based on the original coat of arms designed at Fleming's request by the Rouge Dragon at the College of Arms for ON HER MAJESTY'S SECRET SERVICE. *(Illustration by James Goodner.)*

edition in England for a few years. The *Times* called it a "morbid version of 'Beauty and the Beast,'" and *The Listener* described it as being "as silly as it is unpleasant." More women seemed to like it, however. Esther Howard in *Spectator* found it "surprising," adding that she liked "the Daphne du Maurier touch" and preferred it that way, but doubted that real fans would. Because of the poor reception of the book in England, Fleming stipulated to Eon Productions and Glidrose that only the title of this particular novel could be used by the film makers when the time came to bring THE SPY WHO LOVED ME to the screen. In America, reviewers were cool toward the book as well. Anthony Boucher wrote that the "author has reached an unprecedented low." This was the last Bond novel to be published by Viking Press. Fleming switched to New American Library and NAL immediately began a mass paperback campaign to promote the books, all with uniformly designed covers.

That summer, with his health fluctuating between

Ian Fleming camping up the Bond image. (Photo by Loomis Dean, Life Magazine, *© Copyright 1966 by Time, Inc.)*

good and bad, Fleming decided he would send Bond to Japan for his next novel. The author was anxious to be reunited with his friend Richard Hughes, the *Sunday Times* representative in the Far East. Fleming had met the Australian in 1959 during the THRILLING CITIES tour. For twelve days, Fleming was guided through Japan by Hughes and Torao "Tiger" Saito, the editor-in-chief of a distinguished annual called "This is Japan," published by the Asahi Shimbun. Fleming was to show his gratitude to the two men by creating in their images the characters of "Dikko" Henderson and Tiger Tanaka.

Fleming received considerable exposure in American magazines that summer. The short story, "The Living Daylights," was published in the June issue of *Argosy* under the title "Berlin Escape." The August 10 issue of *Life* featured an article on Fleming. The photographs, taken by Loomis Dean, showed the author camping it up as he posed with guns, playing cards, and a Bentley. Other American magazines, especially men's publications, began featuring Bond serializations. DOCTOR NO was published in *Stag* magazine with the inappropriate title, "Nude Girl of Nightmare Key." A couple of years later, *Stag* published THE SPY WHO

LOVED ME as "Motel Nymph"! *Playboy,* though, did a much classier job with serializations of all the remaining Bond novels beginning with ON HER MAJESTY'S SECRET SERVICE. The appearances of Fleming's work in *Playboy* did much to perpetuate the Bond/Playboy image in the early days of the author's fame in America.

Around this time, Fleming's portrait was painted by his friend Amherst Villiers, whom he had known since the thirties. Villiers had designed superchargers (James Bond had an Amherst Villiers supercharger in his Bentley), and had taken up painting as a hobby. Fleming bought the portrait, and it was used as a frontispiece in a limited edition of ON HER MAJESTY'S SECRET SERVICE.

On October 7, *Dr. No* premiered in London, and was a resounding success. Sean Connery was immediately accepted by the public as James Bond, and Ian Fleming seemed to like it as well. His words were, "Those who've read the book are likely to be disappointed, but those who haven't will find it a wonderful movie." Cubby Broccoli and Harry Saltzman began planning the next film.

In January and February of 1963, Fleming wrote YOU ONLY LIVE TWICE at Goldeneye. The original manuscript was 170 pages long, and was the least revised of the novels. The book ended with another cliffhanger: James Bond has amnesia and is lost somewhere in Russia after leaving Japan.

In April, ON HER MAJESTY'S SECRET SERVICE was published. There was a limited edition of 250 copies, each numbered and signed by the author. The regular edition featured yet another Richard Chopping painting on the jacket, which showed an artist's hand completing a design of Bond's coat of arms (complete with the Bond family motto, "The World is Not Enough"). Reviews were ecstatic. The *Times* called it "perfectly up to snuff, well-gimmicked, well-thrilled, well-jacketed." New American Library published the book a few months later, and it topped the *New York Times* best seller list for over six months. R. M. Stern called it "Solid Fleming . . . Mr. Fleming is a story teller of formidable skill."

In May, *Dr. No* was released in the United States. Bosley Crowther in the *New York Times* thoroughly recommended the film, and it looked as though Eon Productions, in winning the American audience, truly had a successful investment. The second film, *From Russia With Love,* was almost complete, and Fleming had visited the set in Istanbul. He went mostly to see his friend Nazim Kalkavan again, but also because he was curious about what they were doing to his favorite book. *From Russia With Love* premiered in October in England, again to very favorable reviews. Ian and Anne Fleming threw a party for the cast and crew, but the author felt too ill to enjoy himself properly. He finally went upstairs to his room while the party continued.

In November, a James Bond short story entitled "The Property of a Lady" was published in a book called *The Ivory Hammer: The Year at Sotheby's*. Sotheby's specially commissioned Fleming to do a story concerning an auction. It later appeared in *Playboy* magazine. Jonathan Cape finally published THRILLING CITIES that November as well, with a surrealistic painting of Monte Carlo by Paul Davis on its jacket. The book received mixed reviews in both England and America (the American edition was published by NAL).

On November 19, the THUNDERBALL court case finally began. Not only was Fleming being sued by McClory for plagiarism and false attribution of authorship (Whittingham had dropped out as plaintiff due to financial difficulties), but Ivar Bryce was accused of injuring McClory as a false partner in Xanadu Productions. It was an extremely complicated case and the details are still controversial today. The attorneys

for Bryce and Fleming felt that they had a case, as did their friend, Ernest Cuneo. In an affidavit on file in London, Fleming stated that Cuneo had "scribbled off" the basis of a suggested plot for the film. This draft was dated May 28, 1959 and Cuneo assigned all rights in the document to Bryce for the sum of one dollar. Fleming acknowledged this original source in the published copies of THUNDERBALL—the book is dedicated to Ernest Cuneo, "Muse." But it was soon apparent that McClory had a strong case, and Jack Whittingham's testimony would be in his favor. Additionally, a letter dated November 14, 1963, from Fleming's solicitors admitted that the THUNDERBALL novel did reproduce a substantial part of the copyrighted material from the scripts in question.

During the three weeks of the trial, Ian Fleming was not well, although he was in the courtroom every day. His friend Bryce was worried about him, afraid that the stress could possibly cause another heart attack. After days of wrestling with this worry and with the ultimate realization of how weak their case actually was, Bryce decided to throw in the towel rather than watch his friend endure the days to come. After consulting with his counsel and with Fleming, Bryce asked for a settlement. McClory was to put forth his demands.

Ian Fleming, taking a pause from writing YOU ONLY LIVE TWICE in 1963 at Goldeneye. (Photo by Mary Slater.)

In December, the case was settled out of court. McClory would have "no further interest" in Fleming's novel, but publishers were to add the line "This story is based on a screen treatment by Kevin McClory, Jack Whittingham, and the Author" to the title page in subsequent editions. McClory was assigned the copyright to the "The Film Scripts" and the film rights to the THUNDERBALL novel for a consideration paid to Fleming. In addition, Jack Whittingham received a sum of money, and Ivar Bryce paid McClory damages as well as the court costs for all participants. John Pearson claimed that the total cost for the case was estimated at £80,000. (Whittingham afterwards issued a writ against Fleming, but this action died when Fleming himself passed away a few months later.)

1964 was the beginning of what could be called "the spy boom." For the next three or four years, secret agents were definitely marketable, and the media began overexploiting the genre. Ian Fleming's creation was undoubtedly the catalyst, and imitations appeared almost overnight. His books had sold an estimated 30 million copies worldwide by the summer, and it looked as if the phenomenon would never let up.

Television was getting into the act as well. Producer Norman Felton had approached Fleming a couple of years earlier about writing a spy series for TV (the CBS deal had fallen through by 1962). Fleming wouldn't commit to the project, but supposedly gave Felton the names for his leading characters: Napoleon Solo and April Dancer. These characters would be featured on the long-running TV series, "The Man From U.N.C.L.E." Other series with spy formats followed: "I Spy" (1965) with Robert Culp and Bill Cosby; "Mission Impossible" (1966); "Honey West" (1965) with Anne Francis; and of course, "The Avengers," which began on British TV in 1961. "Dangerman," with Patrick McGoohan, ran as a half-hour show in Britain in 1960, but was expanded to a full hour in 1965. In the United States it was called "Secret Agent." Motion picture studios began spawning James Bond imitations and spoofs, most notably the two *Man From U.N.C.L.E.* films, *To Trap a Spy* (1964) and *The Spy With My Face* (1966). Harry Saltzman produced a series of adaptations of Len Deighton novels, starring Michael Caine as Harry Palmer. These were *The Ipcress File* (1964), *Funeral in Berlin* (1966), and *Billion Dollar Brain* (1968). Dean Martin became Donald Hamilton's Matt Helm in *The Silencers* (1966) and two others. James Coburn created an interesting character in Derek Flint in *Our Man Flint* and *In Like Flint* (1966 and 1967). *Modesty Blaise*

(1966) featured a female agent played by Monica Vitti.

The spy world was a glamorous image. Fashion reflected the popularity, and soon designers were creating "007" lingerie and toiletries. Magazine ads featured dashing, handsome spies holding a gun in one hand and a beautiful girl in the other. The appeal of the gadgetry in the films was also reflected in merchandising. James Bond had become England's biggest export next to the Beatles.

The winter of 1964 was Ian Fleming's last in Jamaica. He wrote THE MAN WITH THE GOLDEN GUN, but somehow wasn't satisfied with it. He wrote to William Plomer that it needed tremendous rewriting, and that he was running out of steam. But his spirits were lifted by a surprise visit from none other than James Bond. The author of *Birds of the West Indies* and his wife happened to be in Jamaica at the time, and decided to drop in on Fleming. When he had read in an interview how Fleming had appropriated the name of his hero, James Bond the ornithologist was amused. Mrs. James Bond (Mary Wickham Bond) stated that the couple constantly had trouble with wisecracking porters and airline personnel. Customs officials would ask, "Not carrying any firearms, Mr . . . er, Bond?" And Bond would invariably pat his armpit and reply, "Now if I were carrying firearms, they wouldn't be in my suitcase, would they?" The Flemings and the Bonds had a pleasant visit, and Mrs. Bond later wrote an account of their "adventures" as Mr. and Mrs. James Bond in a book called *How 007 Got His Name*.

In March, Fleming was advised for tax reasons to sell 51 percent of Glidrose Productions. He apparently knew his health was deteriorating; by selling more than half of the shares in his business to a public company, Glidrose would be treated as a separate entity upon the author's death. He eventually negotiated the sale with his golfing friend, Sir Jock Campbell (now Lord Campbell), chairman of Booker Brothers, McConnell & Co. Ltd. and for an estimated $280,000, Booker Brothers became co-owners of James Bond.

YOU ONLY LIVE TWICE was published that March with jacket art by Richard Chopping featuring a toad, dragonfly, pink chrysanthemum, and Japanese character lettering. The *Bookman* said it "must rank among the best of the Bonds." The *Daily Herald* said it was "as damnably readable as ever." The book was a runaway bestseller in England. A few months later, New American Library published the book in the United States, and Anthony Boucher called it "a protracted but enjoyable travelogue of Japan, toward the end of which the author reminds himself to insert some action-adventure.''

In April, *From Russia With Love* premiered in the United States, again to favorable critical and audience reaction. *Life* magazine ran a feature on the film in their April 3 issue, as well as a profile on Sean Connery who was at the time working with Alfred Hitchcock on his film, *Marnie.*

In August, Ian Fleming was asked to be the next captain at the Royal St. George's golf club at Sandwich. Fleming went to his favorite hotel, the Guilford, to attend a committee meeting of the club. On August 11, he suffered his second major heart attack, and was rushed to Canterbury Hospital. His words to the ambulance attendants were typical: "I'm awfully sorry to trouble you chaps."

At 1:00 a.m. on August 12, Ian Fleming died. He was fifty-six years old. At the memorial service held at St. Bartholomew's church on September 15, William Plomer gave a eulogy which poignantly captured the essence of the man. It was later published privately.

Ian Fleming never saw the full extent of Bondmania which erupted in the fall. By that time, the *New York Times* estimated his books alone had earned him $2,800,000. Paperback sales were tripling, and film attendance was beginning to skyrocket. The third film was almost complete, and Fleming's final novel was being revised by his literary executors for publication in the spring of 1965. In October, 1964, CHITTY-CHITTY BANG-BANG was published by Jonathan Cape. The book, with illustrations by John Burningham, was a minor triumph in children's literature. Random House released the book in America and soon, adaptations of the story were published for "younger readers." Actress Shirley Eaton appeared on the cover of the November 6 issue of *Life* magazine, painted entirely in gold paint, publicizing the upcoming release of *Goldfinger.* When the film finally opened in December, the James Bond boom broke through the ceiling.

The year 1965 saw an avalanche of James Bond toys and merchandise. The Milton Bradley Company produced jigsaw puzzles and board games based on *Goldfinger* and *Thunderball,* as well as on James Bond 007 himself. Multiple Toy Makers manufactured a replica of the James Bond attaché case with sniperscope and plastic daggers in the lining. Gilbert produced a number of items, including James Bond and Oddjob action dolls (the latter could throw his bowler hat), as well as four-inch plastic figures of Bond characters and miniature set-pieces. Gilbert even produced a "James Bond 007 Magic Set," which had nothing to do with Bond per se, but was simply a box of magic trick toys with James Bond and spy-related designs. The Philadelphia Chewing Gum Corp. sold a pack of James Bond 007 Bubble Gum trading cards featuring scenes from *Dr. No, From Russia With Love,* and *Goldfinger.*

Multiple Toy Makers' shoulder holster and "missile" gun—"Bond's P.A.K. [Personal Attack Kit]." (Reprinted by permission of Miner Industries, Inc.)

Multiple Toy Makers' attaché case patterned after the one used in From Russia With Love. (Reprinted by permission of Miner Industries, Inc.)

The by-products of "Bondmania" (Photos on pages 27–30 by Pamela Cunningham Hampton)

A. C. Gilbert Co.'s Oddjob dolls. The one on the right tosses his bowler hat by spring action. (Reprinted by permission of Gabriel.)

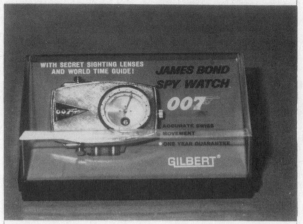

A James Bond "Spy Watch," made by A. C. Gilbert Co. (Reprinted by permission of Gabriel.)

"Action figures" of Dr. No, Oddjob, and Goldfinger, plus a moving laser beam table with James Bond strapped onto it! Made by A. C. Gilbert Co. (Reprinted by permission of Gabriel.)

Battery-operated Aston Martin. Made by A. C. Gilbert Co. (Reprinted by permission of Gabriel.)

Bubble-gum trading card box. (© Copyright 1965 by the Philadelphia Chewing Gum Corp., used by permission.)

Bubble-gum trading cards. (© Copyright 1965 by the Philadelphia Chewing Gum Corp., used by permission.)

A further set was produced a year later featuring *Thunderball.* For the adults, Weldon, Inc. created 007 pajamas and a complete line of 007 sleepware, and the Colgate-Palmolive Co. manufactured a line of toiletries, including "007 Talc." Once the juvenile market was tapped, James Bond was very big business indeed.

Ever since Kevin McClory had obtained the film rights to THUNDERBALL, he had been anxious to begin production. The only problem was that Eon Productions had the market monopolized. Sean Connery was the only James Bond as far as the public was concerned, and McClory had trouble finding a suitable actor for the role. At one point, McClory approached Richard Burton to consider playing Bond, and reportedly, the actor was very interested. McClory says that while he was in the midst of his plans to launch his own production, he was approached by Broccoli and Saltzman about a deal. Perhaps the Eon producers felt that a rival 007 picture would be damaging to their own series. Cubby Broccoli flew to Dublin where he and McClory met at the airport. Here, the deal was made to make *Thunderball,* the fourth James Bond film, which Albert R. Broccoli and Harry Saltzman would *present,* but Kevin McClory would produce. In actuality, the film was produced by all three men, but because of McClory's legal victory in 1963, it was he who received full credit. McClory claims that as a condition of the contract, the copyright to the film rights to the THUNDERBALL novel and screenplays related to the film would revert back to McClory ten years after the domestic release date of *Thunderball.* He agreed not to make further Bond pictures based on "The Film Scripts," during this period.

In late 1964 and early 1965, Leonard Russell, features editor on the *Sunday Times,* commissioned a biography of Ian Fleming and engaged John Pearson, a writer who had assisted Fleming on the "Atticus" column in the newspaper, as the author. Throughout 1965, Russell and Pearson collected reminiscences and letters from Fleming's friends and colleagues, and put together the pieces of the man's many-faceted life. Fleming's personal correspondence was purchased from Anne Fleming as well. Pearson traveled all over the world to interview people like Nazim Kalkavan in Istanbul, Sir William Stephenson in Bermuda, and Richard Hughes in the Far East. *The Life of Ian Fleming* was published by Jonathan Cape a year later. Russell and Pearson had originally planned to share the credit on the book, but since Pearson had done all the work, Russell agreed to let him have full credit.

Board games. (Reprinted by permission of Milton Bradley Co.)

Colgate-Palmolive produced a line of 007 toiletries. (Reprinted by permission of Colgate-Palmolive Co.)

Vanity Fair's Clock Radio. (Reprinted by permission of ERTL, a subsidiary of Kidde, Inc.)

T-shirts and "diplomas" on sale at a New York James Bond Collectors Convention.

In April, THE MAN WITH THE GOLDEN GUN was published posthumously. The jacket illustration was again by Richard Chopping, this time a wrap-around showing a gold-plated Colt .45 revolver, flies and gold bullets. Unfortunately, since Fleming had been unable to do his usual rewriting and revising, the novel was a weak entry in the Bond canon. Kingsley Amis, in the New Statesman, called it "a sadly empty tale, empty of the interests and effects that for better or worse, Ian Fleming made his own." When it was published in August in America, it was received somewhat more enthusiastically. But despite mixed reviews, the book remained a bestseller on both sides of the Atlantic for a long time.

Almost overshadowing THE MAN WITH THE GOLDEN GUN was a book by O. F. Snelling called 007 James Bond: A Report, the first of the books about Fleming's novels. Published late in 1964, it was a best seller. In May, 1965, Jonathan Cape published the "official" study of the Bond oeuvre: The James Bond Dossier by Kingsley Amis. Amis had originally intended to write a simple article on the works, but as he states in his foreword, the article grew to formidable book length. Written with warmth and humor, Amis' book is more a series of essays on different facets of the novels than a scholarly study. Also appearing in 1965 was The Book of Bond, or Every Man His Own 007, published by Jonathan Cape in England and Viking Press in the United States. Kingsley Amis wrote this book as well, using the pseudonym "Lt.-Col. William 'Bill' Tanner" (M's Chief of Staff in the novels). The Book of Bond was an amusing trivia collection with information on James Bond's tastes in clothes, food, drink, etc.

A double bill re-release of Dr. No and From Russia With Love the summer of 1965 made more money than the films' first releases, and Thunderball, released at the end of the year, was the biggest grossing Bond film to that date. The production received the most publicity and news coverage of any of the Bond films, as over 10,000 reporters and photographers flooded the Bahamas to get a glimpse of the proceedings. Many magazines, such as Life, Saturday Evening Post, and Look featured cover stories on the film. An hour-long TV special called "The Incredible World of James Bond" was shown in the fall of 1965, featuring behind-the-scenes looks at Thunderball, plus clips from the previous three films. Thunderball had one of the biggest openings in cinematic history.

The January 7, 1966 issue of Life magazine featured Sean Connery on the cover. But to millions of kids and adults alike, it was "James Bond." This was becoming a problem for the actor who played him. Sean Connery was rapidly losing his identity as an actor capable of other types of roles. It infuriated him when the press only wanted to ask him questions about James Bond, when he'd much rather have talked about the experiences he had making The Hill, a fine film released in 1965 and directed by his friend Sidney Lumet. But what really irritated the actor was that production of the Bond pictures almost always went over the allotted time period, a time Connery felt he could be putting to better use. In a recent interview he related that it took six weeks to film *The Hill,* while *You Only Live Twice* took six *months,* the time it would take to make four small films.

It is not surprising, therefore, that Sean Connery decided he didn't want to be James Bond anymore. His announcement worried Cubby Broccoli and Harry Saltzman who signed Connery to make *You Only Live Twice* on a one-picture basis, releasing him from his original picture-a-year contract. With Connery secure, Eon Productions began work that summer in Japan.

In March, Glidrose Productions released two of Ian Fleming's short stories which Jonathan Cape published as OCTOPUSSY AND THE LIVING DAYLIGHTS (generally referred to simply as OCTOPUSSY). The title story had been written by Fleming in the early sixties but never published. It was also serialized in *Playboy* in 1966.

Celebrated British writer, Kingsley Amis, caught reading an issue of Bondage Magazine *(published by the James Bond 007 Fan Club). Amis was the author of* COLONEL SUN *(using the pseudonym Robert Markham) and* The James Bond Dossier. *(Photo by Raymond Benson.)*

The second story was originally published by the *Sunday Times* in 1962. Richard Chopping's jacket illustration featured a scorpionfish, seashell, and flies on a wood background. The book was received only moderately well, not nearly as well as Fleming's other anthology, FOR YOUR EYES ONLY. In the New American Library edition, illustrations by Paul Bacon were added. When the 1967 paperback edition was released in both countries, a third short story, "The Property of a Lady," (originally written for Sotheby's) was included.

In October 1966, *Life* magazine published a two-part serialization of John Pearson's *The Life of Ian Fleming* and ran a photograph of Ian Fleming behind the wheel of a Bentley on the cover of the October 7 issue. The book was published the same month, and remains the definitive biography of Fleming.

While Eon Productions was busy making *You Only Live Twice,* another James Bond film was in production. Charles K. Feldman, who had bought the rights to CASINO ROYALE from Gregory Ratoff's widow, had finally begun making the picture. At first, Feldman intended to make a serious Bond film and even attempted to interest Broccoli and Saltzman into co-producing. When Feldman was turned down, he decided, at the suggestion of several writers, to make a James Bond spoof. Many writers worked on the script, some uncredited, including Wolf Mankowitz, John Law, Michael Sayers, Ben Hecht, Terry Southern, and Woody Allen. The film also had five directors. Needless to say, *Casino Royale,* released in April of 1967 by Columbia Pictures, was a mess. There are a few funny bits in the film, which starred Peter Sellers, Ursula Andress, David Niven (as "Sir" James Bond), Orson Welles, Woody Allen, and a host of guest stars including William Holden, John Huston, and Deborah Kerr. But mostly, the plot was confusing and many of the gags never worked. *Casino Royale,* in all fairness, shouldn't be considered a James Bond film.

The official Bond was back in the summer of 1967 when *You Only Live Twice* was finally released. It was the first film to totally throw out Ian Fleming's story, and illustrates the increasing outlandishness of the series. James Bond was disappearing as a character, and the sets and gadgets were taking over. In terms of spectacle, however, *You Only Live Twice* was impressive. The production values of the films showed no signs of sagging.

Sean Connery made it clear that *You Only Live Twice* was his last James Bond film. The producers were then forced to begin searching for an actor to replace him in their next project, *On Her Majesty's Secret Service.*

In the spring of 1968, a new James Bond novel was published, written by Robert Markham. Titled COLONEL SUN and published by Jonathan Cape in England (and by Harper and Row in the United States), it featured Salvador Dali-like jacket art by Tom Adams. Robert Markham turned out to be a pseudonym for Kingsley Amis, who had written *The James Bond Dossier.* It was Glidrose's original intention that other writers would have shots at writing Bond books, but they would all use the same pseudonym to avoid confusion. The book received mixed reviews in both countries, mainly because the style was so different from the Fleming books. The *Sunday Times* said that "Mr. Amis is an extremely gifted novelist," but went on to say that James Bond was so personal to Fleming that Amis' work "doesn't ring true." But *The Listener* defended the work, saying that Ian Fleming's "inheritance has been well and aptly bestowed . . . fast-moving action, a rather superior Bond-maiden, violence, knowledgeableness about guns, golf and seamanship . . . Good dirty fun." Kingsley Amis himself considered it a compliment that an American fan wrote and asked him to confirm the rumor that COLONEL SUN had been based on drafts and notes which Ian Fleming had left behind. (It wasn't.) COLONEL SUN seemed to be a misfire at the time, although in retrospect it is a very admirable novel. Because of the somewhat poor reception of the book, Glidrose was silent for quite a while.

A film version of *Chitty-Chitty-Bang-Bang,* produced by Albert R. Broccoli, was released in 1968. Containing a musical score and featuring Dick Van Dyke, it was only moderately successful.

In October, it was announced that an Australian model with no previous acting experience was to be the new James Bond. George Lazenby, a handsome but curiously naive-looking man, was cast opposite Diana Rigg, who played the woman James Bond marries in *On Her Majesty's Secret Service.* Lazenby, suddenly thrust into the limelight of show business, wasn't accustomed to spending most of his free time attending press and publicity functions. In an interview for *Bondage* magazine (published by the James Bond 007 Fan Club), Lazenby also claimed that others treated him as an inferior on the set. As a result of these experiences, some time before the film's release in December of 1969, Lazenby announced that *he* was not going to make any more James Bond films either. The producers, angry that he had announced this fact prior to the film's opening and that he had broken his contract, began to downplay Lazenby in publicizing the film.

On Her Majesty's Secret Service was the first Bond film not to be a runaway success. Lazenby wasn't received well by the critics or the public, and the film reverted to the more serious, less gadgety format of the early Bonds. It also had a down beat ending with Mrs. James Bond being shot to death, as in the novel. The film finally broke even two years later, and has since been profitable and in retrospect, it is actually one of the best films in the series.

THE SEVENTIES AND INTO THE EIGHTIES

On January 1, 1970, the BBC presented a documentary on Ian Fleming for their *Omnibus* series. The program was produced by Kenneth Corden, and John Pearson was the research advisor. The documentary featured many interviews with Fleming's friends and colleagues including Kingsley Amis, Henry Brandon, Cyril Connolly, Noël Coward, William Plomer, and Col. Peter Fleming. Also featured were clips from the recently released *On Her Majesty's Secret Service,* as well as scenes from earlier films. The program was repeated two years later.

With George Lazenby out of the running, Broccoli and Saltzman were forced to find another James Bond. For a while, it was reported that the producers were considering such American actors as Burt Reynolds and John Gavin. But David Picker, then head of United Artists, believed Sean Connery could be persuaded to return to the role. Picker felt that it was Connery audiences wanted to see, not just any James Bond. As reported in Steven Jay Rubin's book, *The James Bond Films,* Picker flew to London and offered Connery one of the most lucrative deals in cinema history—a salary of one-and-a-quarter million dollars (which Connery subsequently donated to the Scottish International Education Trust). In addition, United Artists agreed to back two films of Connery's choice that he could either act in or direct. (One of these films, *The Offense,* was made in 1972 and was again directed by his friend, Sidney Lumet.) Connery accepted, with the additional stipulation that he would be paid an additional $10,000 for every week that went over the scheduled eighteen weeks of shooting.

Diamonds Are Forever, released in December of 1971, was one of the biggest grossing Bonds yet. Sean Connery appeared once again as 007, looking quite a bit older and heavier. But the audiences loved him and screamed for more. But Sean Connery had signed on a one-picture basis only. He was definitely not going to make another James Bond film. So the producers went back to the drawing board once again.

Roger Moore, an admired British actor best known for his television series (*The Saint, The Persuaders*) and light comedy roles, was chosen to star in *Live and Let Die.* Moore, it is said, was originally the producers' choice after Sean Connery. Moore was certainly a more experienced actor than George Lazenby, and he added a style and sophistication to his characterization of Bond that was quite different from Connery's interpretation. In a way, the style of the Bond films was changed to accommodate his characterization. In the Bond films of the seventies, comedy was emphasized more and more, until they became a different sort of animal altogether from the early films, and especially from Ian Fleming's novels.

Audiences and critics alike accepted Roger Moore as James Bond when *Live and Let Die* was released in the summer of 1973. Its box-office success ensured the future of the series, and Eon Productions began planning its next film.

A new rash of toys and by-products flooded the market as a result of the film. There was a James Bond 007 Tarot Game manufactured by U.S. Games Systems, Inc., based on the one used in the film. There were more trading cards, and Corgi Toys sold miniature Bond automobiles and the like. A new generation was out there for the merchandisers to tap.

In August, *James Bond—The Authorized Biography of 007,* was published in England by Sidgwick & Jackson, and in the United States by William Morrow & Co., Inc. It was written by John Pearson, Fleming's biographer. The idea for such a book came from William Armstrong, then head of Sidgwick & Jackson. Glidrose Publications (the name was changed from Glidrose Productions in September, 1972) shared the copyright on the book with Pearson. Pearson was surprisingly successful at making this fictional biography convincing. The premise is that Ian Fleming actually *knew* a James Bond in the Secret Service, and that the Service had authorized Fleming to write the James Bond "novels" so that their enemies would believe that Agent 007 was a fictional character! (Of course, the real James Bond's exploits were not as glamorized as Fleming wrote them.) In the book, John Pearson "interviews" James Bond at age 53, and Bond relates his entire life story, embellishing brief references to his early life which Fleming put in the books. Though it's not an "official" James Bond novel, it stands as one of the most interesting and enjoyable works pertaining to the cult.

The first James Bond 007 Fan Club was started that year at Roosevelt High School in Yonkers, New York, by two students, Richard Schenkman and Bob Forlini. Initially, the members were just a few of their friends. In the summer of 1974, they put out a club magazine, called *Bondage,* and since then, the club has grown considerably. Forlini eventually dropped out, leaving Schenkman to run the club himself. *Bondage*'s first issue was mimeographed, the pages stapled together. Now it is a slick printed magazine with a glossy cover. Today, the fan club has about 1,600 members in the United States and abroad, mostly male. The average age is twenty-one, but Schenkman claims that since *Playboy* wrote about the club in the late seventies, the age has risen to twenty-five. Eon Productions was originally supportive of the club and Cubby Broccoli agreed to an interview in 1978. But since then, the club has not been on the best of terms with the film company for reasons about which Schenkman can only speculate. In *Bondage* No. 5, he published an interview with George Lazenby. In *Bondage* No. 6, he published an interview with Kevin McClory. Neither article probably pleased the film producer. Nevertheless, the club is thriving, and the magazine is member-supported. At the back of this book is an address to write for more information about the James Bond 007 Fan Club.

In December of 1974, United Artists released *The Man With the Golden Gun,* starring Roger Moore again as Bond, and Christopher Lee as Scaramanga. The film, one of the weaker of the series, did fairly well internationally, but it had a poor reception in America and in England. Around this time, it was reported, Cubby Broccoli and Harry Saltzman were not on the best of terms. They had more or less taken turns producing the last two films. Saltzman had gone on location for most of *Live and Let Die,* and Broccoli had taken more control of *Golden Gun.* Now that the new film was out, Harry Saltzman decided to leave. It was rumored that he needed capital for a private venture, and he sold his share in Danjaq, S.A. (the Swiss company made up of Eon Productions and United Artists) to United Artists. Danjaq, S.A., then, became Albert R. Broccoli (Eon Productions) and United Artists.

In January of 1976, the THUNDERBALL film rights reverted back to Kevin McClory. He was also supposedly free to make further pictures based on "The Film Scripts." He therefore began planning to make

his own Bond series. He contacted Len Deighton, author of such thrillers as *The Ipcress File* and *Funeral in Berlin.* McClory took "The Film Scripts" and built a new screenplay. The men collaborated on the script, which was provisionally called *James Bond of the Secret Service,* one of the original titles from "The Film Scripts." One day, McClory was visiting Sean Connery and asked if he might be interested in also collaborating on the script. Connery had always expressed an interest in writing and directing, and surprisingly agreed to the offer. Together, McClory, Deighton, and Connery came up with a screenplay which McClory retitled *Warhead.* It was reported that during the writing of the script, Sean Connery became interested in not only directing the film, but starring as James Bond again as well.

Meanwhile, Eon Productions was preparing production on its latest, *The Spy Who Loved Me,* again featuring Roger Moore. When Broccoli learned of McClory's plans to make *Warhead,* he wasn't too

President Richard Schenkman (standing left) and members of the James Bond 007 Fan Club. (Photo by Charles Reilly, courtesy of Richard Schenkman.)

pleased. As reported by John Brosnan in *James Bond in the Cinema,* further friction was caused when McClory and Sean Connery learned that some of the plot details of *The Spy Who Loved Me* were coincidentally similar to parts of *Warhead.* As a result, Broccoli ordered his scriptwriter to make last-minute changes in *The Spy Who Loved Me* before filming began.

McClory tried in vain from 1976 to 1979 to finance *Warhead* but apparently, too many obstacles were placed in his way. The word on *Warhead* eventually disappeared from the public eye and the production seemed to have fallen through.

But *The Spy Who Loved Me* was released in the summer of 1977, this time produced by Broccoli alone. He proved that he could make a slick, entertaining Bond film without Harry Saltzman, and the film was the biggest success since *Thunderball* in 1965. One character in the film, a henchman called Jaws (portrayed by Richard Kiel), became something of a cult hero with kids, and the character would return in the next Bond film.

For Your Eyes Only was originally announced to be the eleventh Bond film, but due to the success of *Star Wars* and *Close Encounters of the Third Kind,* United Artists and Cubby Broccoli changed their minds. The only Fleming title left which could incorporate an outer space theme was MOONRAKER, and that became the replacement. *Moonraker,* released in the summer of 1979, and starring Roger Moore, represents the low point in the series. Nevertheless, it became the biggest grossing Bond film ever. According to *Variety,* rentals in the United States and Canada only, by 1982, amounted to over $33,000,000.

In the fall of 1980, twenty-year-old Ross Hendry of Harrow, Middlesex, founded The James Bond British Fan Club. Since James Bond was a *British* character, Hendry felt that his hero should not be represented only by an American fan club. In the three years since the club's formation, branches have opened in the United States, Germany, Australia, Norway, and all over England. The club distributes two publications: *007,* the regular club magazine, and *For Your Eyes Only,* a supplemental booklet of "hard-core" Bondian information. Information on how to join The James Bond British Fan Club appears at the back of this book.

In 1980, the Board of Directors of Glidrose decided it was time to bring back the *real* James Bond, the hero of the books. For some time, authors' names were tossed around, and eventually they had a list of six. First on that list was John Gardner.

John Gardner was born in 1926 in the little village of Seaton Delaval, in the northeast of England. He studied at Cambridge and St. Stephen's House, at Oxford. After serving in the Royal Marines during the war, Gardner wrote for the theatre for a while, then decided to try something else. After working on an autobiographical book, Gardner wrote *The Liquidator,* published in 1964. It was an all-out spoof on James Bond, and quite a success. The main character was Boysie Oakes, who worked as an assassin for the British Secret Service. The problem was that Boysie Oakes was a coward and secretly hired hit men to do his dirty work for him! In addition, he became ill on airplanes. Gardner wrote other Boysie Oakes books and two novels about Sherlock Holmes' nemesis, Professor Moriarty. Two later books, *The Garden of Weapons* and *The Nostradamus Traitor,* were more in the realistic style of John Le Carré. Another, *The Director,* deals with backstage drama in the theatre.

Glidrose contacted Gardner through a go-between, who asked the author if he might be interested. A three-book deal was eventually worked out. Glidrose reportedly kept close tabs on Gardner while he wrote the first book, carefully monitoring it. One important change Gardner made was updating James Bond's world to the 1980s, but he kept the character more or less the same age as he was in the sixties. Bond does seem a little older, a little wiser, but he certainly isn't the sixty-one-year-old he should be according to "Fleming's Bond."

In the spring of 1981, Gardner's first Bond book was published. Titled LICENSE RENEWED, it was published in England by Jonathan Cape (in association with Hodder and Stoughton) and in the United States by Richard Marek Publishers. The book was a bestseller, despite lukewarm reviews from critics and Bond fans alike. The British jacket had an attractive Richard Chopping illustration (designed by Mon Mohan) of a Browning 9mm pistol with a string of pearls and yellow roses.

In the summer, the 12th James Bond film was released. *For Your Eyes Only,* which again featured Roger Moore in a tougher, grittier characterization, marked a return to the more serious, original format of the early films. It was the best Bond film since *On Her Majesty's Secret Service* and the film grossed in the $25 million range.

Also that summer, Chicago film historian Jim Schoenberger discovered a kinescope of the original CBS-TV presentation of the hour-long *Casino Royale* in a pile of dusty old film cannisters. A special public showing was arranged, and Barry Nelson (who por-

James Bond's new father: John Gardner. Gardner is posing with Bond's latest wheels: a Saab 900 Turbo. (Photos courtesy of Saab-Scania of America, Inc.)

trayed Bond in the film) appeared to talk about it. Around this same time, Richard Schenkman obtained permission to reprint three of the *Daily Express'* comic strip versions of DIAMONDS ARE FOREVER, FROM RUSSIA, WITH LOVE, and DOCTOR NO. The James Bond 007 Fan Club published the book.

In March, 1982, Albert R. Broccoli received the Irving G. Thalberg award from the American Academy of Motion Picture Arts and Sciences. The Thalberg is an annual award given to producers for outstanding achievement. The Bond films had been deemed the most successful film series of all time, and Broccoli appeared at the Oscar Awards ceremonies on March 29 to receive the trophy. A series of film clips were shown, and Roger Moore presented the award.

Also that spring, producer Jack Schwartzman purchased a license to make one James Bond film based on the original copyright assignment of "The Film Scripts" and the film rights to the THUNDERBALL novel to Kevin McClory. A new script was begun by Lorenzo Semple, Jr., and the film would be directed by Irvin Kershner *(The Empire Strikes Back)*. Most importantly, Sean Connery agreed to return to the role of James Bond. Apparently the film was to be a remake of *Thunderball*. By September, the film was underway with a working title of *Never Say Never Again* (which reportedly was coined by Connery's wife). Connery's co-stars would be Barbara Carrera and Klaus Maria Brandauer, and filming was scheduled to begin in the Bahamas in the fall with Kevin McClory as executive producer.

In May, John Gardner's second James Bond novel was published by Coward, McCann and Geoghegan. Titled FOR SPECIAL SERVICES, the book featured a return of SPECTRE in a newly formed reorganization. LICENSE RENEWED was published in paperback as well, and other Ian Fleming titles were reissued by Berkley Books. FOR SPECIAL SERVICES was published in Britain in September by Jonathan Cape (in association with Hodder and Stoughton) and the jacket, designed and illustrated by Bill Botten, featured a giant python.

A resurgence of the James Bond Phenomenon appeared to be on the horizon in the first half of 1983, the 30th anniversary of the publication of CASINO ROYALE. John Gardner's third Bond novel, ICEBREAKER, was published in America in April by Putnam's and in Britain by Cape/Hodder in the summer. Bill Botten's jacket for the British edition showed a skeleton hand clutching ski equipment in the snow. Despite poor reception by critics in both countries, ICEBREAKER remained on the *New York Times* Bestseller list for several weeks, surpassing the sales of Gardner's previous efforts. Glidrose Publications announced that Gardner

Albert R. "Cubby" Broccoli received the Irving Thalberg Award at the 1982 Oscar ceremony. The proud producer stands alongside his current star, Roger Moore. (Reprinted by permission of the Academy of Motion Picture Arts and Sciences.)

had been signed to continue writing in Ian Fleming's footsteps; there would be even more Gardner/Bonds in the future, with ROLE OF HONOR being title number four.

The thirteenth film in the United Artists/Eon Productions series, *Octopussy,* was released in June by MGM/UA Entertainment Co. It was received extremely well by critics and audiences alike, and in the face of such tough competition as *Return of the Jedi* and *Superman III,* was one of the highest grossing pictures that summer. Although Roger Moore once again announced that *Octopussy* would be his last appearance as 007, it was proclaimed in December, 1983 that he would play Bond a seventh time in *From a View to a Kill* (one of the short story titles from the FOR YOUR EYES ONLY anthology. The title has since been changed to *A View to a Kill.* The film is slated for a summer 1985 release.

Complementing the release of *Octopussy,* a one-hour television special was produced in both England and the United States. "James Bond—The First 21 Years" assessed the two decades of James Bond on film. Several luminaries were interviewed, including Alexander Haig, Burt Reynolds, Alistair Cooke, and even President Ronald Reagan, and each expressed his opinion on the social significance of 007. Other events kept the renewed Bond mania from waning—a "Spy Con" was held in New York in July, bringing together secret agent fans from the surrounding areas. A new generation of 007 lovers had been born.

Kevin McClory and Jack Schwartzman had their share of problems with *Never Say Never Again* in the latter part of the spring and early summer—the Trustees of the Ian Fleming Estate (financed by Eon Productions/Danjaq/UA) brought an injunction against them to stop the release of the film, and fought them with appeal after appeal; but the court ruled in favor of the new Sean Connery Bond. The final appeal court verified McClory's rights in the original copyright assignment. *Never Say Never Again* was released by Warner Brothers on October 7 in the U.S., and has grossed $25,000,000 to date (as per *Variety,* 1/11/84). Encouraged by this success, McClory has been engaged to launch a series of James Bond films based on the copyrights of the "The Film Scripts" and the film rights to THUNDERBALL. Paradise Productions III made an announcement in February 1984 that the first film would be titled *SPECTRE.* Broccoli's reaction to this remains to be seen at the time of writing.

If James Bond survives the eighties, he will have

lived four decades. If the films continue to be made throughout the eighties, James Bond will be the only character in cinema history to span a series of films made over three decades. When Ian Fleming first sat down at Goldeneye and wrote those opening sentences of CASINO ROYALE, he had no idea what he was creating. The James Bond phenomenon has far outlived Fleming, and still shows no signs of dying. If asked today how it felt to be finally successful, Fleming would probably reply as he did in 1964 when an old Etonian friend asked him the question. "Oh," Fleming said with a sigh, "it's all been a tremendous lark."

▫ TWO ▫
Ian Fleming—
A Remembrance

Ian Fleming in a pensive moment in Jamaica, circa 1951. (Photo by Josephine Bryce.)

Many people have attempted to describe Ian Fleming, the man. Those who knew him did so *individually*; his relationships were such that he was a man who appeared to be different things to different people. Ian was a complex person, a man of many moods and conflicts, but with an obvious passion for life and boyish zeal for adventure. His friend Ernest Cuneo describes him as "a knight out of phase; a knight errant searching for the lost Round Table and possibly the Holy Grail, and unable to reconcile himself that Camelot was gone and still less that it had probably never existed." One close friend remembers that it was his "innocence, geniality, merriment, wonderful sense of humor and of the comic; bashfulness under the scorching criticism poured on him—all that and his zest for extracting what cheer he could from the daily situation, and injecting *joie de vivre* into companions, that rendered him so attractive to be with. He was privately, almost secretly, generous minded, and there was nothing petty about him."

Former Attorney General Francis Biddle once said that the British were "an incredibly brave and incredibly boyish people," and Ian Fleming was both of these things. He carried himself with the Etonian air sometimes described as the "consciousness of effortless superiority," which gave him sophistication and nobility; but he also had an almost childlike sense of playfulness, and was willing to try anything once. This mixture of conflicting traits gave Ian Fleming a great deal of charisma. It has been said that he radiated so much energy that he "lit up the room."

Fleming was considered extremely good-looking. He had a fine, high forehead topped by a head of thick brown, almost black, slightly curly hair, which he parted on the left. He had a strong jawline and possessed striking blue eyes. His nose was broken. One close friend said that Fleming carried himself more like an American than an Englishman. In a typical stance, he would rest his weight on his right leg, left foot and shoulders slightly forward. He was very "smooth-muscled," and stood six feet tall, or perhaps a shade under. Ian wasn't a fancy dresser by any means. One might have caught him in a short sleeved white shirt and a blue bowtie with white polka dots. Outdoors, he always carried a battered, soft black felt hat. For casual wear, Fleming chose shorts and cotton shirts, much like James Bond. For swimming in his private cove at Goldeneye, Fleming chose to wear nothing.

Ian Fleming was a man of intense energy and curiosity, with a mind for detail and organization. "He wrote such succinct and trenchant Intelligence reports that I was somewhat scandalized later when he wanted to publish CASINO ROYALE under his own name!" says Clare Blanshard, who had known Fleming since the war. The author was obsessive about accuracy as well. He extracted ideas and fine points with the fervor of a sharp detective, scribbling down notes in a little pad which he always kept with him. He loved questioning people about their jobs, learning what they did, how they did it and why. He was the sort of person who wanted to know a little about everything. He longed to be "learned," like his elder brother, Peter.

Geoffrey Boothroyd, the arms expert who helped "re-arm" James Bond, once said that Fleming wanted to know the *whys* and the *hows* of something, but could care less about all the other details. He would become attached to an object simply because he liked the sound of its name. Boothroyd claimed that Fleming chose a Walther PPK for Bond to use because the name "rolled off the tongue nicely." And Fleming liked "double-barrelled" words, like "Rolls-Royce," "Smith and Wesson," or "Aston Martin." This attraction to the sound of words is nowhere more evident than in the names Fleming gave his characters: Le Chiffre, Hugo Drax, Pussy Galore, Vesper Lynd, Auric Goldfinger, Vivienne Michel, Kissy Suzuki, Tiger Tanaka . . . the list goes on and on.

Fleming appreciated fine craftsmanship, especially in objects of value. He had a fascination for diamonds and how they were cut and polished. He was extremely interested in gold and its metallurgical qualities. Ian respected the *thought* behind all works of art, which underlies his appreciation for books and first editions. He had particular interest in schemes and plots and how they were devised and a passion for crime—not to commit one, but to learn how it was done. Gambling odds intrigued him, and he would pursue a system for beating the odds in almost every game he played. At the end of Chapter Five in a proof copy of MOONRAKER, in which Bond warns M that he is about to be dealt a "Yarborough," Fleming asterisked "Yarborough" and wrote an explanation in ink: "A hand containing no card higher than nine. The odds against it are 1,827 to 1." He was always collecting bits of information to plug into the Bond books.

That Ian Fleming was a lover of nature is certainly apparent in the novels. He liked pretty things, like shells, and took pleasure in collecting them. He loved the underwater world, and enjoyed exploring it in his private cove at Goldeneye. Outdoor sports went hand in hand with Fleming's penchant for nature, for he was an avid skier in his younger days and found mountain climbing especially invigorating. Ernest Cuneo tells a story of a time when he and Ian climbed the mountain next to Cuneo's farm. "Let's climb Goose Egg Mountain," Ian suggested one day, and Cuneo agreed. The two friends, both at this time in their forties, scrambled up the steep cliff. Cuneo remembers tiring halfway up and making an excuse to stop by pointing out the view. A little later, it was Ian who suggested stopping for a "view." "Aha!" Cuneo thought. "Now *he's* tired." Cuneo had worked up a sweat, but Fleming appeared undaunted. After they had reached the top, Fleming proclaimed that it was harder to go down a mountain than to climb it because one's muscles had to fight the force of gravity. Cuneo refuted him, saying that the best way of descending Goose Egg Mountain was to "brake your speed by grabbing a pine bough as you hurtle past it." Fleming accepted the challenge and the two men raced down the cliff like "whirling dervishes," laughing like mad.

Al Hart, editor of the first six Bond books in America, remembers that Ian Fleming had the uncanny ability to make one feel witty. He laughed a lot, and found ways of turning everyday things into absurdities. Fleming's sense of humor was sharp and jocular. He enjoyed a good joke, a nuance, or a play on words. A favorite expression was "What fun!" (a telling clue to his personality). "The Bond books were amusing to him," Al Hart says. "We used to laugh about sections together." Once, while Hart was reading the manuscript of LIVE AND LET DIE, he couldn't help laughing at a certain line of dialogue. Near the end of the book, Bond and Solitaire are tied together, naked, about to be pulled behind Mr. Big's boat over a coral reef. It was over one hundred pages into the story and Bond still had not made it to bed with Solitaire. Now, here

they were, and she says, "I didn't want it to be like this." Hart called Fleming and asked, "Listen, do you want to leave this line like this?" And Fleming, roaring with laughter, said, "Yes! Leave it . . . leave it!!" When the name Pussy Galore first came up, Hart called Fleming again and said, "You can't use this name." And Fleming grandly stated, "Oh yes I will, and not only that, we're going to get away with it!"

Being a bachelor for over forty years tended to make Fleming a bit particular in his ways. Cuneo remembers, "His favorite drink was a martini, and the instructions were maddening. He didn't want the gin 'bruised,' and was painfully specific about both the vermouth and the gin and explained each step to the guy who was going to mix it as if it were a delicate brain operation. Several times I impatiently asked him why the hell he didn't go downstairs and mix it himself, but he ignored me as if he hadn't heard and continued right on with his instructions. Equally annoyingly, he always warmly congratulated the captain when he tasted it as if he had just completed a fleet maneuver at flank speed." While on their celebrated cross-country train ride, Fleming, in grandly pronouncing the oysters and steak as excellent, managed to inflect that slight touch of surprise that makes it patronizing.

Ian Fleming did not necessarily consider himself a gourmet, but did appreciate fine food. He was amused by the sounds of fancy menus and often had a good laugh concocting the meals James Bond ate. Naomi Burton remembers, "A good way of teasing Ian was to tell him we were going to take him out and make him eat one of James Bond's meals. Indeed, "Beef Brizzola" which appears in DIAMONDS ARE FOREVER was a bastardization of a dish served at New York's "21" club. Fleming liked scrambled eggs for breakfast, simple and straightforward. In Jamaica, his favorite meal was ackee and saltfish (codfish), the national Jamaican dish. He also liked baked black crab and fish done in any form.

Fleming's particular "charming conceits" gave critics the excuse to accuse him of snobbery. One of these "charming conceits" was the way he carefully chose his friends and kept them all in separate compartments. He had his golfing friends, and he had his *Sunday Times* friends. He had his acquaintances with whom he shared adventure, and he had his companions with whom he shared his personal problems. None of these friends knew the same Ian Fleming. He would reveal different sides of himself to various people, but was intentionally inconsistent with what he chose to reveal to whom. Some might consider this compartmental-

Relaxing in the sun at Goldeneye. Ian, Anne, Robert Harling, and Ivar Bryce (sitting on ground). (Photo courtesy of owner.)

izing of relationships a form of snobbery; in truth, Fleming simply valued his privacy. He only associated with those he considered "fine people," and couldn't be bothered by those who bored him. Once, while Ian was in New York, a friend of his agent, Naomi Burton Stone, invited him to accompany her for drinks at the Stones' apartment. "You must come and meet Naomi's husband," she told him, but Fleming was evasive. "No, no, I need to do some other things," he told her, making excuses. She persisted, and finally he said, "Oh, all right, but I can only stay for half an hour." He was afraid of getting caught in a situation in which he would have to feign interest in the conversation when he might be bored to tears. But as it turned out, Fleming took to Naomi's husband immediately (they had both served in Naval Intelligence during World War II), and the men talked for hours!

According to one close friend, Fleming was not a snob at all. "Ian exhibited great kindness through his generous ways of dealing with the people he cared for. He was very protective of his friends." Indeed, Fleming was known to do special favors for the people who meant something to him. If he could help a friend in his career, he was always more than willing. He respected those with whom he associated, whether they cleaned the windows or played bridge with him.

Fleming lived his life intensely and to the fullest. He was never one to "wallow" (one of his favorite words,

which he would pronounce with exaggeration as if the word itself were wallowing), and was always intent on extracting the most out of life. His greatest fear was boredom; he dreaded the "soft life," a malady James Bond himself suffered at times. Ivar Bryce, who had known Fleming since childhood, believes that Ian was *always* searching for adventure; and throughout the years, the two friends indulged in many unusual escapes. They were constantly sending letters and telegrams inviting the other to accompany him on some outlandish expedition (such as the trip to Inagua in 1956); every invitation closed with the words, "Fail Not." One time Bryce and Fleming decided to lose weight together. They visited a doctor in New York, who put them on a strict diet and said to come back in two weeks. After the allotted time period, when Bryce met Fleming at the airport he appeared much fatter than he did two weeks earlier. Fleming thought to himself, "Well, I've got this one won." Then Ivar laughed and pulled out a pillow from underneath his overcoat. Actually, he had lost the most weight.

Because Fleming was a vigorous man of action, he

Anne Rothermere (a year before she became Mrs. Fleming) with Ivar Bryce in Jamaica, circa 1951. (Photo by Josephine Bryce.)

was difficult to keep inactive for any lengthy period of time (except when he was at his most mellow during January and February at Goldeneye). James Bond's epitaph at the end of YOU ONLY LIVE TWICE is even more suited to Fleming: "I shall not waste my days in trying to prolong them. I shall use my time." This rather brave attitude, mixed with Fleming's undeniably boyish taste for the romantic, fed lifeblood into the Bond adventures, and for the most part, explains why they are so popular.

Ian Lancaster Fleming was born on May 28, 1908, in appropriately, the Mayfair section of London, England. His father, Valentine Fleming, was a Scot, who worked for his father's prestigious banking firm, Robert Fleming and Company, and who was elected a Tory M.P. for South Oxfordshire in 1910. He was well-liked and also extremely wealthy. His circle of friends included Winston Churchill. Ian Fleming's mother was Evelyn St. Croix Rose, a beautiful woman of Irish, Scot, and Huguenot descent. Eve Fleming was reported to be a romantic, passionate woman, full of surprises and changes. She was a strong-willed, somewhat vain, authoritarian person, capable of standing her ground against any form of challenge. From the beginning, his parents' characteristics (his father's pride, patriotism, geniality, intelligence, and love for the outdoors; and his mother's extravagance, taste, curiosity, and independence) blended to create a multifaceted individual.

John Pearson wrote in *The Life of Ian Fleming* about Fleming's early childhood: "From the start he had one of those natures for which the world is uncomfortable in whatever shape they find it . . ." He was a precocious and sometimes mischievous child, a rebel as far as his family was concerned. According to Pearson, little Ian disliked everything his family loved, such as horses and dogs and family gatherings, and held no particular affection for Scotland.

By August 1914, Valentine Fleming was in the army and had been sent to France where he soon became a major. Eve Fleming was left to care for four sons— Peter, Ian, Richard and Michael. In 1915, Peter and Ian were sent to a boarding school, the Durnford School, near Swanage, on the island of Purbeck. The school was run by a man named Tom Pellatt, who allowed the boys a good deal of freedom. In the next couple of years, young Ian Fleming became interested in adventure and mystery yarns, for Pellatt's wife read aloud the stories of Bulldog Drummond to the boys. Soon,

Fleming was addicted to the works of Sax Rohmer, Robert Louis Stevenson, and other adventure novelists.

Tragedy struck on May 20, 1917. Valentine Fleming was killed in action in France. He was posthumously awarded a D.S.O., and Winston Churchill wrote an appreciation of him in *The Times*. Ian Fleming's father had died a hero, and this incident had a profound effect on the boy's emotional growth. Ian seemed to need a hero, and as a result, he began to idolize his older brother, Peter. As with most upper-crust English families, the emphasis on primogeniture was strong, and Ian was forced to walk in his brother's shadow for a good many years. Peter seemed to be the perfect son: he was well-behaved, extremely bright for his age, and held much promise for success. Ian, on the other hand, was considered eccentric, overly imaginative— the black sheep of the family.

In the autumn of 1921, Eve Fleming, an extremely rich widow, packed Peter and Ian off to Eton. At thirteen, Ian had grown into a handsome boy, and he took great pride in his appearance and personal affectations. (It was reported that Ian's housemaster disapproved of his pungent hair oil.) Ian was never happy at Eton. According to Paul Gallico, Fleming actually loathed it, and constantly felt out of place. But this didn't stop the boy from making some kind of mark for himself. Ian found he was athletic, and was especially good in track. In 1925, Fleming was named *Victor Ludorum* (champion of the games) for the school. He won the title a second time in 1926, while he was still under eighteen. He broke his nose during a football match that year which tended to give his features a somewhat worldly look.

Fleming once related one of his Eton experiences to Paul Gallico. He was due for a birching in the headmaster's office at noon one day for some misdemeanor. But as he was also due to run the steeplechase at noon for the championship, he persuaded the headmaster to move the caning back to 11:45. At the appointed time, Fleming reported to the office and submitted to the punishment. Afterwards, he proudly ran the steeplechase with blood stains on the back of his trunks, and came in second place. Fleming was, from the beginning, a strong advocate of the British stiff upper lip.

But Fleming soon lost interest in his studies at Eton; his marks dropped. Eve Fleming decided to remove her second son from the school and place him into a more rigorous, disciplinary environment. At age eighteen, Fleming was enrolled in the Royal Military College at Sandhurst (England's West Point). In that summer of 1926, Fleming was sent to a "Crammer's" tutoring school to prepare him for the Sandhurst entrance exam. Colonel William Trevor, who ran the school, wrote to Mrs. Fleming that Ian should make an excellent soldier, "providing always that the ladies don't ruin him." For already, Ian Fleming was something of a ladies man. He was extremely good-looking and had a natural ability for meeting and wooing girls. According to Paul Gallico, once Ian escorted a local girl to a nightclub and persuaded another cadet to sign in for him at the evening roll call. Later that night, Fleming was caught climbing into the college and was penalized with thirty days confinement to barracks and no leave for six months.

Actually, Fleming did quite well at Sandhurst. By 1927, he had been placed on His Majesty's List for the King's Royal Rifle Corps. But as the time approached for him to take his commission, it was reported that the army was going to be "mechanized." Fleming, along with a few other cadets, decided he didn't want to spend his time pushing buttons and levers in the army, and refused his commission. He even had the audacity to write his refusal on a postcard, drop it in the mail, and then simply leave the college. Needless to say, his mother was not pleased.

Eve Fleming had heard through friends that an excellent private school had been set up in Kitzbuhel in the Austrian Tyrol, run by Ernan Forbes-Dennis and his wife, the novelist Phyllis Bottome. This school, located high in the mountains in a château called the Tennerhof, held a special place in Fleming's memory for the rest of his life. For it was here when he was in his late teens and early twenties, that he discovered his ambitions and began to think of himself as something other than Peter Fleming's younger brother. The Forbes-Dennises not only provided a rigorous foreign-language program (from which Fleming learned German and French), but also experimented in psychology. The life in the mountains was idyllic, and Fleming soon became an avid skier and mountain climber. He also became very popular with the local girls.

Encouraged by Phyllis Bottome, Fleming began to write in Kitzbuhel and even produced a short story called "Death, On Two Occasions." With the prodding of the Forbes-Dennises, Fleming decided to build a career in the Foreign Office, which was considered a prestigious and difficult profession. To improve his language skills, the Forbes-Dennises sent him to Munich

University in 1928. Fleming soon picked up an adequate knowledge of Russian. In 1929, he enrolled in the University of Geneva to improve his French. One of his notable achievements at the time was receiving permission from Carl Jung to translate a speech Jung had delivered on Paracelsus.

Fleming had many friends during this time, mostly girls. One of his closest friends was Lisl Popper, to whom Fleming left £500 in his will. Fleming told another friend years later that Ms. Popper was one of the few people he had known who cared sufficiently enough about him to tell him the truth about himself. On the BBC's *Omnibus* documentary about Fleming, Lisl Popper told how she and Ian had met. She and a few friends were sitting at a table in a restaurant and one of the youngest and most naive of the girls said, "Can you see the Englishman over there?" The girls all looked and there at another table was Ian Fleming, whom they had never seen before, wearing a navy blue shirt. He was "slim, very good-looking, reading a book, very serious." The girl asked, "How can we meet him?" The others told her to forget it. She persisted. Finally, Lisl explained to her that the English were "shy," and that there was only one thing to do. She should get up, pass the Englishman's table, fall over his feet, and say, in English, "I am sorry." The girl repeated the phrase over and over to make sure she would get it right, then went over and fell over Fleming's feet. "Ian was delighted," and from then on, "We never left each other," Ms. Popper said.

While Fleming was in Geneva, he became engaged to a Swiss girl named Monique. Perhaps for the first time, Fleming was truly in love; and despite the differences in their backgrounds, the young man made a valiant attempt to convince her family and his that theirs was a suitable match. But when Ian's mother met the girl, there was a scene. She did not approve and that was the end of that. Eve Fleming held a very powerful card in her hand: in Valentine Fleming's will, she had been granted power to alter the family's inheritance in any way she saw fit. This meant she could disown any of her sons, and they would be denied the extensive Fleming fortune. After the engagement was broken off, Fleming was reportedly quite bitter, and his attitude toward women became one of careful objectivity. Never again would he become so obsessed with a woman. Fleming, however, later paid something of a tribute to his ex-fiancée: the mother of James Bond was a Swiss named Monique.

In 1931, Fleming took the Foreign Office exam. He placed twenty-fifth out of sixty-two. The failure was a tremendous blow to his pride, and he never told the truth about the defeat. To friends he said that he placed seventh, but that only five candidates were accepted.

Back in England, now that he was out of school and in his early twenties, it was time to look for a suitable job. Luckily, his mother's influence pulled some strings for him: she was friends with Sir Roderick Jones, the head of Reuters News Service. Jones hired young Fleming to work in the news office under the editor, Bernard Rickatson-Hatt. Reuters, at this time, was highly competitive with its American counterpart, United Press International, and was attempting to become one of the leading news agencies in the world. In this fast-paced, demanding environment, Fleming quickly learned the trade of a journalist. He was soon out of the news office and given reporting assignments. And in 1933, Fleming was given a particularly important assignment—covering the trial in Moscow of British citizens who had been accused of spying on the Russian government.

That March, six British and several Russian employees of the Metropolitan-Vickers Electrical Company had been arrested as part of Stalin's great purges of the mid-thirties. The arrests outraged the British government. News agencies from all over the world sent reporters to Moscow to cover the trial, and twenty-four-year-old Ian Fleming was chosen to represent Reuters because he could speak Russian.

Fleming, who already had developed a mind for creating detailed plans of action, came up with a scheme to scoop the other news agencies. He wrote two possible reports of the trial beforehand, one with a guilty verdict and one without. The censors had to approve the articles before they could be phoned or cabled to the appropriate news agency, and Fleming used his charm and panache to strike up a friendship with a censor named Mironov. Mironov, with reluctance, stamped his approval on both stories with the understanding that when the verdict was announced, the appropriate story would be used. Fleming also enlisted the services of a young boy and a man at the cable office. According to Fleming's plan, as soon as the verdict was announced, he would lean out of a window, drop a message to the boy, who would then run to the cable office. There Fleming's other man would fill in the remaining details to the story and cable it to Reuters.

The plan worked beautifully, and Fleming's story was the first to reach London by cable. But Central News beat him by twenty minutes over the telephone. The Central News reporter just happened to be on the phone with his office as the verdict was announced and heard the judge's statement over the building's loudspeaker. Still, Fleming's ingenuity was soon recognized by all the reporters in Moscow who sent Sir Roderick Jones a telegram saying that they all had an "extremely high opinion of his journalistic ability." Fleming was a winner after all.

In October of 1933, Ian Fleming surprised everyone by announcing his resignation from Reuters to take a position as a junior partner in a firm of merchant bankers. He subsequently wrote to Sir Roderick Jones, declining Reuters' offer to be general manager of the Far East office, saying that his family had urged him to take the job. So at the age of twenty-five, Ian Fleming became a stockbroker in the City for the firm of Cull and Company. He later moved to Rowe and Pitman, and remained a junior partner there until 1945.

It seems odd that Fleming would be happy as a stockbroker, but London held a particular fascination for the young man. He was particularly good at organizing and managing; although he aways admitted finding money-making a little boring. It was life *after hours* that held his interest, and the thirties was Fleming's period of bachelor paradise. His circle of friends became more elite. He founded a gentleman's club with a friend, Gerald Coke, and named it *The Cercle,* short for *Le Cercle gastronomique et des jeux de hasard* (The Circle of gastronomy and of games of chance). The members basically were Etonians with whom Fleming shared bridge games and elegant dinners. Living in a bachelor apartment on Ebury Street, Fleming maintained a conservative life as a stockbroker by day, and an indulgent, sometimes mysterious, life by night. He was never one to socialize at parties, save for his gatherings with *The Cercle*. He had many girlfriends, as usual, and would court them by preparing elaborate meals and by serving them champagne in his apartment. And like James Bond, he kept his affairs uncomplicated and noncommittal, as well as extremely private. He soon had a reputation for extraordinary ruthlessness with women, yet these same women found him irresistible.

Ivar Bryce reports that during this period Fleming wrote a collection of poetry called THE BLACK DAFFODIL and had it privately printed. But Fleming was ashamed of the book and soon after burned all available copies. The fact that Fleming would write a book of poetry at this time signifies that he indeed had a romantic view of himself and his lifestyle.

Fleming had always been keen on rare books and first editions, and in 1935, he decided to begin a collection of books that "started something," or "made things happen." A friend from Kitzbuhel, Percy Muir, was a partner in the rare book firm of Elkin Mathews, of which Fleming himself became a partner. Fleming wrote to Muir, instructing him to search for appropriate additions to the collection. Though the idea and the purchases came from Fleming, it was Muir who did the work. Now known as The Fleming Collection, these books became one of the most valuable and important collections of rare first editions in the world. It consists of works by scientists and practical workers whose writings were responsible for what could be called the modern revolution. For instance, included in the collection are the Wright Brothers' first papers on aeronautics; Bell's original description of the telephone; Einstein's work on relativity; the major contributions of Pasteur, Koch, Lister, and others; works of economic and social importance by authors such as Marx, Engels, Lenin, and Hitler; works in psychology by Darwin, Freud, Jung, Pavlov, and others; as well as major literary works by Goethe, Byron, Balzac, Dickens, Maeterlinck, Kipling, Schiller, Tolstoy, and many more. The collection numbered over a thousand when it was completed, and was eventually purchased by the Lilly Library at Indiana University a few years after Fleming's death.

In the spring of 1939, Fleming learned that "funny little questions" were being asked about him; his friends told him that people were asking where he'd been, who he knew—things of that sort. These questions were the first stirrings of a major change of direction in Fleming's life.

War with Germany was imminent. The newly appointed Director of Naval Intelligence, Rear Admiral John Godfrey, was looking for a personal assistant. His predecessor, Sir Reginald Hall, had used a young stockbroker as an assistant during World War I and had found that the man's organizational and business experience proved invaluable. Godfrey decided to look for the same type of individual, and sent inquiries through the Bank of England. Most likely on the recommendation of Montagu Norman, Governor of the Bank of England, Fleming was finally invited to a luncheon with Admiral Godfrey. Fleming was surprised when he found the brother of the senior partner in his own brokerage firm, Admiral Aubrey Hugh-Smith, sitting at the table as well. Godfrey decided Fleming was the man for the job and that spring, Ian Fleming became a lieutenant

(Special Branch) in the Royal Naval Volunteer Reserve. His duties were to assist Godfrey in practically any conceivable manner, but what that meant in essence was that Fleming became the number two man in Naval Intelligence. He was in on the planning and organization of the department, and sometimes represented Godfrey at routine conferences. The headquarters were located in Room 39 of the Ministry of Defense, where Britain's propaganda, subversive activities, political warfare, and undercover operations originated. Although Fleming never actually participated in active operations, he certainly helped plan them. He was known for his imaginative suggestions, even though some of them had to be highly bowdlerized. Admiral Godfrey, who most likely served as the model for M, James Bond's chief, described Fleming as "a benevolent presence" who served as the binding force in a group of men and women working in close proximity to each other and under a great deal of pressure. It was through his "wit, laughter, appreciation of human frailties and willingness to become the butt of others' humour" that Fleming created a position for himself in Naval Intelligence. But he was a good officer as well, and soon was promoted to Commander. "Ian," Godfrey said later, "was a war-winner."

One of Fleming's more active experiences of the war took place in June of 1940, when the Germans almost completely controlled France. The French Naval Commander, Admiral Darlan, was holding out at Le Bourget, refusing to evacuate his fleet to British ports. Fleming proposed that he and a wireless operator be sent to Le Bourget to report on Darlan's situation, and convince him to sail. Once in France, Fleming followed Darlan to Bordeaux, which had become the safest port for evacuation. The town was mobbed with families attempting to leave. Fleming took it upon himself to organize the evacuation and help the British citizens decide what to leave behind and what to take with them. Tons of valuable items including motorcars had to be abandoned. Fleming received orders to make sure that a load of engine parts did not fall into German hands, and that the reluctant ship captains carried the equipment to England. Fleming and his assistant burned the remaining files and papers at the temporary British embassy, and just as they were leaving, King Zog of Albania arrived with his family and the crown jewels. Fleming took responsibility for seeing King Zog aboard, and the party finally left France for Arcachon, where they met a cruiser to Britain.

In February, 1941, Fleming went on a special Naval

Intelligence mission to Tangier, carrying an official diplomatic courier's passport. In June, he and Admiral Godfrey went to Lisbon. On their second evening there, the two men visited the Estoril casino where Fleming rather hoped they could engage a group of Nazis in a game of baccarat and attempt to clean them out. But there were only a few Portuguese in the casino. Nevertheless, Fleming sat down to play and duly lost all of his money. This incident became the main plot of CASINO ROYALE, in which James Bond challenges the evil Le Chiffre to a baccarat game in an attempt to wipe out the the man's finances.

From Lisbon, Fleming and Godfrey flew to the United States, where attempts were in progress to create an American intelligence organization. They visited Sir William Stephenson, the man called "Intrepid," who was the head of the British Security Co-ordination in New York. It was in Stephenson's office on the thirty-sixth floor of the RCA building in Rockefeller Center that Fleming first met Ernest Cuneo, who was working for General William "Wild Bill" Donovan, the father of the OSS—Office of Strategic Services, the forerunner of the CIA. Fleming took to New York immediately, and he enjoyed spending off-hours with Stephenson and Cuneo at "21," or at Stephenson's apartment in the Hotel Dorset.

There is a well known story told of the time Fleming accompanied Stephenson on a profitable intelligence "exercise." The Japanese Consul General's office was located on a floor below Stephenson's office in Rockefeller Center. Stephenson knew that messages were received and transmitted to Tokyo from that office. Very late one night Stephenson, Fleming, and two assistants broke into the Consulate and its locked safe; microfilmed and copied the Japanese code book; replaced the materials; and left the office as they had found it. This incident, highly embellished, would also play a part in CASINO ROYALE. James Bond's first assignment with the Secret Service was to assassinate a Japanese cipher expert by shooting him through the window of a neighboring building.

In June of 1941, Admiral Godfrey left Fleming in the United States with instructions to contribute as much as he could to the development of the American intelligence operation. Fleming accompanied William Donovan to Washington for a weekend, and the two men reportedly worked on a document which most likely helped Donovan in drawing up the original chart of organization for the OSS. Thomas F. Troy, in his book, *Donovan and the CIA*, reports that in the document, dated June 27, 1941, Fleming urged Donovan

to confront those in the government who opposed the institution of an American intelligence operation. Fleming then went on to recommend certain individuals for key positions in what was a sketchy organizational chart and made suggestions on other practical matters such as space and tactics. On the subject of a liaison between the Americans and M.I. 6, Fleming referred to his "previous memo"; what the Naval officer had to say about a collaboration between British and American "secret agents" remains unknown, as that memo has never been found. Although none of Fleming's suggestions ever came to fruition, legend has it that Donovan presented Fleming with a Colt .38 Police Positive revolver inscribed with the words "For Special Services" in appreciation for his contribution.

At one point, Fleming visited the training camp for subversive actions run by Stephenson in Oshawa, Canada, and even took a few of the training courses himself. One of these demanded that he swim a lengthy distance underwater and plant a limpet mine on the hull of a derelict tanker—an experience he later used in his book LIVE AND LET DIE. Fleming also furthered his knowledge of ciphers, and the use of explosives and other subversive weaponry. But he never passed the test to determine whether he was capable of killing a man. It was actually a trial of nerves which required him to break into a room and open fire on a man sitting in a chair. As Fleming approached the door with gun in hand, he simply couldn't bring himself to continue the exercise.

Ernest Cuneo eventually became the liaison between William Donovan and the British Security Coordination, with immediate access to the White House. Often, he was the only American present at the meetings at Rockefeller Center. Cuneo remembers that he and Fleming developed a friendship which consisted mainly of sporting jabs at each other's homeland. Cuneo would denegrate anything British, and Fleming would do the same to everything American. But it was all in good spirit, and the two men became very close friends. Cuneo remembers that Fleming was quite the ladies man during the war. There was a shortage of nylons in Britain, and one day Cuneo walked into the room and threw a few pairs of stockings on Fleming's desk. "Long, medium, and short," Cuneo said. "I assume you're playing the field." Fleming said, gallantly, "Actually, I'm not." Cuneo said, "Good, there are others who are," and he proceeded to take back the nylons. But Fleming snatched them with the speed of a card shark. "I'm not," he said with a straight face. "But

Perhaps Fleming's closest American friend, lawyer and newspaperman Ernest Cuneo. (Photo courtesy of Ernest Cuneo.)

some of my friends are." And the two men roared with laughter.

In late 1941, Fleming created the Number 30 Assault Unit, something he liked to call his "Red Indians," an outfit of Intelligence Commandos who specialized in cleaning out Nazi hideouts after their capture. Fleming's idea for the unit actually came from the Germans. After the battle of Crete in May 1941, a German unit overran a British one and seized all ciphers and technical equipment. Fleming thought the notion of a commando spy outfit was exciting and adapted it for Naval Intelligence. The men in the 30 A. U. were trained in counterespionage techniques and capturing enemy intelligence documents. The outfit began operating in the Middle East, working with the Eighth Army. 30 A.U. worked in North Africa, Sicily, and Italy, and had a strong participation in D-Day. Other units tended to resent them, for at times they were a rowdy bunch who thumbed their noses at discipline. But the accomplishments of the outfit were impressive and 30 A.U.'s reputation was justly famous. Eventually, its control passed from Fleming's hands.

In 1942, Admiral Godfrey became Flag Officer of the Royal Indian Navy, and he was replaced as D.N.I. by Commodore E.G.N. Rushbrooke. Fleming, who retained his close working relationship with the D.N.I., liked to refer to his new commanding officer as "Rush Admiral Rearbrooke."

The air raids had begun in London and the threat of death from bomb blasts existed every day. The war took its toll on Fleming's personal life during this period. First, Muriel, his girlfriend, a dispatch rider, was killed when a bomb struck her flat one night. Then Ian lost his younger brother Michael, who died as a result of wounds as a P.O.W. after Dunkirk.

In the autumn of 1944, Fleming was back in Washington for routine meetings and to attend a special Intelligence conference in Kingston, Jamaica, an island he had never visited. He met his friend Ivar Bryce, who was working for William Stephenson, in Washington, and helped clear Bryce's passage to Jamaica. Bryce owned a home in Jamaica, called Bellevue, and invited Fleming for a three-day visit before the conference. After taking the Silver Meteor to Florida, as James Bond did in LIVE AND LET DIE, the two men departed for the Caribbean. At Bellevue, they were greeted by an enthusiastic housekeeper, an empty cupboard, and terrible weather; it rained the entire three days. But surprisingly, at the end of this time, Fleming asked Bryce to help him search for a piece of land where he could build a house. He had fallen in love with the island. In March of 1945, he began construction of his retreat—which he named "Goldeneye." Fleming was very proud of Goldeneye, especially since he designed it himself. The three-bedroom house was modestly furnished, with a shower adjoining each bed-

The ambience in and around Goldeneye. (Photos by Mary Slater.)

room. His island neighbor, Noël Coward, complained that the house didn't face the sunset, and called the place, "Goldeneye, nose, and throat," The house is still looked after by Violet, the cook and housekeeper. Violet remembers that sometimes for fun, Fleming would purchase cow and donkey carcasses and pitch them into the sea, to watch the sharks feed on them. "Usually he'd invite friends from all over the island to watch with him, and they'd have lots of fun." When Fleming described the sound a shark's jaws make in his books, he knew what he was talking about!

Ian Fleming made valuable contributions to his country during the war, only a few of which have been noted here. It was a serious and demanding time for him, and many said it was his finest hour. Throughout it all, Fleming kept his sense of humor, sharing it with others and helping them through the trying times. His friend Clare Blanshard, who was personal assistant to the Chief of Naval Intelligence—Eastern Theatre recalls a letter from Fleming in May of 1945 in which he wrote that except for filching the archives of the German Navy on the Czechoslovak border and lashing a few German WRNS (women's naval force), he had had no "devilry" for some time. Work had increased since Germany's defeat but it mostly involved fighting over the corpses of the German Navy and bickering for the

"wish-bones"! The war provided Fleming with the opportunity to expand his expertise in many fields, create new circles of friends, and fill his need to make his mark, as his father had done, in the British war effort. He was discharged on November 10, 1945.

Immediately after the war, Fleming took the position of Foreign Manager at Kemsley Newspapers. The job offered many opportunities to travel abroad while pursuing stories for the *Sunday Times*. Fleming's work for the newspaper was outstanding, and he did some of his best writing during this period. He was particularly good at travel-adventure stories. Buried and sunken treasure fascinated him, and he wrote a series of articles on the subject. He went diving with Jacques-Yves Cousteau, and joined an exploration led by Norbert Casteret, a noted French archaeologist, in the Gouffre Pierre Saint-Martin on the Franco-Spanish border. In the spring of 1954, he persuaded Somerset Maugham to allow the *Sunday Times* to serialize a number of articles Maugham was writing on "the ten best novels of the world." Maugham had never allowed a newspaper to serialize his work, but Fleming's enthusiasm for the project, along with the promise that his material would not be edited, convinced Maugham to agree. It was a major coup for Fleming.

In the autumn of 1953, Fleming was offered the role of "Atticus." Although it had prestige, the Atticus column was basically high-class gossip. Nevertheless, it was an honor that Fleming was asked. He took the job on the condition that none of the writing would be altered. John Pearson worked as one of Fleming's assistants on the column. He remembers Fleming's unusual story ideas. Once, Fleming asked Pearson to identify the most ridiculous and expensive Christmas present one could purchase in London. After seeing Pearson's research, Fleming chose to write about a very expensive gold-plated "egg decapitator," which sliced off the top of an egg without breaking the shell. Since Fleming didn't have to sign his own name to Atticus, Pearson notes, the author could reveal his personality without fear of ridicule or direct personal criticism.

In the summer of 1955, Lord Kemsley decided to sell his distinguished bibliographical journal, *The Book Collector,* which was not meeting its expenses. Fleming, who was fond of the publication, bought it from Kemsley. Fleming left the running of the journal to its editor, John Hayward, but managed to obtain funds from American foundations to secure its future. Though he never wrote for *The Book Collector,* Fleming was proud of saving and owning this exceptional source of information.

During the period immediately after the war, Fleming met his future wife. For a better understanding of the effects marriage had on Ian Fleming, one must first look at his attitude toward women in general. His reputation as a ladies man was a controversial one. He reportedly was very cruel and ruthless with the women he courted. His close friend Robert Harling confirms that Ian had "some kind of contempt" for women. According to Lisl Popper, Ian, if given the choice, would much rather have dined with a man than a woman.

One girlfriend from the thirties says that "Ian was cozy and sympathetic when he was in a good mood, but he was never in the same mood two days together, which I suppose was part of the attraction." This same woman also says that Ian would pretend that ordinary events were adventures, or make out that some well-known restaurant was special and secret. He claimed the etiquette of walking on a lady's right was "to have his sword-arm free." He was somewhat ashamed of being a stockbroker because he thought it so unromantic. "The only 'incident' I can remember," she

says, "was when he made me hide in his bedroom when a couple of friends were coming in for half an hour. There was no earthly reason why I shouldn't have stayed and talked to them, particularly as it was in the afternoon, but he thought it exciting to have a girl hidden in his bedroom. I thought it rather silly."

Fleming seemed to tire quickly of the women he knew. Fionn Morgan, his stepdaughter, says that most of the women in his early life were "housekeepers" rather than lovers. In his memoir, *You Only Live Once,* Ivar Bryce tells of receiving a telegram one day in 1938 to meet Ian in Boulogne for a "journey." Ian was there with an American Graham Paige sports car and an American girl named Phyllis. All Ivar could get out of Fleming was that their destination was Kitzbuhel. Ian put Ivar in charge of the luggage, placed Phyllis in between them in the seat and took off. Apparently, Ian and Phyllis had met at a party the previous evening. The girl was intelligent and witty, but Ian soon began snapping at her. By the second day, the tension had increased between them. That night, in Munich, Ian tersely told her he was taking Ivar to dinner where only men could come. Over dinner, Ian said he couldn't take any more of her anglophobic American prejudices. Even though he was pro-American, Ian disliked spoiled American girls loaded with culture. Afterwards, Ivar found a note in his room from Phyllis, begging him to come to her room for a talk. She was very upset. She said she was in love with Ian, but he treated her so cruelly she didn't know what to do. Ivar advised her to forget him and go back to Massachusetts. In the morning, Phyllis appeared at the car, ready to go on but Ian said, "No, Phyllis, no. You are a good girl and I'm sorry this trip has been a flop, but the place for you is home in America. Now goodbye and grow up and be happy. Get in, Ivar, we're late." They drove away, leaving the girl with her baggage in the street. Ivar was distressed and embarrassed by Ian's behavior, but Fleming justified it by saying, "She's got no place, traveling alone with us. She would madden us with her demands, make herself miserable, and achieve nothing. We could have stayed there arguing with her all day. She ought to go home and she has plenty of money to get there, so stop fussing."

If a girl expected love from Ian Fleming in his bachelor days, she was destined to suffer. Bryce remembers that Ian would say to his girlfriends: "You must treat our love as a glass of champagne," which supposedly meant sparkling, delicious, and leaving a euphoric memory in its wake. Yet despite his enormous appetite

A snapshot taken at the airport prior to Ian and Anne Fleming's departure from Jamaica as newlyweds in March, 1952. The calypso band behind them was hired to send the Flemings off with a festive farewell. (Photo by Josephine Bryce.)

for women, Fleming once told a close friend that he had never received much pleasure from a woman. He hated the fact that "men depended on women." Fleming's bitterness toward women may have been caused by the demands and pressures placed upon him by his authoritarian mother when he was younger and from disappointment over the breakup of his engagement to the Swiss girl, Monique. But a close friend contends that it was Muriel, the dispatch rider during the war who was killed in a bomb raid, who was the love of Ian's life. After her death he always said he'd never marry.

But he broke that promise in 1952, at the age of forty-three, when he married a woman who couldn't have been more his opposite. The love affair between Ian and Anne Fleming was a stormy and passionate one. They first met before the war, while Anne (née Charteris) was married to Lord O'Neill. Anne (called "Annie" by her friends), had two children from that marriage, which ended when O'Neill was killed in action during the war. Anne had begun to see Fleming occasionally by this time, but Ian avoided any serious entanglement. So Anne married Lord Rothermere. As the forties drew to a close, Ian and Anne saw more of each other, especially in Jamaica during Ian's winter sojourns. They became good friends with Noël Coward, who entered in his diary on July 10, 1949: "I have

doubts about their happiness if she and Ian were to be married. I think they would both miss many things they enjoy now."

Anne was an extremely beautiful, strong-willed woman. It is quite well known that she enjoyed the company of men over that of women, and she gained distinction by entertaining a long list of notable celebrities at luncheons or dinners which she would host. Among her closest friends were Somerset Maugham, Evelyn Waugh, Sir Isaiah Berlin, Peter Quennell, Cecil Beaton, Malcolm Muggeridge, Noël Coward, and Cyril Connolly. She did have female friends as well, notably Loelia, Duchess of Westminster, Lady Diana Duff Cooper, and Lady Avon (formerly Lady Eden). Anne had a sharp wit and enjoyed that quality in others. Intellectual conversation stimulated her and men reportedly delighted in her company. But Anne could be very cutting with her wit. One close friend of the Flemings remembers a time when three couples were relaxing in the sun at Goldeneye. The men, in jest, each told the story of how they'd had their first woman. After all was said and done, Anne spoke up with, "All right, now I'll tell you how I had *my* first woman!"

The passion and intensity of the relationship must have changed Fleming's mind about marriage. The fact that Anne was already pregnant with his child was merely tangential to his decision. After Anne's divorce from Lord Rothermere, she and Ian were married in Jamaica. According to Noël Coward, one of the witnesses, on the the BBC's *Omnibus* documentary: "It took place in the parochial hall of Port Maria, and Annie was very nervous. And she had on a silk dress— she shook so much it fluttered. I don't know why she was so terrified, but she was . . . The principal official of the ceremony spoke very close to them—he put his face very close—which I don't think they cared for, and so they had to turn their faces away when they said, 'I do, I do.' Very lovely ceremony."

Fionn Morgan, Anne's daughter, says that Ian was a good stepfather and was very interested in his stepchildren. But even she agrees that the marriage was not made in heaven. John Pearson seems to think there was some kind of "sadomasochistic" strain, mentally, in their relationship. Both partners were egocentric, and ultimately this destroyed their happiness. Noël Coward wrote in his diary on Sunday, November 14, 1954:

On Tuesday I dined with Annie and Ian and it was somehow tiresome. Annie is such a darling when she is alone with Ian but when surrounded by her own set—Judy (Montagu), Alastair (Forbes), etc.—she changes completely and becomes shrill and strident, like one of those doomed Michael Arlen characters of the twenties. I am really surprised that Ian doesn't sock her in the chops and tell her to shutup.

Years later, on January 29, 1961, Coward wrote:

. . . their connubial situation is rocky. Annie hates Jamaica and wants him to sell Goldeneye. He loves Jamaica and doesn't want to. My personal opinion is that although he is still fond of Annie, the physical side of it, in him, has worn away. It is extraordinary how many of my friends delight in torturing one another.

In an interview for the *Evening Standard* in 1960, Fleming openly admitted to not caring for his wife's dinner parties. "My wife," he explained, "fully understands my attitude, that I don't care for her parties and literary friends. For one thing, you know, if you are married to a hostess, you find that she will seat the most interesting men next to herself and saddle you with their boring wives. So whenever possible I avoid going to my wife's parties." He went on to say that he would much rather go to a Hamburg striptease joint than to one of Anne's parties. "Give me a cheap joint any day," he said.

It was almost immediately after the birth of their

Ian and Anne Fleming in January, 1962. (Wide World Photo.)

son, Caspar, in August 1952, that the physicality went out of Ian and Anne's relationship. But Fionn contends the couple loved each other in their own way through the end, and couldn't leave each other even though the romance had gone out of the relationship. It is obvious that Anne had a profound effect on his life. Once he became a father, he was very proud. He looked forward to his weekends and arranged his work schedule so that he put in what was called "The Fleming Four-Day Week." The time he spent alone with his family was precious to him. Still, the loss of his bachelor existence frustrated Fleming, and from the beginning of the marriage, he found another outlet from which to release these frustrations—he began writing the James Bond novels.

"For Ian, marriage was an admission of defeat," Robert Harling says. "Hence, the Bond books were an escape." John Pearson also believes that James Bond was a wish fulfillment for Fleming. Noël Coward said that "James Bond was Ian's dream-fantasy of what he would like to be, you know—ruthless and dashing." There is evidence to support this theory. When Fleming sent Ivar Bryce a copy of his most recent book, he wrote in a note that it was the latest installment of his "autobiography." But Fionn Morgan says that "wish fulfillment" is an oversimplification. Ian created the character and it simply grew as Fleming grew as a writer. Ernest Cuneo commented: "I think Bond was a thing apart from him. Though created by him, he seemed to be as detached from Bond as a scientist who has created a robot, and indeed, there were a considerable number of times when I thought Bond bored Fleming to tears. I had the impression that Bond was the mere instrumentation, perhaps unconscious, of this craftsmanship, which is most excellent. Indeed, I think some of Fleming's paragraphs are all but Keatsian, and that a good deal of his writing will survive James Bond. Fleming didn't. As a matter of fact, at that time, he was striving to get James Bond living and wasn't too sure he wouldn't die before."

Fleming himself thought of the books as schoolboy literature. He wrote from Goldeneye to one close friend that he was writing the final pages of a *B.O.P.* (*The Boys' Own Paper* was a boys' magazine from Victorian days which presented adventure stories of a pure, patriotic nature). Naomi Burton believes that Fleming was capable of writing a much more literary work than the Bond books. The problem was that he was afraid of the criticism he would receive from Anne and her intellectual circle. He asked a mutual acquaintance to tell Naomi that he refused to write a "good" book. He admitted having the mind of a mischievous "boy scout" and that was the material his agent would be forced to hawk until he became aged and sagacious and wrote a book about his sad boyhood.

Noël Coward supported this theory. In his diary entry for Sunday, January 25, 1955, he wrote:

I have read Ian's new thriller in proof. It is the best he has done yet, very exciting and, although as usual too far-fetched, not quite so much so as the last two and there are fewer purple sex passages. His observation is extraordinary and his talent for description vivid. I wish he would try a nonthriller for a change; I would so love him to triumph over the sneers of Annie's intellectual friends.

It is said that Fleming wanted to dedicate CASINO ROYALE to Anne but she objected. She told him that "you do not dedicate a book like this to *anyone*."

Fionn Morgan says that Anne did not actually disapprove of James Bond; she was unhappy with the image and way of life the character had brought to Fleming. "She was secretly proud of him but publicly felt she had to stick to her guns that they weren't of high literary value." William Plomer said that Fleming felt "eclipsed" by James Bond in his later years. And indeed, Fleming's lifestyle did change in the last few years of his life. Fionn Morgan also states that he was probably the type of man who couldn't handle success well; he attempted to live up to an expected image. His smoking and drinking increased, and as a result, his health deteriorated. One close friend says that Ian was terribly unhappy the last few years of his life—he was frustrated with his marriage and the slowness of success, but mainly with his inability to live the life of his fantasy.

It is no wonder that the later Bond novels have a peculiar tone of impending doom and despair. Some of the painful and traumatic incidents through which Bond lives perhaps alleviated the plight of Fleming's own existence. Through James Bond, he could escape from the routine boredom of the "soft life," which was precisely what his reality had become. It was something he had fought until he was forty-three, but he had succumbed to it and there was no turning back. This striving for adventure and extracting excitement and stimuli from the daily situation became the motivation behind the writing of the James Bond novels. Despite the overwhelming success of the books, James Bond was an extremely personal creation for Ian Fleming. It was his very own escape route—his custom-made drug. Even though at times he wanted to forget all about James Bond, he found himself writing the latest opus every winter of every year. It was the intensity and energy with which Fleming struggled against the "soft life" that finally killed him.

Fleming once told Ivar Bryce that "after age fifty, one must really *love* every day—if one is allowed to." *This* perfectly captures the essence of Ian Fleming. He was a man who wanted the most out of life; he was constantly striving to achieve a goal which, once won, could not fully satisfy him. The man's lust for life is what made him the personality his friends like to remember. As James Bond lives on in new novels and motion pictures, it is fitting to picture Ian Fleming as William Plomer described him in his memorial address at St. Bartholomew's Church: ". . . on top of the world, with his foot on the accelerator, laughing at absurdities, enjoying discoveries, absorbed in his many interests and plans, fascinated and amused by places and people and facts and fantasies, an entertainer of millions, and for us a friend never to be forgotten."

□ THREE □
James Bond—
A Portrait

Ian Fleming behind the wheel of a 4½-litre Bentley (but does it have an Amherst Villiers supercharger?), the same car James Bond drives in CASINO ROYALE *and* MOONRAKER. *After the automobile's demise in the latter novel, Bond drives a Mark II Continental Bentley in the remaining Fleming series. (Photo by Loomis Dean, Life Magazine. © Copyright 1962 by Time, Inc.)*

BACKGROUND AND EARLY LIFE

The James Bond character remains fairly elusive in the early novels; not until the fifth book, FROM RUSSIA, WITH LOVE, does a personality truly begin to develop. Some of Bond's vague personal life is touched on in the third novel, MOONRAKER, but it is in GOLDFINGER (the seventh novel) that Ian Fleming provides a more complete picture of the character's "normal" life. In the twelfth novel, YOU ONLY LIVE TWICE, the details of James Bond's childhood and school years are finally presented in the form of an obituary. John Pearson, Ian Fleming's biographer, published an intriguing book in 1973 entitled *James Bond—the Authorized Biography of 007*, which embellishes the few incidents in Bond's early life that are mentioned in the Fleming series. In addition, Pearson creates a completely fleshed-out existence since Bond's birth, according to Pearson, in 1920. I will not attempt to summarize these additional events in Bond's life created by Pearson, but only deal with the facts provided by Fleming. It should also be noted that the James Bond character of the novels is quite different from the figure as presented on film. The literary Bond is much more realistic; he's a serious individual with very human qualities. (The film version of James Bond is a larger-than-life superhuman, and this character will be examined in Part Five.)

Commander James Bond, C.M.G., R.N.V.R., was born of a Scottish father, Andrew Bond of Glencoe, and a Swiss mother, Monique Delacroix, from the Canton de Vaud. John Pearson selects November 11 (Armistice Day), 1920, as Bond's birthday, but there is no evidence pointing to this in the Fleming novels. The obituary appearing in YOU ONLY LIVE TWICE asserts that Bond was seventeen when he left school; and by "claiming the age of nineteen," he entered a branch of what was subsequently to become the Ministry of Defense in 1941. If, as Fleming states, Bond was seventeen in 1941, then he was actually born in 1924.

Andrew Bond was a foreign representative of the Vickers armaments firm; therefore, Bond's early life was spent abroad. While living in Germany, the young James Bond acquired a first-class command of French and German.

Fleming reveals the only clue to Bond's childhood interests in the opening chapter of ON HER MAJESTY'S SECRET SERVICE, while the character reminisces at the beach:

It reminded him almost too vividly of childhood—of the velvet feel of the hot powder sand, and the painful grit of wet sand between young toes when the time came for him to put his shoes and socks on, of the precious little pile of sea-shells and interesting wrack on the sill of his bedroom window ('No, we'll have to leave that behind, darling. It'll dirty up your trunk!'), of the small crabs scuttling away from the nervous fingers groping beneath the seaweed in the dancing waves—always in those days, it seemed, lit with sunshine— and then the infuriating, inevitable 'time to come out.' It was all there, his own childhood, spread out before him to have another look at. What a long time ago they were, those spade-and-bucket days! How far had he come since the freckles and the Cadbury milk-chocolate Flakes and the fizzy lemonade! (ON HER MAJESTY'S SECRET SERVICE, Chapter 1)

When he was eleven years old, both of Bond's parents were killed in a climbing accident in the Aiguilles Rouges above Chamonix. The youth came under the guardianship of an aunt, Miss Charmian Bond; he went to live with her at the "quaintly named hamlet of Pett Bottom near Canterbury in Kent." Aunt Charmian, a most learned and proficient lady, completed Bond's early education and prepared him for an English public school. Since he had been entered at birth by his father for Eton, Bond passed satisfactorily into the school at "age 12 or thereabouts."

Like Fleming, Bond left Eton early. Bond's career there was "brief and undistinguished." After only two halves, Bond allegedly got into some trouble with one of the boys' maids, and Aunt Charmian was asked to remove him. Bond was then sent to Fettes, his father's old school, where the environment was "somewhat Calvinistic, and both academic and athletic standards were rigorous." The youthful Bond was inclined to be solitary by nature, but he established strong friendships among the traditionally famous athletic circles at the school. Bond fought twice for the school as a lightweight and also founded the first serious judo class at an English public school.

A sketch of Ian Fleming's description of James Bond. The bone structure resembles that of Hoagy Carmichael, and the eyes and mouth hold a hint of "cruelty." (Illustration by George Almond.)

The losing of his innocence in Paris at the age of sixteen is the next major development in Bond's life:

If he wanted a solid drink he had it at Harry's Bar, both because of the solidarity of the drinks and because, on his first ignorant visit to Paris at the age of sixteen, he had done what Harry's advertisement in the *Continental Daily Mail* had told him to do and had said to his taxi-driver, 'Sank Roo Doe Noo.' That had started one of the memorable evenings of his life, culminating in the loss, almost simultaneous, of his virginity and his notecase.

("From a View to a Kill," FOR YOUR EYES ONLY)

At the early age of seventeen, Bond left school. Fleming mentions in FROM RUSSIA, WITH LOVE that Bond attended the University of Geneva for a while (as did the author). There, he presumably was taught to ski by Hannes Oberhauser of Kitzbuhel. Like Fleming, Bond was happiest in Kitzbuhel. There are references to this in the short story, "Octopussy."

Bond's first work with the British Secret Service was before the war, according to a brief reference in CASINO ROYALE. Reportedly, he sat in the casino at Monte Carlo for two months watching a Roumanian team "work their stuff with the invisible ink and the dark glasses." According to the Head of S., Bond and the Deuxieme "bowled them out in the end," and Bond turned in a million francs he had won. Bond couldn't have been more than fifteen or sixteen at the time. (When Ian Fleming began writing the novels, he didn't intend to pen as many as he did. As more and more books were written, Fleming had to tinker with Bond's early life—that is, change dates—so that Bond would be the appropriate age. In CASINO ROYALE, for example, Bond claims he bought his 4½-litre Bentley "almost new in 1933." Bond's age couldn't have been more than nine! Dates like these were corrected in later novels.)

Bond entered a branch of what was subsequently to become the Ministry of Defense in 1941. He was given the rank of lieutenant in the Special Branch of the Royal Naval Volunteer Reserves, and ended the war with the rank of Commander. After the war, the head of the Secret Service, M, became aware of Bond's service record. He accepted Commander Bond's post-war application to continue working for the Ministry in which he had risen to the rank of Principal Officer in the Civil Service.

Bond was awarded a Double-0 number in the Service for two jobs briefly described in CASINO ROYALE. The first was in New York. A Japanese cipher expert was cracking British codes on the thirty-sixth floor of the R.C.A. building in Rockefeller Center, where the Japanese had their consulate. Bond took a room on the fortieth floor of the next-door skyscraper, and he could look across the street into the decoder's room. Bond was helped by a colleague and a couple of Remington thirty-thirties with telescopic sights and silencers. The guns were smuggled to Bond's room, where the men sat for days waiting for the chance to gun down the cipher expert. Since the windows at Rockefeller Center were of heavy glass, a bullet would deflect and miss a target on the inside. Therefore, Bond's colleague shot first in order to blast a hole through the window so that Bond could shoot the Japanese through the opening. Bond was successful—he shot the cipher expert in the mouth as the man turned to gape at the broken window.

The second job was in Stockholm. Bond's assignment was to kill a Norwegian who was doubling against the British for the Germans. The Norwegian had managed to get two British agents captured and probably killed. Bond eliminated the double agent in the man's bedroom, using a knife. Bond claims that this particular job wasn't as clean as the first one.

For those two jobs, Bond was awarded the number 007, which gave him the license to kill in the line of duty. In 1954, Bond was appointed a C.M.G. (Companion to the Order of St. Michael and St. George) for his duties with the Ministry, and M notes that these duties were performed with "outstanding bravery and distinction, although occasionally, through an impetuous strain in his nature, with a streak of the foolhardy that brought him in conflict with higher authority." But

Bond possessed what M calls "The Nelson Touch" in moments of the highest emergency, and "somehow contrived to escape more or less unscathed from the many adventurous paths down which his duties led him."

Today, James Bond would be in his late fifties. John Gardner, in resurrecting the Bond series with the publication of LICENSE RENEWED, has more or less picked up the Bond character from the sixties and placed him intact in the 1980s relatively unchanged. This is a little disconcerting for Bond fans who have followed the character since the beginning. Avoiding any specific reference to age, the only clue that Gardner gives to Bond's advancing years is that a little grey is showing at his temples.

APPEARANCE

The first impression of James Bond's appearance is uttered by Vesper Lynd in CASINO ROYALE:

"He is very good-looking. He reminds me rather of Hoagy Carmichael, but there is something cold and ruthless in his . . ."
(CASINO ROYALE, Chapter 5)

This sentence is never finished due to an interruption (and a nasty one at that—an explosion outside smashes the window over the table at which Vesper is sitting). Later on, Bond examines himself in the mirror:

His grey-blue eyes looked calmly back with a hint of ironical inquiry and the short lock of black hair which would never stay in place subsided to form a thick comma above his right eyebrow. With the thin vertical scar down his right cheek the general effect was faintly piratical. Not much of Hoagy Carmichael there, thought Bond, as he filled a flat, light gunmetal box with fifty of the Morland cigarettes with a triple gold band. Mathis had told him of the girl's comment.
(CASINO ROYALE, Chapter 8)

In the next novel, LIVE AND LET DIE, not much is added to this basic description. Again, Bond is looking into a mirror and notices that the "thick comma of black hair" has lost some of its tail. He notes that nothing could be done about the thin vertical scar down his right cheek—the FBI had experimented with Covermark—or about the "coldness and hint of anger in his grey-blue eyes." But there was the "mixed blood of America in the black hair and high cheekbones," which might pass him off as an American except, Bond notes, with women.

And, in MOONRAKER:

Bond knew that there was something alien and un-English about himself. He knew that he was a difficult man to cover up.

(MOONRAKER, Chapter 4)

For the first time, Bond is described in MOONRAKER as being "rather saturnine"—an adjective which could have applied to Fleming himself.

Finally, in FROM RUSSIA, WITH LOVE, a complete picture of Bond's face is found in SMERSH's file:

It was a dark, clean-cut face, with a three-inch scar showing whitely down the sunburned skin of the right cheek. The eyes were wide and level under straight, rather long black brows. The hair was black, parted on the left, and carelessly brushed so that a thick black comma fell down over the right eyebrow. The longish straight nose ran down to a short upper lip below which was a wide and finely drawn but cruel mouth. The line of the jaw was straight and firm. A section of dark suit, white shirt and black knitted tie completed the picture.

(FROM RUSSIA, WITH LOVE, Chapter 6)

The dossier goes on and states other statistics: Bond's height is 183 centimetres (a little over six feet). His weight is seventy-six kilograms (a little over 167 pounds), and he has a slim build.

Since then, Bond has always been described as having "dark, rather cruel good looks." This is the quality which women find irresistible.

CLOTHING AND OTHER PERSONAL HABITS

James Bond usually wears a dark-blue serge suit with a white shirt made of silk. Bond's suits are almost always single-breasted and very lightweight. For casual wear, Bond sports a sleeveless dark blue Sea Island cotton shirt and navy blue tropical worsted trousers. Bond likes comfortable soft leather or moccasin shoes, usually in black (he abhors shoelaces). At times Bond wears a black, knitted silk tie.

Bond also likes pajamas. In CASINO ROYALE, he wears a pajama coat from Hong Kong. (Bond is teased a bit by his American colleagues during the LIVE AND LET DIE case—"We mostly sleep in the raw in America, Mr. Bond.")

Bond takes cold showers. Sometimes he takes a cold shower immediately following a very hot one. The stinging temperature of a cold shower stimulates the nerves in his body. He uses Pinaud Elixir, "that prince among shampoos," and prefers Guerlain's "Fleurs des Alpes" over Camay. Bond usually begins his day with twenty slow pushups, "lingering over each one so that his muscles have no rest." Then, he rolls over and performs leg lifts until "his stomach muscles scream." Next, he touches his toes twenty times and moves on to arm and chest exercises combined with deep breathing "until he is dizzy."

James Bond's cultural interests are not very extensive. His reading habits only serve either functional or recreational purposes. His bookshelf at home includes Tommy Armour on *How to Play Your Best Golf All the Time* and Ben Hogan's *Modern Fundamentals of Golf. Scarne on Cards* is a particular favorite and reference guide for cheating and gambling, and Patrick Leigh-Fermor's *The Traveller's Tree* provides handy information on Haitian voodoo cults. He is especially fond of Eric Ambler thrillers, and is reading *The Mask of Dimitrios* en route to Istanbul in FROM RUSSIA, WITH LOVE. Bond claims that he only reads *The Times,* but has been caught on occasions with *The Daily Express, Country Life,* and the *Evening Standard. The Daily Gleaner* amuses him when he's in Jamaica. And from what the reader can gather, Bond has little or no taste in art, music, or theater.

Bond is an outstanding athlete. An expert swimmer both below the surface and above, Bond excels in every sort of water sport. He is able to swim a couple of miles without tiring. He is an avid skier, and has won something called a "Golden K." He actually learned the sport at the Hannes Schneider School at St. Anton in the Arlberg. Bond seems to have a thorough knowledge of every kind of game imaginable; but his favorite, other than card games, is golf. His favorite course is the Royal St. Mark's at Sandwich. Bond also enjoys mountain climbing, a fondness he acquired as a youth in Kitzbuhel.

James Bond has no real hobbies, but he does love fast cars. The early novels feature Bond driving one of the last of the 4½-litre Bentleys with a supercharger by Amherst Villiers. Bond kept it serviced every year, allowing a former Bentley mechanic in London to tend it with "jealous care." It was a battleship-grey convertible coupe and was capable of reaching ninety miles per hour with thirty in reserve. But the Bentley met its maker when Hugo Drax's henchman, Krebs, caused it to collide with a heavy roll of newsprint.

The remainder of Fleming's novels featured Bond in a Mark II Continental Bentley which he acquired after its previous owner crashed into a telephone pole. Bond bought the car and had the bend in the chassis straightened and fitted with new power: a Mark IV engine with 9.5 compression. Fleming spends an entire page of Chapter 7 in THUNDERBALL describing the outstanding features of the car and adding that "she went like a bird and a bomb and Bond loved her more than all the women at present in his life, rolled, if that were feasible, together." Bond demands that his car start immediately (in all types of weather), and, after that, by all means stay on the road.

During the Goldfinger affair, Bond is issued a company car in the form of an Aston Martin D.B. III fitted with some unusual specifications. Although not the armory appearing in the film version, the D.B. III includes switches to alter the type and color of Bond's front and rear lights if he was tailing or being followed at night; reinforced steel bumpers; a trick compartment in which to keep a long-barrelled Colt .45; and a radio pick-up tuned to receive an apparatus called the Homer. One must assume Bond was forced to return the Aston Martin to the company car pool after the case, since he never uses it again in subsequent adventures. He resumes life with his beloved Bentley, and is surprised when it reaches a speed of 125 m.p.h. for the first time

The famous Aston Martin D.B.V used in the films Goldfinger, Thunderball, *and* On Her Majesty's Secret Service. *Note machine guns behind the front parking lights and the bulletproof shield behind the back windshield. (Photos courtesy of Aston Martin Lagonda Inc.)*

The later Bond films feature a Lotus Esprit which is able to dive like a submarine. (Photo courtesy of Rolls-Royce Motors Inc.)

John Gardner's Bond drives a Saab 900 Turbo with interesting accessories. Note "secret" compartments, fire-extinguishing system, and blinding headlight behind license plate. (Photos courtesy of Saab-Scania of America, Inc.)

(while chasing his future wife on the road to Royale-les-Eaux). He worries about the crankshaft bearings for a moment, but later Bond hears "no expensive noises."

John Gardner's Bond now drives a Saab 900 Turbo. It, too, is equipped with accessories, such as the capacity to blind tailing drivers with extremely bright rear lights. It has its own fire extinguishing system, and contains a secret compartment in which to hide large prints of art or other items.

Unlike the accusations Q makes about 007's treatment of his equipment in the films, the Bond of the novels is a perfectionist in his care for and use of weaponry. From the very beginning, the point is made clear:

His last action was to slip his right hand under the pillow until it rested under the butt of the .38 Colt Police Positive with the sawn barrel. Then he slept . . .

(CASINO ROYALE, Chapter 1)

This fanatical practice has saved Bond's life more than once, even though it causes his bed partners some dismay. During THE SPY WHO LOVED ME, Vivienne Michel wonders why Bond sleeps with his body away from hers, with his right hand under the pillow. She discovers the reason a little while later, after Bond has had to use the gun on a gangster attempting to break into their cabin:

Now I realized why he had lain like that, with his right hand doubled under the pillow. I guessed that he always slept like that. I thought his must be rather like a fireman's life, always waiting for a call. I thought how extraordinary it must be to have danger as your business.

(THE SPY WHO LOVED ME, Chapter 14)

Bond takes care to clean his weapons regularly, always making sure each part is in working order. In the first five novels, Bond's standard equipment consisted of a very flat .25 Beretta automatic with a skeleton grip inside a light chamois leather holster slipped over his left shoulder so that it hung about three inches below his armpit. But Major Boothroyd and M put a stop to Bond's use of the Beretta after it snagged in Bond's jacket during an attempted draw in FROM RUSSIA, WITH LOVE. In DOCTOR NO, Boothroyd calls the Beretta a "ladies' gun," much to Bond's dismay. M's orders are final, and Bond is forced to continue the series with a Walther PPK 7.65mm. It's about a .32 caliber as compared with the Beretta's .25. The Walther is carried in a Berns-Martin triple-draw holster made of stiff saddle leather. For a longer range, Bond is issued a Smith &

Beretta .25. Bond used this gun in Ian Fleming's first five novels. It had a blue finish, a 2″ barrel and is 4.75″ over-all. To the best of our knowledge, the "Jetfire" model was used. A silencer was also used twice with the gun. (Photo courtesy of Beretta U.S.A. Corp.)

Walther PPK, 7.65mm, with a blue finish. Bond used this model in a .32 calibre, rather than a .22 calibre, as shown here. Fleming stated that Bond's model had a spur at the bottom of the clip (this helped in gripping the weapon). The model used in the films does not have a spur. The Walther PPK has a 3.27″ barrel, and is 6.1″ over-all. The gun was used in the remaining Fleming books. (Photo courtesy of Interarms Inc.)

Wesson Centennial Airweight. This .38 caliber revolver is hammerless, so it won't catch in clothing.

John Gardner's Bond is issued a Browning 9mm in the 1980s, which has been replaced by the Heckler & Koch VP70, and, in ICEBREAKER, by the H&K P7. He also keeps an unauthorized Ruger Super Blackhawk .44 Magnum in a secret compartment in his Saab. Throughout the years, Bond has occasionally used the previously mentioned .38 Colt Police Positive; a .45 Colt; a Savage 99F with a Weatherby 6 x 62 telescope;

Smith & Wesson Centennial Airweight Revolver, Model 42, which holds five .38 Special rounds. Bond is issued this gun along with the Walther PPK in DOCTOR NO. *Although Fleming appropriated the revolver for long-range shooting, it is actually a short-range gun and disappeared from the books probably because the author was embarrassed by this technical error. (Photo courtesy of Smith & Wesson Inc.)*

The modern version of the Berns-Martin "triple-draw" holster, now called the Bianchi Model 9R. Bianchi Gunleather acquired the Berns-Martin design. (Photo courtesy of Bianchi Gunleather.)

John Gardner's Bond is issued a Browning 9mm in LICENSE RENEWED. *The gun has a blue finish and carries a seven-shot clip (but also has an eighth round in the breech). (Photo courtesy of Browning Inc.)*

John Gardner's Bond illegally keeps a Ruger Super Blackhawk .44 Magnum Revolver in a secret compartment of his Saab. The gun has a blue finish and is a six-shot model with a 7.5″ barrel. (Photo courtesy of Sturm, Ruger & Company, Inc.)

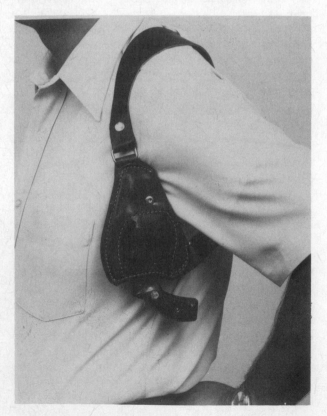

FOR SPECIAL SERVICES *finds Bond using a Heckler & Koch VP70 automatic, a rapid-firing weapon. This model was replaced by the P7 in* ICEBREAKER. *(Photo courtesy of Heckler & Koch, Inc.) (Thanks to Lloyd Jones for technical information.)*

and a Winchester .308 caliber International Experimental Target rifle.

Bond likes to spend the money he makes. In MOON-RAKER, he muses that it is his ambition to have "as little as possible in his banking account when he was killed, as, when he was depressed he knew he would be, before the statutory age of forty-five." Bond tells his future father-in-law, Marc-Ange Draco, that "too much money is the worst curse you can lay on anyone's head . . . that is the only kind of money to have—not quite enough." But Bond does enjoy spending money won from gambling—something he calls "found money."

Bond had always been a gambler. He loved the dry riffle of the cards and the constant unemphatic drama of the quiet figures round the green tables. He liked the solid, studied comfort of cardrooms and casinos, the well-padded arms of the chair, the glass of champagne or whisky at the elbow, the quiet unhurried attention of good servants. He was amused by the impartiality of the roulette ball and of the playing cards—and their eternal bias. He liked being an actor and a spectator and from his chair to take part in other men's dramas and decisions, until it came to his own turn to say that vital "yes" or "no," generally on a fifty-fifty chance.

Above all, he liked it that everything was one's own fault. There was only oneself to praise or blame. Luck was a servant and not a master. Luck had to be accepted with a shrug or taken advantage of up to the hilt. But it had to be understood and recognized for what it was and not confused with a faulty appreciation of the odds, for, at gambling, the deadly sin is to mistake bad play for bad luck. And luck in all its moods had to be loved and not feared. Bond saw luck as a woman, to be softly wooed or brutally ravaged, never pandered to or pursued.

(CASINO ROYALE, Chapter 7)

This philosophy of Bond's runs throughout the novels thematically. Too often Bond must depend on luck to bring him through a crisis or a decision. Though he hates to admit it, luck plays an important part in his work as a secret agent.

For miscellany's sake, Vivienne Michel notes that Bond's handwriting is very clear and even, and that Bond uses a real pen and not a ball-point. One of Bond's favorite expressions is "So that's the score!" and it should be noted that James Bond is not too shy to sing aloud. He first meets Honeychile Rider in DOCTOR NO by joining her in a verse of "Marion."

* * *

FOOD, DRINK, AND DRUGS

Quite naturally, Ian Fleming's taste for luxurious meals, fine liquor, and elegant surroundings is shared by James Bond. Bond explains himself to Vesper Lynd over dinner in CASINO ROYALE:

"You must forgive me," he said. "I take a ridiculous pleasure in what I eat and drink. It comes partly from being a bachelor, but mostly from a habit of taking a lot of trouble over details. It's very pernickety and old-maidish really, but then when I'm working I generally have to eat my meals alone and it makes them more interesting when one takes trouble."

(CASINO ROYALE, Chapter 8)

Later on, Fleming emphasizes Bond's particularities:

James Bond was not a gourmet. In England he lived on grilled soles, oeufs cocotte and cold roast beef with potato salad. But when travelling abroad, generally by himself, meals were a welcome break in the day, something to look forward to, something to break the tension of fast driving, with its risks taken or avoided, the narrow squeaks, the permanent background of concern for the fitness of his machine.

(ON HER MAJESTY'S SECRET SERVICE, Chapter 2)

James Bond is actually a *gourmand*. Only Bond would insist that his eggs be boiled precisely for three and a third minutes. Breakfast is Bond's favorite meal of the day. When he's in England, the breakfast is always the same and consists of very strong coffee (from De Bry in New Oxford Street, brewed in an American Chemex) of which he drinks two large cups, black and without sugar. That single egg is a very fresh, speckled brown egg from French Marans hens owned by some friend of his housekeeper, May, in the country. It is served in a dark blue egg cup with a gold ring around the top. It amuses Bond to maintain that there is such a thing as "the perfect boiled egg." Next comes two thick slices of whole-wheat toast, "a large pat of deep yellow Jersey butter and three squat glass jars containing Tiptree 'Little Scarlet' strawberry jam; Cooper's Vintage Oxford marmalade and Norwegian Heather Honey from Fortnum's." Breakfast is a ritual for Bond, and his day never seems to go well without it.

Bond likes scrambled eggs, too, although he usually has these for lunch rather than breakfast. Bond always relays specific orders on how to make his special scrambled eggs, usually eaten with smoked salmon. Fleming provides the recipe in a short story entitled "007 in

New York,'' which appears in his travelogue, THRILL-ING CITIES:

Scrambled Eggs ''James Bond''
For FOUR individualists:
    12 fresh eggs
    salt and pepper
    5-6 oz. fresh butter
Break the eggs into a bowl. Beat thoroughly with a fork and season well. In a small copper (or heavy-bottomed saucepan) melt four oz. of the butter. When melted, pour in the eggs and cook over a very low heat, whisking continuously with a small egg whisk.

While the eggs are slightly more moist than you would wish for eating, remove pan from heat, add rest of butter and continue whisking for half a minute, adding the while finely chopped chives or fines herbes. Serve on hot buttered toast in individual copper dishes (for appearance only) with pink champagne (Taittainger) and low music.

("007 in New York," THRILLING CITIES)

The time Bond spends with Felix Leiter on a case is usually over a meal. While snooping in Harlem, Leiter insists on having "the national dish"—Little Neck clams and fried chicken Maryland with bacon and sweet corn. These men are always attempting to impress each other by ordering the other man's meal before he can speak to the waiter. On one occasion in New York, while Bond is in the washroom of Sardi's (one of his favorite New York establishments), Leiter "takes a chance" and orders smoked salmon and Brizzola (Leiter insists it's the best cut of beef, straight cut across the bone, roasted and then broiled). Bond is pleased with the meal, and is impressed that the Brizzola is so tender he can cut it with a fork. At a "Chicken in the Basket" in upstate New York, the men enjoy scrambled eggs and sausages with hot buttered rye toast. Bond likes these little American roadside eateries, and Fleming's descriptive powers add to their "flavor."

But the men show an extreme distaste for the commercialism of the tourist traps in the Bahamas. At the Royal Bahamian in Nassau, Bond and Leiter are disgusted by the menu:

From the pretentious dishes, "For Your Particular Consideration," printed in Ornamental Gothic, Bond chose Native Seafood Cocktail Supreme followed by Disjointed Home Farm Chicken, Sauté au Cresson, which was described in italics as "Tender Farm Chicken, Broiled to a Rich Brown, Basted with Creamery Butter and Disjointed for Your Convenience. Price 38/6 or dollars 5.35." Felix Leiter went for the Baltic Herring in Sour Cream followed by "Chopped

Tenderloin of Beef, French Onion Rings (Our Renowned Beef is Chef-Selected from the Finest Corn-fed, Mid-Western Cattle, and Aged to Perfection to Assure You of the Very Best). Price 40/3 or dollars 5.65."

When they commented sourly and at length about the inflated bogosity of tourist-hotel food and particularly the mendacious misuse of the English language to describe materials which had certainly been in various deep-freezes for at least six months, they settled down on the balcony to discuss Bond's findings of the morning.

(THUNDERBALL, Chapter 12)

During the above meal, Felix Leiter throws down his knife and fork and says, "This is hamburger and bad hamburger. The French onion rings were never in France, and what's more, they're not even rings. They're oval."

When he's in Jamaica, Bond enjoys something called "paw-paw with a slice of green lime, a dish piled with red bananas, purple star-apples, and tangerines, scrambled eggs and bacon, Blue Mountain coffee, Jamaican marmalade (almost black), and guava jelly." The Blue Mountain coffee is supposedly the "best in the world."

The dinner meals are always something exquisite. On his first date with Vesper Lynd, he tells her to order expensively. Vesper tells the waiter:

"I'd made two choices," she laughed, "and either would have been delicious; but behaving like a millionaire occasionally is a wonderful treat, and if you're sure . . . well, I'd like to start with caviar and then have a plain grilled rognon de veau with pommes soufflés. And then I'd like to have fraises des bois with a lot of cream. Is it very shameless to be so certain and so expensive?" She smiled at him inquiringly.

"It's a virtue, and anyway it's only a good plain wholesome meal." He turned to the maitre d'hotel. "And bring plenty of toast.

"The trouble always is," he explained to Vesper, "not how to get caviar, but how to get enough toast with it.

"Now," he turned back to the menu, "I myself will accompany Mademoiselle with the caviar; but then I would like a very small tournedos, underdone, with sauce Béarnaise and a coeur d'artichaut. While Mademoiselle is enjoying the strawberries, I will have an avocado pear with a little French dressing. Do you approve?"

(CASINO ROYALE, Chapter 8)

Once, while in Miami, Bond has what he calls "the most delicious meal he had had in his life." Bond is wined and dined by an American millionaire, Mr. Junius Du Pont, and he is afforded the opportunity to indulge. He has stone crabs containing the tenderest, sweetest shellfish meat he has ever tasted. The meat is perfectly set off by the dry toast and slightly burned taste of melted butter. After each helping of crab, champagne cleans his palate for the next. Once this meal is bloating his belly, Bond is momentarily disgusted with himself.

The most celebrated of all the Bond dinners occurs in MOONRAKER, when Bond dines with M at Blades Club. Fleming devotes an entire chapter to the meal, and although the reader may not be familiar with much of the food consumed, Fleming's tasty descriptions are mouth watering. M orders caviar, devilled kidney with a slice of bacon, peas, and new potatoes. This is followed by strawberries in kirsch and a marrow bone. Bond has lamb cutlets, the same vegetables as M, asparagus with Hollandaise sauce, and a slice of pineapple. Along with all that, Bond has sliced smoked Scotch salmon on toast. The salmon has "the delicate glutinous texture only achieved by the Highland curers—very different from the desiccated products of Scandinavia." The cutlets are again so tender he can cut them with a fork. And M, of course, is in heaven with his marrow bone—something he can't resist.

The most amusing dinner sequences appear in YOU ONLY LIVE TWICE, as Tiger Tanaka initiates Bond into the culinary delights of Japan. At one point, Bond is "wrestling" with his octopus and rice, and is about to savor a lobster specialty:

Lacquer boxes of rice, raw quails' eggs in sauce, and bowls of sliced seaweed were placed in front of them both. Then they were each given a fine oval dish bearing a large lobster whose head and tail had been left as a dainty ornament to the sliced pink flesh in the centre. Bond set to with his chopsticks. He was surprised to find that the flesh was raw. He was even more surprised when the head of his lobster began moving off his dish and, with questing antennae and scrabbling feet, tottered off across the table. "Good God, Tiger!" Bond said, aghast. "The damn thing's alive!"

Tiger hissed impatiently, "Really, Bondo-san. I am much disappointed in you. You fail test after test. I sincerely hope you will show improvement during the rest of your journey. Now eat up and stop being squeamish. This is a very great Japanese delicacy."

James Bond bowed ironically. "Shimatta!" he said. "I have made a mistake. It crossed my mind that honourable Japanese lobster might not like being eaten alive. Thank you for correcting the unworthy thought."

(YOU ONLY LIVE TWICE, Chapter 9)

Bond also has the opportunity to try Kobe beef, which is reported to be the finest in the world. At one point, he is awarded the treat of tasting a *fugu* feast. *Fugu* is the Japanese blowfish equipped with poisonous glands, but the meat is the staple food of *sumo* wrestlers because of its strength-giving qualities. Bond thinks the fish tastes like nothing, not even fish. But "it was very pleasant on the palate and Bond was effusive in his compliments because Tiger, smacking his lips over each morsel, obviously expected it of him."

"And now, my friend, I have ordered dinner, a good dinner, to be served us up here. And then we will go to bed stinking of garlic and, perhaps, just a little bit drunk. Yes?"
From his heart Bond said, "I can't think of anything better."
(ON HER MAJESTY'S SECRET SERVICE, Chapter 23)

This statement implies that James Bond likes to drink. From the moment James Bond gives a waiter special instructions for mixing a martini in CASINO ROYALE, we know that he is especially a hard-liquor man:

"A dry Martini," he said. "One. In a deep champagne goblet."
"Oui, Monsieur."
"Just a moment. Three measures of Gordon's, one of vodka, half a measure of Kina Lillet. Shake it very well until it's ice-cold, then add a large thin slice of lemon-peel. Got it?"
(CASINO ROYALE, Chapter 7)

And thus is born the famous James Bond martini, "shaken but not stirred." After the martini is brought to the table and tasted, Bond tells the barman that if he can obtain a vodka made with grain instead of potatoes, he'll find the drink even better than it is. Later on in the book, Bond dubs his original martini "The Vesper," after the heroine of the first Bond novel. Actually, Fleming was contested over his use of Kina Lillet, which contains quinine and might be very bitter in a martini. Simple Lillet vermouth would have been more appropriate. The martini is contagious, for even Felix Leiter develops a taste for it. He chastizes a bartender in THUNDERBALL for not following instructions in making it. Bond's standard variation of the martini is simply vodka, medium dry.

Bond also has a taste for champagne. When he's not drinking martinis or ice-cold vodka straight up, he almost always orders champagne (especially the pink variety). While dining with M at Blades, the wine waiter suggests Bond try the Dom Perignon '46, to go with the real pre-war Wolfschmidt vodka from Riga. Once Bond has both drinks in front of him, he shocks M with some unusual table practices:

When M. poured him three fingers from the frosted carafe Bond took a pinch of black pepper and dropped it on the surface of the Vodka. The pepper slowly settled to the bottom of the glass leaving a few grains on the surface which Bond dabbed up with the tip of a finger. Then he tossed the cold liquor well to the back of his throat and put his glass, with the dregs of the pepper at the bottom, back on the table.

M. gave him a glance of rather ironical inquiry.

"It's a trick the Russians taught me that time you attached me to the Embassy in Moscow," apologized Bond. "There's often quite a lot of fusel oil on the surface of this stuff—at least there used to be when it was badly distilled. Poisonous. In Russia, where you get a lot of bath-tub liquor, it's an understood thing to sprinkle a little pepper in your glass. It takes the fusel oil to the bottom. I got to like the taste and now it's a habit. But I shouldn't have insulted the club Wolfschmidt," he added with a grin.

M. grunted. "So long as you don't put pepper in Basildon's favourite champagne," he said drily.

(MOONRAKER, Chapter 5)

Bond's traditional drink at Royale-les-Eaux is Taittinger's Blanc de Blancs. Bond consumes a bottle of this one evening before visiting the casino, immediately followed by half a bottle of Mouton Rothschild '53, and a glass of ten-year-old Calvados with three cups of coffee!

Bond also likes bourbon on the rocks. His favorite brands are Old Grand-dad, Walker's de luxe, Jack Daniels, and I. W. Harper's. When drinking gin, he prefers Gordon's or Beefeater. Other favorite cocktails include an Old-Fashioned or a Negroni (one-third gin, one-third Campari, one-third red Cinzano). He is particular about certain drinks in specific countries. For instance:

James Bond had his first drink of the evening at Fouquet's. It was not a solid drink. One cannot drink seriously in French cafes. Out of doors on a pavement in the sun is no place for vodka or whisky or gin. A *fine á l'eau* is fairly serious, but it intoxicates without tasting very good. A *quart de champagne* or a *champagne á l'orange* is all right before luncheon, but in the evening one *quart* leads to another *quart,* and a bottle of indifferent champagne is a bad foundation for the night. Pernod is possible, but it should be drunk in company, and anyway Bond had never liked the stuff because its licorice taste reminded him of his childhood. No, in cafes you have to drink the least offensive of the musical-comedy drinks that go with them, and Bond always had the same thing, an Americano—bitter Campari, Cinzano, a large slice of lemon peel, and soda. For the soda he always stipulated Perrier, for in his opinion expensive soda water was the cheapest way to improve a poor drink.

("From a View to a Kill," FOR YOUR EYES ONLY)

Bond always orders his drinks double. Once, in THE MAN WITH THE GOLDEN GUN, he feels a little guilty ordering his third double (but Mary Goodnight wouldn't know it as a double when it came anyway).

Finally, Bond does not drink tea. He hates it. "It's mud," he says. He believes it is one of the main reasons for the downfall of the British Empire. After he had said this to one of the girls from the canteen at headquarters, the expression "cup of mud" began seeping through the building.

Bond smokes cigarettes made especially for him by Morlands of Grosvenor Street. They are a special blend of Balkan and Turkish mixture, and each cigarette bears three gold bands. Bond keeps his cigarettes in a wide, gunmetal case which holds fifty. He also sports a black, oxidized Ronson lighter. Bond smokes around sixty cigarettes a day. This habit catches up with him in THUNDERBALL—Bond's medical report indicates that these cigarettes have a higher nicotine content than the mass-produced varieties. After his experience at Shrublands health spa, Bond's tobacco intake is reduced to around twenty or twenty-five cigarettes a day.

John Gardner's Bond has arranged for Morlands to create a special cigarette with a tar content slightly lower than any currently available on the market. A year later, Bond quits using the Morlands cigarettes and commissions H. Simmons of Burlington Arcade to create a low-tar cigarette for him. These still retain the distinctive gold bands (along with Simmons' trademark).

Bond basically stays away from other drugs, but he does have a habit of using Benzedrine before a particularly dangerous assignment. He takes some of these tablets before his swim through Shark Bay in LIVE AND LET DIE, as well as before swimming to Dr. Shatterhand's Castle of Death in YOU ONLY LIVE TWICE. During the exquisite dinner with M at Blades, Bond is brought an envelope containing the white powder; he discreetly mixes it with his champagne. "Now what?" asks M, with a "trace of impatience."

"Benzedrine," he said. "I rang up my secretary before dinner and asked her to wangle some out of the surgery at Headquarters. It's what I shall need if I'm going to keep my wits about me tonight. It's apt to make one a bit over-confident, but that'll be a help too." He stirred the champagne with a scrap of toast so that the white powder whirled among the bubbles. Then he drank the mixture down with one long swallow. "It doesn't taste," said Bond, "and the champagne is quite excellent."

M. smiled at him indulgently, "It's your funeral," he said—
(MOONRAKER, Chapter 5)

In another instance, Bond uses Benzedrine at the Dreamy Pines Motor Court, before tackling the likes of Horror and Sluggsy. He explains to Vivienne Michel that it will keep him awake. The one thing he doesn't want to happen that particular evening is fall asleep.

In Harlem, Bond and Leiter go to several nightclubs where marijuana is smoked freely. Bond sniffs the stuff and immediately knows what it is. And there's a point in THUNDERBALL when Leiter suggests that a traffic accident could actually have been an attempt on Bond's life. Bond dismisses this by saying, "You've been taking mescaline or something. It's a damned good sequence for a comic strip, but these things don't happen in real life." I doubt whether Bond or Leiter ever experimented with hallucinogens; but it is possible, since both of them have spent time in the Caribbean, where mescaline is plentiful.

James Bond is not a man of many vices; only particular ones.

HOME AND OFFICE LIFE

James Bond lives in a comfortable flat on a square lined with plane trees off the King's Road in Chelsea. His flat is on the ground floor of a converted Regency house, and it is looked after by his elderly Scottish housekeeper, May. Bond's bedroom is "smallish," and is decorated with white and gold Cole wallpaper with deep red curtains. The sitting-room is lined with books, but Bond's reading tastes are never fully explored in the novels. There is an ornate Empire desk at which Bond likes to sit when he is studying *Scarne on Cards* or other such technical manuals. May serves Bond's meals on Minton china, of a dark blue and gold and white; the coffee pot and silver are Queen Anne. There are two telephones—a regular personal phone, and a red one with a direct line to headquarters. The red phone almost always rings at inopportune times. But the flat in Chelsea is within ten minutes driving time to the office.

When Bond is not on an assignment abroad, one wonders what he does with his spare time. One paragraph gives us a small clue:

It was the beginning of a typical routine day for Bond. It was

only two or three times a year that an assignment came along requiring his particular abilities. For the rest of the year he had the duties of an easy-going senior civil servant—elastic office hours from around ten to six; lunch, generally in the canteen; evenings spent playing cards in the company of a few close friends, or at Crockford's; or making love, with rather cold passion, to one of three similarly disposed married women; week-ends playing golf for high stakes at one of the clubs near London.

(MOONRAKER, Chapter 1)

It's hard to imagine Bond having a "few close friends" because they are never mentioned—Bill Tanner, M's Chief of Staff, is supposedly Bond's best friend at the office.

Bond almost never brings women home to his flat. Only once in the entire series does this happen: Tiffany Case comes to live with Bond in between books, after DIAMONDS ARE FOREVER. John Pearson, in his fictionalized biography of 007, presents these scenes in which Tiffany comes to blows with May; the two women cannot get along in the same flat, and eventually Tiffany becomes disenchanted and leaves. Although the story is fleshed out by Pearson, the incident is only vaguely hinted at in FROM RUSSIA, WITH LOVE.

The Secret Service (M.I.6) is housed on the eighth floor of a tall, grey building near Regent's Park. The Ministry-of-Works, as it was then called, is a "bustling world of girls carrying files, doors opening and shutting, and muted telephone bells." The doors to the offices have no numbers. If a person had business on the eighth floor, one had to be fetched by a secretary and brought to the particular office one was visiting.

Bond shares an office with two other members of the Double-0 section—008 and 0011. There is hardly a time when all three members of the section are in the office on a particular day, so there is no fighting for the attentions of their attractive secretary, Loelia Ponsonby. The total number of personnel in the Double-0 section is never mentioned.

Bond takes no holidays, but is usually awarded a fortnight's leave at the completion of each assignment, in addition to any sick leave that might be necessary (it almost always is). Bond earns, in 1955, fifteen hundred pounds a year, but he also has an additional one thousand pounds a year free of tax of his own. While on a job, Bond has an unlimited expense account, so for the other months of the year he spends in London, he lives very well on his roughly two thousand pounds a year net. In 1955, an English pound equalled approximately $2.80, which made Bond's salary, in American money, roughly $4,200 a year. Once, while staying in a luxurious hotel in Miami as a guest of Mr. Du Pont, Bond muses that were he spending his own money on the room (at $200 a night), he would lose his entire salary for a year in three weeks.

Routine office work usually consists of wading through piles of secret papers. These papers are circulated among the top members of the Service, and after reviewing, Bond simply signs "007" on the list, and places the document in his OUT tray. Sometimes Bond is called on to perform night duty. What this amounts to is basically the same secret-paper weeding, but in addition, Bond must, of all things, answer the Universal Export telephone. When M informs Bond that it is time that all senior officers do "their spell of routine," Bond protests. But after a few nights of the work, Bond begins to enjoy it. It gives him time to work on a handbook he is writing on secret methods of unarmed combat (Bond titles it *Stay Alive!*) which he hopes may become a standard manual for the Service.

Universal Export is the standing cover name for the British Secret Service until around 1963. By then, almost all enemy operatives know about it, so the name is changed to Transworld Consortium around the time of THE MAN WITH THE GOLDEN GUN.

ATTITUDES TOWARD HIS PROFESSION

It was part of his profession to kill people. He had never liked doing it and when he had to kill he did it as well as he knew how and forgot about it. As a secret agent who held the rare Double-0 prefix—the license to kill in the Secret Service—it was his duty to be as cool about death as a surgeon. If it happened, it happened. Regret was unprofessional—worse, it was death-watch beetle in the soul.

(GOLDFINGER, Chapter 1)

James Bond's duties as Principal Officer in the British Secret Service include diverse roles requiring diverse skills. But his most important function—never said in so many words—is to perform the role of executioner for the British government. That's putting it bluntly, but the "privilege" of holding a Double-0 number means that James Bond must kill people in the line of duty. It is something that he has accepted and is expected to perform. Many times an assignment involves nothing *but* the elimination of an enemy op-

erative. Bond performs this unpleasant task as best as he can without second thoughts—but even James Bond is not immune to the repercussions of this burden on his psyche. The opening chapter of GOLDFINGER finds Bond glumly reflecting on a recent assignment—involving a nasty killing—and attempting to block the regrets from his mind. He forces himself to justify his actions:

What the hell was he doing, glooming about this Mexican, this capungo who had been sent to kill him? It had been kill or get killed. Anyway, people were killing other people all the time, all over the world. People were using their motor cars to kill with. They were carrying infectious diseases around, blowing microbes in other people's faces, leaving gas-jets turned on in kitchens, pumping out carbon monoxide in closed garages. How many people, for instance, were involved in manufacturing H-bombs, from the miners who mined the uranium to the shareholders who owned the mining shares? Was there any person in the world who wasn't somehow, perhaps only statistically, involved in killing his neighbor?

(GOLDFINGER, Chapter 1)

Bond is lucky that he has a strong sense of patriotism. After a killing, it helps to remind himself that the act was performed for the good of England. The short story, "For Your Eyes Only," is built around the premise that Bond will personally carry out the execution of the men who murdered some personal friends of M. When M reveals the situation to Bond, it is Bond who volunteers the appropriate action, knowing full well that there is no legal evidence against the murderers to bring them to trial.

Bond said, "I wouldn't hesitate for a moment, sir. If foreign gangsters find they can get away with this kind of thing they'll decide the English are as soft as some other people seem to think we are. This is a case for rough justice—an eye for an eye."

M went on looking at Bond. He gave no encouragement, made no comment.

Bond said, "These people can't be hung, sir. But they ought to be killed."

("For Your Eyes Only," FOR YOUR EYES ONLY)

M makes no reply, but simply hands over the file on the case. What Bond will do is left unsaid. It is always left unsaid.

A full account of Bond's philosophy toward killing unfolds in Chapter 20 of CASINO ROYALE. While recuperating in the hospital after his torturous ordeal with Le Chiffre, Bond tells his friend Mathis that if he were faced with the task again, he would kill Le Chiffre out of personal vendetta rather than for the sake of his country. He goes on to argue that, in these modern times, ''heroes and villains keep on changing parts.'' He takes a step further by concluding that perhaps Le Chiffre served a high purpose of creating a norm of evil by which an opposite norm of good could exist. Mathis eventually laughs at Bond's serious brooding; he assures Bond that his tune will change with more experience under his belt—it is still very early in Bond's career.

''Well, when you get back to London you will find there are other Le Chiffres seeking to destroy you and your friends and your country. M. will tell you about them. And now that you have seen a really evil man you will know how evil they can be, and you will go after them to destroy them in order to protect yourself and the people you love. You won't wait or argue about it. You know what they look like now and what they do to people. You may be a bit more choosy about the jobs you take on. You may want to be certain that the target really is black; but there are plenty of really black targets around. There's still plenty for you to do. And you'll do it. And when you fall in love and have a mistress or a wife and children to look after, it will seem all the easier.''

Mathis opened the door and stopped on the threshold.

''Surround yourself with human beings, my dear James. They are easier to fight for than principles.''

He laughed. ''But don't let me down and become human yourself. We would lose such a wonderful machine.''

(CASINO ROYALE, Chapter 20)

This last statement is telling. Bond *does* become more of a machine when it comes to the unpleasant task of killing. He learns, throughout the course of the series, that thinking twice about death can result in mental catastrophe. Almost thirty years after the CASINO ROYALE affair, Bond is asked by Q'ute (Ann Reilly of Q Branch) how it feels to kill a person:

''While it's happening, you don't think much about it,'' Bond answered flatly. ''It's a reflex. You do it and you don't hesitate. If you're wise, and want to go on living, you don't think about it afterward either. I've known men who've had breakdowns—go for early retirement on half pension—for thinking about it afterward. There's nothing to tell, my dear Q'u—Ann. I try not to remember. That way I remain detached from its reality.''

(LICENSE RENEWED, Chapter 5)

A somewhat cynical attitude, to be sure, but it has kept Bond sane over the years.

James Bond's loyalty to England is a strong motivating force in his attitude toward his profession, and he defends this position on more than one occasion. There is one point in YOU ONLY LIVE TWICE when Tiger Tanaka takes advantage of Bond's pride in England in order to persuade him to perform an execution for Tiger's government. Tiger finds this touchy spot in Bond's character and jabs at it with accusations that Britain is a weak little nation. Bond loses his temper:

Bond said angrily, ''Balls to you, Tiger! And balls again! Just because you're a pack of militant potential murderers here, longing to get rid of your American masters and play at being *samurai* again, snarling behind your subservient smiles, you only judge people by your own jungle standards. Let me tell you this, my fine friend. England may have been bled pretty thin by a couple of world wars, our welfare-state politics may have made us expect too much for free, and the liberation of our colonies may have gone too fast, but we still climb Everest and beat plenty of the world at plenty of sports and win Nobel Prizes. Our politicians may be a feather-pated bunch, but I expect yours are, too. All politicians are. But there's nothing wrong with the British people—although there are only fifty million of them.''

(YOU ONLY LIVE TWICE, Chapter 8)

This outburst causes Tiger to applaud. Amends are made, and soon Bond has agreed to assassinate Dr. Shatterhand for the Japanese in exchange for a secret ciphering method needed by the British.

Despite the many courageous and dangerous duties Bond performs for his country, the Secret Service does not allow him to accept medals or awards in recognition of his actions. Several times in the series Bond declines some sort of reward from various countries—even from the Prime Minister of England himself. He is always appreciative, but stands firmly on the Service's policy. Only once does M allow the rules to bend. At the end of THE MAN WITH THE GOLDEN GUN, the Prime Minister proposes to recommend to Queen Elizabeth that Bond be immediately knighted. This would take the form of amending Bond's C.M.G. to a K.C.M.G. M congratulates Bond and gives the approval for Bond to accept the honor. But surprisingly, Bond refuses:

James Bond wiped his forehead with his handkerchief. Of course he was pleased! But above all pleased with M.'s commendation. The rest, he knew, was not in the stars. He had never been a public figure, and he did not wish to become one. He had no prejudice against letters after one's name, or before it. But there was one thing above all he treasured. His privacy. His anonymity. To become a public person, a person, in the snobbish world of England, of any country, who would be called upon to open things, lay foundation stones, make after-dinner speeches, brought the sweat to his armpits. "James Bond!" No middle name. No hyphen. A quiet, dull, anonymous name. Certainly he was a Commander in the Special Branch of the R.N.V.R., but he rarely used the rank. His C.M.G. likewise. He wore it perhaps once a year, together with his two rows of lettuce, because there was a dinner for the Old Boys—the fraternity of ex-Secret Service men that went under the name of The Twin Snakes Club. A grisly reunion held in the banqueting hall at Blades, it gave enormous pleasure to a lot of people who had been brave and resourceful in their day but now had old men's and old women's diseases and talked about dusty triumphs and tragedies. Tales which, since they would never be recorded in the history books, must be told again that night, over the Cockburn '12, when "The Queen" had been drunk, to some next-door neighbour such as James Bond who was only interested in what was going to happen tomorrow. That was when he wore his lettuce and the C.M.G. below his black tie—to give pleasure and reassurance to the Old Children at their annual party. For the rest of the year, until May polished them up for the occasion, the medals gathered dust in some secret repository where May kept them.

(THE MAN WITH THE GOLDEN GUN, Chapter 17)

No, Bond cannot imagine being called *Sir* James Bond. He sends a reply to M explaining that he is a Scottish peasant, has always been a Scottish peasant, and that he would not feel at home being anything else.

ATTITUDES TOWARD WOMEN AND MARRIAGE

One of the less redeeming qualities Ian Fleming bestowed upon his major character is the author's own chauvinistic attitudes toward women. But one must keep in mind the time period in which Fleming wrote the Bond novels—the feminist movement in the fifties was a far cry from what it is today. At first glance, one would label Bond's treatment of women in the series as ruthless and uncaring; and granted, this is true to some extent, especially in the first novel, CASINO ROYALE. But on further study, James Bond's attitude toward women is not a degrading one—it is a *protective* one (which many women might find just as chauvinistic). Although most of the Bond women can certainly fend for themselves, Bond adopts the position of the *machismo* white knight saving the damsel in distress from the evil dragon. Although he probably wouldn't admit it, James Bond is a romantic at heart. He loves women as long as their involvement with him remains

a short-term fantasy. And one must remember that the Bond women do not mind this. They, too, are independent people who are not looking for eternal entanglement any more than Bond is himself. Female fans of the Fleming novels understand this, and enjoy the Bond *oeuvre* on the basis that it *is* only fantasy life. The critics who accuse Fleming of chauvinism overlook the obvious good things Bond does for the women in the novels. For example, he is *always* a gentleman and treats his ladies with utmost respect. He has not once hit a woman (save for female villains like Irma Bunt or Rosa Klebb). And, despite what he may think when the woman is not present, Bond is always extremely kind to her. This is nowhere more evident than in THE SPY WHO LOVED ME, in which Bond goes out of his way to become involved in the personal problems of Vivienne Michel. Not only does he risk his life to save hers, but he takes great pains to see that the horrible experience at the Dreamy Pines Motor Court leaves no scars on Vivienne. Even Bond's future father-in-law commends him on the respectable way Bond has treated Tracy di Vicenzo:

"Your gentlemanly conduct in the casino, for which"—he looked across at Bond—"I now deeply thank you, was reported to me, as of course were your later movements together." He held up his hand as Bond shifted with embarrassment. "There is nothing to be ashamed of, to apologize for, in what you did last night. A man is a man and, who knows?—but I shall come to that later. What you did, the way you behaved in general, may have been the beginning of some kind of therapy."

(ON HER MAJESTY'S SECRET SERVICE, Chapter 5)

Marc-Ange Draco is referring to an incident in which Bond volunteered to pay off the gambling debt which Tracy foolishly brought upon herself (she made a bet with no money to back her up). Later that same evening, Bond and Tracy became lovers. Marc-Ange contends that Bond's actions may have prevented a suicide attempt by Tracy.

There *have* been three women in the series with whom Bond has fallen in love. Vesper Lynd, the heroine of CASINO ROYALE, is a thorn in his side at the beginning of the adventure; but he soon finds himself totally captivated by the woman. Toward the novel's end, he is considering proposing to Vesper. But this romance is short-lived: Vesper, a double agent, kills herself before Bond is able to pop the question. This hurts Bond deeply, and he carries this scar with him through the rest of the series. It is mentioned in ON

HER MAJESTY'S SECRET SERVICE that Bond visits Vesper's grave annually. The second woman is Tiffany Case, the heroine of DIAMONDS ARE FOREVER, with whom he lives for a while in his flat off King's Road; but subsequent clashes not only with May but with Bond's very organized life bring about the end of this relationship. Tiffany eventually meets and falls in love with an American serviceman. The third woman is Tracy, whom Bond marries in ON HER MAJESTY'S SECRET SERVICE. But the marriage ends in tragedy—Tracy is murdered by Ernst Stavro Blofeld only minutes after the wedding. Additionally, Bond lives with Kissy Suzuki for a year in YOU ONLY LIVE TWICE, but he is amnesic at the time. He eventually leaves her, not knowing that she is pregnant with his child.

CASINO ROYALE features Bond at his most chauvinistic:

. . . And then there was this pest of a girl. He sighed. Women were for recreation. On a job, they got in the way and fogged things up with sex and hurt feelings and all the emotional baggage they carried around. One had to look out for them and take care of them.

(CASINO ROYALE, Chapter 4)

And a little later in the novel, we learn Bond's overall feelings concerning affairs:

With most women his manner was a mixture of taciturnity and passion. The lengthy approaches to a seduction bored him almost as much as the subsequent mess of disentanglement. He found something grisly in the inevitability of the pattern of each affair. The conventional parabola—sentiment, the touch of the hand, the kiss, the passionate kiss, the feel of the body, the climax in the bed, then more bed, then less bed, then the boredom, the tears, and the final bitterness—was to him shameful and hypocritical. Even more he shunned the mise-en-scene for each of these acts in the play—the meeting at the party, the restaurant, the taxi, his flat, her flat, then the week-end by the sea, then the flats again, then the furtive alibis and the final angry farewell on some doorstep in the rain.

(CASINO ROYALE, Chapter 22)

When it comes to the subject of marriage, Bond tells Tiffany Case that "most marriages don't add two people together. They subtract one from the other." She asks him what sort of woman he would marry.

. . . He lit a cigarette thoughtfully. "Somebody who can make Sauce Béarnaise as well as love," he said.

"Holy mackerel! Just any old dumb hag who can cook and lie on her back?"

"Oh no. She's got to have all the usual things—" Bond examined her. "Gold hair. Grey eyes. A sinful mouth. Perfect figure. And of course she's got to be witty and poised and know how to dress and play cards and so forth. The usual things."

"And you'd marry this person if you found her?"

"Not necessarily," said Bond. "Matter of fact, I'm almost married already. To a man. Name begins with M. I'd have to divorce him before I tried marrying a woman. And I'm not sure I'd want to do that. She'd get me handing round canapes in an L-shaped drawing-room. And there'd be all those ghastly, 'Yes you did No I didn't' rows that seem to go with marriage. It wouldn't last. I'd get claustrophobia and run out on her. Get myself sent to Japan or somewhere."

"What about children?"

"Like to have some," said Bond shortly, "But only when I retire. Not fair to the children otherwise. My job's not all that secure."

(DIAMONDS ARE FOREVER, Chapter 22)

Once, while at a social party in Nassau, Bond makes the remark that if he married, he would want an airline hostess. His friend, the Governor, asks him why.

"Oh, I don't know. It would be fine to have a pretty girl always tucking you up and bringing you drinks and hot meals and asking if you had everything you wanted. And they're always smiling and wanting to please. If I don't find an air hostess, there'll be nothing for it but marry a Japanese. They seem to have the right ideas too." Bond had no intention of marrying anyone. If he did, it would certainly not be an insipid slave. He only hoped to amuse or outrage the Governor into a discussion of some human topic.

("Quantum of Solace," FOR YOUR EYES ONLY)

As the series progresses, Fleming reveals more details concerning Bond and his women. For example, on one-night stands:

Bond had taken her to the station and had kissed her once hard on the lips and had gone away. It hadn't been love, but a quotation had come into Bond's mind as his cab moved out of Pennsylvania Station: "Some love is fire, some love is rust. But the finest, cleanest love is lust." Neither had had regrets. Had they committed a sin? If so, which one? A sin against chastity? Bond smiled to himself. There was a quotation for that too, and from a saint—Saint Augustine: "Oh Lord, give me Chastity. But don't give it yet!"

(GOLDFINGER, Chapter 5)

And once, Bond daydreams what it would be like playing the field in Heaven:

There must be a whole lot of them, going up together. Would

Tilly be on the same trip? Bond squirmed with embarrassment. How would he introduce her to the others, to Vesper for instance? And when it came to the point, which would he like the best? But perhaps it would be a big place with countries and towns. There was probably no more reason why he should run into one of his former girl friends here than there had been on earth. But still there were a lot of people he'd better avoid until he got settled in and found out the form. Perhaps, with so much love about, these things wouldn't matter. Perhaps one just loved all the girls one met. Hm. Tricky business!

(GOLDFINGER, Chapter 16)

Concerning homosexuality:

Bond came to the conclusion that Tilly Masterson was one of those girls whose hormones had got mixed up. He knew the type well and thought they and their male counterparts were a direct consequence of giving votes to women and "sex equality." As a result of fifty years of emancipation, feminine qualities were dying out or being transferred to the males. Pansies of both sexes were everywhere, not yet completely homosexual, but confused, not knowing what they were. The result was a herd of unhappy sexual misfits— barren and full of frustrations, the women wanting to dominate and the men to be nannied. He was sorry for them, but he had no time for them.

(GOLDFINGER, Chapter 19)

Concerning women drivers:

Women are often meticulous and safe drivers, but they are very seldom first-class. In general Bond regarded them as a mild hazard and he always gave them plenty of road and was ready for the unpredictable. Four women in a car he regarded as the highest danger potential, and two women as nearly as lethal. Women together cannot keep silent in a car, and when women talk they have to look into each other's faces. An exchange of words is not enough. They have to see the other person's expression, perhaps in order to read behind the other's words or to analyze the reaction to their own. So two women in the front seat of a car constantly distract each other's attention from the road ahead and four women are more than doubly dangerous, for the driver has to hear, and see, not only what her companion is saying but also, for women are like that, what the two behind are talking about.

(THUNDERBALL, Chapter 11)

One must also examine, when studying Bond's attitudes toward women, the opposite point of view as well. It is important to emphasize here that women characters find James Bond sexually attractive. Period.

James Bond is a handsome and virile specimen of the human race. He has a sexual persona strong enough to turn the most diehard Lesbian, such as Pussy Galore, into a heterosexual. This perhaps takes the point to the extreme, but the message is clear: James Bond represents an ultimate male sexual fantasy figure for women. This is obvious in the following excerpt:

Ariadne studied Bond's profile. As always, her employers' instructions had been confined to essentials. She had been told only to induce the Englishman to go with her to a designated area where fellow-workers would take over the operation from her. What would happen to him afterwards was no concern of hers—officially. But, more and more, the question bothered her as a woman, a woman who had learnt to recognize on sight the kind of man who knew how to love. Bond was such a man. She was certain, too, that he found her desirable. She had always been a loyal servant of her cause, and not for a moment did she seriously contemplate disobeying orders, allowing Bond to take her home after dinner and do with her whatever he wanted. Ariadne only wished, passionately, that it had been possible. That mouth was made to give her brutal kisses, not to become distorted in a grimace of agony; those hands existed to caress her body, not to be stamped on by the torturer's boot. These images were so painfully vivid that she could find almost nothing to say as the taxi approached the slopes of the Acropolis.

(COLONEL SUN, Chapter 6)

Of course, one cannot take the sexual conduct of the Bond novels too seriously—the books *are* fantasies. Criticizing what may seem like an overindulgence in sexual frivolity would destroy the erotic fantasy of the stories. And that is a key element in the success of the James Bond character, as well as the series as a whole.

OUTLOOK

James Bond lives his life as best he can without looking back. To dwell in the past only creates cavities in the soul. Because he believes, when he's depressed, that he will not live past the age of forty-five, Bond tackles each day with a mania for experiencing whatever sensations it might offer. For a man surrounded by so much cold-hearted death, Bond loves life. He thrives on the adventure his assignments bring. Danger is a drug that stimulates Bond—his mind is clearest when his life is threatened. The worst disease a man can catch, according to both Bond *and* Fleming, is boredom. He dreads what he calls "the Soft Life." Once, while attempting to shake himself out of one of these particular periods which attack him *every so often*, Bond recalls a quotation from somewhere: "Those whom the Gods wish to destroy, they first make bored." Bond has undergone much physical pain in his time: having his testicles battered with a carpet beater; feeling the little finger of his left hand pulled back slowly until it snaps; wincing as a blowtorch scorches the side of his face; collapsing while being kicked by two men wearing heavy boots; crawling through a torture-infested obstacle course; and feeling the orifices of his head probed by thin wires—but nothing is as painful to Bond as ennui.

Therefore, Bond lives his life to the fullest. And he takes it seriously—the early James Bond is as humorless as a statue. Only in the later novels did Fleming imbue his character with a sense of humor. Perhaps Fleming had been influenced by the direction the character in the films was going. The Bond of the twelfth novel, YOU ONLY LIVE TWICE, is much like the stoical, nonchalant characterization of Sean Connery.

This attitude of thriving on and devouring life's experiences is the most important element in James Bond's character. It is the basis for the success of all the appealing ingredients of the novels—it allows for a fantasy life to be fully realized. There is a subtle but revealing moment in ON HER MAJESTY'S SECRET SERVICE when the eccentric Griffon Or at the College of Arms suggests that James Bond is a descendent of Sir Thomas Bond of Bond Street. Bond dismisses the ridiculous notion, but does decide to adopt the Bond family motto: "The World is Not Enough."

□ FOUR □
The Novels

THE JAMES BOND NOVELS

TITLE	PLACES	GIRL(S)	VILLAIN(S)	VILLAIN'S EMPLOYER
CASINO ROYALE (first published 1953)	Royale-les-Eaux (resort in N.E. France)	Vesper Lynd	Le Chiffre	SMERSH (but labor relations not good)
LIVE AND LET DIE (1954)	New York; Florida; Jamaica	Solitaire	Mr. Big	SMERSH
MOONRAKER (1955)	London; Kent	Gala Brand	Hugo Drax	USSR
DIAMONDS ARE FOREVER (1956)	French Guinea; London; New York; Saratoga; Las Vegas; Spectreville; L.A.	Tiffany Case	Jack Spang (Rufus B. Saye); Seraffimo Spang	Syndicate (The Spangled Mob)
FROM RUSSIA WITH LOVE (1957)	USSR; London; Istanbul; Orient Express; Paris	Tatiana Romanova	Rosa Klebb; Red Grant	SMERSH
DOCTOR NO (1958)	London; Jamaica; Crab Key Island	Honeychile Rider	Doctor Julius No	USSR (but on freelance terms)
GOLDFINGER (1959)	Miami; London; Kent; N. France; New York; Ft. Knox	Pussy Galore; Tilly Masterson; Jill Masterson	Auric Goldfinger	SMERSH
FOR YOUR EYES ONLY (1960) 1. "From a View to a Kill"	Paris and environs	Mary Ann Russell	Russian spy group	USSR
2. "For Your Eyes Only"	Jamaica; London; Ottawa; N. Vermont	Judy Havelock	Von Hammerstein	Self-employed
3. "Quantum of Solace"	Nassau, with anecdote set in Bermuda	None	None	None
4. "Risico"	Rome; Venice and environs; Santa Maria	Lisl Baum	Kristatos	USSR
5. "The Hildebrand Rarity"	At sea off Chagrin Island (Indian Ocean)	Liz Krest	Milton Krest	Self-employed

This chart is based on one by Kingsley Amis appearing in *The James Bond Dossier,* published by Jonathan Cape, Ltd. I have updated it and substituted my own "highlights" and "remarks." (Used by permission of Jonathan Cape, Ltd.)

All of the novels and stories shown are by Ian Fleming except for COLONEL SUN (by Robert Markham), LICENSE RENEWED, FOR SPECIAL SERVICES, and ICEBREAKER (all by John Gardner)—R.B.

VILLAIN'S PROJECT	MINOR VILLAIN(S)	BOND'S FRIENDS	HIGHLIGHTS	REMARKS
Winning at casino to recoup misappropriated SMERSH funds	Assorted Bulgars	Rene Mathis; Felix Leiter	Camera bomb; Bond's baccarat duel with Le Chiffre; carpet beater torture; shooting of Le Chiffre	Most atmospheric of all novels; most serious and violent of all novels; Bond at his coldest and most ruthless
Financing SMERSH operators with pirate hoard	The Robber; Tee Hee; assorted Negro hoods	Felix Leiter; Quarrel	Encounter in Harlem with Mr. Big; fight in fish warehouse; Bond's swim; climax in coral lagoon	Fleming Sweep at its best; one of most exciting novels, though lacking in characterizations
Destroying London with nuclear rocket	Willy Krebs; assorted German scientists	None	Bridge game at Blades; chase with newsprint roll wreck; ordeal with blowtorch and steam hose	Lack of suspense, but stronger in character development; best glimpse of Bond's London life
Running diamond smuggling pipeline out of Africa into USA	Wint; Kidd; Shady Tree	Felix Leiter; Ernest Cureo	Bond/Leiter reunion; mud bath sequence; railroad chase	Weakest of early books because changes of locales are too fast; contains some tense moments, however
Assassinating Bond	General G.; Kronsteen; Krilencu	Darko Kerim; Vavra; Mathis	Assassination planning; gypsy camp sequence; shooting of Krilencu; fight with Grant; fight with Klebb	Best book in series; most successful blend of action and character
Playing hell with U.S. missiles by beaming wrong "instructions" at them	Assorted Chigroes	Quarrel; Pleydell-Smith	Centipede ordeal; "dragon"; No's establishment; obstacle course; fight with squid	Most implausible of books, yet one of the most exciting and suspenseful; very imaginative
Seizing all the gold in Ft. Knox	Oddjob	Felix Leiter	Canasta ploy; golf game; Oddjob's demonstration; Fort Knox operation; climax in plane	Slower moving than most; lacks suspense; rich in characterization
Ambushing SHAPE dispatch riders	None	None	Discovery of hideout in woods; shooting of executioner	Compressed and well-told yarn
Blackmailing, murdering, etc.	Gonzales	None	Bond/M scene; gun and bow-and-arrow battle	Best story in collection; good characterizations
None	None	The governor	None	A Maughamish anecdote recounted to Bond; full of character; never boring
Dope running aimed at demoralizing England	Smugglers	Colombo	Tape-recorder ploy; beach chase; quayside gun battle	Changes locale too fast for a short story; good characters
Catching rare fish and flogging it to Smithsonian Institute; wife beating	None	Fidele Barbey	Catching of fish; death of Krest	Very different sort of story; Bond's human side shows strongly

TITLE	PLACES	GIRL(S)	VILLAIN(S)	VILLAIN'S EMPLOYER
THUNDERBALL (1961)	Sussex; Paris; London; Bahamas	Domino Vitali; Patricia Fearing	Ernst Blofeld; Emilio Largo	SPECTRE
THE SPY WHO LOVED ME (1962)	Adirondacks; flashbacks to London and Toronto	Vivienne Michel	Horror; Sluggsy	Mr. Sanguinetti
ON HER MAJESTY'S SECRET SERVICE (1963)	Royale; London; Swiss Alps; "Quarterdeck"; Munich	Tracy di Vicenzo; Ruby Windsor	Ernst Blofeld	SPECTRE
YOU ONLY LIVE TWICE (1964)	London; Tokyo; Kyoto; Fukuoka; Kuro Island	Kissy Suzuki	Ernst Blofeld	Self-employed
THE MAN WITH THE GOLDEN GUN (1965)	London; Jamaica	Mary Goodnight	Pistols Scaramanga	Castro and the USSR
OCTOPUSSY (1966) 1. "Octopussy"	Jamaica, with flashback to Kaiser mountains in Germany	None	Major Dexter Smythe	Self-employed
2. "The Living Daylights"	London; West Berlin	None	"Trigger"	USSR
3. "The Property of a Lady"	London	None	Unidentified resident director of KGB in London	USSR
COLONEL SUN (1968)	London; Athens; Vrakonisi (island between Greece and Turkey)	Ariadne Alexandrou	Colonel Sun	Red China
LICENSE RENEWED (1981)	Dublin; London; Scotland; Paris; Perpignan	Lavender Peacock; Q'ute	Anton Murik	Self-employed
FOR SPECIAL SERVICES (1982)	London; New York; Washington DC; Amarillo, Texas; Cheyenne Mountain; Louisiana	Cedar Leiter; Nena Bismaquer; Q'ute	Blofeld's Heir	SPECTRE
ICEBREAKER (1983)	Libya; Finland; USSR	Paula Vacker; Rivke Ingber	Konrad von Glöda (Aarne Tudeer)	National Socialist Action Army

VILLAIN'S PROJECT	MINOR VILLAIN(S)	BOND'S FRIENDS	HIGHLIGHTS	REMARKS
Blackmailing Western governments by threat of hijacked nuclear bombs	Count Lippe; Petacchi	Felix Leiter	Rack ordeal; hijacking of bombs; *chemin de fer* game with Largo; swim under *Disco;* finding plane; underwater battle	Fast moving and exciting; rich in detail
Burning down motel for insurance, and burning Vivienne too	None	None	Cinema seduction; Bond's entrance; night battle with thugs	Female viewpoint handled with imagination, but somewhat flawed; last third of novel thrilling
Infecting Britain with crop and livestock pests	Irma Bunt	Marc-Ange Draco	Beach scene; arrival of Campbell; ski escape; battle at Piz Gloria; murder of Tracy	One of the best of the later novels; full of detail and suspense; tragic ending
Enticing people to commit suicide in private poisonous garden	Irma Bunt	Tiger Tanaka; Dikko Henderson	Discovery of Shatterhand's identity; exploration of garden; fight with Blofeld	Another one of the best books; atmospheric and haunting; more symbolic than most; travelogue interesting but unnecessary
Damaging Western interests, especially sugar, in Caribbean	Hendriks; assorted hoods	Felix Leiter; Nick Nicholson	Assassination attempt on M; train battle; duel in swamp	Weakest novel in series; lacks the rich detail from other novels; unfinished
Living off stolen Reichsbank gold	None	None	Flashback scene on mountain top	Not much here; more of a morality tale than a secret service story
Assassinating Western agent who is attempting to escape from USSR to West Berlin	None	Capt. Paul Sender (though not really a friend)	M/Bond scene; shooting of Trigger	Best story in this collection; interesting twist at end
Pushing the bid at an auction as high as possible to pay off a Russian agent	Maria Freudenstein	Kenneth Snowman	None	Weak ending; lacks suspense; solving of mystery too easy
Sabotaging USSR summit conference and making it look like the British did it	Von Richter; assorted terrorists	Niko Litsas; Bill Tanner	Scene at "Quarterdeck"; sea battle; torture scene; climactic battle	Rich in detail but lacks Fleming Sweep; more political than most; more violent than most
Blackmailing major powers with threat to cause meltdowns in six nuclear power plants around the world	Mary Jane Mashkin; Franco; Caber	None	Fight with Caber; high frequency torture; fashion show sequence; fight on plane	More like the films than the novels, but moves quickly and is suspenseful; updating a little disconcerting
Gaining control of the Space Wolf Satellites	Markus Bismaquer; Walter Luxor; Mike Mazzard	Felix Leiter (briefly)	Plane hijack; elevator incident; Grand Prix; raid on Cheyenne Mountain; encounter with Blofeld	New SPECTRE and Blofeld twist interesting and involving; moves quickly but lacks rich detail
Bringing about a "Fourth Reich" with a new fascist army	Kolya Mosolov	Brad Tirpitz	Snow plow battle; ice water torture; Fencer attack on Ice Palace	Fun but has no real depth; good locations; Nazi plot a little trite

INTRODUCTION

James Bond was introduced to the world in 1953 with the publication of CASINO ROYALE. Fleming had predicted his first novel to be "the spy story to end all spy stories," but had no idea how accurate the prediction was, or what was to follow. In all, Ian Fleming wrote twelve James Bond novels and two collections of short stories. The series was continued after Fleming's death by Kingsley Amis (under the pseudonym of Robert Markham) with COLONEL SUN, and most recently, by John Gardner with LICENSE RENEWED, FOR SPECIAL SERVICES, and ICEBREAKER. Examining the series as a whole, a special world was indeed created—a landscape of fantasy and adventure to which readers could escape. Fleming himself admitted that he wrote "unashamedly for pleasure and money." He said the books were written for "warm-blooded heterosexuals in railway trains, airplanes or beds." But the *oeuvre* deserves closer study because Fleming's style is unique, and the development of the James Bond character throughout the series is fascinating. The books should be examined chronologically, because there is a definite continuity from one novel to the next. Fleming's growth as a writer is apparent in comparing later novels with earlier ones.

Fleming's series can be divided into two groups: the early novels (CASINO ROYALE, 1953, through FOR YOUR EYES ONLY, 1960) and the later novels (THUNDERBALL, 1961, through OCTOPUSSY, published posthumously in 1966.) The early novels have an engaging style that concentrates on mood, character development, and plot advancement. In the later novels, Fleming injected more "pizzazz" into his writing—his work became richer in detail and imagery. By the time THUNDERBALL was published in 1961, Fleming had truly become a master storyteller; he was painting images with exacting detail and creating sweeping suspense. The only later novel which does not fit this bill is the last, THE MAN WITH THE GOLDEN GUN, published posthumously in 1965. The later novels also have a peculiar tone not found in the early ones: a feeling of imminent disaster and despair. This is perhaps because these later novels were written when Fleming's health was failing—he had suffered his first heart attack in 1961. His own feelings of "bodily decay" crept into the books.

But the series is *not* without humor, as many critics have complained. The novels are full of Ian Fleming's sense of humor, which can be cynical, melodramatic, and sly. It is the character of James Bond *himself* who is without humor. The humor is in the writing. For example, most of the meals James Bond eats do not exist. The so-called "Beef Brizzola" which Felix Leiter insists James Bond order at Sardi's in DIAMONDS ARE FOREVER is an invented dish. Fleming often pulls the reader's leg with his celebrated menus. The villains' obligatory "Welcome to Doomsday" speeches are another give-away that the novels are not to be taken in total seriousness. Just try reading one of the speeches, Dr. No's, for example, aloud.

☐ STYLE

Perhaps the most striking stylistic element of the Fleming novels is their ability to sweep the reader along from chapter to chapter at a breakneck pace. Fleming once said that if his novels failed to do this, he would consider himself an unsuccessful writer. The important thing, he maintained, was to keep the plot *moving*. Fleming would sit at his desk at Goldeneye and type the entire novel without looking back at what he'd written. By driving through the initial story, Fleming established a fast, urgent pace. Hooks at the end of chapters were added to pull the reader into the next. Only once or twice does the "Fleming Sweep" fail in the series.

Another major stylistic element is the almost fanatical detail—especially trivial detail: brand names of objects; technical data about gadgets; specific ingredients of foods and drinks; and minute descriptions of scenic surroundings. Kingsley Amis, in his excellent book, *The James Bond Dossier,* calls this stylistic element "Fleming Effect." Fleming is so convincing in his descriptions that the reader rarely questions the factual accuracy of the detail. Only those with fanatical expertise have raised objections over some of the more blatant errors Fleming made. (And Fleming always seemed to enjoy when a mistake was pointed out to him; witness the case with Geoffrey Boothroyd.) All of this can be attributed to Fleming's experience as a journalist. Fleming's prose is rich and colorful, painting distinct and *believable* images. It's not important, really, whether the facts are right. The details are there merely to heighten the realism of the action.

Structure in Fleming's novels usually follows a specific formula. In most cases, the novel begins with a "teaser" chapter: the scene is set in the middle of the story, with Bond already on a designated assignment. The second chapter then flashes back to the beginning, as Bond receives his orders from his crusty old chief, M. The story then proceeds until it catches up with the opening chapter. The first part of the novel includes clue gathering, chance encounters with the villain and/or his henchmen, and the development of the romantic interest. The middle of the story usually involves a journey to the villain's headquarters which almost always leads to Bond's capture. The climax of the story involves, in Kingsley Amis' words, Bond being "wined and dined, lectured on the aesthetics of power, and finally tortured by his chief enemy" (three of Fleming's favorite situations). But Bond manages to make the villains eat their words by the novel's end. In seven of the books, Bond returns from his mission via the hospital. But his ordeal is worth it, for Bond usually ends up with a girl in his arms on the last page.

Only a few times does Fleming depart from his formula, choosing instead to experiment with the structure. Oddly enough, the results are some of the most interesting novels in the series (FROM RUSSIA, WITH LOVE; THE SPY WHO LOVED ME; and YOU ONLY LIVE TWICE). CASINO ROYALE, the first novel, is quite different from the basic Fleming formula, as well. The structure of each novel is discussed in its own section.

☐ THEMES

The most obvious theme, of course, recurring throughout the Bond series is that of Good vs. Evil. The image of Saint George and the dragon is actually alluded to no less than three times. Fleming provides an entire chapter on the philosophies of Good and Evil in CASINO ROYALE, and YOU ONLY LIVE TWICE is an allegorical novel told in epic terms. In this later novel, James Bond represents all that is Good while his archenemy, Ernst Stavro Blofeld, represents everything that is Evil.

This theme accounts for why the Bond books are so popular. Wish fulfillment, character identification,

you name the terms; what the reader ultimately finds attractive in the books is the vanquishing of Evil by Good, and the ease with which the reader can identify with the action. Fleming's treatment of his major character allows the reader to slip into James Bond's persona and view the world through his eyes. Of course, other elements enter into it—the attraction of the adventures (locales, characters, etc.), the women, and the novel's general embrace of worldly pleasures.

Another strong recurring theme is gambling, not only the casino variety, but in day-to-day situations. Fleming, a serious gambler, brought into the novels the essence of challenges in decision making. Bond takes risks in almost everything he does. Many times he takes a chance on a hunch or intuition—and sometimes the gamble doesn't pay off. For instance, Bond recklessly weighs the odds against Dr. No's dragon tank and orders his companion, Quarrel, to help him fight it with nothing but pistols. Quarrel ends up burned to death while Bond and his female friend are captured. Bond doesn't believe in luck—he states this explicitly in CASINO ROYALE —he "only bets on even chances." The plot of FROM RUSSIA, WITH LOVE involves a gamble on Bond's part (as well as the Secret Service) to trust Tatiana Romanova, who claims she is in love with him. She will give the British a coveted secret coding machine belonging to the Russians if Bond will come and take her to the West. Bond gambles when he hides Goldfinger's plans for the robbery of Fort Knox under a toilet seat in an airplane, hoping that an attendant will find the piece of paper and forward it to Felix Leiter. And, after learning that Scaramanga plans to kill him on a train ride, Bond gambles and allows himself to be taken along for the ride as a sitting duck. Fleming has taken the risks of the casino and put them into everyday life, or rather, the everyday life of James Bond.

Friendship is another recurring theme. In almost every novel, Bond has a male ally with whom he shares the adventure. In six cases, that ally turns out to be the American CIA agent, Felix Leiter, probably Bond's closest friend outside of England. Bond seems to depend on these male alliances, and the links between him and his friends are emotionally felt in the writing. This is especially true in LIVE AND LET DIE, when Leiter loses an arm and a leg to a shark, and in DOCTOR NO, when Quarrel is burned alive. Even though Bond ultimately accomplishes his mission alone (for instance, Leiter is forced to leave the underwater battle early in THUNDERBALL because of a malfunctioning breathing apparatus), the ally serves to add another dimension to Bond's character, and ultimately, to the thematic continuity of the novels.

Other themes crop up in individual novels, as do revenge and patriotism in YOU ONLY LIVE TWICE. Sometimes Fleming injects his books with cynicism, which isn't precisely a theme, but an element which reveals much of the author's view of the world. At times, the cynical tone is misanthropic, as in the first novel, CASINO ROYALE. Here, Fleming seems downright bitter. The endings of CASINO ROYALE, MOONRAKER, FROM RUSSIA, WITH LOVE, ON HER MAJESTY'S SECRET SERVICE, and YOU ONLY LIVE TWICE explore the tragic, the melancholic, and the wistful. Bond himself is a true cynic—he is suspicious of love, and is afraid of his emotions. It is Fleming's own view of the world which pervades his novels and creates distinctive moods.

Finally, one must accept the fact that the Bonds are fantasies. By no means did Fleming intend for them to be anything else. The extremely tongue-in-cheek sexual frivolity of the novels plays on the adolescent fantasies of sexual skill which mature readers have never wholly forgotten. These fantasies are most likely far more thrilling and sensational than the reader's reality. Male readers can live the adventures *through* Bond, and escape into a world where one is tough enough to withstand torture yet can retain enough energy to make love to a beautiful woman later. Female readers could imagine that they, too, were independent free spirits like the Bond women, unfettered by the duties of home and family—traveling to exotic places and meeting handsome spies. Once one has accepted the fact that Fleming is pulling the reader's leg and is laughing to himself, these fantasies and dreams can be enjoyed by any reader who is willing to allow his or her senses to be aroused.

□ CHARACTERS

James Bond's character has been examined in an earlier section. An overview of the series reveals that Bond becomes more human with each successive novel. In CASINO ROYALE, Bond is such a cold, ruthless individual that the reader is barely able to identify with him. Not until MOONRAKER does Fleming begin to flesh out a "normal" life for Bond. Here, the reader is treated to scenes of Bond's daily office life and social outings. In FROM RUSSIA, WITH LOVE, a scene at Bond's flat is included, and the reader meets the agent's elderly Scottish treasure of a housekeeper, May. In GOLDFINGER,

Fleming's prose has a stream of consciousness quality: in this novel, Bond's interior monologue allows the reader to discover the character's more personal thoughts.

The Bond-girl   The most obvious fantasy element of the Bond novels is the heroine. Kingsley Amis sums up her physical attributes in *The James Bond Dossier:*

Physically, the Bond-girl varies little from book to book. Her hair oscillates between blond (clear favorite) and black or dark brown with no intermediate shades. It is never coiffured. Her eyes are an almost invariable blue (only two exceptions). She is often suntanned. She has a wide mouth, a small nose, and high cheekbones. Her hands are strong and practical, with nails unpainted and filed short. Her physique is generally good, with some hints of assistance from tennis or swimming. She is tall, five foot seven or above, and not thin. Her most frequently mentioned feature is her fine, faultless, splendid, etc., breasts.

(Kingsley Amis, *The James Bond Dossier,* Chapter 5)

Amis goes on to say that the Bond-girl is not 100 percent perfect. For example, Honeychile Rider has a broken nose, and Domino Vitali limps because one leg is slightly shorter than the other.

The Bond-girl is quite independent. She usually has no family ties, and any relatives quickly disappear (such as Domino's brother or Judy Havelock's parents). Tracy di Vicenzo has a father (who also becomes a Bond ally), and Kissy Suzuki lives with her parents; but these women go their own way and make their own decisions. The Bond-girl, contrary to popular belief, is not merely a sex object. She is a free spirit, and is certainly more liberated than most women ever dreamed of being in the late fifties and early sixties.

The Bond-girl is an athletic, outdoors-type of woman: she is usually proficient with guns if she needs to be; she can run and swim as well as any man; and at several points in the series, she actually saves Bond's life. She shows a resourcefulness, in most cases, equal to Bond's. The Bond-girl was ahead of her time; in fact, she resembles a woman of the eighties more than one of twenty years ago.

Fleming improved his female characters in successive novels. Vesper Lynd, the heroine of CASINO ROYALE, is a bit two-dimensional; but this is rectified in the second novel, LIVE AND LET DIE, by Solitaire and her involvement with the supernatural. Tatiana Romanova has political ideals for which she is fighting. Honeychile Rider is a nature-girl by choice. Tracy di Vicenzo is a woman running from her life as the daughter of a rich gangster. And Vivienne Michel, the narrator of THE SPY WHO LOVED ME, is determined to make it on her own in America. Vivienne is perhaps Fleming's most successful female creation. In this experimental book, the reader is placed inside the heroine's head for a change. Thus, one is able to examine James Bond objectively from a female point of view.

It should also be noted here that James Bond does not always get the girl at the end of each adventure. In MOONRAKER, heroine Gala Brand is actually engaged to another man, and she walks off into the distance with *him* rather than Bond. In "The Hildebrand Rarity," one of the five short stories from FOR YOUR EYES ONLY, Bond helps Liz Krest with no intention of becoming involved with her. And Tilly Masterson, with whom Bond joins forces in GOLDFINGER, is a Lesbian and will have nothing to do with Bond physically.

But most important, the Bond-girl is essential to the plot. She is never an accessory to the action (as she is sometimes in the films), but always an integral part of the story. The Bond-girl is second only to the villain in the full realization of a James Bond novel.

The Bond-villain Bond's enemies are usually physically grotesque and exhibit a particularly nasty penchant for sadism. Yet they are often quite intelligent and some border on genius. The Bond-villain is a super-human in terms of Evil as Bond is super-human in terms of Good. Only thrice does the Bond villain fall short of this standard: Scaramanga in THE MAN WITH THE GOLDEN GUN, the Spang brothers in DIAMONDS ARE FOREVER, and the two hoods in THE SPY WHO LOVED ME. The major villains (Ernst Stavro Blofeld, Doctor No, Auric Goldfinger, Mr. Big, Hugo Drax, etc.) are intent on causing a global incident (blackmailing Western powers with stolen atomic bombs; wrecking the U.S. missile program; robbing Fort Knox; financing the Communist spy network in America). These men want to be *great* criminals. Mr. Big tells Bond that he will be "the first great Negro criminal." Blofeld tells Bond, "I have one of the greatest brains in the world." It is this megalomania that unites the Bond villains into a common group. Amis makes the point that each villain/Bond scene is like a father/bad boy scene, in which the father calmly chastises the bad boy for some wrong doing—and then proceeds to apply the belt.

Physically, the villain is almost always over six feet or under five-foot-five. He's usually overweight. The villain's eyes are blue or black. Two major adversaries,

Le Chiffre and Blofeld, have pupils which are entirely surrounded by the whites of their eyes. Some villains depend on specific props: Dr. No's mechanical pincers, Rosa Klebb's poisoned knitting needles, Le Chiffre's benzedrine inhaler, and Blofeld's suit of armor (in YOU ONLY LIVE TWICE). And finally, as Amis again notes, there is sometimes a "glint of red" in the villain's eyes.

Ernst Stavro Blofeld is Bond's archenemy. Appearing in three of the novels, he perpetrates evil of such magnitude (even murdering Bond's wife in ON HER MAJESTY'S SECRET SERVICE) that he seems a devil incarnate. Blofeld changes his appearance and methods in each of the three books; therefore, it is difficult to know him as a complete character. Both Hugo Drax (MOONRAKER) and Auric Goldfinger (GOLDFINGER) are certainly more completely drawn. With these two adversaries, Fleming typified the essential Bond-villain.

M Aside from Bond, the character who appears most frequently in the series is, of course, James Bond's chief, Admiral Sir Miles Messervy, known only as "M." (M's real name is not revealed until THE MAN WITH THE GOLDEN GUN. Furthermore, Fleming was never consistent about punctuating the initial "M"—sometimes a period followed the initial, and sometimes not.)

M is most likely based on Ian Fleming's real commanding officer in Naval Intelligence during World War II, Rear Admiral John H. Godfrey. But, as John Pearson speculates, it is also possible that, since as a boy Fleming would call his mother M, much of Eve Fleming may be behind the demanding old autocrat.

M is a crusty codger getting on in years. Several times Fleming refers to the admiral's "damnably clear grey eyes" inside a "weather-beaten face." As the head of the Secret Service, M earns five thousand pounds a year, plus the use of an old Rolls-Royce and driver. In addition, M receives perhaps fifteen hundred pounds Naval pay (as a vice-admiral on the retired list). This meager salary leaves M with just enough money to afford a beautiful, small Regency manor house on the edge of Windsor Forest, affectionately called Quarterdeck. The front door holds the clapper of the brass ship's-bell of "some former H.M.S. *Repulse*, the last of whose line, a battle cruiser, had been M's final seagoing assignment." Quarterdeck was looked after by M's former Chief Petty Officer, Hammond, and his wife, until their tragic deaths in COLONEL SUN.

The only clue to M's personal life is that his "stock bachelor hobby" is painting in water colors. Flowers are the only subjects that he paints.

The Admiral's familiar office is guarded by the faithful Miss Moneypenny. Entrance to the office is gained by waiting until the green light above the door pops on (Fleming was also inconsistent with the color of this light—sometimes it's blue or red).

M can be difficult to work for. As Kingsley Amis notes in *The James Bond Dossier:*

His demeanor or voice is described as abrupt, angry (3 times), brutal, cold (7 times), curt, dry (5), frosty (2), gruff (7), hard (3), impatient (7), irritable (2), moody, severe, sharp (2), short (4), sour (2), stern and testy (5), which divides out as an irascibility index of just under 4.6 per book.

(Kinglsey Amis, *The James Bond Dossier,* Chapter 7)

M also has many idiosyncrasies as far as the Service goes:

M had certain bees in his bonnet. They were famous in the Service, and M knew they were. But that did not mean that he would allow them to stop buzzing. There were queen bees, like the misuse of the Service, and the search for true as distinct from wishful intelligence, and there were worker bees. These included such idiosyncrasies as not employing men with beards, or those who were completely bilingual, instantly dismissing men who tried to bring pressure to bear on him through family relationships with members of the Cabinet, mistrusting men or women who were too "dressy," and those who called him "sir" off-duty; and having an exaggerated faith in Scotsmen. But M was ironically conscious of his obsessions, as, thought Bond, a Churchill or a Montgomery was about his. He never minded his bluff, as it partly was, being called on any of them.

("Risico," FOR YOUR EYES ONLY)

He especially does not like the Service getting involved with drugs—he feels that's the territory of the Special Branch of Scotland Yard. In the short story, "Risico," M testily sends Bond on an assignment involving drug traffic into England. He curtly hands Bond the file on the case, and with almost no briefing, sends Bond on his way. (He usually at least gives Bond a few minutes of his time to *explain* the case.)

At one point in THUNDERBALL, M admits to Bond that he thinks the agent is "reliable" but almost never shows any more approval of Bond's work for the Service. He allows Bond to conduct the Service's business in almost any way the agent chooses, but doesn't always approve of Bond's methods. When Bond reveals his plan to play golf with Goldfinger in order to spy on him, M's response is:

"Fine way for one of my top men to spend his time." The sarcasm in M.'s voice was weary, resigned. "All right. Go ahead. But if what you say is right, you'd better see that you beat him."

(GOLDFINGER, Chapter 7)

M doesn't approve of Bond's womanizing, either. In FROM RUSSIA, WITH LOVE, before M reveals that a Russian girl named Tatiana Romanova is in love with Bond, he asks the agent about his relationship with Tiffany Case. Bond replies that Tiffany has gone back to the states and will probably marry a Marine Corps major she met.

M. gave one of the brief smiles that lit up his eyes more than his mouth. "I'm sorry if it went wrong, James," he said. There was no sympathy in his voice. He disapproved of Bond's "womanizing," as he called it to himself, while recognizing that his prejudice was the relic of a Victorian upbringing. But, as Bond's chief, the last thing he wanted was for Bond to be permanently tied to one woman's skirts. "Perhaps it's for the best. Doesn't do to get mixed up with neurotic women in this business. They hang on your gun-arm, if you know what I mean. Forgive me for asking about it."

(FROM RUSSIA, WITH LOVE, Chapter 12)

The reader will always know something suspicious is up when M addresses Bond as "James" rather than "007." It usually means there is business coming up that is non-Service oriented. In MOONRAKER, M asks Bond to do a personal favor for him: accompany M to Blades Club and determine if Hugo Drax is really a cheat at cards. Bond is only too happy to do so. In the short story, "For Your Eyes Only," M more or less persuades Bond to volunteer to avenge the deaths of a pair of M's personal friends. Fleming reveals a different side of M in this story. The problem of the Havelocks' murder troubles M a great deal, and he feels guilty about involving the Service in the business. He mysteriously asks Bond, "James, has it ever occurred to you that every man in the fleet knows what to do except the commanding admiral?" Bond replies that he supposes "it's the same as saying that supreme command is the loneliest post there is."

M jerked his pipe sideways. "Same sort of idea. Someone's got to be tough. Someone's got to decide in the end. If you send a wavering signal to the Admiralty you deserve to be put on the beach. Some people are religious—pass the decision on to God." M's eyes were defensive. "I used to try that sometimes in the Service, but He always passed the buck back again—told me to get on and make up my own mind. Good for one, I suppose, but tough. Trouble is, very few people keep tough after about forty. They've been knocked about by life—had troubles, tragedies, illnesses. These things soften you up.''

("For Your Eyes Only," FOR YOUR EYES ONLY)

When Bond attempts to relieve M's worries by saying that he accepts unpleasant assignments because he assumes the cause is just, M tells him:

"Dammit.'' M's eyes glittered impatiently. "That's just what I mean! You rely on *me*. You won't take any damned responsibility yourself.'' He thrust the stem of his pipe toward his chest. "I'm the one who has to do that. I'm the one who has to decide if a thing is right or not.'' The anger died out of his eyes. The grim mouth bent sourly. He said gloomily, "Oh, well, I suppose it's what I'm paid for. Somebody's got to drive the bloody train.'' M put his pipe back in his mouth and drew on it deeply to relieve his feelings.

Now Bond felt sorry for M. He had never before heard M use as strong a word as "bloody." Nor had M ever given a member of his staff any hint that he felt the weight of the burden he was carrying and had carried ever since he had thrown up the certain prospect of becoming Fifth Sea Lord in order to take over the Secret Service.

("For Your Eyes Only," FOR YOUR EYES ONLY)

More of the weight on M's shoulders is revealed in THE MAN WITH THE GOLDEN GUN when it is learned that his predecessor as the head of the Secret Service was assassinated by one of his own men in the Universal Export office. As a result of this, M is protected by a bulletproof plate which falls from a slit in the ceiling at the touch of a button. The admiral, then, must constantly be on his guard at the office—which may explain his usual businesslike and rather stiff manner in dealing with employees.

The best glimpse of M at his most vulnerable appears in COLONEL SUN. Here, M is kidnapped and drugged by a terrorist group. Bond sees him once at the beginning of the novel. The admiral is under the drug's influence and appears zombielike and helpless. Toward the end of the book, Bond himself is captured by the terrorists and is placed in the same room with M. M has been tortured, suffering burns on his chest. The episode again reveals the human side of M as he is forced to deal with the violence of Bond's work on the same level as his top agent.

Felix Leiter Bond's ally in six of the Fleming novels is the American CIA agent from Texas, Felix Leiter.

After Leiter loses a right arm and a leg to a shark in LIVE AND LET DIE, the CIA lets him go; however, he finds work with Pinkerton's Detective Agency. Leiter remains with Pinkerton's until THUNDERBALL, in which Allen Dulles (the CIA chief) puts Leiter on the reserve force. Leiter is again placed on the reserves in THE MAN WITH THE GOLDEN GUN.

Leiter, when Bond meets him in CASINO ROYALE, is about thirty-five. He is tall and thin, and wears his clothes "loosely from his shoulders like Frank Sinatra." Although his movements and speech are slow, Bond gets the feeling that there is plenty of speed and strength in Leiter, and that he would be a "tough and cruel fighter." Fleming goes on to describe him:

As he sat hunched over the table, he seemed to have some of the jackknife quality of a falcon. There was this impression also in his face, in the sharpness of his chin and cheekbones and the wide wry mouth. His grey eyes had a feline slant which was increased by his habit of screwing them up against the smoke of the Chesterfields which he tapped out of the pack in a chain. The permanent wrinkles which this habit had etched at the corners gave the impression that he smiled more with his eyes than with his mouth. A mop of straw-coloured hair lent his face a boyish look which closer examination contradicted.

(CASINO ROYALE, Chapter 7)

Bond also reflects that "good Americans were fine people and that most of them seemed to come from Texas.''

One of the ties between the Englishman and the American may be that they enjoy being "barroom rivals.'' There is almost always an obligatory scene in which the two visit a bar and drink themselves silly. In CASINO ROYALE, Bond educates Leiter on the making of a "real" martini, and Leiter remembers the formula in subsequent novels. In THUNDERBALL, Leiter seems to have studied martinis thoroughly, for he, in turn, educates a barman in a Nassau hotel on the ingredients of a real martini. Leiter knows when he's being had; the martinis at the hotel are served with inadequate portions of liquor. Leiter explains to the barman:

". . . here's one who's dry behind the ears. A good barman should learn to be able to recognize the serious drinker from the status-seeker who wants just to be seen in your fine bar.''

(THUNDERBALL, Chapter 14)

Kingsley Amis, in *The James Bond Dossier*, seems

to think that Leiter has no personality. But Leiter's personality is clearly revealed in his manner of speech, the subjects about which he speaks, as well as through several of the character's idiosyncrasies. For instance, Leiter is a jazz fan, and he escapes a nasty scrape in LIVE AND LET DIE by "arguing the finer points of jazz" with his black captor. Leiter tells Bond many anecdotes about America while giving him guided tours of New York, Saratoga, or Florida. He and Bond have a good laugh at the "old folks" of St. Petersburg, and they take pleasure in complaining about the commercialism of the Bahamas' hotels.

Most important, though, is the fact that Leiter reinforces the friendship theme running through the series. The bond between the two men is extremely heartfelt. Felix Leiter, of all of Bond's allies, brings to the series a warmth and joviality which is missing most of the time.

Among the other Bond allies appearing in the novels are René Mathis (twice), Quarrel (twice), Darko Kerim, Marc-Ange Draco, Tiger Tanaka, and Niko Litsas. All of these allies not only serve some plot function, but emphasize the friendship theme.

□ OTHER CHARACTERS

Other recurring characters include Bond's secretary, Loelia Ponsonby, until she runs off and marries. Bond insists on calling her Lil because he knows she hates it; but he enjoys having what he considers "a beautiful secretary." Miss Ponsonby is "tall and dark with a reserved, unbroken beauty to which the war and five years in the Service had lent a touch of sternness." Loelia mothers Bond, as well as the two other members of the Double-0 section, worrying herself to death when they are in danger. By the time of ON HER MAJESTY'S SECRET SERVICE, Loelia has married a rich member of the Baltic Exchange and is replaced by the very attractive Mary Goodnight (who also becomes the Bond-girl of THE MAN WITH THE GOLDEN GUN). Miss Goodnight begins her role in the series with "blue black" hair, and ends it as a blond.

Miss Moneypenny is another familiar character, though not as much is made of her in the novels as in the films. Moneypenny, it is said, has a secret desire for Bond and "dreams hopelessly" about him. But she never does anything about it. She is much more overt about her affection in the films. Moneypenny is also best friends with Loelia Ponsonby, and they share the office gossip. In MOONRAKER, both women are caught wearing the same style blouse on the same day!

Bill Tanner, M's Chief of Staff, is mentioned sporadically through the novels, but becomes a more substantial entity in YOU ONLY LIVE TWICE, THE MAN WITH THE GOLDEN GUN, and COLONEL SUN. Tanner is "about Bond's age" and supposedly is Bond's "best friend in the Service." There is no corroboration of this beyond the fact that the two men are always making references to having lunch together. At the beginning of COLONEL SUN, though, they are playing golf together and have drinks at the club house afterwards. Tanner seems to share Bond's feelings about M, and the pair usually cracks jokes behind the old man's back. (It is also interesting to note that Tanner is only referred to as "Bill" or "Chief of Staff" until YOU ONLY LIVE TWICE, in which we learn his last name.)

Sir James Molony is a famous neurologist assigned to handle cases in the Service. He is called to look after Bond a few times, and is responsible for rehabilitating the agent after he is almost killed by Rosa Klebb's poison-tipped shoe; nursing Bond through depression after the death of Tracy; and "de-brainwashing" 007 after the assassination attempt on M. Molony seems to become more important with each successive appearance; in YOU ONLY LIVE TWICE, the neurologist has become a Nobel Prize winner!

A final character worth mentioning is Bond's Scottish housekeeper, May. One of May's endearing traits is that she calls no man "sir" except for English kings and Winston Churchill. Therefore, she addresses Bond with, "Good morning—s," which Bond presumes is the next best thing. May mothers Bond more than any other woman in his life. After he returns from his stay at Shrublands health spa, he is obsessed with health food. May is mortified by it all, and tells Bond:

"Ye can tell me to mind my own business and pack me off back to Glen Orchy, but before I go I'm telling ye, Mister James, that if ye get yerself into anuither fight and ye've got nothing but yon muck in yer stomach, they'll be bringing ye home in a hearse. That's what they'll be doing."

(THUNDERBALL, Chapter 7)

May serves as comic relief in her brief scenes and is one of the more colorful characters with whom Fleming populates the special world of James Bond.

*   *   *

CASINO ROYALE (1953)

The first James Bond novel begins with the distinctive style and texture that Ian Fleming brings to all of his work:

The scent and smoke and sweat of a casino are nauseating at three in the morning. Then the soul-erosion produced by high gambling—a compost of greed and fear and nervous tension—becomes unbearable, and the senses awake and revolt from it.

James Bond suddenly knew that he was tired. He always knew when his body or his mind had had enough, and he always acted on the knowledge. This helped him to avoid staleness and the sensual bluntness that breeds mistakes.

(CASINO ROYALE, Chapter 1)

Immediately the senses of the reader are bombarded by images that highlight the environment of the story. There is a preoccupation with sights, sounds, smells, textures, and tastes. Due to Fleming's experience as a journalist, his writing exhibits a reporter's attention to detail.

Though it lacks many of the qualities (such as the greater depth of the Bond character) which improve the later books, CASINO ROYALE is one of the best novels in the series. It is harsh, stark, and extremely atmospheric, as well as highly readable.

The story concerns one of the USSR's chief agents in France, a certain Le Chiffre, who is operating as undercover paymaster of the Communist-controlled trade union in Alsace. Recently he carelessly appropriated USSR funds to finance a chain of brothels for his own profit. Now under pressure to repay his debt to the Soviets, Le Chiffre is gambling for high stakes at the casino at Royale-les-Eaux, a resort in northern France. NATO would greatly benefit if Le Chiffre's luck should fail, for his subsequent humiliation and destruction would lead to the collapse of the Communist trade union. Agent 007, James Bond, is sent to Royale-les-Eaux to do battle with Le Chiffre over the baccarat table. Bond succeeds in defeating Le Chiffre, but he later finds himself at the mercy of the villain. Bond is captured and tortured, but his life is unwittingly saved by a member of SMERSH, the USSR's organization for eliminating spies and traitors. The man from SMERSH executes Le Chiffre for his treachery and leaves Bond unconscious. After recuperating, Bond begins an intense love affair with heroine Vesper Lynd, who is revealed at the novel's end to be a double agent working for Russia. Torn between duty and her love for Bond, she commits suicide; this wounds Bond deeply,

and he makes a resolution to fight back against SMERSH and other forces of evil in the world.

□ STYLE AND THEMES

CASINO ROYALE is more a novella than a complete novel. It is short and compressed. Its brevity is certainly an asset, and the pages seem to fly by. This is the Fleming Sweep at work. The end of each brief and concise chapter pulls the reader into the next. This pace is sustained to the conclusion.

The book introduces the narrative structure that became a hallmark of the Bond novels: the opening chapter is a "teaser," dealing with an event that takes place somewhere in the middle of the story. The second chapter goes back in time to the beginning of the adventure—Bond receives his assignment from M and the story proceeds from there.

There is abundant detail in the novel's settings, especially when it comes to props. Bond doesn't use a mere cigarette lighter, but a black, oxidized Ronson lighter. Special attention is paid to each item; every object has a brand name. We are told the ingredients of Bond's breakfast, and the vintage of champagne served. This stylistic element (what Kingsley Amis calls "Fleming Effect") heightens the prose to such an extent that everything is ultimately believable. After writing his first draft, Fleming took great pains to research the facts and these graphic details are among the most distinctive ingredients of the *oeuvre*.

But other elements set CASINO ROYALE apart from the rest of the series. First, the character of James Bond is darker, colder, and more ruthless—until he falls in love. Then, we see a side of James Bond not often revealed in the series. The agent actually contemplates marriage! He views the prospect with caution, doubt, and suspicion, but also with curiosity. Ian Fleming wrote the novel just prior to his own marriage. Perhaps many of his own fears and curiosities were transferred to the leading character. But James Bond never makes it to the altar in this novel. Bond takes the tragedy of Vesper's death hard, and he becomes something of an unfeeling stone wall. Second, the tone of the story is the most serious of all the books in the series. It is also one of the most violent. Third, the climax occurs, curiously enough, only two-thirds of the way through the narrative. The last third is a moody denouement concerning the love affair between Bond and Vesper. This structure might have been deadly, but Fleming manages to keep the story suspenseful and well paced. Fourth, the novel is more atmospheric than any other in the series except, perhaps, YOU ONLY LIVE TWICE. CASINO ROYALE has shadowy, melancholic imagery which is vividly conjured in the opening chapter and lingers until the story's tragic and cynical conclusion. This ending on a down note is not in keeping with most of the Bonds; the cynicism of the author is at its strongest here.

A major theme in the book is that of gambling—not only in the casino, but also in the form of risk-taking in crisis situations. When Vesper wishes Bond good luck before his baccarat game, he replies that he doesn't believe in luck—he needs to depend on life without it. "I only bet on even chances, or as near them as I can get," Bond says. Contrary to this assertion, Bond gambles on some rather *uneven* chances throughout the story. When he is down to his last sixteen million francs, Bond takes the risk of challenging Le Chiffre again. This time he loses everything. Felix Leiter, however, saves the day with the CIA's gift of thirty-two million francs. Bond takes another chance in pursuing the Citroen after Le Chiffre abducts Vesper. He knows very well the risk he is taking—he even considers letting the kidnappers go, which would serve Vesper right for allowing herself to be tricked and captured. But Bond ultimately follows them and winds up trapped in the villain's clutches as well.

Another theme in the novel is the constant questioning of what is Good and what is Evil. As Bond is recovering in the hospital after his ordeal with Le Chiffre, he relates a philosophy to his French friend Mathis:

"For those . . . jobs I was awarded a Double 0 number in the Service . . . A Double 0 number in our Service means you've had to kill a chap in cold blood in the course of some job . . . that's all very fine—the hero kills two villains; but when the hero Le Chiffre starts to kill the villain Bond and the villain Bond knows he isn't a villain at all, you see the other side of the medal. The villains and heroes get all mixed up."

(CASINO ROYALE, Chapter 20)

Here, Bond is doubting his profession to the extent that he considers resigning once he returns to London. Mathis laughs at Bond and assures him that he's only imagining things. Once he has recovered, Bond will want nothing more than to go after SMERSH simply for the principle of saving his loved ones from evil. Mathis is proven right.

□ CHARACTERS

Bond is entirely humorless in this first novel, and he treats his job with conviction and importance. He wants nothing to do with Vesper Lynd at first, and only toward the end of the novel does he loosen up in her presence. His male chauvinism is at its strongest in CASINO ROYALE. Bond isn't happy with being assigned a partner in the first place, and his frustration is further enhanced when he learns that the partner is a woman. When Vesper is kidnapped by Le Chiffre, Bond loses all patience and thinks:

These blithering women who thought they could do a man's work. Why the hell couldn't they stay at home and mind their pots and pans and stick to their frocks and gossip and leave men's work to the men? And now for this to happen to him, just when the job had come off so beautifully: for Vesper to fall for an old trick like that and get herself snatched and probably held to ransom like some bloody heroine in a strip cartoon. The silly bitch.

(CASINO ROYALE, Chapter 15)

Nevertheless, Bond winds up falling in love with Vesper, and his thoughts turn completely around:

But somehow she had crept under his skin, and over the last two weeks his feelings had gradually changed.

He found her companionship easy and unexacting. There was something enigmatic about her which was a constant stimulus. She gave little of her real personality away, and he felt that, however long they were together, there would always be a private room inside her which he could never invade. She was thoughtful and full of consideration without being slavish and without compromising her arrogant spirit.

(CASINO ROYALE, Chapter 23)

After thinking this, Bond walks into his room to find his bath prepared. He says to Vesper, "Darling, the bath's absolutely right. Will you marry me?" Though this is said in jest, at the end of this chapter Bond decides:

That day he would ask Vesper to marry him. He was quite certain. It was only a question of choosing the right moment.

(CASINO ROYALE, Chapter 24)

But, once Bond discovers that Vesper was in reality a double agent working for the Russians, he pushes away the love he felt and hardens his heart. (He sheds tears as well.) Making a call to headquarters to inform the authorities that she was a traitor, he says, "Yes, dammit, I said 'was.' The bitch is dead now."

The "bitch," Vesper Lynd, makes a startling impression on Bond. She has black hair and blue eyes, and she carries herself with confidence and professionalism. As a character, she is fairly interesting but is not as three-dimensional as subsequent female figures in Fleming's books; she is one of the author's lesser female efforts. Vesper is cold and sterile, in much the way that Bond is. Maybe this is inherent in women working for the law. (Gala Brand in MOONRAKER, a policewoman, is also very stiff.) Vesper does seem braver in moments of danger than other heroines, but she falls apart toward the end of the novel once she realizes that SMERSH is on to her. Her character is out of step with the other Bond-girls in that she manages to wrap Bond around her little finger in the last third of the story. He falls for her, and falls hard. She begins dictating the rules of the relationship: he sees her when she's ready to be seen, and he leaves when she orders him from her room. Her suicide is a bit melodramatic—surely if Vesper had told Bond the truth about herself, he might have gotten her to safety. But the ending as Fleming wrote it emphasizes the melancholy, cynical, and bitter mood of the novel.

Le Chiffre is an ugly and perverted villain, and one of Fleming's lesser creations. His role in the story is small, but his nastiness is underscored enough to make a lasting impression on the reader. The image of the man sitting at the baccarat table and using his benzedrine inhaler in public is quite repellent. The torture scene is particularly effective, as he calmly assures Bond that the game of "Red Indians" is now over. Repeating the phrase, "My dear boy," as he speaks, the character begins the typical fatherlike treatment of the "bad boy" Bond. (Supposedly, Fleming picked up the "My dear boy" expression from his friend Noël Coward, and used it as a joke.) Le Chiffre is the only villain in the series to be killed by his own people.

M's role in this first novel is a small one. The reader learns that he is Bond's superior, and that the agent respects him a great deal. The only character traits mentioned are that M is very businesslike and rather crusty.

Two familiar characters of the series, René Mathis of the Deuxieme and Felix Leiter of the CIA, are introduced in this story. Mathis is an old acquaintance of Bond and is the primary ally. His character is interesting simply because he is the only one in the book who has a sense of humor. Mathis is very helpful, and he seems to understand what Bond is going through during the recovery process in the hospital. He succeeds in lifting Bond's spirits when the agent is morose and bedridden.

More important, though, is Bond's encounter with Felix Leiter, the CIA agent from Texas who will accompany the Englishan on further adventures. Leiter is amiable and boyish, and Fleming succeeds in giving the character a personality that is distinctly American. Leiter performs the important function of fulfilling Bond's need for male friendship. Not much else is revealed about Leiter's character in CASINO ROYALE, but he is an immediately likeable figure. Fleming was wise in using Leiter as the "cavalry to the rescue" when Bond loses all his money at the baccarat table.

□ HIGHLIGHTS AND OTHER INGREDIENTS

A notable element of CASINO ROYALE is the opening chapter, which creates a compressed view of James Bond's special world. A mood is established that surrounds the central character throughout the novel. At the end of this chapter, Bond slips into bed with his gun under the pillow—a nice touch, and a wonderful hint of the stringent discipline with which Bond will approach his job.

The highlight of the novel is, of course, the baccarat game. Fleming is particularly masterful in describing gaming contests, and the sequence is exciting. Even if the reader is unfamiliar with baccarat, Fleming makes it easy to follow the rudiments and subtleties of the game. The author intensifies the suspense of the sequence by allowing Bond to lose three consecutive hands before Leiter comes to his rescue.

The carpet-beater torture scene is both ingenious and revolting. Bond is tied naked to a chair with an opening in the seat. Le Chiffre sits next to Bond with a carpet beater in his hand. The paddle is placed under the open seat of Bond's chair, and Le Chiffre holds the handle over his knee. With a flick of the villain's wrist, the carpet-beater slams into Bond's buttocks and genitals. The reader can feel Bond's senses being ravaged by the pain; indeed, the agent will never undergo such a fiendish torture again (except, perhaps, for the one in COLONEL SUN). Critics have accused Fleming of being overly sadistic here, an indictment that is a testament to the scene's disturbing effectiveness.

One criticism of the novel could be that Fleming is rather pretentious in his use of the French language and the trappings of the elite, rich world of gambling casinos, expensive food, and beautiful women. But then, all of the Bond novels have this—it is a basic element of the author's style. Another criticism is that Bond himself is much too stonelike in this adventure. Subsequent novels improve on this, and Bond does become more human—even developing something of a sense of humor, which is totally absent here. Perhaps he takes Mathis' advice at the end of Chapter 20 to heart: to surround himself with human beings.

After all is said and done, one can argue that CASINO ROYALE is an extremely impressive first novel. A distinctive style is immediately apparent, and the narrative moves with uncompromising speed and conviction. It is one of the best of the adventures, capsulizing Bond's world into an intense, fascinating, and moody piece of fiction.

LIVE AND LET DIE (1954)

Fleming's second novel, LIVE AND LET DIE, improves upon CASINO ROYALE in many ways. First, the Fleming Sweep is at full force; here is perhaps the best example of this stylistic element. Second, Fleming uses even greater detail in descriptions of environments. More care seems to have been taken in revising and polishing. Finally, LIVE AND LET DIE contains one of Fleming's best plots, full of very exciting sequences. The novel is a little dated today (especially in its treatment of blacks) and is weak in terms of characterization. But the story is hard-hitting and violent in a way that none of the others are.

The story concerns Mr. Big, a powerful black businessman believed to be a member of SMERSH. Recently, gold coins from a seventeenth-century pirate hoard have been turning up in pawn shops and banks in Harlem and Florida. The source is thought to be a treasure hidden in Jamaica by the English pirate Bloody Morgan. M suspects that the pirate treasure is being used to finance the Soviet espionage system in America, and that Mr. Big is the man behind the smuggling operation. James Bond's investigation takes him from New York to Florida, where he and CIA agent Felix Leiter discover Mr. Big's United States port of entry for the smuggling. After Leiter is severely mutilated by a shark, Bond travels to Jamaica alone. He makes an underwater swim to locate Mr. Big's hideout, but is discovered by Mr. Big's men. 007 and the heroine, Solitaire, are tied together and dragged through the water behind Mr. Big's boat; but before their bodies are torn to shreds by a coral reef, a limpet mine previously planted by Bond destroys Mr. Big's boat. The pirate hoard is recovered and M grants Bond a "passionate leave," which will naturally be spent with Solitaire.

□ STYLE AND THEMES

LIVE AND LET DIE is longer than CASINO ROYALE, but moves just as quickly. The chapters are again short and compressed, almost always ending with hooks to lead the reader to the next. Fleming builds suspense with a masterly touch as Bond follows Mr. Big's trail to the Isle of Surprise. Since it is known very early that Mr. Big is the villain and is certainly behind the gold smuggling operation, the suspense comes in Bond's piecing the clues together; getting out of one scrape and into another; and moving forward toward the final confrontation with Mr. Big. The Fleming Sweep never achieves a more engaging rhythm and flow than here.

If CASINO ROYALE was abundant with detail, LIVE AND LET DIE takes the descriptive writing a step further by incorporating more exotic locales. Fleming's chronicle of the underwater world in Chapter 19 is vivid and awesome. Critics have always mentioned that the author's descriptive powers are most effective in describing gaming contests and life in the sea. Fleming's picture of America in the fifties is also very interesting and sometimes amusing:

It was no waste of time to start picking up the American idiom again: the advertisements, the new car models, and the prices of second-hand ones in the used-car lots; the exotic pungency of the road signs: SOFT SHOULDERS—SHARP CURVES—SQUEEZE AHEAD—SLIPPERY WHEN WET; the standard of driving; the number of women at the wheel, their menfolk docilely beside them; the men's clothes; the way the women were doing their hair; the Civil Defense warnings: IN CASE OF ENEMY ATTACK KEEP MOVING—GET OFF BRIDGE; the thick rash of television serials and the impact of TV on billboards and shop windows; the occasional helicopter; the public appeals for cancer and polio funds; THE MARCH OF DIMES—all the small fleeting impressions that were as important to his trade as are broken bark and bent twigs to the trapper in the jungle.

(LIVE AND LET DIE, Chapter 1)

Throughout the series of novels, Fleming can't resist the temptation to use his reporter's eye for detail and include a wealth of information about the particular locale in which his hero travels. CASINO ROYALE has a bit of this with its descriptions of the resort in Northeast France; LIVE AND LET DIE introduces the reader to one of Fleming's favorite locations, Jamaica, where all of the Bond novels were written. Because Fleming loved the West Indies and the tropical island world, many Bond adventures take place in similar locales. In visiting such exotic sites, Bond (and the reader) are introduced to local sights and customs via a "tour-guide." For example, through the voice of Quarrel, the Cayman Islander with whom Bond joins forces, we learn that two prevailing winds influence Jamaica's climate—the "Undertaker's Wind," which "blows all the bad air out of the island at night," and the "Doctor's Wind," which "blows all the sweet air in from the sea in the morning."

This "Undertaker's Wind" (also a working title for the novel) is used as a metaphor for Bond's mission on the island—Quarrel comments that the agent will be "blowing all the bad air from the island" when he finally eliminates Mr. Big. This metaphor leads directly to Fleming's major theme, which fulfills the prediction Mathis made toward the end of CASINO ROYALE: that Bond would surely seek out the bad men of the world and terminate their existence. When the FBI agent, Captain Dexter, tells Bond early in the novel that the official policy with Mr. Big so far (since they have no concrete evidence against him) was "live and let live," Bond replies, "In my job when I come up against a man like this one, I have another motto. It's 'live and let die.' "

The friendship theme is quite strong in this story, and the male allies are important: Felix Leiter has a strong supporting role, and Quarrel becomes a prominent figure. The friendship between Bond and Leiter comes to fruition here. From the first chapter, in which the American surprises the Englishman by greeting him in a hotel room, to the tragic incident in which Leiter almost loses his life to a shark, the men are inseparable. They barhop through Harlem together, sharing meals, conversation, and clue-gathering. Despite their differences in background, the men hit it off as if they have been friends since childhood. Bond seems to depend on this alliance with a male friend—it means more to him, sometimes, than his relationship with any woman in the novels. Bond even has trouble keeping the emotion from choking his voice when he learns that Leiter, after having lost half an arm and half a leg, will live after all.

Bond's heart was full. He looked out of the window. "Tell him to get well quickly," he said abruptly. "Tell him I miss him."

(LIVE AND LET DIE, Chapter 17)

This kind of emotion reveals itself infrequently; the loyalty Bond feels toward his friends is as strong as his commitment to his job.

☐ **CHARACTERS**

James Bond becomes more human in LIVE AND LET DIE. The strict coldness that enveloped the character in CASINO ROYALE is gone. He is a much warmer, more likeable man from the opening chapter. Fleming takes further care with smaller details of Bond's life: we learn he likes to wear pajamas, even after being told that "Americans sleep in the raw." Bond's face is fully described for the first time (CASINO ROYALE had basically given an impression of his features), emphasizing that there is a hint of the "mixed blood of America" in his hair and cheekbones.

Bond's attitude toward women has lightened as well. In CASINO ROYALE, Bond curses Vesper for allowing herself to be abducted by Le Chiffre. In LIVE AND LET DIE, Bond trusts Solitaire immediately when she calls him at the hotel with a plea to help her escape from Mr. Big. But then, Solitaire is "one of the most beautiful women Bond has ever seen." From the beginning he is friendlier with Solitaire than he ever was with Vesper Lynd, as the following indicates:

For better or worse he had decided to accept Solitaire, or rather, in his cold way, to make the most of her . . . he reflected it was going to be fun teasing her and being teased back, and he was glad that they had already crossed the frontiers into comradeship and even intimacy.

(LIVE AND LET DIE, Chapter 10)

Felix Leiter becomes a more complete character in this story as well. His jovial, boyish qualities are an excellent complement to Bond's seriousness. It is like a breath of fresh air when the Texan appears in any of the novels. Leiter acts as Bond's guide to America, as Quarrel does for Jamaica. Much of Fleming's sense of humor is revealed in the Texan's speeches:

"You can get through any American conversation," advised Leiter, "with 'Yeah,' 'Nope,' and 'Sure.' The English word to be avoided at all costs," added Leiter, "was 'Ectually,' " Bond had said that this word was not part of his vocabulary.

(LIVE AND LET DIE, Chapter 4)

At one point in the story, Leiter escapes a beating from one of Mr. Big's hoods by "arguing the finer points of jazz" with him. After making a crack about the clarinet—"an ill woodwind that nobody blows good"—Leiter is suddenly friends with his captor. The hood, who had been ordered to "hurt Leiter considerably," worries about what he should do with the

American agent. Finally, he simply knocks Leiter out with a blackjack.

Solitaire, whose real name is Simone Latrelle, is a mysterious, appealing heroine, and one of Fleming's better female characters. Her connection with the occult adds an enigmatic dimension to her personality that Vesper Lynd lacked. Solitaire had been raised in Haiti, is experienced in the world of voodoo rituals, and is telepathic. Mr. Big especially believes in her powers; he trusts the girl enough to let her make decisions for him. During Bond's first encounter with the villain, Mr. Big brings Solitaire to determine whether Bond is lying or telling the truth. Mr. Big asks Bond who he is and the agent replies with a cover story. Solitaire looks at Bond, and he suspects there is some kind of message for him behind her eyes. And, as he hoped, Solitaire informs Mr. Big that Bond "speaks the truth."

The heroine's immediate attraction to Bond is a little contrived, but it certainly serves the plot's purposes. She sees in Bond her only chance to escape from Mr. Big, who has kept her a prisoner for a year. Her desperate phone call to Bond is highly suspicious, too— yet Bond instinctively trusts her. Solitaire, who has long blue-black hair, and, like Bond, has a "sensual mouth which holds a hint of cruelty," is a woman with an "iron will." One of Bond's first impressions of her is that her face is "one born to command." She literally casts a spell on Bond, and it is strong enough to nab the world's most elusive secret agent.

Mr. Big is only an adequate villain. He tells Bond that he is the "first of the great Negro criminals." In choosing a black man for his villain, Fleming wasn't necessarily making a statement about blacks, as some critics complained. Granted, Fleming's portrait of the black hoods is none too favorable. Their speech is overwritten, with exaggerated colloquialisms, and none of the minor villains seems very bright. But Mr. Big himself is quite brilliant. (SMERSH would never pick a man with no brains to run such an important operation for them, whether he was black or white.) Mr. Big is meticulous in manner, speaks slowly and distinctly, and knows exactly what he wants. He states that there have already been great black writers, doctors, athletes, etc., but never a "great Negro criminal." Mr. Big explains that he takes "subtle pains" to outwit his opponents, and that he is, by nature, a wolf. The obligatory lecture scene is terrific: the villain ties Bond up and proceeds to expound philosophy. Though it seems unrealistic for a villain to do this, it usually gives Bond a chance to free himself. But the sequence also allows the villain to have his big moment. He has Bond in the palm of his hand, and like a cat, can't resist the temptation to play with the prey before devouring it.

Another Bond ally, Quarrel, is introduced in LIVE AND LET DIE. A native of the Cayman Islands, Quarrel immediately brings the novel some local color. Few characters in the series are more likeable than he. Quarrel's relationship with Bond is explored only briefly in this novel, but it flowers later in DOCTOR NO.

M is still a cardboard figure in this second novel. The Bond/M scene in LIVE AND LET DIE is not quite as brief as that in CASINO ROYALE, but nothing new is revealed about Bond's chief. The scene is "all business," and M doesn't mince words.

☐ HIGHLIGHTS AND OTHER INGREDIENTS

LIVE AND LET DIE is a touch more violent than most of the novels, except for CASINO ROYALE and COLONEL SUN. The scene in which Tee-Hee breaks Bond's little finger generates a good deal of suspense. One can empathize with Bond here as he watches the finger being pulled back until it snaps.

Leiter's mishap with the shark is intensely violent, although the actual incident occurs "off screen." The image of Bond finding Leiter wrapped in a bloody bedsheet is nightmarish and seems to haunt the remainder of the novel. The sequence is easily recalled when Leiter reappears in subsequent books.

The fight in the fish warehouse is exciting. Bond has just discovered Mr. Big's method for smuggling the gold coins and is suddenly interrupted by The Robber, one of Mr. Big's henchmen. Many fish tanks are shattered by bullets as their guns blaze. After a few explosive moments, Bond feigns an injury, tempting The Robber to investigate. Bond hits him and The Robber falls through a trap door over a shark pool. Apparently, the trap had been meant for Bond.

Finally, the climactic sequences in the lagoon are dramatic and intense. Mr. Big's death, as witnessed by Bond, is revolting and horrific. After the *Secatur* explodes, the surviving crew members find themselves swimming in shark- and barracuda-infested waters. Mr. Big goes down in the jaws of one of these predators.

LIVE AND LET DIE, then, stands as one of the best of the early novels. The plot moves excitingly and urgently, and a good deal of suspense is generated. The book's only fault is that characterizations are still incomplete, especially that of James Bond. But this problem is corrected in the next novel.

MOONRAKER (1955)

Fleming's third novel is different in tone and atmosphere from the previous two books: MOONRAKER is a much more thoughtful, introspective novel; it has less action; and the characters are further developed and well-rounded. Though there are some weak passages in the book (due to a curious lack of suspense), MOONRAKER stands out among the early novels as the first in which James Bond becomes a three-dimensional human being.

The story concerns James Bond's investigation of Sir Hugo Drax, a wealthy and respected national hero of sorts. Drax recently announced that he will donate ten million pounds for the defense of Britain. The weapon is the Moonraker, a nuclear rocket built to Drax's specifications at his own plant in Kent. The rocket is now complete and a test flight is scheduled in a few days. The problem bothering M is that Drax cheats at cards. As a favor for M, Bond accompanies his chief to Blades Club, where the men play bridge with Drax and a partner. Sure enough, Bond catches Drax cheating and beats the man at his own game. But the next day, M learns that an RAF security man was murdered the previous evening at Drax's plant; Bond is sent to investigate as the RAF's replacement. 007's suspicions are confirmed when an attempt on his and undercover policewoman Gala Brand's lives is made. Drax becomes wise to Bond and Gala and eventually traps them in a room close to the launching pad. Here, Drax reveals his plan to destroy London as revenge for Germany, and that the USSR is backing him. Using his teeth, Bond manages to light a blowtorch and uses it to free Gala. She cuts Bond loose and together they reset the rocket gyros so that it will splash down in the North Sea rather than London. As they hoped, the Moonraker comes down in the North Sea right on top of the submarine carrying Drax and his companions to Russia.

☐ STYLE AND THEMES

The Fleming Sweep is not as prominent here as in CASINO ROYALE and LIVE AND LET DIE, mainly due to the scarcity of action sequences. Much of the novel's plot advancement lies in James Bond's *thinking* the action through; the reader is invited into Bond's mind as he ponders and reflects on the many mysteries behind Hugo Drax. Also, the story takes place in England—around London and near Kent. There is no hopping from country to country, which is a major contributor to the Fleming Sweep. There are but a few passages of real action (the car chase, the blowtorch and steam hose ordeals). This is not to say that MOONRAKER is boring. On the contrary, it is a fascinating book, simply because of what it reveals about the James Bond character.

Fleming's penchant for detail is stronger than ever in MOONRAKER. For example, the author describes the elegant card club, Blades:

At the far end, above the cold table, laden with lobsters, pies, joints, and delicacies in aspic, Romneys' unfinished full-length portrait of Mrs. Fitzherbert gazed provocatively across at Fragonard's *Jeu de Cartes*, the broad conversation-piece which half-filled the opposite wall above the Adam fireplace. Along the lateral walls, in the centre of each gilt-edged panel, was one of the rare engravings of the Hell-Fire Club in which each figure is shown making a minute gesture of scatalogical or magical significance. Above, marrying the walls into the ceiling, ran a frieze in plaster relief of carved urns and swags interrupted at intervals by the capitals of the fluted pilasters which framed the windows and the tall double doors, the latter delicately carved with a design showing the Tudor Rose interwoven with a ribbon effect.

(MOONRAKER, Chapter 5).

The novel also brings back the moodiness of CASINO ROYALE, but without the cynicism. The plot involves the solving of a mystery rather than an action-filled, country-hopping pursuit of a super villain. This in itself adds to the sinister atmosphere of the book. There is also a distinct feeling of melancholy in the writing; perhaps this is due to Fleming's own sensitivities to middle age which he has passed on to his leading character.

The major theme of the novel is, again, gambling. Bond takes a number of chances, hoping that his own resourcefulness and timing will prevail over fate. He literally gambles in a high-stakes game at Blades by attempting to out-cheat Drax at bridge. Bond wagers on Drax's trustworthiness during his first two days at the Moonraker plant, and risks burning his face terribly when he lights a blowtorch with his teeth. Finally, the biggest gamble occurs when Bond re-sets the gyros to change the Moonraker's course to aim for the homing device aboard Drax's submarine in the North Sea.

Fleming seems to be emphasizing the need to take risks in order to receive full satisfaction from life's adventures. These risks may be dangerous, and may ultimately be fatal. But each new day might contain an adventure filled with such a challenge, and one must be a gambler to face it with any hope of survival.

Early in the novel, Fleming hints at impending doom, not only for Bond and England, but for the entire world. This occurs at the end of Chapter 3, when Bond notices a flashing neon sign and is alarmed by what he believes it says:

Startled at the great crimson words, Bond pulled in to the curb, got out of the car and crossed to the other side of the street to get a better view of the big skysign.

Ah! That was it. Some of the letters had been hidden by a neighboring building. It was only one of those Shell advertisements. "SUMMER SHELL IS HERE" was what it said.

Bond smiled to himself and walked back to his car and drove on.

When he had first seen the sign, half-hidden by the building, great crimson letters across the evening sky had flashed a different message.

They had said: "HELL IS HERE . . . HELL IS HERE . . . HELL IS HERE."

(MOONRAKER, Chapter 3)

The novel was written in 1954 and published in 1955, in the middle of the Cold War. Fear of the Bomb was worldwide. Fleming was perhaps a little too critical of the Russians during this period of political paranoia; but at the time, the threat of a nuclear war was felt widely. Today the plot seems somewhat contrived.

☐ CHARACTERS

In MOONRAKER, for the first time, James Bond becomes something more than a cardboard figure. Glimpses of a personal life are seen, such as a visit to Bond's flat off King's Road in Chelsea. We meet his secretary at the office, Loelia Ponsonby, and learn what he does at headquarters while not on an assignment. We ride with him in his Bentley. But most important, the author shares with the reader Bond's inner thoughts and feelings. As John Pearson observes in his biography of Fleming:

MOONRAKER was the most serious novel Fleming had written so far. Here the James Bond books begin to reveal themselves as the undercover autobiography of Ian Fleming. MOONRAKER completed his identification with his hero and gave him the chance of stating what he saw as the central problem of his own life, the malaise of middle age. It showed him attempting to map out some sort of solution in the dream of action, daring, maleness, sex, and high living.

(John Pearson, The Life of Ian Fleming)

Bond also reveals the first touch of a sense of humor. When M tells him that Drax's employees number fifty-two, Bond visualizes a "pack of cards and a joker."

Hugo Drax is one of Fleming's most successful villainous characters. German-born Drax was educated in England. How such an ugly, boisterous, and mysterious man could work his way up England's social and political ladders to become Sir Hugo Drax, knighted miner of columbite and defender of Britain, is highly questionable. Nevertheless, Drax is a fascinating character. He is larger than life—"physically big—about six foot tall" and he has a large square head with "tight reddish hair parted in the middle." His hair dips down in a curve toward his temples to cover as much as possible the scar tissue from plastic surgery that Drax had during the war. A bushy red mustache and long bushy whiskers growing at the level of his ear lobes completes the image. Bond reflects that Drax resembles a "ringmaster at a circus." The man is a loud-mouthed vulgarian and his flamboyance brings a richness to the novel that the characters of Le Chiffre and Mr. Big lack. There is also a childishness to Drax that makes him even more interesting. He loses his temper at the end of the celebrated bridge game at Blades, causing quite a scene. The image of a knighted social figure such as Drax ranting and raving in an elegant public place only heightens his colorfulness.

While Drax is a superior villain, the heroine of the book is relatively weak. Gala Brand seems to be a throwback to the rather stiff characterization of Vesper Lynd. She has no real interest in Bond (she's engaged to be married, although we don't learn this until the end of the book), which automatically dampens the sexual interest of the story. (She is one of the few women in the series that Bond fails to bed.) She is a policewoman and keeps her attitude professional and businesslike. She does loosen up a bit when Bond accompanies her to the beach for a swim (before being almost buried alive by a landslide), and after the couple's escape from their captors toward the end of the novel. Shortly after Bond meets Gala, he attempts to engage her in conversation but fails miserably. She answers only with polite monosyllables and refuses to meet his eye. Bond feels that her "frigid indifference" is overacted. At one point, he would like to give her a "sharp kick on the ankle" in order to get a response. But, he admits, Gala has probably been well chosen by Scotland Yard. She's "another Loelia Ponsonby. Reserved, efficient, loyal, virginal—a professional."

M is more fully developed in MOONRAKER. For the first time, M appears outside of the office for a social gathering. Bond is only too happy to accept M's invitation to dine at Blades, and as a personal favor determine how Drax is cheating at bridge. M is very cordial and pleasant at the dinner table, and for once, he seems more like a warm human being than the cold, crusty old admiral behind the desk at Universal Export. But the morning after Bond humiliates Drax at Blades, M becomes his usual self. Bond enters the office with a hangover, and M says, curtly, "You look pretty dreadful, 007 . . . Sit down." But M reveals an appreciation for Bond at the end when the Prime Minister phones to congratulate the Service on a job well done. The Prime Minister wants to honor Bond with an award for saving England, but it is against the Service's regulations for an agent to accept medals and decorations. This pleases M anyway, and he tells Bond of the P.M.'s wishes.

M. gave one of the rare smiles that lit up his face with quick brightness and warmth. Bond smiled back. They understood the things that had been left unsaid.

(MOONRAKER, Chapter 25)

☐ HIGHLIGHTS AND OTHER INGREDIENTS

The major feature of MOONRAKER is the bridge game at Blades. Though it's not essential to the plotline, it serves to reveal an excellent insight into Hugo Drax's character. It also showcases Fleming's talent for describing gaming contests. The few chapters concerning the bridge game are exciting, suspenseful, and fascinating, surpassing the baccarat game in CASINO ROYALE. Bond prepares for the card battle by first reading up on cheating tricks in *Scarne on Cards*. He stacks decks of two colors (since he's unsure which color deck Drax will be using) and uses one to deal a "Culbertson hand." This leads Drax to believe he has the winning hand, when in reality, Bond has the superior one. The bidding builds to a high pitch until Bond calmly reveals his hand to a much surprised Hugo Drax. The writing of the scene is nothing short of brilliant.

Another highlight is the car chase toward the end of Part Two. Krebs' newsprint roll ploy is ingenious, and it's one of the few action sequences in the story. The blowtorch incident and subsequent events leading to the blast-off of the Moonraker are also exciting and fast-paced. It is in Part Three that the novel begins to resemble the style of the previous books, as Bond and Gala frantically attempt to alter Drax's plans of destroying London. There is one tense moment when the couple hides in a ventilation shaft to avoid Drax's guards. The guards search for the couple by spraying steam hoses into each shaft. Bond and Gala bravely withstand the intense heat without giving themselves away. The guards eventually give up and evacuate the area for the liftoff.

The final unique element in MOONRAKER, which is exemplified especially at the end, is its undertone of melancholy. This moodiness is brought about by Bond's thoughts and reflections about his job, Gala Brand, and women in general. For once, we get a sense that James Bond may be a very lonely man; this melancholy is nowhere better exhibited than in the final paragraphs. Bond has just learned that Gala Brand is engaged and plans to marry the very next day:

And now what? wondered Bond. He shrugged his shoulders to shift the pain of failure—the pain of failure that is so much greater than the pleasure of success. An exit line. He must get out of these two young lives and take his cold heart elsewhere. There must be no regrets. No false sentiment. He must play the role which she expected of him. The tough man of the world. The Secret Agent. The man who was only a silhouette.

She was looking at him rather nervously, waiting to be relieved of the stranger who had tried to get his foot in the door of her heart.

Bond smiled warmly at her. "I'm jealous," he said. "I had other plans for you tomorrow night."

She smiled back at him, grateful that the silence had been broken. "What were they?" she asked.

"I was going to take you off to a farmhouse in France," he said. "And after a wonderful dinner I was going to see if it's true what they say about the scream of a rose."

She laughed. "I'm sorry I can't oblige. But there are plenty of others waiting to be picked."

"Yes, I suppose so," said Bond. "Well, goodbye, Gala." He held out his hand.

"Goodbye, James."

He touched her for the last time and then they turned away from each other and walked off into their different lives.

(MOONRAKER, Chapter 25)

Quite a downbeat ending for James Bond. But in a way, these final paragraphs present a summation of the solitary life a secret agent must lead. Fleming dubs his character "the man who is only a silhouette." It is here that the shadowy, cold world of James Bond becomes a lonely reality.

DIAMONDS ARE FOREVER (1956)

Fleming's fourth novel, DIAMONDS ARE FOREVER, zips from location to location at a breakneck pace. Like LIVE AND LET DIE, the new novel is another country-hopping story which is fueled by the Fleming Sweep. In the former novel, there are logical reasons for the action moving from one locale to another as the plot develops; but in DIAMONDS ARE FOREVER, this is not the case. Both plot advancement and change of locale seem contrived here, and as a result, DIAMONDS ARE FOREVER, although it has some tense moments and some interesting character developments, is probably the weakest of the early Bonds.

The story concerns a diamond smuggling operation running from a British-owned mine in French Guinea to America. The British Treasury suspects the House of Diamonds of controlling the pipeline. James Bond impersonates one of the pipeline's carriers and meets a contact in London, the scintillating American blonde named Tiffany Case, and together they smuggle the diamonds to New York. Meanwhile, the Service learns that the European vice president of the House of Diamonds, Rufus B. Saye, is none other than Jack Spang, who with his twin brother, Seraffimo Spang, runs a syndicate in America known as "The Spangled Mob." Bond's assignment, then, is to follow the pipeline to Las Vegas, where Seraffimo is located. Seraffimo Spang soon learns that Bond is an imposter and instructs his hoods to kidnap the agent and bring him to Spectre-ville, a ghost town near Las Vegas which Spang had purchased and decorated as a Wild West "resort." Bond is brutally beaten by Spang's henchmen, Wint and Kidd. But with the help of Tiffany, Bond escapes and manages to derail Spang's locomotive, with Spang inside, during a nocturnal chase out of Spectreville. Tiffany and Bond board the *Queen Elizabeth* for London, unaware that Wint and Kidd are also on board. Tiffany is captured by the hoodlums, but is eventually

rescued by Bond in a furious battle with the killers. Finally, Bond traces the pipeline back to French Guinea, where he encounters Jack Spang attempting to close down his operation. With a Bofors artillery gun, Bond knocks Spang's helicopter out of the sky.

□ STYLE AND THEMES

The Fleming Sweep, after taking a bit of a rest in MOONRAKER, returns at full force in DIAMONDS ARE FOREVER. This novel moves just as quickly as LIVE AND LET DIE, managing to maintain a constant level of excitement. But unfortunately, the plot suffers from too many loose ends. For example, Bond's assignment is to impersonate a diamond smuggler carrying a load of gems from London to New York. He must then attempt to trace the diamond pipeline to its final destination. None of Bond's actions after arriving in New York lead him to Las Vegas on his own—he is more or less pushed there by happenstance. A few of the sequences are gratuitous, such as the Saratoga race track visit and the auction aboard the *Queen Elizabeth*. Some events are *never* explained. For instance, why does Bond wear a disguise to call upon Rufus B. Saye at the House of Diamonds in London? If it was merely to mask his appearance, it is unnecessary. (He never encounters Rufus Saye/Jack Spang face-to-face again.) And though Tiffany Case has Francs' name and description, Bond does *not* wear a disguise when they first meet in her hotel room. She doesn't notice any difference between Bond's and Francs' looks.

Fleming's plot device for the rapid changes of locale once Bond arrives in America is the Mob finding a way to pay off the agent (as Peter Francs) for delivering the diamonds. First he is instructed to bet on a fixed horse at Saratoga. Bond purposely helps Felix Leiter disqualify the fixed horse so he will have an excuse to be sent elsewhere by the Mob. Bond is then sent to Las Vegas (in a very roundabout way) to play blackjack at a particular time of day. This seems like a rather expensive and ineffective means to pay off an employee—sending him all over the country and footing the bill. But otherwise, Bond would have no cause to visit Las Vegas, and would therefore never meet Seraffimo Spang.

Another flaw in the story is the lack of a central villain. The Spang brothers hardly qualify, since Jack Spang appears in only two chapters, and Seraffimo appears in only one. (They are mentioned throughout, however.) In the early stages of the story, Bond is constantly warned by M, the Chief of Staff, and Felix Leiter that he is up against very dangerous people—even a group like SMERSH supposedly comes nowhere near the power of the Spangled Mob. This menace is never really demonstrated. In fact, the Spangled Mob seems such a poorly organized outfit (they can't even pay off a diamond smuggler without first running him all over the country) that it is hardly worth James Bond's time. Therefore, despite the few instances of real danger (such as the Acme mud bath sequence, the car/cab chase in Las Vegas, and the "Brooklyn stomping" by Wint and Kidd), the novel is fairly tame.

Fleming's use of detail, however, is still rich and flamboyant. As in LIVE AND LET DIE, descriptions of America are interesting and amusing. This time, though, there is a hint of superiority mixed with a curious affection toward some aspects of American culture. For instance, Fleming is laughing under his breath when he describes a roadside diner in New York State:

At 12:30 they stopped for lunch at a "Chicken in the Basket," a log-built, "frontier-style" roadhouse with standard equipment—a tall counter covered with the best known name-brands of chocolates and candies, cigarettes and cigars, a juke box blazing with chromium and coloured lights that looked like something out of science-fiction, a dozen or more polished pine tables in the centre of the raftered room and as many low booths along the walls, a menu featuring fried chicken and "fresh mountain trout" which had spent months in some distant deep-freeze, a variety of short-order dishes, and a couple of waitresses who couldn't care less.

(DIAMONDS ARE FOREVER, Chapter 10)

Some things, however, are viewed with a touch of disgust. While Bond is in Las Vegas, he has these thoughts about what is basically an American institution in the middle of the midwestern desert:

The first thing he noticed was that Las Vegas seemed to have invented a new school of functional architecture which he dubbed the Gilded Mousetrap School, its main purpose being to channel the customer-mouse into the central gambling trap whether he wanted the cheese or not . . . It was, essentially, an inelegant trap, obvious and vulgar, and the noise of the machines had a horrible mechanical ugliness which beat at the brain . . .

With an occasional silvery waterfall the metal cup would overflow and the gambler would have to go down on his knees to scrabble for a rolling coin. Or, strictly speaking, her knees, for they were mostly women, as Leiter had said—elderly women of the prosperous housewife class. Droves of them stood at the banks of machines like hens in an egg

battery, conditioned by the delicious coolness of the room and the hypnosis of the spinning wheels to go on laying it on the line until their roll was gone.

Then, as Bond watched, a change-girl's voice cried, "Jackpot!" and some of the women raised their heads and the picture changed. Now they reminded Bond of Dr. Pavlov's dogs, saliva drooling at the treacherous bell that brought no dinner, and he shuddered at the empty eyes and the flaccid skin and the half open mouths and the thoughtless minds.

(DIAMONDS ARE FOREVER, Chapter 16)

Raymond Chandler, in his review of the book, said that for the first time, the sleaziness of Las Vegas had been accurately portrayed. The picture painted here is certainly not a pretty one.

The major theme of the novel is explicitly expressed in the title, and Fleming underscores the point in Chapter 24 in relation to death. Bond has just killed Wint and Kidd, and is looking forward to the prospect of holding Tiffany in his arms "forever":

Forever?

As he walked slowly across the cabin to the bathroom, Bond met the blank eyes of the body on the floor.

And the eyes of the man . . . spoke to him and said: "Mister, nothing is forever. Only death is permanent. Nothing is forever except what you did to me."

(DIAMONDS ARE FOREVER, Chapter 24)

Then Fleming turns to this image at the end of Chapter 25, after Bond has shot down Spang's helicopter:

So this great red full stop marked the end of the Spangled Mob and the end of their fabulous traffic in diamonds. But not the end of the diamonds that were baking at the heart of the fire. They would survive and move off again across the world, indestructible, as permanent as death.

And Bond suddenly remembered the eyes of the corpse which had once had a Blood Group F. They had been wrong. Death is forever. But so are diamonds.

(DIAMONDS ARE FOREVER, Chapter 25)

Diamonds, then, serve as a metaphor for death—and Bond, who carries the diamonds from London to New York, is the messenger of death who brings about the destruction of the Spangled Mob.

Another theme, and a recurring one, is that of friendship. One of the highlights in DIAMONDS ARE FOREVER is Bond's reunion with Felix Leiter, whom he had last seen as a bundle of bloody bedsheets in a Florida motel. Their scenes together are again a breath of fresh air, mainly because Leiter is such a warm and friendly character. Bond seems to remove his cold, stone-faced exterior when he's around the Texan. The friendship is important to both men; this is apparent in their conversation and actions. Bond again allows some emotion to reveal itself when he says goodbye to Leiter toward the end of the novel:

Bond felt a lump in his throat as he watched the lanky figure limp off to his car after being warmly embraced by Tiffany Case. "You've got yourself a good friend there," said the girl.
　"Yes," said Bond, "Felix is all of that."
(DIAMONDS ARE FOREVER, Chapter 21)

Surprisingly, the recurring theme of gambling is not as prominent here as one would expect, since the novel incorporates locations which would seem to play up this aspect: the Saratoga race track, Las Vegas, etc. No luck or gambling is involved here—the race at Saratoga is fixed, and the blackjack deal in Vegas is stacked.

□ CHARACTERS

While DIAMONDS ARE FOREVER lacks structural development, this flaw is almost salvaged by the character development. More of Bond's personal beliefs and ideals are explored by the author, such as his views on marriage. His conversations with Tiffany Case are revealing and are among the highlights of the book. In Chapter 22, over dinner, he and Tiffany share their own views of the perfect mate. Bond jokingly tells her that he would want "somebody who can make Sauce Béarnaise as well as love." But he goes on to add that she must have the "usual things"—and then proceeds to describe Tiffany's features. But he admits that his job does not allow him to consider marriage. It is here that he makes the comment that he is "married to a man named M."

One senses from these paragraphs that Bond seriously wants to settle down and marry. He does fall for Tiffany (as much as he falls for any woman), and it seems that not since Vesper Lynd has a woman had such an effect on him. In the next novel we learn that he and Tiffany continued their affair after the conclusion of DIAMONDS ARE FOREVER, and that she moved into his flat in London. So apparently, there may have been some sort of love between the couple.

Another insight into Bond's character is revealed as he is waiting at the Tiara Hotel in Las Vegas to win his payoff at the blackjack table. He is disgusted with his cover, allowing the Mob to push him around and order him here and there. He admits that he feels "homesick for his real identity." This is a throwback to the similar thoughts he felt at the end of MOONRAKER, when he likens his life as a secret agent to that of a "man who is only a silhouette." In essence, Bond is reflecting that perhaps he doesn't live his "real identity" often enough—that his life is taken up far too much by that of a cover. This is one of the first signs that Bond has doubts about his profession—doubts which continue to plague him throughout the series.

Tiffany Case, the heroine of DIAMONDS ARE FOREVER, is Fleming's first fully developed female character. The trouble is that she is neurotic as hell. Tiffany is constantly wavering between hot and cold—she has a "come here, come here, get away, get away" attitude which Bond finds most frustrating. She uses Bond to buy her expensive meals and keep her company, but if he makes advances—look out! She has a way of being cruel and stand-offish in most of the story; but she relents in the end and finally accepts Bond's ardor.

Tiffany has had a hard life, so her neurotic tendencies are not surprising. According to Leiter, Tiffany's mother ran a whorehouse in San Francisco and one day decided not to pay the local gang's protection money. The group raided the house and raped Tiffany, who was only sixteen at the time. Leiter presumes this is why the girl won't have anything to do with men; but this, of course, is before James Bond comes along. After a series of other misfortunes, Tiffany met Seraffimo Spang in Reno. Spang looked after her and employed her in the Mob.

She is blond with cool grey eyes. She carries herself with brazen sexuality, yet seems to project an invisible message reading "Hands Off!" Bond imagines her eyes saying: "Sure. Come ahead and try. But, brother, you'd better be good." She's a tough girl, but underneath this wall of ice is a lonely, insecure woman. Tiffany has moments of temper at trivial remarks made by Bond, and never lets him know where he stands with her until they are four days into the trip aboard the *Queen Elizabeth* at the novel's end. On their second meeting, she flat out tells him that she isn't going to sleep with him; yet, when they part at her insistence later that same evening, she "angrily" grabs Bond and kisses him hard on the lips, saying she "doesn't want to lose him." Bond is both confused and intrigued by the woman.

Felix Leiter returns in this novel to accompany Bond

to Saratoga, and again pops up in the nick of time in Las Vegas. Leiter no longer works for the CIA—Allen Dulles let him go after he lost his arm and leg. Now he works for Pinkerton's Detective Agency, "The Eye That Never Sleeps." Leiter does not seem bitter at all about carrying a steel hook for a right hand or limping through life with a wooden leg. He is as cheerful and buoyant as ever. Perhaps this conscious negation of his physical handicaps is one reason why Leiter remains a useful friend to Bond. Their reunion on the streets of New York is a joyful moment: they immediately proceed to their usual form of entertainment, i.e., eating and drinking. Leiter remembers Bond's formula for a vodka martini and orders it for Bond, as well as taking the liberty of ordering the Englishman's meal. Even though this is only their third adventure together, they act as if they've known each other for years. Leiter is once again very helpful as Bond's "tour guide." He explains everything Bond needs to know about the Saratoga race track, Las Vegas gambling statistics, etc.

It is these scenes with Leiter and Tiffany that make DIAMONDS ARE FOREVER a pleasure to read.

Nothing new is added to M's character. After the more revealing sequences in MOONRAKER, M is back to his stone-faced, crusty old self in the opening chapters of DIAMONDS ARE FOREVER.

The Spang brothers, as villains, are hardly worth mentioning. They are not present through most of the novel, and they are in no way complete characters. Suffice it to say that the Spangs are American gangsters with a flair for organization, but come nowhere near the caliber or flamboyance of Hugo Drax.

Other mentionable characters are Ernest Cureo, the Las Vegas cab driver who sells his services to Bond; "Shady" Tree, the wise-guy hunchback working for the Mob in New York; and Wint and Kidd, the extremely dangerous homosexual hit men for the Mob. These characters, though minor, are interesting and help advance the plot.

□ **HIGHLIGHTS AND OTHER INGREDIENTS**

As mentioned above, the true highlights of the novel are Bond's relationships with Tiffany and Leiter. The action sequences are dull. The scene in the Acme Mud and Sulphur Bath, in which Wint and Kidd execute a traitorous jockey, though tense, is not really necessary to advance the plot. The railroad chase from Spectre-ville is exciting, but Bond and Tiffany escape from the situation with such ease that it's hardly worth it.

For these reasons, though fast-moving and interesting in terms of character, DIAMONDS ARE FOREVER does not carry the weight of the previous three Bonds.

FROM RUSSIA, WITH LOVE (1957)

The fifth James Bond novel is perhaps the most successful of the series: Fleming has managed to blend excellent characterizations with a highly suspenseful and clever story; the Fleming Sweep operates at a confident pace; the detail in the prose is rich and colorful; and the novel contains purely romantic elements that are missing from most of the other books. In addition, the structure of FROM RUSSIA, WITH LOVE is different from its predecessors—Fleming attempted something new by not bringing in his central character until Chapter 11, almost a third into the book. The novel concludes with a surprise-shocker ending, another offbeat change from the previous books. Fleming himself admitted that he was "attempting to elevate the Bond books to a higher literary level." If not for the cliffhanger ending, FROM RUSSIA, WITH LOVE could stand as the definitive James Bond novel.

The story concerns SMERSH's plot for revenge against the British Secret Service, and in particular, against James Bond. Kronsteen, SMERSH's master planner, creates an elaborate scheme to trap Bond and eliminate him in an embarrassing fashion. Rosa Klebb, Head of Operations and Executions, hand-picks an assassin, Red Grant, as well as a beautiful, innocent Russian girl, Tatiana Romanova, (also known as Tania) to act as pawns in SMERSH's ploy. The Secret Service learns from their man in Istanbul, Darko Kerim, that the girl, Romanova, is willing to defect to the West and hand over a much coveted Spektor Coding Machine (owned by the Russians) if James Bond will come to Istanbul and rescue her. She claims that she fell in love with the agent after seeing his photograph in the KGB file. Although M and Bond both suspect a trap, the bait of a Spektor Coding Machine is too tempting to pass up. Once Bond is in Istanbul, Tania finally makes contact with the agent by surprising him in his hotel suite. She insists on escaping via the Orient Express, and the next day they join Kerim aboard the famous train. But three KGB men are also aboard. Using his well-respected authority, Kerim manages to have two of the men removed for ticket violations; but the third man and Kerim end up killing each other in a struggle. Shortly after, Red Grant boards the train. After drugging the girl, Grant reveals his true identity and explains the entire scheme to Bond. After a furious battle, Bond kills Grant and manages to escape from the train with the girl and the Spektor. Later in Paris, Bond locates Rosa Klebb in a hotel room. The woman attempts to stab Bond with poison-tipped knitting needles, but Renè Mathis of the Deuxième arrives in time to take the woman away. Before she is arrested, however, she kicks Bond in the shin with a poison-tipped blade concealed in her shoe.

□ STYLE AND THEMES

The most obvious change in structure from the previous Bonds is that the first ten chapters deal exclusively with the villains. James Bond does not appear until Chapter 11. In these first ten chapters (subtitled "Part One: The Plan"), Fleming creates a base from which the plot grows. He reveals the inner workings of SMERSH, the Soviet murder organization which Bond has battled in previous adventures. The detail with which Fleming describes the villains' plotting is fascinating. The first three chapters deal with the background of Red Grant, the chief executioner of SMERSH. Then the narrative jumps back in time to a meeting of the Praesidium, which consists of the heads of each department in SMERSH. There, a General G. and his colleagues designate James Bond as a target for a "major Soviet Intelligence victory." The task of creating the *konspiratsia* is given to Kronsteen, a master chess player. His plan is then turned over to Rosa Klebb, Head of Operations, who is responsible for its execution. After Klebb picks a beautiful, innocent Russian girl, Tatiana Romanova, as a lure to bring Bond within SMERSH's grasp, the narrative returns to Red Grant as he is assigned to kill the Englishman.

All of these details could have easily been related in two or three chapters, but Fleming stretches out the conspiracy to a complete story. By doing so, he fully develops each character and each phase of SMERSH's plan. By the end of Part One, a complete exposition has been laid for what seems like a foolproof plan to eliminate the hero. Suspense gradually builds throughout the ten chapters until it reaches a plateau—and then James Bond is smoothly introduced into the action.

The Fleming Sweep steadily propels the plot. Once Bond enters, the story advances with breathtaking excitement. And Fleming teases the reader along the way: for example, Bond does not meet Tania until Chapter 20. The anticipation of this meeting is prominent throughout the preceding chapters. Even the gypsy camp sequences, which may at first seem extraneous to the plot, take on a new meaning once it is learned that the Russians are attempting to eliminate Darko Kerim so that Bond will be alone to fall more easily into their trap. FROM RUSSIA, WITH LOVE is Fleming's longest novel thus far, but the Sweep makes it seem half as long.

Another major difference in the structure is the end. For the first time, Fleming creates a shocking surprise ending: the villains win! Throughout the story, Bond manages to escape each little trap the Russians have set for him; but in the last few paragraphs, Rosa Klebb manages to kick Bond with a poisoned steel-tipped shoe. In the final sentences, Bond begins to feel dizzy and has trouble breathing. The last sentence of the novel reads: "Bond pivoted slowly on his heel and crashed headlong to the wine-red floor." Wham! No explanation. No promise of a resurrection. James Bond is dead. Or is he?

As a plot twist, the surprise ending is effective. In a way, the novel might not have worked as well without it. Because Fleming first elaborately details SMERSH's plot to kill Bond, the feeling of imminent danger is always present. Bond is unaware of the assassination plot as he is taken through the action like a pawn, and the suspense builds to a shattering climax aboard the Orient Express. Once Bond escapes this danger, the tension is momentarily relieved until he meets Rosa Klebb in Paris. The excitement is boosted once again, but Bond's friend Mathis and the authorities arrive in time to take Klebb away. But with that unexpected kick in the shin, all the danger and imminent disaster that have hung over Bond throughout the novel finally hit home. The execution of the plan is complete, even though the original plot was circumvented.

FROM RUSSIA, WITH LOVE is one of Fleming's most romantic novels, in which romantic fantasy serves as the story's major theme. In fact, the *idea* of the story is romantic—a handsome spy travels to a foreign land to rendezvous with a beautiful enemy spy who claims she's in love with him. It is a quintessential thriller-fantasy plot which plays on whatever romantic dreams a reader may have. This notion is summed up as Tania watches Bond sleep aboard the Orient Express:

How extraordinary, this passionate tenderness that had filled her ever since she had seen him last night standing naked at the window, his arms up to hold the curtains back, his profile, under the tousled black hair, intent and pale in the moonlight. And then the extraordinary fusing of their eyes and their bodies. The flame that had suddenly lit between them—between the two secret agents, thrown together from enemy camps a whole world apart, each involved in his own plot against the country of the other, antagonists by profession, yet turned, and by the orders of their governments, into lovers.

(FROM RUSSIA, WITH LOVE, Chapter 21)

FROM RUSSIA, WITH LOVE is also Fleming's sexiest novel thus far, with intensely passionate love scenes.

The "life is a gamble" theme continues in this novel as well. M and Bond are not fools; not even they can pass up the opportunity to seize the Spektor Coding Machine which Tania has promised to bring—no matter what the odds. Whether or not the girl's story of being in love with Bond is true, M wants to take the risk of sending Bond to Istanbul. The whole idea *smells* like a trap, but M's enthusiasm convinces Bond he should risk it:

Bond was sold. At once he accepted all M.'s faith in the girl's story, however crazy it might be. For a Russian to bring them this gift, and take the appalling risk of bringing it, could only mean an act of desperation—of desperate infatuation if you liked. Whether the girl's story was true or not, the stakes were too high to turn down the gamble.

(FROM RUSSIA, WITH LOVE, Chapter 12)

Bond comes to terms with his mission while on the plane to Istanbul, as he reflects, sourly, that he is "pimping for England":

For that, however else one might like to describe it, was what he was on his way to do—to seduce, and seduce very quickly a girl whom he had never seen before, whose name he had heard yesterday for the first time. And all the while, however attractive she was—and Head of T had described her as "very beautiful"—Bond's whole mind would have to be not on what she was, but on what she had—the dowry she was bringing with her. It would be like trying to marry a rich woman for her money. Would he be able to act the part? Perhaps he could make the right faces and say the right things, but would his body dissociate itself from his secret thoughts and effectively make the love he would declare? How did men behave credibly in bed when their whole minds were focused on a woman's bank balance? Perhaps there was an erotic stimulus in the notion that one was ravaging a sack of gold. But a cipher machine?

(FROM RUSSIA, WITH LOVE, Chapter 13)

From these thoughts come the doubts and worries that the whole thing may be a trap. Bond is gambling on M's faith in the mission, and his hunch that the girl isn't bluffing, and most importantly, on his own sexual prowess to succeed. Even M puts this weight on Bond's shoulders when the agent asks M what happens if he doesn't come up to Tatiana's expectations:

"That's where the work comes in," said M. grimly. "That's why I asked those questions about Miss Case. It's up to you to see that you *do* come up to her expectations."

(FROM RUSSIA, WITH LOVE, Chapter 12)

□ CHARACTERS

James Bond's character is further developed in FROM RUSSIA, WITH LOVE. In a scene at Bond's flat off of King's Road, some of his personal habits are revealed (such as his penchant for doing twenty slow push-ups immediately after waking). May, Bond's "Scottish treasure" of a housekeeper, is also introduced. But more importantly, Bond feels bored with his life and feels that he is in danger of "becoming soft." Self-doubt begins to plague Bond more and more.

Bond even has a rare moment of authentic fright—not of a villainous torture, but of air travel. When the flight to Istanbul runs into a storm, Bond's thoughts reveal his manner of protecting himself from the outside world:

In the centre of Bond was a hurricane-room, the kind of citadel found in old-fashioned houses in the tropics. These rooms are small, strongly built cells in the heart of the house, in the middle of the ground floor and sometimes dug down into its foundations. To this cell the owner and his family retire if the storm threatens to destroy the house, and they stay there until the danger is past. Bond went to his hurricane-room only when the situation was beyond his control and no other possible action could be taken. Now he retired to this citadel, closed his mind to the hell of noise and violent movement, and focused on a single stitch in the back of the seat in front of him, waiting with slackened nerves for whatever fate had decided for B.E.A. Flight No. 130.

(FROM RUSSIA, WITH LOVE, Chapter 13)

In this sequence, Bond is almost sorry he didn't heed Loelia Ponsonby's advice. She had been worried that Bond was flying on Friday the thirteenth. But he prefers to fly on this day because it's "less crowded."

When dealing with Tania, Bond reveals even more human qualities. He is awkward and nervous the first time he meets her. He is especially disgruntled at having to ask about the Spektor machine while she is seducing him:

And now for the question he had been shirking. He felt a ridiculous embarrassment. This girl wasn't in the least what he had expected. It was spoiling everything to ask the question. It had to be done.

"What about the machine?"

Yes. It was as if he had cuffed her across the face. Pain showed in her eyes, and the edge of tears.

She pulled the sheet over her mouth and spoke from behind it. Her eyes above the sheet were cold.

"So that's what you want."

"Now listen." Bond put nonchalance in his voice. "This machine's got nothing to do with you and me. But my people in London want it." He remembered security. He added blandly, "It's not all that important. They know all about the machine and they think it's a wonderful Russian invention. They just want one to copy. Like your people copy foreign cameras and things." God, how lame it sounded!

(FROM RUSSIA, WITH LOVE, Chapter 20)

Yes, it does sound lame, and Bond feels foolish because of it.

Bond is even subject to moments of guilt. While he and Kerim are enjoying an evening out at the gypsy camp, Bulgars attack in an attempt to kill Kerim and the gypsies' leader. Kerim makes some careless mistakes and almost gets himself murdered, but Bond saves his life:

Bond stopped in his tracks. "You bloody fool," he said angrily. "Why the hell can't you take more care! You ought to have a nurse." Most of Bond's anger came from knowing that it was he who had brought a cloud of death around Kerim.

(FROM RUSSIA, WITH LOVE, Chapter 17)

Kerim apologizes; Bond feels ashamed and disgusted with all the bloodshed that has occurred.

In one moment, Bond becomes nostalgic and reflects on his early years. As his plane is flying over Switzerland, he is reminded of a time when, as a teenager, he had climbed mountains with some companions:

And now? Bond smiled wryly at his reflection in the Perspex as the plane swung out of the mountains and over the grosgrained terazza of Lombardy. If that young James Bond came up to him in the street and talked to him, would he recognize the clean, eager youth that had been him at seventeen? And what would that youth think of him, the secret agent, the older James Bond? Would he recognize himself

beneath the surface of this man who was tarnished with years of treachery and ruthlessness and fear—this man with the cold arrogant eyes and the scar down his cheek and the flat bulge beneath his left armpit? If the youth did not recognize him what would his judgment be? What would he think of Bond's present assignment? What would he think of the dashing secret agent who was off across the world in a new and most romantic role—to pimp for England?

(FROM RUSSIA, WITH LOVE, Chapter 13)

With each successive novel, Fleming develops a more complex major character.

Tatiana Romanova is an appealing heroine. She is intriguing, intelligent, and is certainly the sexiest female in the books thus far. Often compared to Greta Garbo by her friends, Tania has "fine dark brown silken hair" (she admits she copies a hair style once used by Garbo). Her deep blue eyes are set wide apart, with unusually long lashes. She has the ever-present Fleming-female "wide mouth" (apparently the author thought this an erotic feature on women), and soft, pale skin with an "ivory sheen at the cheekbones." Her arms and breasts are "faultless" and "only a purist would disapprove of her behind."

Besides being beautiful, Tania is a firm believer in her country—she is very patriotic and would do anything to serve Mother Russia. At the time she is assigned to seduce James Bond, she is serving as a Corporal of State Security. She is well-mannered and would never do anything that isn't *kulturny*. Except, perhaps, seduce a handsome enemy spy. Tania is brave (or she would not be able to begin accomplishing the task given her by Colonel Klebb), yet she is also shy and girlish. The image of her lying naked and peeking out with a giggle from under a sheet in Bond's bed, is a mixture of every man's fantasy of the little girl and the seductress—and she knows it!

It is disappointing that Fleming does not relate what becomes of Tania after the novel's end. The life of the previous heroine, Tiffany Case, is neatly summed up in Chapters 11 and 12 (she has gone to America to marry a serviceman). But in this book, and the following one, Tania's post-Bond life is not mentioned. It must be assumed that, as Bond predicts, she is taken into the bowels of the Western government and thoroughly interrogated and probed for Soviet information, and then, most likely, relocated in Canada.

Bond's ally in FROM RUSSIA, WITH LOVE, is Darko Kerim Bey, one of Fleming's most colorful characters. Patterned after a real-life Turkish friend of the author, Kerim embodies the richness that one finds in figures like Quarrel and Colombo. Kerim has a "wonderfully warm dry handclasp." He is taller than Bond, and has smiling blue eyes in a large, smooth, brown face with a broken nose. He is "vaguely gypsy-like" in his fierce pride and in his curling black hair and crooked nose. Bond thinks he looks like a "vagabond soldier of fortune," an effect which is heightened by a gold ring worn in his right earlobe.

Kerim is a wild, romantic fellow. He takes great pride in relating to Bond his adventures and experiences growing up and becoming the head of Station T. He is friend to the gypsies, and once took a gypsy woman home in order to "tame her." He accomplished this task by chaining her to the floor under his dining table and throwing scraps of food to her. This may seem barbaric, but Kerim insists that when his mother found the girl and ordered Kerim to release her, the girl refused to go! (Another example of Fleming at his most chauvinistic.)

At one point in the story, Kerim states a philosophy which could be applied to Fleming himself. He tells Bond:

"I am greedy for life. I do too much of everything all the time. Suddenly one day my heart will fail. The Iron Crab will get me as it got my father. But I am not afraid of The Crab. At least I shall have died from an honourable disease. Perhaps they will put on my tombstone 'This Man Died from Living Too Much."

(FROM RUSSIA, WITH LOVE, Chapter 15)

Rosa Klebb, although she doesn't appear in many chapters, is an excellent villainess. For once, the major adversary is female—a new Fleming twist. And she, like most of her male counterparts, is hideous in appearance. Klebb is in her late forties—a short, squatty woman with thick legs. Kronsteen thinks that in her uniform she looks like a "badly packed sandbag." He compares her to the *tricoteuses* of the French Revolution—the women who sat and knitted as the guillotine claimed its victims. Klebb has pale, "thick chicken's skin," and she conveys coldness, cruelty, sadism, and strength: Klebb is a very tough number. And in the end, she wins. The woman also has Lesbian tendencies, and attempts to seduce Tania in her office in one of the novel's more revolting sequences.

Red Grant is also a very menacing character, sharing the role of villain with Klebb. It is he who is slated to do the dirty work of killing Bond, but botches it up. What Grant lacks in brains he makes up for in strength and viciousness. He is a handsome Englishman (ac-

tually half German) with golden hair—a "Golden Boy." He is also mad as a hatter; in his teens, when exposed to the full moon, he would go on "killing excursions." He began killing animals, and, as he grew older, advanced to murdering people. He is Fleming's first seriously frightening psychotic. The author does add a bit of humor to the character by having Grant, as Captain Nash, call Bond "old man" throughout his escapade.

A new side of M is revealed in FROM RUSSIA, WITH LOVE. One learns of M's disapproval of Bond's "womanizing." But even M realizes that Bond is a handsome man and is attractive to women. He doesn't for a moment disbelieve Tania's story of being in love with Bond, though Bond is incredulous. M "smiles at the mixture of expressions on Bond's face." When Bond says that her story sounds crazy, M replies:

"Now wait a moment," M.'s voice was testy. "Just don't be in too much of a hurry simply because something's turned up you've never come across before. Suppose you happened to be a film star instead of being in this particular trade. You'd get daft letters from girls all over the world stuffed with Heaven knows what sort of rot about not being able to live without you and so on. Here's a silly girl doing a secretary's job in Moscow. Probably the whole department is staffed by women, like our Records. Not a man in the room to look at, and here she is, faced with your, er, dashing features on a file that's constantly coming up for review. And she gets what I believe they call a "crush" on these pictures just as secretaries all over the world get crushes on these dreadful faces in the magazines." M. waved his pipe sideways to indicate his ignorance of these grisly female habits. "The Lord knows I don't know much about these things, but you must admit they happen."

(FROM RUSSIA, WITH LOVE, Chapter 12)

M, with his Victorian ways, is quite amusing here. Even he admits that Bond is a man with whom women must reckon.

Other characters worth mentioning include the chess master Kronsteen, the evil "Wizard of Ice" who plans the entire *konspiratsia* against Bond; General G., the head of SMERSH, who briefly represents the supreme command behind this Soviet murder organization; Vavra, the gypsy friend of Kerim who helps defend Bond and the Turk against an attack on their lives; and even René Mathis, Bond's friend from CASINO ROYALE, who makes a brief appearance at the novel's end. All of these characters add to the varied personalities, exotic locales, and dramatic action that make FROM RUSSIA, WITH LOVE a vivid adventure.

□ HIGHLIGHTS AND OTHER INGREDIENTS

A major highlight, as mentioned before, is the assassination planning in the first third of the novel. Not only does it build suspense, but it reveals the inner workings of SMERSH. The gypsy camp sequence is full of texture and detail, and again serves Fleming's urge to create local color. The girl fight, which received hostile criticism when the novel was first published, is tense and explosive—probably the most violent scene in the book. The chapter is appropriately entitled "Strong Sensations," as the author graphically describes the sweat and smell of the writhing female bodies.

The Orient Express chapters are exciting, not only because the story is approaching its climax, but because of the colorful history of the famous train itself. When he sees the sign for the Orient Express at the train depot, Bond admits to himself that it must be "one of the most romantic signs in the world."

The fight with Red Grant on the train is gripping. Thanks to some stupid mistakes due to Grant's overconfidence, Bond is able to trick the killer and escape from what has seemed a hopeless situation. The fact that Grant is stabbed in the groin may perhaps be a little sadistic, but it certainly serves as a tremendous catharsis to the build-up of tension.

Bond's encounter with Rosa Klebb provides a final thrill. It is amusing at first, as Bond and Klebb pleasantly greet each other as if one of them were accidentally in the wrong room. But Bond eventually drops all pretense and says cheerfully, "It's no use! You are Rosa Klebb. And you are Head of Otdyel II of SMERSH. You are a torturer and a murderer. You wanted to kill me and the Romanov girl. I am very glad to meet you at last." But the laugh is soon stifled as Klebb attacks Bond with poisoned knitting needles. And Klebb gets the last laugh.

It is in this book that Fleming provides Bond with the first of the "spy gadgets" that will appear from time to time in the novels, and used to an absurd extreme in the films. In FROM RUSSIA , WITH LOVE, the Armourer provides Bond with an attaché case with secret compartments for money, ammunition, and a silencer for his Beretta. The case also contains two throwing knives hidden in the lining. In his fight against Grant, one of these knives saves his life. The gadget, in the context of the novel, is believable and acceptable.

If one were to be overly critical, FROM RUSSIA, WITH LOVE could not represent the Bond series as a whole because of the surprise ending in which Bond doesn't win. But because of its extremely successful blend of full characterizations with a highly original, fascinating, and suspenseful plot, FROM RUSSIA, WITH LOVE remains a high point in the James Bond series.

DOCTOR NO (1958)

Many fans consider DOCTOR NO the best James Bond novel. After experimenting with the structure of FROM RUSSIA, WITH LOVE, Fleming returns to the standard formula in the new novel. In terms of sheer excitement and thrills, DOCTOR NO ranks very high. It also has a simple, direct plot; a very appealing heroine; and the best villain since Hugo Drax. It isn't surprising that DOCTOR NO was also chosen to be the first James Bond film. The book's only fault is the implausibility of some of its situations. In fact, DOCTOR NO has elements bordering on the fantastic, which could label it the first James Bond science fiction story.

The story concerns James Bond's investigation of the disappearance of Commander John Strangways and his secretary from Station C in Jamaica. Strangways was working on a case involving the Audubon Society and its trouble with the maintenance and operation of a bird sanctuary on the island of Crab Key. The man who owns the island, Dr. Julius No, promised to maintain the sanctuary when he purchased the land years ago. Recently, however, Audubon wardens paid a visit to the island, and only one man came back alive. Badly burned, the warden kept mumbling something about a "dragon." After arriving in Jamaica, Bond and his friend Quarrel unravel clues which suggest that Strangways was murdered. After an attempt is made on Bond's life by Dr. No's underlings in Kingston, 007 and Quarrel take a boat to Crab Key in the dead of night. There, they meet an innocent, beautiful "nature girl," Honeychile Rider. Eventually, the dragon appears, and it is revealed to be a tanklike vehicle painted to resemble a creature. It claims Quarrel as a victim with its built-in flame thrower, and Bond and the girl are taken prisoner. They are brought to Dr. No's establishment, an elaborate headquarters run by slave labor. Over an elegant meal, Dr. No reveals his secret plan to use a specially developed radio beam which can deflect the course of any United States test missiles launched from nearby Turks Island. Bond undergoes several horrors in a specially-prepared obstacle course, which empties into an enclosed inlet containing a man-eating giant squid. Bond miraculously survives the ordeal and escapes to find Dr. No overseeing the loading of bird guano (his cover business) onto a tanker. Bond overpowers a crane operator and uses the machine to bury Dr. No under a pile of guano. Bond then locates Honey and they escape to safety.

□ STYLE AND THEMES

Having "killed" Bond in FROM RUSSIA, WITH LOVE, Fleming had to resurrect him in the opening chapters of DOCTOR NO. But the story begins in Fleming's usual way: the first chapter deals with events before Bond enters the picture (the murder of Strangways), and is followed by Bond's meeting with M in the next chapter. The chapters all follow a logical cause-and-effect sequence, and the Fleming Sweep takes the reader through them at the usual brisk pace. The chapters are longer than usual, however, though fewer in number. More information and action is packed into each chapter of DOCTOR NO than Fleming has attempted in previous books. The novel is structurally flawless.

The book can also be called Fleming's most imaginative. Each sequence seems to go one step beyond what is expected. For example, Bond's trek through the obstacle course builds to a peak with the addition of one bizarre impediment after another. First, Bond is met by an electric shock when he attempts to break the wire grille covering the ventilation tunnel which leads to the gauntlet. Next, he must climb a sheer vertical shaft. Bond encounters heat next, as he must crawl across steaming metal. The next obstacle is a cage full of tarantulas, through which Bond cuts his way with a knife and homemade spear. At the end of the course, Bond plummets into a large inlet where he battles a giant squid. The sequence goes even further, and the reader is asked to believe that Bond is not only able to *walk* after his ordeal, but can then also pilot a crane in order to bury Dr. No in—of all things—guano! Fleming's imagination may have run a little too rampant here.

The major theme of DOCTOR NO is an examination of the meaning of power. Bond, throughout the novels, has many conversations on this subject with the villains. Dr. No believes that power can only be secured by privacy. He quotes Clausewitz's first principle of obtaining power: to operate from a secure base. From there, he says, "one proceeds to freedom of action." Bond argues with the villain, saying that power is really

an illusion. Dr. No scoffs at Bond's "play on words," saying that all concepts are illusions—concepts such as beauty, art, money, death, and, he adds, probably life. Dr. No has secured a private base of operations on Crab Key Island from which he can cause havoc with U.S. test missiles. He has also provided himself with protection of a mythical nature—a "dragon" that roams the island in search of trespassers. Because his domain is so private, he evokes a fear of the unknown in all of the Jamaicans. Dr. No capitalizes on this fear, using it as the base of his power. And it works very well—that is, until Bond comes along. Bond isn't superstitious and can see through Dr. No's scarecrow tactics. He proves to Dr. No, by the novel's end, that the power of which the madman boasts is truly an illusion.

The theme of friendship is quite strong in DOCTOR NO. Quarrel, the Cayman Islander from LIVE AND LET DIE, is back as Bond's ally. When Quarrel insists that Bond take out a life insurance policy on him before they set sail to Crab Key, the Englishman doesn't hesitate to help him. The affection Bond has for Quarrel is summed up in the last chapter, as he sadly reflects on Quarrel's death:

Bond thought of the burned twist down in the swamp that had been Quarrel. He remembered the soft ways of the big body, the innocence in the grey, horizon-seeking eyes, the simple lusts and desires, the reverence for superstitions and instincts, the childish faults, the loyalty and even love that Quarrel had given him—the warmth, there was only one word for it, of the man.

(DOCTOR NO, Chapter 20)

Bond is genuinely hurt by Quarrel's death, and the loss is felt by the agent throughout the final chapter of the book.

□ CHARACTERS

For the first time, hostility flares between Bond and M. M, rather angry with Bond for allowing Rosa Klebb to get the best of him in FROM RUSSIA, WITH LOVE, orders Bond to turn in the reliable Beretta .25 in exchange for new guns provided by the Armourer. To top that, M sends Bond on what the Admiral calls a "holiday" assignment in the sun. Bond resents it:

He's got it in for me over the last job. Feels I let him down. Won't trust me with anything tough. Wants to see. Oh well!

He said: "Sounds rather like the soft life, sir. I've had almost too much of that lately. But if it's got to be done . . . If you say so, sir."

"Yes," said M. "I say so."

(DOCTOR NO, Chapter 2)

As the conversation continues, Bond's anger builds. After receiving the details of the assignment, Bond rises to leave the office and makes a move to retrieve the Beretta. M stops him and snidely orders Bond to leave the Beretta and to make sure he holds onto his new guns.

Bond looked across into M's eyes. For the first time in his life he hated the man. He knew perfectly well why M was being tough and mean. It was deferred punishment for having nearly got killed on his last job. Plus getting away from this filthy weather into the sunshine. M couldn't bear his men to have an easy time. In a way Bond felt sure he was being sent on this cushy assignment to humiliate him. The old bastard.

(DOCTOR NO, Chapter 3)

But, of course, the holiday in the sun doesn't turn out as such, and Bond suffers some of the worst tortures and dangers he's ever faced. At the end of the novel, Bond sends a nasty cable to M:

Bond had enciphered a short signal to M via the Colonial Office which he had cooly concluded with: "REGRET MUST AGAIN REQUEST SICK LEAVE STOP SURGEONS REPORT FOLLOWS STOP KINDLY INFORM ARMOURER SMITH AND WESSON INEFFECTIVE AGAINST FLAMETHROWER END IT."

(DOCTOR NO, Chapter 20)

Bond reveals a paternal side in his attitude toward Honey. At first glance, one might think Bond is a little patronizing toward the girl, who is, despite her womanly virtues, a most childlike female. But in actuality, Bond assumes a protective stance with Honey, constantly and compassionately reassuring her that everything will turn out all right (even though they have been beaten, captured, and swept away inside a mechanical dragon). Once inside Dr. No's "mink-lined prison," Bond conceals his own doubts and pretends they are perfectly safe. Honey is perhaps more terrified by their soft treatment inside the "hotel suite": she isn't accustomed to such luxury. Bond rescues her from this anxiety:

*　　*　　*

Bond laughed. He laughed with real pleasure that her fear had been drowned in the basic predicament of clothes and how to behave, and he laughed at the picture they made—she in her rags and he in his dirty blue shirt and black jeans and muddy canvas shoes.

He went to her and took her hands. They were cold. He said, "Honey, we're a couple of scarecrows. There's only one problem. Shall we have breakfast first while it's hot, or shall we get out of these rags and have a bath and eat the breakfast when it's cold? Don't worry about anything else. We're here in this wonderful little house and that's all that matters. Now then, what shall we do?"

She smiled uncertainly. The blue eyes searched his face for reassurance. "You're not worried about what's going to happen to us?" She nodded at the room. "Don't you think this is all a trap?"

"If it's a trap we're in it. There's nothing we can do now but eat the cheese. The only question is whether we eat it hot or cold."

(DOCTOR NO, Chapter 13)

As Honey becomes more relaxed, she turns playful. She flirts and provokes, while Bond does his best to resist temptation. He friskily scolds her:

"Shut up, Honey. And stop flirting. Just take this soap and the sponge and start scrubbing. Damn you! This isn't the time for making love. I'm going to have breakfast." He reached for the door handle and opened the door. She said softly, "James!" He looked back. She was sticking her tongue out at him. He grinned savagely back at her and slammed the door.

(DOCTOR NO, Chapter 13)

For the first time in the series, Bond reflects on a past love affair. When he and Quarrel arrive at Beau Desert, Bond remembers the LIVE AND LET DIE adventure:

Yes, there it was, the stretch of deep, silent water—the submarine path he had taken to the Isle of Surprise. It sometimes came back to him in nightmares. Bond stood looking at it and thinking of Solitaire, the girl he had brought back, torn and bleeding, from that sea. He had carried her across the lawn to the house. What had happened to her? Where was she? Brusquely Bond turned and walked back into the house, driving the phantoms away from him.

(DOCTOR NO, Chapter 7)

Moments of nostalgia are rare for Bond. It happens once in FROM RUSSIA, WITH LOVE as he's flying to Istanbul, and occurs only a few more times in the series.

DOCTOR NO provides another example of Bond's loyalty to his male ally in his response to Quarrel's untimely death. The dragon tank has incinerated the Cayman Islander, and Bond has surrendered to Dr. No's men. But he insists on paying his last respects to his dead friend before allowing himself to be taken away:

Bond walked on towards the smoking clump of bushes. He got there and looked down. His eyes and mouth winced. Yes, it had been just as he had visualized. Worse. He said softly, "I'm sorry Quarrel." He kicked into the ground and scooped up a handful of cool sand between his manacled hands and poured it over the remains of the eyes. Then he walked slowly back and stood beside the girl.

(DOCTOR NO, Chapter 12)

Honeychile Rider is a provocative, sensual heroine. She is a childlike nature girl, but also physically very much a woman. Honey is blond with deep blue eyes under lashes "paled by the sun." Again, there is the wide mouth, and she has a jawline that is "determined." Bond notices that she has the face of one who fends for herself. Once, though, she failed—her nose is badly broken as a result of a fight with an old lover. But this fault is quickly overlooked, and Bond believes she is one of the most beautiful girls in Jamaica. He compares her to Botticelli's Venus.

Honey, having had no formal schooling, taught herself by reading the encyclopedia. Though intelligent, she is also incredibly naive, which is the main reason she is so appealing and endearing. She is playful, yet she can be confident and imperious in defending her beliefs. She certainly knows much more about animals and insects than Bond, and she uses this knowledge of nature to escape what almost certainly would have been, for anyone else, a fiendish death. Bond overlooks her lack of education, for what is immediately attractive in Honey is her purity of heart. Honey is the most well-meaning, sincere female character in the series.

Doctor Julius No, a wickedly successful villain, is half-Chinese, half-German, and is at least six inches taller than Bond. His appearance is extremely perverse: bald, a skull-like face, jet black eyes and no eyelashes, a cruel and authoritative mouth, and a receding chin. At the ends of Dr. No's arms are pairs of steel pincers. As he walks, he gives the appearance of gliding, rather than actually stepping. To Bond, he looks like a "giant venomous worm wrapped in grey tin-foil."

Once again, the villain is quite mad. Bond is forced to listen to Dr. No's personal history while being wined and dined, as usual, and then is taken away to be tortured to death. Dr. No's theories of power are all but shot down by Bond, but because Dr. No speaks with such conviction and deliberate thought, he sometimes sounds frighteningly correct. The doctor's treatment of his guests (the facade of a luxurious hotel, the elegant meal and dinner conversation, and the ultimate dessert of a fiendish death) takes on the aspect of therapy prescribed by an authentic doctor. The calm method of dealing with patients before the operation is all too familiar to Dr. No. He is aloof toward others' pain and suffering, which only heightens the sense of madness about him. The doctor is a truly extraordinary character.

Quarrel is warm, jovial, and, very simply, fun. There is no prejudice or discrimination in the relationship between Bond and Quarrel. To Bond, Quarrel is more than just a friend or an ally. He represents something genuinely good that is rare in people, and Bond respects this. He has amusing character traits, for example:

Bond smiled to himself at the way Quarrel, like most West Indians, added an 'h' when it wasn't needed and took it off when it was.

(DOCTOR NO, Chapter 4)

This is in reference to Quarrel's previous words about a friend who once "fought wit' a big hoctopus."

Quarrel, like Honey, is intelligent, but lacks education. He is superstitious and naive. He believes in dragons, voodoo, and other mythical frights which are created by the villains in LIVE AND LET DIE and DOCTOR NO to scare people precisely like Quarrel. And sadly, Quarrel has good reason to be frightened. The dragon he has feared becomes a reality in the form of a flame-thrower. But Quarrel is a good hand when it comes to a more realistic form of danger. When Bond orders Quarrel to lose a car that is following them, Quarrel grins with excitement; for the first time since he last saw Bond, Quarrel is experiencing action again and loves it.

M is nothing short of a perfect bastard in DOCTOR NO. He begins his scene in the novel in a foul mood, and he doesn't let up. He is angry at 007 for bungling his last assignment, and punishes Bond by stripping him of his beloved Beretta .25.

M swivelled back to face him. "Sorry, James," he said, and

there was no sympathy in his voice. "I know how you like that bit of iron. But I'm afraid it's got to go. Never give a weapon a second chance—any more than a man. I can't afford to gamble with the Double-0 Section. They've got to be properly equipped. You understand that? A gun's more important than a hand or a foot in your job."

(DOCTOR NO, Chapter 2)

Ironically, it's precisely Bond's hands and feet which save him in this adventure: he works the controls of a crane to kill Dr. No, and coincidentally finds his gun with the unconscious pilot of the machine *after* he has done the dirty work.

M is at his most tyrannical in this story. He doesn't stand for any floundering from Bond. He also feels that Bond's assignment is a waste of the Service's time and funds, and nothing sets off M like misuse of the Service. DOCTOR NO provides yet another side of the inscrutable M.

□ HIGHLIGHTS AND OTHER INGREDIENTS

FROM RUSSIA, WITH LOVE was a sexual breakthrough in the James Bond novels (being far more provocative and titillating than its predecessors), and DOCTOR NO goes a step further. Honeychile Rider embodies pure sexual fantasy: Bond discovers her naked on the beach of Crab Key. And what does she do when she realizes Bond is watching her? She covers her pubic area and her broken nose—*not* her exposed breasts. Although the novel still leaves much to the imagination, the antics between the couple, especially in the hotel suite/prison, are highly erotic.

DOCTOR NO is also more violent than the preceding three novels. Quarrel's death is ghastly, and Bond's ordeal in the obstacle course is harrowing. Bond is also forced to kill several times in cold blood, such as when he shoots the guard wading through the river. Bond feels obligated to apologize to Honey after killing the guard, explaining that it "had to be done."

The dragon is also an interesting creation, one that simultaneously teases and frightens. Still, the obstacle course and the subsequent fight with the giant squid are the major highlights of the story. This sequence is Fleming at his most outrageous. Although the situation is nearly impossible, the conviction and pace with which Fleming writes negates this fault.

Fleming's ability to build suspense is exemplified no better than in the sequence with the centipede. This section is one of the author's most outstanding and thrilling. Bond is asleep in his hotel room in Kingston, when:

Something had stirred on his right ankle. Now it was moving up the inside of his shin. Bond could feel the hairs on his leg being parted. It was an insect of some sort. A very big one. It was long, five or six inches—as long as his hand. He could feel dozens of tiny feet lightly touching his skin. What was it?

Then Bond heard something he had never heard before—the sound of the hair on his head rasping up on the pillow. Bond analysed the noise. It couldn't be! It simply couldn't! Yes, his hair was standing on end. Bond could even feel the cool air reaching his scalp between the hairs. How extraordinary! How very extraordinary! He had always thought it was a figure of speech. But why? Why was it happening to him?

The thing on his leg moved. Suddenly Bond realized that he was afraid, terrified. His instincts, even before they had communicated with his brain, had told his body that he had a centipede on him.

Bond lay frozen. He had once seen a tropical centipede in a bottle of spirit on the shelf in a museum. It had been pale brown and very flat and five or six inches long—about the length of this one. On either side of the blunt head there had been curved poison claws. The label on the bottle had said that its poison was mortal if it hit an artery. Bond had looked curiously at the corkscrew of dead cuticle and had moved on.

The centipede had reached his knee. It was starting up his thigh. Whatever happened he mustn't move, mustn't even tremble. Bond's whole consciousness had drained down to the two rows of softly creeping feet. Now they had reached his flank. God, it was turning down towards the groin! Bond set his teeth. Supposing it liked the warmth there! Supposing it tried to crawl into the crevices! Could he stand it? Supposing it chose that place to bite? Bond could feel it questing amongst the first hairs. It tickled. The skin on Bond's belly fluttered. There was nothing he could do to control it. But now the thing was turning up and along his stomach. Its feet were gripping tighter to prevent it falling. Now it was at his heart. If it bit there, surely it would kill him. The centipede trampled steadily on through the thin hairs on Bond's right breast up to his collar bone. It stopped. What was it doing? Bond could feel the blunt head questing to and fro. What was it looking for? Was there room between his skin and the sheet for it to get through? Dare he lift the sheet an inch to help it? No. Never! The animal was at the base of his jugular. Perhaps it was intrigued by the heavy pulse there. Christ, if only he could control the pumping of his blood. Damn you! Bond tried to communicate with the centipede. It's nothing. It's not dangerous, that pulse. It means you no harm. Get on out into the fresh air!

As if the beast had heard, it moved on up the column of the neck and into the stubble on Bond's chin. Now it was at the corner of his mouth, tickling madly. On it went, up along the nose. Now he could feel its whole weight and length. Softly Bond closed his eyes. Two by two the pairs of feet, moving alternatively, trampled across his right eyelid. When it got off his eye, should he take a chance and shake it off—rely on its feet slipping in his sweat? No, for God's sake! The grip of the feet was endless. He might shake one lot off, but not the rest.

With incredible deliberation the huge insect ambled across Bond's forehead. It stopped below the hair. What the hell was it doing now? Bond could feel it nuzzling at his skin. It was drinking! Drinking the beads of salt sweat. Bond was sure of it. For minutes it hardly moved. Bond felt weak with the tension. He could feel the sweat pouring off the rest of his body on to the sheet. In a second his limbs would start to tremble. He could feel it coming on. He would start to shake with an ague of fear. Could he control it, could he? Bond lay and waited, the breath coming softly through his open, snarling mouth.

The centipede started to move again. It walked into the forest of hair. Bond could feel the roots being pushed aside as it forced its way along. Would it like it there? Would it settle down? How did centipedes sleep? Curled up or at full length? The tiny millipedes he had known as a child, the ones that always seemed to find their way up the plughole into the empty bath, curled up when you touched them. Now it had come to where his head lay against the sheet. Would it walk out on to the pillow or would it stay on in the warm forest? The centipede stopped. Out! OUT! Bond's nerves screamed at it.

The centipede stirred. Slowly it walked out of his hair on to the pillow.

Bond waited a second. Now he could hear the rows of feet picking softly at the cotton. It was a tiny scraping noise, like soft fingernails.

With a crash that shook the room Bond's body jackknifed out of bed and on to the floor.

(DOCTOR NO, Chapter 6)

GOLDFINGER (1959)

The seventh James Bond novel marks a turning point in the series. It is a transitional novel, separating the early books from the later ones in that James Bond's character becomes increasingly obsessed with the mortal trappings of life. In GOLDFINGER, Fleming discloses his major character's thoughts more often, thus enabling one to dig deeper into Bond's feelings. As in MOONRAKER, the narrative takes on a tone that is more

reflective than suspenseful. As a thriller, GOLDFINGER is decidedly weak—it lacks suspense, much of the plot is impractical and improbable, and sometimes there is no logic in the sequence of events. However, GOLDFINGER is very successful in terms of characterizations and mood. More is revealed about James Bond than in any of the other novels, and the supporting characters are well-drawn and interesting as well.

The story concerns James Bond's investigation of Auric Goldfinger, touted as the richest man in England. Goldfinger is suspected of smuggling gold out of England. Bond's job is to discover how he does it. After a prologue in Miami in which Bond learns that Goldfinger cheats at canasta, the agent exposes the scheme and has a brief affair with Goldfinger's secretary, Jill Masterson. Later, in London, Bond is ordered to meet Goldfinger socially in order to spy on him; the agent does this by accepting a challenge for a golf game. Again, Goldfinger attempts to cheat during the game, but Bond wins the match with a little cheating of his own. By means of an ingenious homing device located in 007's Aston Martin, the agent tracks Goldfinger's Rolls-Royce into Northern France. While spying on Goldfinger's factory, Bond learns that gold is melted onto the Rolls-Royce in England and stripped in France. But in the woods near the factory, Bond encounters one Tilly Soames, who is revealed to be Jill Masterson's sister. Tilly is attempting to avenge her sister's death— Goldfinger ordered that Jill be covered from head to toe in gold paint, causing her to suffocate. Bond and Tilly are captured by Goldfinger's Korean bodyguard, Oddjob; but instead of killing the pair, Goldfinger forces them into his employ as "secretaries" for Operation Grand Slam. It is revealed that SMERSH is backing Goldfinger to commit the biggest crime in history: the robbery of Fort Knox. Goldfinger's party is flown to New York, where gang leaders from all over the country are enlisted to help in the operation. Bond takes a risk by writing down the details of Goldfinger's plan and hiding the paper beneath the lavatory seat of Goldfinger's plane. The paper promises a reward to anyone finding the paper and delivering it to Felix Leiter. D-Day finally arrives, but Goldfinger's plan goes awry as seemingly dead soldiers scattered over the area spring to life. Tilly is killed by Oddjob's steel-rimmed bowler hat and Goldfinger and his party escape, even though Operation Grand Slam has failed. The next day, Bond is kidnapped by Goldfinger and strapped into an airplane en route to Russia. But with the help of Pussy Galore, one of the gang leaders who is sweet on Bond, he uses his resourcefulness to escape. Using a knife concealed in the heel of his shoe, Bond breaks a window in the pressurized cabin, causing Oddjob to be sucked out into oblivion. As the plane plummets, he and Goldfinger lock their hands around each other's throats—but 007 emerges the victor. The plane crashlands near a friendly weather station, and Bond and Pussy are rescued.

□ STYLE AND THEMES

GOLDFINGER is Fleming's longest, densest novel. The book, like MOONRAKER, is divided into three parts, entitled respectively, "Happenstance," "Coincidence," and "Enemy Action." These titles refer to Goldfinger's words alluding to the three occasions of meeting Bond: "once is happenstance, twice is coincidence, and a third time is enemy action." The three parts of the book, then, relate to the encounters between Bond and Goldfinger in these terms. The main gambit of the novel (the plan to rob Fort Knox), though, only takes place in the third part. While the first two-thirds of the book contains some interesting segments, that part has no real bearing on Goldfinger's plans per se.

The story is much more episodic than previous books, even DIAMONDS ARE FOREVER. There is no logic to the rapid changing of locales throughout the novel. The major switch of territory (Europe to New York) is especially difficult to accept. In this sequence, Bond and Tilly Masterson are held captive by Goldfinger. Bond offers his and Tilly's services if Goldfinger will spare their lives. Goldfinger accepts the offer, which is not only stupid on his part, but unbelievable. First, Bond, a few minutes before this, attacked and attempted to strangle Goldfinger. Second, it seems obvious that Tilly's only reason for being there is to avenge the death of her sister, Jill. Why would Goldfinger want to keep the two of them around? He claims it's because he needs two English-speaking people to help him with the planning of Operation Grand Slam. If this is true, it seems SMERSH would have provided the personnel.

The plot to rob Fort Knox, though carefully detailed, still smacks of implausibility. Oddly enough, this section is the only part of the book which generates real excitement. In fact, the last three chapters of GOLDFINGER are the *only* truly gripping sections. Even DIAMONDS ARE FOREVER contains more suspense than GOLDFINGER.

The gambling theme is present again. The novel is full of games: the canasta game in the first part, and the golf match in the second. Operation Grand Slam is treated as a game by Goldfinger. And throughout the story, Bond must accomplish his assignment by strictly gambling on hunches. At one point after having dinner with Goldfinger, Bond reflects on the man's claim that he wouldn't be surprised if he and Bond met again soon:

Bond turned the phrase over and over in his mind. He undressed and got into bed thinking of it, unable to guess its significance. It could mean that Goldfinger intended to get in touch with Bond, or it could mean that Bond must try and keep in touch with Goldfinger. Heads the former, tails the latter. Bond got out of bed and took a coin from the dressing-table and tossed it. It came down tails. So it was up to him to keep close to Goldfinger!

(GOLDFINGER, Chapter 11)

This certainly illustrates the gambling temptation both Bond and Fleming share. The entire novel incorporates this heads-or-tails feeling. Another example is when Bond takes the chance of leaving the details of Operation Grand Slam on a rolled piece of paper underneath the lavatory seat of a chartered airplane. His only hope is that some flight attendant will find the message and deliver it, as instructed, to Felix Leiter at Pinkerton's. Naturally, this is what eventually happens. But it is doubtful that any flight attendant would accept the message as authentic.

Another theme which more or less runs throughout the series is finally stated explicitly: the parallel between Fleming's hero and St. George. This occurs after Goldfinger reveals he will open the vault at Fort Knox by using an atomic warhead. Bond thinks:

And now! Now it was not a rabbit in the rabbit hole, not even a fox, it was a king cobra—the biggest, most deadly inhabitant of the world! Bond sighed wearily. Once more into the breach, dear friends! This time it really was St George and the dragon. And St George had better get a move on and do something before the dragon hatched the little dragon's egg he was now nesting so confidently. Bond smiled tautly. Do what? What in God's name was there he could do?

(GOLDFINGER, Chapter 18)

The foregoing passage reveals Bond's inner thoughts. This technique, which resembles stream of consciousness narration, recurs throughout GOLDFINGER, and seems to be used by Fleming to voice his own ideas through Bond's personal reflections. Fleming's identification with Bond is at its strongest in GOLDFINGER.

☐ CHARACTERS

The most successful element of GOLDFINGER is its rich characterizations. James Bond, especially, is at his most developed. Because he reflects and daydreams almost constantly in the story, many personal sides of the character are revealed. Much of Bond's thinking on death in his profession and his attitudes toward women are revealed in GOLDFINGER. There is even a passage which discloses Bond's feelings toward homosexuality and Lesbianism. Most of these quotes from GOLDFINGER appear in Part Three, which deals with the Bond character in more detail. But other revelations on Bond are worth bringing up here.

Bond muses over his approach to women as he is driving through Eastern France into Switzerland and is passed by Tilly Masterson in her Triumph:

That *would* happen today! The Loire is dressed for just that—chasing that girl until you run her to ground at lunchtime, the contact at the empty restaurant by the river, out in the garden under the vine trellis. The *friture* and the ice-cold Vouvray, the cautious sniffing at each other and then the two cars motoring on in convoy until that evening, well down to the south, there would be the place they had agreed on at lunch—olive trees, crickets singing in the indigo dusk, the discovery that they liked each other and that their destinations could wait. Then, next day ("No, not tonight. I don't know you well enough, and besides I'm tired") they would leave her car in the hotel garage and go off in his at a tangent, slowly, knowing there was no hurry for anything, driving to the west, away from the big roads. What was that place he had always wanted to go to, simply because of the name? Yes, Entre Deux Seins, a village near Les Baux. Perhaps there wasn't even an inn there. Well, then they would go on to Les Baux itself, at the Bouches du Rhône on the edge of the Camargue. There they would take adjoining rooms (not a double room, it would be too early for that) in the fabulous Baumanière, the only hotel-restaurant in France with Michelin's supreme accolade. They would eat the *gratin de langouste* and perhaps, because it was traditional on such a night, drink champagne. And then . . .

Bond smiled at his story and at the dots that ended it. Not today. Today you're working. Today is for Goldfinger, not for love. Today the only scent you may smell is Goldfinger's expensive after-shave lotion, not . . . what would she use? English girls made mistakes about scent. He hoped it would be something slight and clean.

(GOLDFINGER, Chapter 12)

It is amusing that Bond can daydream about this girl he has never seen, suddenly force himself to concentrate on the mission at hand, and then find himself falling right back into daydreaming again. Bond is an incurable woman-chaser, especially of those driving fast cars. This passage unmasks the rascal that Bond can allow himself to be.

GOLDFINGER marks another change in Bond's character: he begins to take everything less seriously. For instance, he takes pleasure in verbally abusing the deadly Oddjob, although he knows Oddjob could probably kill him with one karate chop. Jibing at the Korean seems to bolster Bond's spirits:

Half an hour later, Bond was sitting on the edge of his bunk thinking, when the door without a handle opened abruptly. Oddjob stood in the entrance. He looked incuriously at Bond. His eyes flickered carefully round the room. Bond said sharply, "Oddjob, I want a lot of food, quickly. And a bottle of bourbon, soda and ice. Also a carton of Chesterfields, king-size, and either my own watch or another one as good as mine. Quick march! Chop-chop! And tell Goldfinger I want to see him, but not until I've had something to eat. Come on! Jump to it! Don't stand there looking inscrutable. I'm hungry."

Oddjob looked redly at Bond as if wondering which piece to break. He opened his mouth, uttered a noise between an angry bark and a belch, spat drily on the floor at his feet and stepped back, whirling the door shut. When the slam should have come, the door decelerated abruptly and closed with a soft, decisive, double click.

The encounter put Bond in good humour. For some reason Goldfinger had decided against killing him. He wanted them alive. Soon Bond would know why he wanted them alive, but so long as he did, Bond intended to stay alive on his own terms. Those terms included putting Oddjob and any other Korean firmly in his place, which, in Bond's estimation was rather lower than apes in the mammalian hierarchy.

(GOLDFINGER, Chapter 16)

So Bond is revealed to be a bigot as well. This aspect of his character is not particularly evident elsewhere in the series, though one should notice that 95 percent of the villains in the novels are non-British. But this is the only instance in which Bond/Fleming actually derides a race. From this point on, taunts directed at Oddjob abound. Once, Bond knocks on the door keeping him captive to order breakfast for Tilly. When Oddjob opens the door an inch, Bond says, "All right, Oddjob. I'm not going to kill you yet," and then gives the food order. Finally, the James Bond character is developing a sense of humor, which is a new pleasure for the reader.

Auric Goldfinger may be Fleming's most successful villain to date. He is certainly equal in villainous stature to Hugo Drax. This particular nemesis is short (not more than five feet tall), and has a huge, round head sitting on a thick, blunt body. The first thing that strikes Bond about Goldfinger is that "everything is out of proportion." The millionaire, when Bond first meets him, has a fetish for sunburn. Bond assumes this is to conceal the man's ugliness, because without the "red-brown camouflage the pale body would be grotesque." But beyond Goldfinger's hideous appearance, Bond thinks the man has the face of a "thinker, perhaps a scientist, who is ruthless, sensual, stoical and tough." The fact that Goldfinger is short arouses Bond's suspicions as well—short people have inferiority complexes and strive all their lives to be big. Bond believes that short people cause all the trouble in the world.

Goldfinger, in contrast to the flamboyance of Drax, is methodical and deliberate. Where Drax would be rash and prone to lose his temper, Goldfinger is silent and calm. Goldfinger at least looks before he leaps, and this is quite evident in the care with which he plans his crimes. The canasta ploy in Part One of the novel is very clever. Goldfinger does lower himself to sophomoric cheating tricks during the golf game, such as making unnecessary noise while Bond is attempting to putt or planting his ball in an advantageous spot. But his Operation Grand Slam, as he puts it, is the "Crime de la Crime." Goldfinger goes into such detail in describing this plot that Bond cannot help but be impressed. After hearing these plans, Bond, for the first time in the story, is worried about the outcome of the situation.

Added to Goldfinger's brilliance is, as usual, a touch of the perverse. Goldfinger likes to have his women painted gold once a month, because he enjoys "making love to gold." Usually, he leaves a strip down the woman's back unpainted, allowing her skin to breathe. But when the woman happens to be a traitor, like Jill Masterson, she may find herself unlucky enough to be completely covered in gold paint. A nasty hobby.

Pussy Galore (her name is Fleming at his most outrageous) is an unbelievable heroine. For one thing, she is supposedly a Lesbian, and a tough one at that. And, through most of her scenes in the book, this is true. But Fleming's own fantasy gets in the way, and he allows Pussy to fall for Bond. There is no gradual development of Pussy's changing attitude toward Bond. It seems that if she were the hard-nosed criminal she's supposed to be, a man like Bond, no matter how handsome, would mean nothing to Pussy. It seems unlikely that a committed Lesbian would make the sexual switch so abruptly. The switch *is* hinted at earlier: Pussy calls Bond "Handsome" from the moment she meets him, which already seems to be a contradiction of her description. Perhaps when Pussy witnesses the murder of her fellow syndicate heads at the hands of Goldfinger, she decides to take Bond's side. Anyway, in the last scene of the book, Pussy passes a note to Bond telling him that she is "with him." Bond takes the cue and, with Pussy as an added incentive, attacks Oddjob and Goldfinger. In the final paragraphs of the book, Bond and Pussy are alone and safe in a weather station. They embrace. Bond comments that he thought she only liked women. Pussy replies that "she never met a man before." Well, we know that Bond is good, but is he *that* good? This is quite a switch for a woman who, on her first appearance in the book, warns Bond that "all men are bastards and cheats." Pussy is also the oldest of the Bond-girls. Fleming describes her as being in her early thirties, with pale, "Rupert Brooke" good looks, high cheekbones and a beautiful jawline. Pussy is aggressive and tough, but, since she is more Fleming fantasy than accurate reality, she also exudes a "sexual challenge all beautiful Lesbians have for men." This is a myth, and it's possible that there are many Lesbians who might be offended by this description.

Tilly Masterson is also a Lesbian, and unlike Pussy, conforms to the stereotype. At least she is never attracted to Bond physically, and once Bond realizes Tilly is a Lesbian, he is never attracted to her. Tilly wears masculine clothes, and there is "something faintly mannish and open-air" about the woman's behavior and appearance. Tilly doesn't bother with makeup, and her hair is untidy, with "bits that stray." But she is good-looking, Bond admits, and carries herself with confidence and challenge. As Bond gets to know Tilly, it begins to dawn on him why she is so cool toward him. At one point, she flatly tells him that if he ever touches her, she'll kill him.

Fleming uses Tilly's Lesbianism as a character flaw— a fatal one. When there is the chance for Bond and Tilly to escape from Goldfinger, Tilly hesitates a moment; she wants to remain with Pussy Galore. This hesitation gives Oddjob just enough time to fling his steel-rimmed hat at Tilly, breaking her neck. Even Bond blames her sexual preference for her death. He tells Felix, "Poor little bitch. She didn't think much of men . . . I could have got her away if she'd only followed me."

Is Fleming saying something here about homosexuality? In contrasting Pussy with Tilly, it is obvious that Bond himself makes the difference in the two characters' survival. It's presumptuous of Fleming, but then,

GOLDFINGER was written in 1958, when attitudes toward this subject were more repressive and the general public more benighted.

Jill Masterson, who appears briefly, is a more typical Bond-girl. Described as a "classic English beauty," Jill immediately falls for Bond (which unhappily, and in contrast to Pussy, marks her for Goldfinger's death list). Jill is more or less a "party girl"—the kind of girl with whom Bond can freely have an affair and have no regrets, or so he thinks. He certainly regrets it later when he finds out he was the cause of her murder. Jill's function in the novel, though, is to serve as a catalyst to get the story rolling, so to speak.

Oddjob is an interesting minor villain, who provides not only the few mysterious elements in GOLDFINGER, but some of the humor as well. Oddjob, a Korean, and "one of the three men in the world holding a black belt in karate" (surely in 1959 there were more than three), is only menacing when he's angry. Otherwise, he's a particularly funny character whose vocabulary consists of nothing but grunts like, "Arrgh!" and "Garch a har?"

Felix Leiter appears briefly at the end of GOLDFINGER, again in the form of "cavalry to the rescue." He saves Bond's life and the Englishman admits that Felix is "always good" at doing so. Felix, who still works for Pinkerton's, is the same amiable character who is so refreshing to have around. It's too bad his appearance is so brief.

M is getting crabby in his old age. After being in such a foul temper in DOCTOR NO, M's sarcastic mood in GOLDFINGER seems only slightly more pleasant. After teaching Goldfinger a lesson during the canasta ploy, Bond decides to do a little research on the man and asks C.I.D. Records to run a trace on Goldfinger. Later, after being summoned to M's office for an assignment, Bond laughs at the coincidence that the assignment concerns Goldfinger:

"What's the matter?" M's voice was testy. "What the hell is there to laugh about?"

"I'm sorry, sir." Bond got hold of himself. "The truth is, only last night I was building his face up on the Identicast." He glanced at his watch. In a strangled voice he said, "Be on its way to C.I.D. Records. Asked for a Trace on him."

M was getting angry. "What the hell's all this about? Stop behaving like a bloody schoolboy."

Bond said soberly, "Well, sir, it's like this . . ." Bond told the story, leaving nothing out.

(GOLDFINGER, Chapter 5)

But M finds another reason to attack Bond. After hearing 007's story, M asks Bond what happened to the $10,000 that Goldfinger was forced to pay Bond.

"Gave it to the girl, sir."

"Really! Why not to the White Cross?"

The White Cross Fund was for the families of Secret Service men and women who were killed on duty.

"Sorry, sir." Bond was not prepared to argue that one.

"Humpf." M had never approved of Bond's womanizing. It was anathema to his Victorian soul. He decided to let it pass.

(GOLDFINGER, Chapter 5)

□ HIGHLIGHTS AND OTHER INGREDIENTS

Fleming expands his use of sex in GOLDFINGER: there are *three* Bond-girls in this one, even though Bond eventually "conquers" only two of them. But the sexual activity still remains tame when compared to today's standards.

The canasta ploy and golf match are highlights in the novel, but, as mentioned before, neither have a real bearing on the main plot. But these sections do substantiate the statement that Ian Fleming is at his best when describing gaming contests. Each detail of the card game and the golf match is thought out and related in a suspenseful manner.

There is an increase of gadgetry in GOLDFINGER. Bond is equipped with an Aston Martin D.B. III containing a secret compartment for hiding objects such as gold bricks. It also is equipped with an ingenious homing device used for tracking another car. One simply has to plant the transmitter on the car being followed, and the Aston Martin picks up the signal within a safe distance. The film version of GOLDFINGER expanded the accessories of the Aston Martin to include machine guns, oil slicks, bulletproof shields, and smoke screens. Fleming's imagination was wild, but not that wild! In addition, Bond is outfitted with shoes that house small throwing knives in the heels. One of these knives comes in handy at the novel's end, when Bond decides upon the perfect method of ridding himself of Oddjob.

The Secret Service headquarters also owns a machine called the Identicast, which enables the user to assemble a person's facial features on a screen until a likeness of the individual is formed. These machines were actually recently developed at the time of the novel.

In comparing GOLDFINGER to the preceding novels, there is no doubt that it is weak. The lack of suspense and the absence of a truly believable plot account for this. But the revelations about James Bond and other aspects of the agent's world keep the novel interesting. Apparently, combining strong characters with a logical, suspenseful plot was difficult for Fleming to accomplish—only in a handful of the novels does the combination work successfully. But GOLDFINGER is certainly not boring, for it shows an ever-maturing style and development.

FOR YOUR EYES ONLY
(1960)

Fleming's eighth offering is an anthology of five short stories. The subtitle for the book in England is "Five Secret Occasions in the Life of James Bond" (in America it is "Five Secret Exploits of James Bond"). All five stories have something interesting to offer, and they are all up to standard. FOR YOUR EYES ONLY proves that Fleming is as adept at writing short stories as full-length novels. A couple of the stories are experimental in nature, while the other three are straightforward secret service adventures.

□ "FROM A VIEW TO A KILL"
The story concerns James Bond's investigation of the murder of a NATO dispatch-rider who was shot in the back while driving a BSAM motorbike from SHAPE headquarters in Versailles to his base in Saint-Germain. After gathering clues, Bond disguises himself as a SHAPE dispatch-rider, and drives a BSA down the same road. As expected, the assassin attempts to repeat the crime. But Bond is ready for him; when the killer draws his gun, Bond brakes and skids around to shoot him. After killing the man, Bond rides back to the underground Russian hideout which had been camouflaged with a rose bush. Station F forces help the agent clean up the case.

This opening story is a tightly knit, compressed yarn which easily holds one's interest in a single sitting. It has a typical Fleming structure: the story opens with an incident (the murder of the SHAPE rider); James Bond is then assigned to investigate that incident; the agent does preliminary fact finding; and he finally un-ravels the mystery and closes the case. The opening scene, as usual, is set up with care and deliberation. It immediately grabs the reader's attention and sets a mood which remains through the end.

The Fleming Sweep moves at a steady pace, carrying one through the sequence of events that lead Bond to the Russian espionage team's hideout. The story is rich in the familiar Fleming detail: the description of the woods include images of colors and sounds which are among Fleming's most textured.

A possible theme in the story may be Fleming's own criticism of the fact that British Intelligence has a bad habit of criticizing smaller branches located in other areas. Fleming seems to express the opinion, through the thoughts of Bond and M, that each little subgroup (such as SHAPE) is jealous of the other and believes that all the branches should mind their own business. This is the basic problem with Colonel Schreiber, the head of SHAPE in Versailles. He insists that his team has done everything it can to investigate the murder; he looks down his nose at Bond, who has come into the case from another department of the Service.

As far as characterizations go, there are no new insights into James Bond. It is revealed, though, that he lost his virginity at age sixteen in Paris. The female character, Mary Ann Russell, is not very well drawn. She saves Bond's life at the end, which is the first time Fleming has allowed a female to do so. Bond has just exposed the hideout beneath the rose bush, as Station F forces appear from the woods with drawn guns. But one of the Russians knocks Bond off balance and aims a gun at his head. A shot rings out, killing the Russian just in time. It is revealed that Mary Ann fired the shot.

The highlights of the story include the opening murder scene, the discovery of the hideout in the woods, and the subsequent attack by Bond and the forces from Station F. The hideout in the woods incorporates another gadget: the entrance is a fake rose bush which splits into halves, revealing the hole in the ground. A periscope disguised as a rose is in the center of the bush. The attack on the hideout happens quickly and is exciting, especially once the rest of the forces appear to aid Bond.

"From a View to a Kill" is a sharp piece of fiction in the traditional Fleming mold.

□ "FOR YOUR EYES ONLY"
In this story, a middle-aged couple named Havelock

are murdered in their home in Jamaica by a Major Gonzales and two hit men working for one von Hammerstein. It so happens that the Havelocks are personal friends of M. Bond volunteers to assassinate the men as a favor to his chief. As 007 is spying on the killers' cabin in the woods of Vermont, he encounters a girl armed with a bow and arrow. The girl is Judy Havelock, daughter of the murdered couple. She has tracked down von Hammerstein and is seeking revenge. She succeeds in piercing von Hammerstein's back with an arrow as he dives into the lake. All hell breaks loose at this point, and Bond manages to pick off Gonzales and the two hit men in an explosive gun battle.

The title story in the collection is by far the most successful. In a way, it is a "mini novel": it has all the elements of a Bond novel compressed into a well-told and exciting short story. Again, there is a typical Fleming structure: an incident at the opening of the story involving a murder; Bond's interview with M; fact gathering and the introduction of the heroine to complicate the plot; and finally the showdown with the villains. The story sweeps along from scene to scene in the manner of the longer books, yet there is no problem with keeping the logic intact in switching locales.

The theme in "For Your Eyes Only" deals with the question of determining justice outside the boundaries of the law. In this instance, James Bond volunteers to assassinate the murderers of some personal friends of M. Since the killers have fled to America, there isn't much British police can do. The American officials can merely cancel the men's visas, which would only put them on the run again. M, who has taken a personal interest in the case because he was best man at the Havelocks' wedding, knows he cannot simply order Bond to go and "do justice." In fact, no orders are ever spoken. Bond volunteers to execute the justice that a court of law, in this case, could never rule. Therefore, Bond becomes a personal "hit man" for M. There is no question that von Hammerstein and his colleagues are evil and must be destroyed. The question remains as to whether their rights should or shouldn't be respected. Fleming doesn't attempt to answer the question, but only reveals his particular stance by allowing Bond to "do his duty."

There are no new revelations in Bond's character. However, a bit of a sense of humor is revealed when he first meets Judy Havelock in the woods near the killers' cabin. Since she is dressed in hunter's clothes, he amuses himself by addressing her as "Robina Hood."

Judy Havelock is a determined, vengeful girl. Even though little information is imparted about the character, a clear picture emerges from the details with which Fleming describes her. Apart from the usual striking good looks (blond hair, sensual wide mouth, etc.), she has the "vibrations of a wild animal." She's tough, and will not stand for anything but what she hopes to achieve, which is to avenge the death of her parents. Her insistence and confidence convinces Bond that she means business, and he allows her to have the first shot at von Hammerstein. Judy proves her competence by shooting an arrow through the villain's back. Only after all the killers are dead, and she is wounded, does she become someone more traditionally feminine whom Bond can pamper and protect.

The major highlight of the story, though, is the scene between Bond and M. So much is revealed about the Admiral here: his feelings about his responsibilities, and the weight of the Service on his shoulders. Finally, one can see the fatherly figure whom Bond admires so much. Gone is the crabbiness that characterized him in the previous two novels. M is at a stalemate, and has turned to Bond as his only hope in resolving the Havelock case. Bond is flattered and warmly pleased that M has turned to him in this matter, and the relationship between the two men is never more revealing.

"For Your Eyes Only," of all the short stories Fleming wrote, is certainly the best.

☐ "QUANTUM OF SOLACE"

This story is in the form of an anecdote told to Bond by his friend, the Governor in Nassau. One Philip Masters, a shy, naive, and vulnerable sort of chap, had fallen in love with an attractive airline hostess named Rhoda Llewellyn. The couple eventually married; but in time, Rhoda became bored and unhappy and began an affair with a young golf pro. Masters reacted like a wounded puppy; his work efficiency slipped and his disposition became morose. Masters was transferred to Washington for a special six-month project. In his absence, Rhoda's affair ended, and she decided to reconcile with her husband. But when Masters returned, he was a changed man. He didn't want Rhoda's reconciliation. During the year, the couple kept up social appearances as if they were still happily married, but alone at home they never spoke. Finally, Masters left Rhoda, alone and practically destitute. A social friend eventually found her a job in Jamaica and provided her the funds to move. There, after a few years, she met a rich Canadian and they married. The Governor then reveals that Bond has met Rhoda Llewellyn—she was a woman with whom he had chatted at a party earlier that evening.

"Quantum of Solace" is an offbeat, experimental story for Fleming. Kingsley Amis describes it as a "Maughamish" anecdote; this is not surprising, since Fleming was a Maugham fan as well as a personal acquaintance of the writer. It is not a Secret Service story, but a morality tale as told to Bond by his friend, the Governor. It doesn't resemble any other work by Fleming, and this is precisely why it is so intriguing. The story is rich in characterization and feeling, and it is apparent that Fleming enjoyed writing it simply as a departure from the usual Bond.

The theme is that no adventure story can top a real-life human drama. Bond comes to this conclusion at the end of the story, as he is leaving the Governor's house to finish up the assignment on which he is currently working. He reflects that his present job is "dull and unexciting."

Interwoven with this theme is the premise of the title. The "quantum of solace" is a theory the Governor holds about the amount of comfort on which love and friendship is based. He maintains that unless there is a certain degree of humanity existing between two people, there can be no love. This quantum can be measured numerically, with zero as the absolute absence of any kind of love. When Philip Masters and Rhoda Llewellyn were married, the quantum of solace between them was very high; but at the end of their relationship, it was zero. Apparently, Fleming believes in this theory himself. His rather rocky marriage must have given him cause to create the theory and incorporate it into a story.

Again, nothing new is revealed about Bond, except, perhaps, more of his views on marriage. Otherwise, Bond is merely a sounding board for the Governor's story. But Bond is also made to seem more human than usual, simply because he reacts with compassion to the story; he is able to relate it to his own life. The Governor (his name is never revealed) is a friendly chap who is actually speaking in Fleming's voice. As a character, he is unimportant. The truly important characters in this story are Philip Masters and Rhoda Llewellyn. Masters, though shy and vulnerable, is quite intelligent and resourceful. Rhoda is pretty, ambitious, and a much more aggressive character than her husband. This is what finally breaks up the couple. No sides are taken by the author in the story of this divorce;

both partners become equally cruel to each other. Rhoda, perhaps, pays the most for her wrong doings, but she at least emerges from the story a happier person than Masters, who will spend the rest of his life in a civil service post in Nigeria.

The story, with its surprise ending of Rhoda turning out to be Mrs. Harvey Miller, somehow rings true to life, and it is ultimately very moving. Even though "Quantum of Solace" has no intrigue, action, or thrills, it has a quality which is missing from most of the other Bond stories—human drama.

□ **"RISICO"**

In this story, James Bond is assigned to break up a drug smuggling racket operating from Italy to Britain. He is ordered to offer an informant named Kristatos a large amount of money to stop the drug flow. Kristatos agrees to Bond's offer only if the Englishman will kill the head of the drug smuggling operation. He says the leader is Enrico Colombo. Unbeknownst to Bond and Kristatos, Colombo has managed to record the men's conversation by an ingenious wire-tap located in an empty chair at their table. Later, Colombo has Bond captured and brought aboard the smuggler's ship, the *Colombina*. There, Colombo insists that it is actually Kristatos who is running the drug operation. The next morning, the *Colombina* arrives at Santa Maria, where men are loading what appear to be rolls of newsprint onto a ship. The *Colombina*'s crew attacks the smugglers. Kristatos is discovered in the warehouse, and Bond shoots him before he can escape. Once back at sea, Colombo explains that the Russians were backing Kristatos.

Fleming returns to the usual format in "Risico," with Bond pursuing and breaking up, for the first time in the series, a drug smuggling racket. There are structural problems, though. The story begins in the flash-forward manner: there is an opening scene which takes place before any exposition is made, then a jump back in time to M's office where Bond receives his assignment. In the traditional Fleming novel, this flashback technique usually works; but in a story as short as "Risico," it is damaging because there is not enough space to flesh out a fully realized situation and then go back to illustrate the exposition. Also, the change of locale happens too quickly. "Risico" could have been expanded to an exciting, lengthier novella. But as it stands, the story is too frantically overcrowded with scene changes, plot developments, characterizations, and exposition. "Risico" is rich with detail, though, and contains some fine characters. Its main problem is a lack of focus.

Whatever theme the story contains, the Kristatos character more or less states it at the beginning: "In this business there is much risk." The point is driven home far too many times in the story, finally becoming a little trite.

The characters are interesting: aside from the usual Bond (nothing new here), there is the colorful ally Colombo. Colombo is reminiscent of Darko Kerim in FROM RUSSIA, WITH LOVE. He is that familiar heart-of-gold type of man, brash and extroverted, with a penchant for bragging and boasting. He, like Kerim, embraces life and lives it day to day with no expectation of tangible rewards. Kristatos is a slimy villain, although not much is known about him. It is a clever twist that the author leads one to believe that Kristatos is the ally and Colombo is the villain at the beginning of the story. Lisl Baum, as a heroine, is practically nonexistent. She appears briefly and is never successfully incorporated into the plot.

But M is back to his stuffy self in "Risico." Here Fleming reveals the various idiosyncrasies in M's running of the Service, as well as his disgust at involving the organization in a drug smuggling case.

As usual Fleming's descriptive travel passages are excellent: he paints a clear picture of Venice and the Lido peninsula. The final shootout at Santa Maria is exciting and well done; but overall, "Risico" suffers from Fleming's insistence on confining its sprawling storyline within undersized boundaries.

□ **"THE HILDEBRAND RARITY"**

In this story, James Bond has a week's leave in the Seychelles Islands before returning to England. His friend, Fidele Barbey, tells him that a rich American, one Milton Krest, has offered them a job of helping him hunt for a rare fish called "The Hildebrand Rarity." The boorish Mr. Krest has no qualms about showing that he is boss of his attractive wife, Liz. She doesn't seem to mind, but Bond senses that she actually fears her husband. During a tour of Krest's luxurious yacht, Bond notices a stingray tail hanging on the wall of the master cabin. Krest admits to using it on his wife, calling it "The Corrector." Krest has set up The Krest Foundation as a tax shelter, and has recently been collecting rare animals for the Smithsonian Institution by bribing owners with large amounts of money. But Liz foolishly

reveals that the tax people will reclaim their yacht if Krest fails to bring back a catch this time. As a result, Krest uses "The Corrector" on his wife that night.

Krest is very drunk the night after the Hildebrand Rarity is found, and he insults Bond and Barbey. He goes to sleep in a hammock on deck. As Bond listens to him snore, the sound is interrupted by a choking, gurgling sound. When he investigates, 007 finds that the rare fish has been stuffed into Krest's mouth. Bond throws Krest's body over the side. Back in port, neither Barbey nor Liz Krest admit to the murder, and they all pretend that Krest fell overboard.

"The Hildebrand Rarity" is another off-beat experiment for Fleming, and is probably the most successful story in the anthology after "For Your Eyes Only." It is straightforward structurally, and each sequence proceeds logically from the previous one. Although it isn't a secret service story, it contains elements of intrigue, danger, and murder.

The theme of the story is similar to that of "Quantum of Solace." Here, the question is: how much abuse can a person take before rebounding with offensive action? Krest is a boorish, sadistic braggart. One wonders why the couple married in the first place. The murder of Krest is an act of retribution, to be sure. Although the murderer is never revealed, it is strongly hinted that Liz Krest killed her husband; it makes the most sense that she is the culprit.

The story has well-drawn characters. A new side of Bond is revealed: his temper. Throughout the story, Bond must do everything he can to restrain himself from striking Milton Krest. But his better judgment reminds him not to become involved in family quarrels. He is attracted to Liz Krest, but keeps his distance. He feels sorry for her having to put up with such a disgusting husband, but he allows the situation to work itself out. His opportunity to help her comes after he has discovered Krest's dead body. Bond throws it overboard so that there will be extreme difficulty in proving Krest was murdered.

Another humanitarian side of Bond emerges as he is helping Krest find the Hildebrand Rarity. Feeling disgust for Krest and compassion for the beautifully striped fish, Bond allows the creature to swim away before Krest can kill it with a poison chemical. But unfortunately, the fish swims back into the area as the poison spreads through the water. Finally, Bond, against his true feelings, plucks the dead fish from the water and resignedly hands it over to Krest with a disgruntled, "Here."

Milton Krest is a nasty, perverted villain; it's too bad he couldn't have been used in a longer novel. He's well drawn, and exemplifies the worst qualities of a certain type of pigheaded rich American. Krest, who throws insults left and right, is an obnoxious boor. The reader will certainly share Bond's constant urge to hit the man.

Liz Krest is also a well-developed character. Externally, she is pleasant and at ease, but internally she is frightened and yearns for a savior. Her actions in the story illustrate her need to be liberated from her marriage. She confides in Bond, for which her husband punishes her. Another interesting note about Liz Krest: she joins Gala Brand and Tilly Masterson as the only three females in the Bond series who do not eventually sleep with the agent.

Fidele Barbey is a Quarrel-like character who is Bond's friend and ally in the story. A native of the Seychelles Islands, Barbey simply adds to the local color. The man is warm at heart, friendly, and jovial. He is a pleasure.

Aside from the rich characterizations, Fleming's usual masterly descriptions of the underwater world make the story top-notch. The colors, textures, and shapes of the sea are easily visualized through Fleming's words. The story is clever, the moods are vibrant, and the narrative is lush. "The Hildebrand Rarity" is a rare gem, indeed.

THUNDERBALL (1961)

The ninth James Bond novel, THUNDERBALL, is a terrific book. It is the beginning of what could be called the Blofeld Trilogy, which also includes ON HER MAJESTY'S SECRET SERVICE and YOU ONLY LIVE TWICE. THUNDERBALL also marks the change from the earlier novels to the later, more mature books. The later Bond novels are distinguished by the usual Fleming Sweep and rich detail, but also feature the excellent characterizations which work so well in FROM RUSSIA, WITH LOVE and GOLDFINGER. There is, in addition, a change in the character of James Bond: he seems to be more aware of his own mortality and the decay that overtakes the body as one becomes older. The later novels are moody and sometimes extremely dark. The Blofeld Trilogy, especially, stands out as the series' most introspective and far-reaching novels in terms of the James Bond character.

In THUNDERBALL, M sends James Bond to Shrublands Health Spa because the agent's health has been very poor lately. There, Bond encounters one Count Lippe, and unravels mysterious clues linking Lippe with criminal organizations. The setting then switches to Paris for a meeting of SPECTRE. Its leader, Ernst Stavro Blofeld, announces the commencement of Plan Omega: the stealing of two atomic bombs from a hijacked NATO plane. SPECTRE demands that England and the United States pay a ransom of one hundred million pounds in gold bullion or the bombs will be used. The massive espionage effort to retrieve the bombs in the few short days before the deadline is called Operation Thunderball. Bond's territory is the Bahamas, as M believes this area to be the most likely landing site for the plane. After arriving in Nassau, Bond immediately investigates suspicious incoming parties of businessmen. He learns that the *Disco Volante*, a yacht carrying Emilio Largo and a treasure-hunting group, is in the area. Bond manages to meet Largo's mistress, Domino, in order to probe her for information about the Italian. Throughout the next couple of days, Bond and CIA agent Felix Leiter gather clues: Bond, during an underwater reconnaissance, discovers that the *Disco Volante* has a trap door in the hull; the men locate the sunken NATO plane; and Bond convinces Domino that Largo killed her brother—who was in fact the hijacker of the NATO plane. She agrees to help Bond determine if the bombs are aboard the *Disco*. Bond and Leiter join the forces of a Polaris submarine in order to shadow the *Disco* as it sails for its "treasure hunt" one night. Bond assembles a volunteer frogman team, and the group successfully ambushes Largo and his men underwater; the SPECTRE team is caught redhanded with the bombs. During the battle, Largo gains an advantage over Bond, but he is speared in the back by Domino. The bombs are recovered, but Blofeld cannot be found in Paris.

□ STYLE AND THEMES

THUNDERBALL follows the usual Fleming formula developed in LIVE AND LET DIE and perfected in DOCTOR NO. James Bond, after initial incidents, travels to a location hoping to unearth clues to solve the current problem; finds the villain in his base of operations; and ultimately destroys the villain's objective. THUNDERBALL, as discussed in Part One, is based on an original screen treatment by Fleming, Jack Whittingham, and Kevin McClory; therefore, this novel cannot be attributed to Fleming alone. Some changes *were* made from the original story, but the plot line came from a group effort. But the writing is pure Fleming, and only he could embellish the story as he has done in THUNDERBALL.

The Fleming Sweep moves as well as ever. Since the plot requires Bond and his colleague Felix Leiter to solve the Thunderball case within a specified time limit, the novel has an exciting urgency. SPECTRE's deadline approaches nearer and nearer as Bond and Leiter, bit by bit, unravel what seem like invisible clues. By the time Bond leads the *Manta* frogmen in the underwater battle with SPECTRE, the book has reached a rapid and critical pace.

Kingsley Amis claims that THUNDERBALL is the best example of "Fleming Effect." Reading THUNDERBALL gives you a general knowledge of health resorts, the architecture and lifestyles around the Boulevard Haussmann in Paris, underwater technical maneuvering, yachts, food in the Bahamas, Polaris submarines, and emergency medical care for victims who step on sea-egg spines. THUNDERBALL is deliberate and meticulous in its detail, yet extremely readable and entertaining; it is like a textbook with a sense of humor. The underwater sequences are beautifully crafted; the imagery and textures of this favorite among Fleming setpieces stand out:

Inside, Bond's torch shone everywhere into red eyes that glowed like rubies in the darkness, and there was a soft movement and scuttling. He sprayed the light up and down the fuselage. Everywhere there were octopuses, small ones, but perhaps a hundred of them, weaving on the tips of their tentacles, sliding softly away into protecting shadows, changing their camouflage nervously from brown to a pale phosphorescence that gleamed palely in the patches of darkness. The whole fuselage seemed to be crawling with them, evilly, horribly, and as Bond shone his torch on the roof the sight was even worse. There bumping softly in the slight current, hung the corpse of a crew member. In decomposition, it had risen up from the floor, and octopuses, hanging from it like bats, now let go their hold and shot, jet-propelled, to and fro inside the plane—dreadful, glinting, red-eyed comets that slapped themselves into dark corners and stealthily squeezed themselves into cracks and under seats.

(THUNDERBALL, Chapter 17)

This eerie scene, when Bond and Leiter finally locate the sunken Vindicator NATO aircraft, contains some of Fleming's more chilling images.

The gambling theme is very strong in THUNDERBALL. In fact, Operation Thunderball is solved entirely on *hunches* made by Bond and Leiter. They walk blindly into the situation: Bond, after obtaining information from the customs office, assumes his only hope of finding the SPECTRE agents in the Bahamas is by checking out any suspicious newcomers to the area. Largo, with his treasure hunt, is a prime suspect; and by chance, Bond finds Largo's mistress, the elusive Domino. After speculations atop coincidences in almost every sequence, Bond and Leiter point the finger at Largo; but they realize there is no concrete evidence. Even at the end of the novel, as the *Manta* pursues the *Disco Volante,* their only hope is that Largo's men can be caught red-handed transporting the bombs. Their gamble pays off, of course, but not without a little help from Domino.

Bond's philosophy on luck is repeated before he wipes out Largo at *chemin de fer.* "Luck," he tells himself, "is strictly for the birds." Yet it is pure luck that enables Bond to solve the case of Operation Thunderball.

The friendship theme is also very strong. The union between Bond and Leiter is the tightest it has ever been. It seems all they want to do is drink each other under the table after gorging themselves with meals. The loyalty these two men have for each other is one of the warmest qualities of the book—the sequence in which Bond meets the CIA agent at the airport and realizes it's none other than Leiter, is an uplifting moment.

□ CHARACTERS

James Bond continues to develop in THUNDERBALL. Two more scenes at Bond's flat are included, as well as a humorous sequence involving his housekeeper May. Bond's sense of humor seems sharper, and, in the moments when he is feeling good, he is remarkably pleasant. (Quite a change from the cold, ruthless man he is in CASINO ROYALE.) Bond has also developed a particular saying, which must have been a habitual phrase used by Fleming: "So that's the score!" It is one of Bond's most oft-used expressions.

As mentioned before, Bond, in THUNDERBALL and the following books, is more aware of his own mortality. At the beginning of the story he is very unfit, and is ordered to "dry out" at a health resort. Bond reflects Fleming's own penchant for living to excess and the results are showing. The story opens with Bond, plagued by a terrible hangover, attempting to shave. He cuts himself and blames it on his dull job at the office (there have been no exciting assignments in months). But the situation is worse than he realizes: M humiliates Bond by reading aloud the medical report from the agent's last physical:

"This officer," he read, "remains basically physically sound. Unfortunately his mode of life is not such as is likely to allow him to remain in this happy state. Despite many previous warnings, he admits to smoking sixty cigarettes a day. These are of a Balkan mixture with a higher nicotine content than the cheaper varieties. When not engaged upon strenuous duty, the officer's average daily consumption of alcohol is in the region of half a bottle of spirits of between sixty and seventy proof. On examination, there continues to be little definite sign of deterioration. The tongue is furred. The blood pressure a little raised at 160/90. The liver is not palpable. On the other hand, when pressed, the officer admits to frequent occipital headaches and there is spasm in the trapezius muscles and so-called "fibrositis" nodules can be felt. I believe these symptoms to be due to this officer's mode of life. He is not responsive to the suggestion that over-indulgence is no remedy for the tensions inherent in his professional calling and can only result in the creation of a toxic state which could finally have the effect of reducing his fitness as an officer. I recommend that No. 007 should take it easy for two to three weeks on a more abstemious regime, when I believe he would make a complete return to his previous exceptionally high state of physical finess."

(THUNDERBALL, Chapter 1)

The medical report's forecast is proven correct, for when Bond leaves the Shrublands health clinic a few weeks later, he feels "better than he ever has before." As a result, Bond's good humor and cheerfulness are obnoxious to everyone around him. Loelia Ponsonby becomes irritated that he arrives early in the morning and leaves the office late, supplying her with more work. May, the housekeeper, tut-tuts and nags Bond that the food he is eating since leaving Shrublands will kill him. To this, Bond has a surprising response:

In the old days, James Bond would have told May to go to hell and leave him in peace. Now, with infinite patience and good humor, he gave May a quick run through the basic tenets of "live" as against "dead" foods. "You see, May," he said reasonably, "all these denaturized foods—white flour, white sugar, white rice, white salts, whites of egg—these are dead foods. Either they're dead anyway like whites of egg or they've had all the nourishment refined out of them. They're slow poisons, like fried foods and cakes and coffee and heaven knows how many of the things I used to eat.

And anyway, look how wonderfully well I am. I feel absolutely a new man since I took to eating the right things and gave up drink and so on. I sleep twice as well. I've got twice as much energy. No headaches. No muscle pains. No hangovers. Why, a month ago there wasn't a week went by but that on at least one day I couldn't eat anything for breakfast but a couple of aspirins and a prairie oyster. And you know quite well that that used to make you cluck and tut-tut all over the place like an old hen. Well"—Bond raised his eyebrows amiably—"what about that?"

(THUNDERBALL, Chapter 7)

But, as usual, at the end of the novel Bond is wounded, exhausted, and sick from his ordeal. Ending up at the hospital (again), he slumps next to Domino's sickbed and falls asleep—his battered body beginning its familiar slow recuperation for its next bout of punishment.

Additionally, more is revealed about Bond's attitudes toward women. He is especially flirtatious with Domino:

She was getting friendly. "I expect you'll have the same effect on the old women with pincenez and blue rinses."
"Do they eat boiled vegetables for lunch?"
"Yes, and they drink carrot juice and prune juice."
"We won't get on, then. I won't sink lower than conch chowder."
She looked at him curiously. "You seem to know a lot about Nassau."
"You mean about conch being an aphrodisiac? That's not only a Nassau idea. It's all over the world where there are conchs."
"Is it true?"
"Island people have it on their wedding night. I haven't found it to have any effect on me."
"Why?" She looked mischievous. "Are you married?"
"No." Bond smiled across into her eyes. "Are you?"
"No."
"Then we might both try some conch soup some time and see what happens."

(THUNDERBALL, Chapter 11)

But, the hardened Bond does not disappear altogether. When the time comes for Bond to inform Domino that her brother is dead, she blames him. Bond says in a "cold, matter-of-fact voice" that it was Largo who killed her brother. Bond still puts up a wall to hide his emotions.

During his scenes with Domino, Bond seems to be reaching for something he has never had (something he *might* have had with Vesper Lynd); perhaps Bond is searching for a true love this time. He appears to be weary of his age-old pattern of going through women like assignments.

Felix Leiter has a larger role in THUNDERBALL than he has had thus far in the series. This time, Leiter has been drafted back into the CIA because of the urgency of Operation Thunderball. Allen Dulles (CIA chief) knows that Leiter and Bond work well together, so the Texan has been assigned to the Bahamas territory. Bond and Leiter constantly kid each other. For example, in the following scene, the men are using the cover of a property-seeking English businessman and his American lawyer when they meet in a hotel restaurant:

Bond joined Leiter at a corner table. They both wore white dinner jackets with their dress trousers. Bond had pointed up his rich, property-seeking status with a wine-red cummerbund. Leiter laughed. "I nearly tied a gold-plated bicycle chain round my waist in case of trouble, but I remembered just in time that I'm a peaceful lawyer. I suppose it's right that you should get the girls on this assignment. I suppose I just stand by and arrange the marriage settlement and later the alimony."

(THUNDERBALL, Chapter 14)

Leiter doesn't seem to have any bitterness about the loss of his right hand and leg. Toward the end of the book, the Texan insists on joining Bond in the underwater ambush of Largo's men:

Felix Leiter interrupted. He said obstinately, "And don't think you're going to leave me behind eating Virginia ham. I put an extra foot-flipper on this"—he held up the shining hook—"and I'll race you over half a mile any day, gammy leg and all. You'd be surprised the things one gets around to improvising when someone chews off one of your arms. Compensation it's called by the medics, in case you hadn't heard about it . . ."

Leiter turned to Bond. "You goddam shyster. Thought you were going to leave your old pal behind, didn't you? God, the treachery of you Limeys! Perfidious Albion is right, all right."

Bond laughed. "How the hell was I to know you'd been in the hands of rehabilitators and therapists and so on? I never knew you took life so seriously. I suppose you've even found some way of petting with that damned meathook of yours."

Leiter said darkly, "You'd be surprised. Get a girl round the arm with this and you'd be amazed the effect it has on their good resolutions."

(THUNDERBALL, Chapter 22)

*　　*　　*

Domino Vitali is probably the most appealing heroine since Tatiana Romanova. Bond, to himself, calls her a bitch on first encountering her, but he certainly falls for her the next time he sees the girl. Despite his negative feelings about women drivers, Bond thinks Domino "drives like a man." She takes a "man's pleasure in the feel of her machine." Bond believes she has a "gay, to-hell-with-you face that would become animal in passion." Domino has soft charcoal slits for eyes and a proud, sensual mouth. She has a determined chin and a jaw line with "royal command"—Domino holds herself with self-righteous authority. Bond compares her to a "beautiful Arab mare who would only allow herself to be ridden by a horseman with steel thighs and velvet hands—and then only when he had broken her to bridle and saddle."

But later, Bond discovers a different Domino. He sees through the hardened outer shell and inside finds an insecure girl yearning to break away from what could only be called captivity by Largo. And when asked if her limp bothers him (one of her legs is slightly shorter than the other), Bond replies that it "makes her something of a child." Domino is perhaps the bravest of all the Bond heroines. She doesn't confess when Largo catches her with the Geiger counter camera aboard the *Disco Volante,* even after fiendish torture. And finally, she saves Bond's life in the nick of time by ignoring her wounds and swimming after Largo with spear in hand.

Emilio Largo is an adequate villain; he is not the main antagonist here—Blofeld is that—but he inhabits more of the story. He is a well-drawn character, full of tough malevolence. He is a handsome Italian, looking as if he came from the face of an ancient Roman coin. Fleming describes him as resembling a satyr, with ears that are almost pointed. He is a first-rate athlete with enormous hands of "steel." Largo is an adventurer; two hundred years ago he might have been a pirate, Fleming tells the reader. He is a womanizer, an evil one, and the perfect man for SPECTRE. He has nerves of iron. If his role in the novel were as large as, say, a Dr. No or a Goldfinger, Largo might have been one of the most successful Fleming villains.

Ernst Stavro Blofeld, the leader of SPECTRE, is Bond's archenemy of the series. Because he appears in three books (hence, the Blofeld Trilogy), Blofeld, due to his intelligence and severity, becomes the antithesis of the Bond character. Although he appears in only two chapters of THUNDERBALL, enough of the character's aura is presented to allow it to penetrate into every chapter of the book. It is always Blofeld that

Bond is battling, even though Bond is not aware of the fact at this time.

Blofeld's appearance changes in each successive novel. In THUNDERBALL, he is a man who seems to "suck the eyes out of one's head." He has a powerful animal magnetism ascribed to great men of history, such as Genghis Khan, Alexander the Great, and Napoleon. He is a large man, weighing about 280 pounds, and had once been all muscle. His face suggests only cruelty under his black crew-cut, cruelty to an "almost Shakespearian degree." He has no vices, and has always been an "enigma to everyone who has known him." The dark irises of his eyes, like Le Chiffre's, are totally surrounded by white; they are doll-like in their effect. Blofeld is meticulous, unscrupulous, and all-knowing. He sees all, hears all, and when he desires, destroys all. He is a brilliant mastermind in planning schemes and supervising details. He succeeds in every project he undertakes—until Bond comes along, of course. An amusing and significant footnote to all this is that Blofeld's birthdate, May 28, 1908, is identical to that of Fleming's.

M is his usual crusty old self in THUNDERBALL. He takes private pleasure in sending Bond to Shrublands at the beginning of the story. Apparently, M had tried the place himself a few weeks earlier and loved it. There is also a rare moment in the series when M, while briefing Bond on his assignment, admits that 007 is "a reliable man." He tells Bond the entire top secret details of Operation Thunderball. He reveals these secrets because of a hunch (the gambling theme again) that SPECTRE is hiding in the Bahamas. Though Bond is dubious, he goes along with his chief and travels to the islands without the slightest hope of finding any clues.

□ HIGHLIGHTS AND OTHER INGREDIENTS

There are many outstanding passages in THUNDER-BALL, such as the entire Shrublands sequence (including Bond's ordeal with "the rack"). All of the underwater scenes involving SPECTRE's hijacking of the bombs and Bond exploring the hull of the *Disco Volante* and the hidden Vindicator plane are eerie and atmospheric. But the most exciting sequence, and perhaps one of Fleming's most brilliant evocations of tension, is the *chemin de fer* game between Bond and Largo. Note in the following excerpt the dramatic tension between the two characters:

Largo turned round to face Bond. Smiling with his mouth, he narrowed his eyes and looked carefully, with a new curiosity, at Bond's face. He said quietly, "But you are hunting me, my dear fellow. You are pursuing me. What is this? Vendetta?"

Bond thought: I will see if an association of words does something to him. He said, "When I came to the table I saw a spectre." He said the word casually, with no hint at double meaning.

The smile came off Largo's face as if he had been slapped. It was at once switched on again, but now the whole face was tense, strained, and the eyes had gone watchful and very hard. His tongue came out and touched his lips. "Really? What do you mean?"

Bond said lightly, "The spectre of defeat. I thought your luck was on the turn. Perhaps I was wrong." He gestured at the shoe. "Let's see."

The table had gone quiet. The players and spectators felt that a tension had come between these two men. Suddenly there was the smell of enmity where before there had been only jokes. A glove had been thrown down, by the Englishman. Was it about the girl? Probably. The crowd licked its lips.

Largo laughed sharply. He switched gaiety and bravado back on his face. "Aha!" His voice was boisterous again. "My friend wishes to put the evil eye upon my cards. We have a way to deal with that where I come from." He lifted his hand, and with only the first and little fingers outstretched in a fork, he prodded once, like a snake striking, toward Bond's face. To the crowd it was a playful piece of theater, but Bond, within the strong aura of the man's animal magnetism, felt the ill temper, the malevolence behind the old Mafia gesture.

Bond laughed good-naturedly. "That certainly put the hex on me. But what did it do to the cards? Come on, your spectre against my spectre!"

Again the look of doubt came over Largo's face. Why again the use of this word? He gave the shoe a hefty slap. "All right, my friend. We are wrestling the best of three falls. Here comes the third."

(THUNDERBALL, Chapter 15)

Another aspect of THUNDERBALL needs mentioning, and that is the invention of SPECTRE itself. When Fleming and his colleagues were writing the screen treatment in 1959, the Cold War was beginning to thaw; the conflict between East and West was not as critical as people had believed earlier in the fifties. Therefore, it became unfashionable to have the Soviets as villains. SMERSH, although mentioned from time to time in remaining novels, was not to be used again as the enemy organization. In its place was born SPECTRE, an international group of terrorists. Fleming and his collaborators unwittingly created a foreshadowing of today's fear of international terrorists. Kingsley Amis calls THUNDERBALL one of the most implausible of all the books. This may have been true in the early sixties, but today, in the nervous eighties, the situation in THUNDERBALL is frighteningly real. It is highly possible for a terrorist group to gain control of an atomic weapon. The consequences of such an occurrence would be disastrous, and it is this aspect of THUNDERBALL which makes it more realistic and alarming today. As a result, THUNDERBALL is more relevant now than it was two decades ago. Fleming, in letting his imagination run away with SPECTRE and its plot of hijacking atomic bombs (with the help of the imaginations of Kevin McClory and Jack Whittingham), produced, unwittingly, a strong case against the arms race.

THE SPY WHO LOVED ME
(1962)

The tenth James Bond novel is unique among the series. It stands alone as an enigma; it is a truly strange, experimental book for Ian Fleming. This is because the story is told in first person from the point of view of the heroine. And James Bond doesn't enter the tale until two-thirds into the book! It is also controversial—Bond fans either love it or hate it. Women tend to like it more than male readers, which is not surprising. It may have been a novel written expressly for female readers. There are several fine points in the novel, but there are just as many weak ones. In short, THE SPY WHO LOVED ME is a mixed bag.

The opening section of the story outlines heroine Vivienne Michel's growth to maturity, focusing mainly on her first two relationships with men. Both experiences leave her feeling rejected by men, London, and the world, so Vivienne decides to travel abroad. She flies to Canada, purchases a Vespa motor scooter, and sets off from Quebec to Florida. The road eventually leads her to the Dreamy Pines Motor Court in New York State. After spending one night here, the managers offer her a temporary job for a few days until the motel is closed for the season. She is left alone on closing day with a promise that the owner will arrive in the morning to pay her. But that night, two hideous gangsters, Horror and Sluggsy, arrive, explaining they're from the "insurance company." Before she is badly beaten, a stranger appears at the door. Vivienne discreetly lets him know her situation, and the man gallantly offers to help. He introduces himself as James

Bond, and says he is a policeman. The thugs reluctantly allow him to stay after Bond insists he must have a room for the night. Later, 007 tricks the thugs into thinking they have shot him in his bed, and they proceed to set the cabins on fire. Bond rescues Vivienne from her cabin and finally confronts Horror and Sluggsy in a furious gun battle. Both men end up in the nearby lake. Bond and Vivienne retire to the only remaining cabin, but Sluggsy, still alive, attempts to kill the couple one more time. The ever-alert 007 whips out his gun from under the pillow and kills the hoodlum. In the morning, Bond is gone, but Vivienne finds a poignant note left by the mysterious agent who will "live in her heart forever."

☐ STYLE AND THEMES

Until Bond enters the picture, THE SPY WHO LOVED ME might be called Fleming's unintentional attempt at a "true confessions" tale. Vivienne's love life is right out of a soap opera; yet this is contrasted with the gritty, brutal terror which envelops the last third of the novel.

Stylistically, the best thing the book has going for it is its brevity. Since it is the shortest novel Fleming wrote (even shorter than CASINO ROYALE), the corniness of the soap opera exposition and flashbacks does not intrude too much. The chapters still contain the distinctive Fleming Sweep and rich detail (even though, in a disclaimer at the beginning of the book, Fleming insists he found the manuscript on his desk one day—it is "co-authored" by Vivienne Michel herself). Reading THE SPY WHO LOVED ME is a breeze due to the pace of the writing.

The female perspective is imaginative and revealing. It's almost as if a female Fleming were narrating the tale. For the most part, one can believe that the author is female until the subject centers on sex. Somehow, things Vivienne Michel says about sex do not always ring true. In the following excerpt, Vivienne relates how she feels after first making love with Bond:

All women love semi-rape. They love to be taken. It was his sweet brutality against my bruised body that had made his act of love so piercingly wonderful. That and the coinciding of nerves completely relaxed after the removal of tension and danger, the warmth of gratitude, and a woman's natural feeling for her hero. I had no regrets and no shame. There might be many consequences for me—not the least that I might now be dissatisfied with other men. But whatever my troubles were, he would never hear of them. I would not pursue him and try to repeat what there had been between us. I would stay away from him and leave him to go his own road, where there would be other women, countless other women, who would probably give him as much physical pleasure as he had had with me. I wouldn't care, or at least I told myself that I wouldn't care, because none of them would ever own him—own any larger piece of him than I now did. And for all my life I would be grateful to him, for everything. And I would remember him forever as my image of a man.

(THE SPY WHO LOVED ME, Chapter 14)

To be sure, many women would argue with the statement that "all women love to be semi-raped." Also, there is a touch of egotism in Fleming's writing—is this a woman thinking about her idea of a perfect man, or is it Ian Fleming imagining that he or his hero actually *is* the perfect man?

Probably the most interesting aspect of the novel is the objective view of James Bond; it is a view that hasn't been taken in previous novels. It is a more depersonalized look at the man—he is seen from the outside rather than from the inside, as is usually the case. For instance, despite what Bond personally believes about women, in this book he is genuinely a kind, considerate man who treats Vivienne with utmost respect and care. He doesn't appear at all to be the ruthless, cold-hearted, and jaded male Bond believes himself to be. Because of this viewpoint, many new revelations are made about the James Bond character.

The themes in the novel are very black and white. The story can easily be paralleled with St. George and the dragon once again. A handsome knight saves the damsel in distress from the dragon, which in this case, is represented by the two thugs, Horror and Sluggsy. The only difference is that the knight does not ride away with the damsel in his arms at the story's end. He rides off alone, leaving the maiden safe but with a permanent scar on her heart.

Another theme, brought back from CASINO ROYALE, is the notion that there is no difference between the good guys and the bad guys. At the end of the novel, Vivienne is treated to a fatherly lecture by Police Captain Stonor:

"In the higher ranks of these forces, among the toughest of the professionals, there's a deadly quality in the persons involved which is common to both—to both friends and enemies." The captain's closed fist came softly down on the wooden table-top for emphasis, and his inward-looking eyes burned with a dedicated, private anger. "The top gangsters, the top F.B.I. operatives, the top spies and the top counter-spies are coldhearted, coldblooded, ruthless, tough killers, Miss Michel. Yes, even the 'friends' as opposed to the 'enemies.' They have to be. They wouldn't survive if they weren't. Do you get me? . . . So the message I want to leave with you, my dear—and I've talked to Washington and I've learned something about Commander Bond's outstanding record in his particular line of business—is this. Keep away from *all* these men. They are not for you, whether they're called James Bond or Sluggsy Morant. Both these men, and others like them, belong to a private jungle into which you've strayed for a few hours and from which you've escaped. So don't go and get sweet dreams about the one or nightmares from the other. They're just different people from the likes of you—a different species."

(THE SPY WHO LOVED ME, Chapter 15)

In fact, when Vivienne first set eyes on Bond, she believed that he was another one of the gangsters.

□ CHARACTERS

Vivienne Michel is Fleming's most successful female characterization. Since the story is related through the eyes of Viv, the inner thoughts of a Bond-heroine are finally revealed.

Vivienne has blue, clear eyes and an "inquiring" forehead. There is a "tumble" of ordinary dark brown hair which curves to the right and left in waves. She has high cheekbones, and a mouth that is "so big that it often looks sexy when she doesn't want it to." Vivienne, described as having a sanguine temperament, was born a French-Canadian Catholic near Quebec. Orphaned at an early age, Viv lived with her aunt until she was sent to a girls' school in England. Since being orphaned, Viv's nature has always been an independent one. She usually makes her own decisions, and only rarely would she allow herself to be influenced by other people. Twice, she did so, and both instances hurt her deeply. They were love affairs with, respectively, the boy to whom she lost her virginity, and an employer who became very close to her. Both men treated her badly.

Fleming makes no attempt to conceal the fact that Vivienne has been a victim of life. The first part of the book, which deals entirely with flashbacks to her past life and romances, plays upon the reader's sympathy for the girl. She's always been mistreated: at school by classmates, by Derek, and by Kurt; only when she is alone does she seem to be happy. Yet, even then, she longs for something to rescue her from her drab existence.

Viv is a willful, tough girl—she holds her own against the two thugs who threaten her. She probably could hurt the men, but could never stop them from killing her. At one point, she attempts to attack one thug with an ice pick; she fails, but her attempt is admirable.

Fleming makes the point that Vivienne has had an unsatisfactory sex life until she meets James Bond.

I had never before made love, full love, with my heart as well as my body. It had been sweet with Derek, cold and satisfying with Kurt. But this was something different. At last I realized what this thing could be in one's life.

(THE SPY WHO LOVED ME, Chapter 14)

Another egocentric pat on the back for Fleming and his hero; but in another way, it is the only time one is aware of what Bond's partner really *does* feel about his lovemaking. The feelings of the woman are emphasized. This is something that had been ignored in past novels, and it allows Vivienne Michel to seem that much more realistic.

As mentioned earlier, Fleming's attempt at writing in female first-person is successful and imaginative for the most part. It's amusing that Vivienne is able to write descriptively about trivial subjects, just like Ian Fleming. Nevertheless, as Vivienne describes her wants, desires, and fears, they are believable. Only the first part of the novel tends to drag with sentimentality and a play for the reader's sympathy. Once the thugs enter the story, one is easily caught up in Vivienne's narrative; the reader willingly suspends disbelief that someone other than Ian Fleming is telling the tale.

James Bond steps down to a supporting role in THE SPY WHO LOVED ME. Bond is viewed objectively as a perfectly ordinary English gentleman, but a gentleman with nerves of steel, raw courage, and the ability to tackle two ruthless gangsters and save a damsel in distress.

Perhaps the most revealing aspect about Bond in this novel (aside from interesting personal details, such as his dislike of Camay soap) is that he is extremely kind to women. The coldness with which he views the opposite sex in CASINO ROYALE seems to be gone, or at least he's keeping these thoughts to himself. From the moment he realizes Vivienne is in trouble, the agent bends over backward to help her. He is gentle with Viv, and supportive in her ordeal. The note he leaves her at the end of the story is warm and encouraging. He goes out of his way to make sure the authorities trouble Vivienne as little as possible so that she may be on her way to Florida quickly. Bond also arranges that any reward for the deaths of the two gangsters be given to Viv. Even though the note, in a way, is another "Dear Viv" letter, he leaves his address and welcomes her to contact him at any time.

James Bond is a true fantasy figure in this novel. He comes out of the night from nowhere at just the right moment, saves Vivienne from death, and disappears into thin air, as if he never existed. This is Fleming at his most romantic. Vivienne sums up the mystery and wonderment of the man in this way:

I think I know why I gave myself so completely to this man, how I was capable of it with someone I had met only six hours before. Apart from the excitement of his looks, his authority, his maleness, he had come from nowhere, like the prince in the fairy tales, and he had saved me from the dragon. But for him, I would now be dead, after suffering God knows what before. He could have changed the wheel on his car and gone off, or, when danger came, he could have saved his own skin. But he had fought for my life as if it had been his own. And then, when the dragon was dead, he had taken me as his reward. In a few hours, I knew, he would be gone—without protestations of love, without apologies or excuses. And that would be the end of that—gone, finished.

(THE SPY WHO LOVED ME, Chapter 14)

The other two characters in the story, Horror and Sluggsy, are sickening villains, but do not attain to the stature of a major Bond villain. They are merely second-rate professional killers, which in a way, makes them all the more believable in this sort of story. They are frightening, however, and Fleming has succeeded in creating a true sense of terror from their evil actions.

☐ HIGHLIGHTS AND OTHER INGREDIENTS

Fleming has managed to keep THE SPY WHO LOVED ME a continuation of the series, despite the first-person female perspective. There is even a mention of SPECTRE, and of the fact that all the allied nations are still looking for Ernst Stavro Blofeld since the completion of Operation Thunderball—a reminder to the reader that this novel is part of the Bond saga, and the search for Blofeld will continue in the next book, which is the second part of the Blofeld Trilogy.

The most impressive scene in the book is the entrance of Bond. The story, by this time, has reached a peak of excitement: Horror and Sluggsy are just about to get down to the nitty gritty with Vivienne. Things look grim for the girl when the door buzzer suddenly rings. Vivienne answers it and sees a dark stranger outside. There is a sinister, dangerous quality about the stranger until he smiles and says he has had a "puncture." Vivienne is so relieved that the man is English and not a gangster, she almost embraces him immediately. But she retains her cool and, using discreet signals, lets Bond know what is happening. If this situation were in a film, the audience would surely applaud and cheer at this wonderful entrance of the hero. It is utterly romantic and works beautifully.

As mentioned before, THE SPY WHO LOVED ME isn't for everyone. On the negative side are a few problems with the believability of the female perspective, as well as the soap opera story in the first half of the book. The positive aspects include its fast pace, the excitement and thrills of the final third (which contains the same ingredients of sex and violence found in the rest of the series), and the objective view of Bond, which is different and revealing. If the reader has any sort of romantic inclination, THE SPY WHO LOVED ME can be enjoyed as the most escapist fantasy of the series.

ON HER MAJESTY'S SECRET SERVICE (1963)

The second novel in what could be called the Blofeld Trilogy, ON HER MAJESTY'S SECRET SERVICE, is a James Bond story of epic proportions. It is one of the longest of the Bond novels, and contains two seemingly unrelated tales which finally converge at the book's end. One of these plotlines concerns Bond's pursuit of Ernst Stavro Blofeld, the leader of SPECTRE, since the organization's demise at the end of Operation Thunderball. The subplot is a love story involving the marriage of James Bond. How these two stories come together at the conclusion of the novel is tragic, and the otherwise fairly upbeat book ends on a sad, wistful note. ON HER MAJESTY'S SECRET SERVICE is immediately one of Ian Fleming's best novels, despite a couple of slow patches. As one reviewer at the time of publication put it, the book is "solid Fleming."

The novel opens with a series of events chronicling the beginning of a romance between James Bond and Tracy di Vicenzo, a countess who is the daughter of Marc-Ange Draco. Draco is head of the Union Corse,

a French equivalent of the Mafia. Marc-Ange offers Bond a sum of money if he will marry Tracy. Bond refuses, but agrees to continue seeing Tracy as "therapy" if Draco will tell him where Blofeld can be found. A useful lead comes from the College of Arms. Blofeld is attempting to prove that he is the Count de Bleuville, and has asked the college to authenticate his claim. Bond arranges to impersonate Sir Hilary Bray, a college emissary, and travels to Piz Gloria, Blofeld's headquarters in Switzerland, to be met by the count's personal secretary, Fraulein Irma Bunt. The count is doing research on allergies, and Bond meets the current patients: ten beautiful girls from different areas of England. As the days go by, Bond is mystified by Blofeld's intentions at Piz Gloria. After the count becomes suspicious of "Sir Hilary," 007 creates some makeshift ski clothes, steals a pair of skis, and makes a downhill escape from Piz Gloria. In the village below, he runs into none other than Tracy. Together, they escape in her car. In a moment of inspiration, Bond proposes to Tracy, and she happily accepts. Later, in London, it is surmised that Blofeld is attempting biological warfare against England. Apparently, the allergy patients are being brainwashed, then sent home to their families (who are all in the crop and/or livestock business), where they will unwittingly contaminate England's food supply with deadly chemicals. Bond then persuades Marc-Ange Draco to help him destroy Piz Gloria. Accompanied by a Union Corse helicopter team, they infiltrate Blofeld's headquarters and wire explosives. During the battle with the SPECTRE team, Bond locates Blofeld and chases him in a furious bobsled race down a dangerous chute. But Blofeld escapes by tossing a hand grenade in front of Bond's sleigh; but 007 is not hurt badly. Later, on New Year's Day, Tracy di Vicenzo becomes Mrs. James Bond. But the honeymoon is shattered by an explosion of gunfire. Bond glimpses Blofeld's face in the ambush car before he blacks out. He awakes in a highway patrolman's arms, turns, and sees that Tracy is dead.

□ STYLE AND THEMES
After the experimental THE SPY WHO LOVED ME, about which critics and fans were not overly enthusiastic, Fleming decided to return to his reliable, successful Bond formula. ON HER MAJESTY'S SECRET SERVICE is a straight thriller on the one hand, complete with all of the identifiable Fleming elements (the Fleming Sweep, the rich detail, a super villain, etc.); but on the other

hand it is a special chapter in the James Bond saga. In ON HER MAJESTY'S SECRET SERVICE, James Bond falls in love and marries. But, as in FROM RUSSIA, WITH LOVE, the author pulls the rug from under his hero at the novel's end, and Bond's new bride is tragically killed.

Most of the novel is taken up with Bond finally locating the hideout of Blofeld and infiltrating it by means of a peculiar cover: as an emissary from the College of Arms, to whom Blofeld grants permission to come to the hideout and prove that Blofeld is a count in the direct line of the de Bleuville clan. The Fleming Sweep in this part of the story moves with confidence and readability—the suspense builds gradually until the climactic ski escape, which stands as one of Fleming's most exciting passages. After an interlude, the story continues and builds to another climax culminating with the bobsled chase at the novel's end.

ON HER MAJESTY'S SECRET SERVICE is full of rises and falls in the action, which keep this sprawling narrative consistently interesting. There are only two sections that are unnecessarily detailed, interrupting the Fleming Sweep. This happens once when Bond visits the College of Arms and is forced to listen to the eccentric Griffon Or attempt to link Bond with Sir Thomas Bond of Bond Street. The second instance is at M's house, called Quarterdeck, where the Minister of Agriculture and Fisheries reads a lengthy report concerning biological warfare. The journalistic aspects of both these sections are impressive, as are all Fleming's descriptions of technical data, but here they simply bog down the story.

Kingsley Amis, as well as other critics, complained that the structure of this work is flawed because the two separate plotlines seem unrelated. Actually, the two plots *do* come together at the novel's end—Bond's new bride, Tracy, is murdered by Bond's archenemy, Blofeld. The circle is complete. And this is where the main theme of the novel is centered. The title, ON HER MAJESTY'S SECRET SERVICE, implies that Bond is totally under the jurisdiction of his government; everything he does is, and always will be, in the line of duty. Does this also mean that his professional calling will affect his personal life, and if so, can he escape this? Apparently not, for Bond's personal and professional lives unfortunately come together at the end of the story, with tragic consequences. Therefore, Bond's marriage and subsequent life as a widower fall sadly under the same "powers that be" which control his professional life. Bond will always be, as long as he lives, "on her majesty's secret service."

The gambling theme is ever present as well. The main action begins when Bond covers for Tracy at the *chemin de fer* table at Casino Royale in the opening chapters. Tracy, at this point in the story, is unhappy, foolish, and suicidal. She recklessly gambles and loses a good deal of money at the table; she then admits to not having the money to pay the debt. Bond, ever the gentleman, pays the debt in order to meet her. This is a gamble on Bond's part. This act of nobility is what begins the chain of events which leads Bond down two different paths through the girl Tracy—one path toward Blofeld, and the other toward marriage. Bond makes other risky gambles, especially once he has entered the Swiss Alps headquarters of SPECTRE. There, Bond is impersonating Sir Hilary Bray, and must be extremely careful not to let his cover slip. The entire deceit of masquerading as an emissary from the College of Arms is a tremendous risk; the cover, one must admit, is pretty flimsy. Bond takes additional chances such as stealing a plastic strip of ski binding and using it to deactivate the electronic lock on his door at Piz Gloria, and confiding in Ruby to gain an ally.

□ CHARACTERS

ON HER MAJESTY'S SECRET SERVICE contains major revelations about James Bond. At the beginning of the novel, Bond is unhappy. He has drafted a letter of resignation to M, which he plans to rewrite and dictate to his secretary in a couple of days. Bond is fed up with boredom, a malady Ian Fleming himself always hated. M has kept Bond in pursuit of Blofeld since the close of Operation Thunderball two years before. His adventure in Canada the previous year in THE SPY WHO LOVED ME apparently was related to the search for Blofeld as well. But once Blofeld's scent is finally uncovered, Bond regains his old energy and drive. Even then, it is quite apparent that Bond is ready for a change in his life. And that change comes about in the form of Tracy.

ON HER MAJESTY'S SECRET SERVICE presents a James Bond in love. Ever since the death of Vesper Lynd in CASINO ROYALE, Bond has visited the resort in northern France, Royale-les-Eaux, annually:

He had come a long way since then, dodged many bullets and much death and loved many girls, but there had been a drama and a poignancy about that particular adventure that every year drew him back to Royale and its casino and to the small granite cross in the little churchyard that simply said "Vesper Lynd. R.I.P."

(OHMSS, Chapter 2)

(It is interesting to note that ON HER MAJESTY'S SECRET SERVICE marks the ten-year anniversary of the James Bond novels—it is only fitting that Fleming should bring up memories of that first book.) It is apparent in the above passage that Bond is longing for an addition to his life, or he wouldn't return to the little gravestone every year. And it is no accident that Bond meets the woman he will marry in the same location as he met Vesper Lynd. Royale will always hold a special place in the life of James Bond.

Bond is attracted to Tracy first by the way she drives her car—she passes him on the highway toward Royale. Bond loves fast cars, especially if they're driven by beautiful women. Next, Bond is intrigued by her looks, and by what the concierge at the hotel tells him. The woman driving the Lancia, it seems, is a "lady who lives life to the full." Finally, at the gambling table, Bond is impressed by the sheer guts of the woman. She gambles for big stakes and loses with no money to back her up. It is then, in speaking with Tracy, that Bond discovers she is a "bird with a wing, perhaps two wings, down." She tells him that she would always be able to pass Bond in a fast car because *he* wants to live. Apparently, *she* doesn't. To pay her debt to Bond, Tracy promptly takes him to her bedroom and the affair begins. Tracy's neurotic, suicidal tendencies only urge Bond to discover more about her. He spies on her the next day, following her to the beach. There, the couple is abducted by two men from the Union Corse, which happens to be run by Tracy's father, Marc-Ange Draco. Draco "kidnapped" Bond in order to bribe the Englishman into marrying Tracy because he believes it would make Tracy happy.

Here, the love story is interrupted and the Blofeld story takes over until almost two-thirds into the book, when Bond miraculously runs into Tracy after his harrowing escape from Piz Gloria. Tracy is a new woman now; it is two months since Bond has seen her. Psychiatric treatment has been a success, and she is now happy and full of energy. Tracy helps Bond flee to safety and one thing leads to another. Over breakfast the next day, Bond comes to some surprising realizations:

Bond suddenly thought, Hell! I'll never find another girl like this one. She's got everything I've ever looked for in a woman. She's beautiful, in bed and out. She's adventurous, brave, resourceful. She's exciting always. She seems to love me. She'd let me go on with my life. She's a lone girl, not cluttered up with friends, relations, belongings. Above all, she needs me. It'll be someone for me to look after. I'm fed up with all these untidy, casual affairs that leave me with a bad conscience. I wouldn't mind having children. I've got no social background into which she would or wouldn't fit. We're two of a pair, really. Why not make it for always?

Bond found his voice saying those words that he had never said in his life before, never expected to say.

"Tracy. I love you. Will you marry me?"

She turned very pale. She looked at him wonderingly. Her lips trembled. "You mean that?"

"Yes, I mean it. With all my heart."

(OHMSS, Chapter 19)

This is quite a burst of emotion from the cold and ruthless individual who appeared ten years previously in CASINO ROYALE!

Bond has second thoughts while sleeping on the plane en route to London. He has a nightmare involving an elegant party at some kind of "grand townhouse." He and Tracy are dressed to a T—she loaded with jewels, he in tails. Tracy is chattering gaily and Bond wishes he were playing a game of bridge at Blades. Commander and Mrs. James Bond are announced as they enter the party, and a hush falls over the crowd. Bond awakes, sweating. He asks himself what he has done, but then realizes that he has just been having a nightmare. His marriage wouldn't be like that, he tells himself.

Bond even begins to enjoy the actual planning of the wedding:

. . . he was surprised to find that all this nest-building gave him a curious pleasure, a feeling that he had at last come to rest and that life would now be fuller, have more meaning, for having someone to share it with. Togetherness! What a curiously valid cliché it was!

(OHMSS, Chapter 26)

There is one moment when Bond realizes that he must come to grips with the fact that someone actually cares about him now; someone who cares if he is hurt, or is entering a dangerous situation. Bond now has someone else in his life to think about. When Tracy first sees Bond after the wrap-up of the Piz Gloria operation, she cries over his cuts and bruises. She chastises him because he "seems to think it doesn't matter to anyone."

Bond reached out and pressed her hand on the wheel. He hated "scenes." But it was true what she said. He hadn't thought of her, only of the job. It never crossed his mind that anybody really cared about him. A shake of the head from his friends when he went, a few careful lines in the obituary columns of *The Times,* a momentary pang in a few girls' hearts. But now, in three days' time, he would no longer be alone. He would be a half of two people. There wouldn't only be May and Mary Goodnight who would tut-tut over him when he came back from some job as a hospital case. Now, if he got himself killed, there would be Tracy who would at any rate partially die with him.

(OHMSS, Chapter 26)

The wedding is a small affair, but Bond is extremely happy with it. As Tracy drives the Lancia away from the reception, Bond relaxes in the seat next to her as if a tremendous load has been taken from him. He tells her that all he wants is "to look after her." And when Tracy asks if she should try and lose the approaching red Maserati on their tail, he replies, "No. Let him go. We have all the time in the world." Unfortunately, these words are the last that Tracy will hear, for their dreams are shattered by the evil Ernst Stavro Blofeld. The bullets, probably meant for Bond, strike the driver of the Lancia, who happens to be Tracy. The Lancia crashes, and Bond comes to in the arms of a policeman. Bond puts up his defensive wall when he realizes what has happened; he refuses to admit she is dead:

He pressed her against him. He looked up at the young man and smiled his reassurance.

"It's all right," he said in a clear voice as if explaining something to a child. "It's quite all right. She's having a rest. We'll be going on soon. There's no hurry. You see"—Bond's head sank down against hers and he whispered into her hair—"you see, we've got all the time in the world."

(OHMSS, Chapter 27)

All of the cynical and melancholic trappings with which Fleming has endowed his hero have never equalled the power of this sad ending to a chapter in the life of James Bond.

La Comtesse Teresa di Vicenzo, otherwise known as Tracy, is not one of Fleming's most successful heroines. She is harder to define as a character than Honeychile Rider, Domino Vitali, Tatiana Romanova, or Vivienne Michel. Perhaps it is this enigmatic quality that Bond falls in love with. At the beginning of the story she is quite neurotic. It seems any other woman acting this way would turn James Bond off; but not Tracy. Her dangerous but confident driving impresses him. Tracy has a "beautiful golden face" with blue eyes and "shocking" pink lips. Her golden hair reaches her shoulders. She possesses an "ice-cold will" and knows exactly what she wants. Tracy grew up in wealthy

surroundings, since her father, a Corsican, is the head of the French Mafia. Her mother, Marc-Ange tells Bond, was English but extremely wild. Tracy inherited these wild qualities, and a volatile temperament. She has been married once before to Count Guilio di Vicenzo, but he left her with a daughter who died of spinal meningitis soon after. Since her daughter's death, Tracy has been in a deep depression. She is ready to end it all when James Bond suddenly walks into her life. After seeking psychiatric help, Tracy changes and becomes a happier, carefree individual. She is, in Bond's words, "brave and resourceful"—she certainly deserves the credit for helping Bond escape the clutches of Blofeld's men after the ski chase from Piz Gloria. Her skillful driving saves them both more than once in this sequence. Aside from all of this, not much more can be ascertained from what Fleming provides the reader about the woman James Bond marries. Instead, we see only how she affects Bond himself, which is perhaps more important anyway.

Ernst Stavro Blofeld returns in OHMSS as a major villain. He has changed his appearance considerably since THUNDERBALL: his weight is now down from 280 pounds to about 168 pounds; he has "longish, carefully tended" silvery white hair; and the right nostril of his aquiline nose has been eaten away by what looks like tertiary syphilis. Blofeld has also changed the color of his eyes by wearing dark-green tinted contact lenses. But the brain has not changed. The villain is still capable of inventing an ingenious plot to destroy England, and even Bond is mystified by Blofeld's actions until late in the story. Apparently, Blofeld is seeking revenge on England for the destruction of SPECTRE's last plan. And although it is never actually stated whether the men surrounding Blofeld at Piz Gloria are members of SPECTRE, it is certainly suggested. The same cell-group structure of three men still exists, and the punishments for failure are very SPECTRE-like. For instance, one guard, who "interfered" with one of the beautiful allergy patients, took a ride early one morning down the bobsled chute—*sans* bobsled!

Exactly where Blofeld has found the means to build his fortress and purchase an entire Alp is not explained, but one must accept the fact that the villain has unlimited capital at his disposal. His hatred for England is not explained either. There is no doubt, however, that Blofeld is a resourceful, clever, but ultimately sick man.

Irma Bunt, Blofeld's mistress and secretary, is basically a rehash of Rosa Klebb. Their descriptions are similar: Bunt is a "toad-like" woman with a square, brutal face. Bond describes her to himself as "Irma La not so Douce.'' Irma Bunt is successful in that she exudes a great deal of hostility and danger, and is responsible for putting Blofeld onto Bond's trail at the novel's end.

Marc-Ange Draco is a successful Bond ally, even though he, too, is a rehash of earlier allies, especially Drako Kerim. Draco has a "delightful face, lit with humor and mischief and magnetism." His handshake is, of course, warm, firm, and dry. The man is so pleasant that it's difficult to believe he is the head of the French equivalent of the Mafia. But then again, every time he appears in the story, Draco is in the presence of his future son-in-law. Perhaps this makes the man more of a human being than one would expect a criminal chieftain to be. Draco adds humor to the book; he is always embracing Bond (at one point, Bond, to himself, wishes that Marc-Ange wouldn't do that). It is evident that Marc-Ange has a heart of gold; his feelings for his daughter circumvent everything else. When Bond asks for the "wedding present" of helping him infiltrate Blofeld's hideaway in the Alps, Draco doesn't hesitate. After all, Bond has refused every other favor Draco has offered!

M has some interesting scenes in the story. One lengthy passage takes place at M's home, Quarterdeck. Bond visits his chief on Christmas day and joins him in a traditional dinner prepared by Mrs. Hammond. M is particularly pleasant on Christmas—perhaps this is because he is at home rather than at the cold office across from Regent's Park. However, in an earlier sequence, when Bond explains his plan to impersonate an emissary from the College of Arms in order to meet Blofeld, M is quite sarcastic:

And who the hell are you supposed to be?

M more or less repeated Bond's question when, that evening, he looked up from the last page of the report that Bond had spent the afternoon dictating to Mary Goodnight. M's face was just outside the pool of yellow light cast by the green-shaded reading lamp on his desk, but Bond knew that the lined, sailor's face was reflecting, in varying degrees, scepticism, irritation and impatience. The "hell" told him so. M rarely swore and when he did it was nearly always at stupidity. M obviously regarded Bond's plan as stupid, and now, away from the dedicated, minutely focused world of the Heralds, Bond wasn't sure that M wasn't right.

(OHMSS, Chapter 8)

But M, who has admitted in the past that Bond is reliable, allows 007 to have his way and follow through with the plan, foolhardy as it may be.

It is also worth mentioning here that Loelia Ponsonby, Bond's secretary, has left in order to marry. She is replaced by Mary Goodnight, who becomes slightly more important to the series than her predecessor.

□ **HIGHLIGHTS AND OTHER INGREDIENTS**

There are several excellent passages in OHMSS. Once Bond has been impersonating Hilary Bray at Piz Gloria, the action is tense and involving. The sequence in which Shaun Campbell, from Station Z in Zurich, is caught spying on the fortress is terribly suspenseful. Bond certainly "sweats it out" while waiting to see whether or not Campbell will blow the Hilary Bray cover.

The ski chase down the Piz Gloria Alp is perhaps the best sequence of the book. Taking up the better part of two chapters, the chase is yet another example of the way in which Fleming's journalistic abilities enhance his story-telling. His description of the snow, the weather, the skiing maneuvers, the avalanche, and the guard's death in the snow plow are masterful. Bond's changing of the "right turn" sign on the cliff road, causing the SPECTRE car to fly over the edge, is another amusing and thrilling highlight. And the book reaches a stunning climax with the now-famous bobsled chase between Bond and Blofeld. The most important highlight, however, is Bond's marriage and its tragic end.

Another interesting note worth mentioning is that the "film star, Ursula Andress" is noticed among the visitors at Piz Gloria ski club. Irma Bunt comments on what a "wonderful tan she has." This isn't surprising, since in 1962 the actress had just completed filming *Dr. No,* the first James Bond film, in Jamaica.

YOU ONLY LIVE TWICE (1964)

The twelfth James Bond novel, and the third in the Blofeld Trilogy, represents another unique, experimental departure for Ian Fleming. It differs from the other Bonds primarily in its allegorical and symbolic aspects. Conjuring more mood and atmosphere than any Bond tale since CASINO ROYALE, YOU ONLY LIVE TWICE is a haunting, foreboding novel which marks what might have been a totally new direction for Fleming had he not died in 1964. It is the last novel Fleming was able to complete (his literary executors completed the last book, THE MAN WITH THE GOLDEN GUN); and, despite an overindulgence in the "travelogue" aspects, YOU ONLY LIVE TWICE stands out as one of the most successful books in the series.

The opening finds James Bond depressed since the death of his wife, Tracy. It is suggested that Bond be given an "impossible" assignment; something so challenging that he would be forced to snap out of his present condition. M then strips Bond of his Double-0 number and "promotes" him into the diplomatic section. His assignment is to go to Japan and persuade Tiger Tanaka, head of the Japanese Secret Service, to share with Britain Japan's new secret ciphering method known as Magic 44. After a month of bandying, Tanaka finally agrees to hand over Magic 44 if Bond will perform a service for Japan. A Westerner named Dr. Shatterhand has recently purchased a castle on the island of Kyushu, bringing with him legitimate credentials from horticultural and botanical societies in Europe. Shatterhand and his wife stocked their garden with poisonous tropical plants and deadly animals. This "Garden of Death" has begun to attract Japanese people who wish to commit suicide. The Japanese Prime Minister has instructed Tanaka to hand over Magic 44 if Bond will infiltrate the castle and assassinate Dr. Shatterhand. A plan is formed: Bond will stay with the Ama family of Kissy Suzuki on Kuro Island (across the bay from Kyushu), swim the channel one night, and make his way to the castle. Before embarking for Kuro, however, Bond learns that Shatterhand and his wife are none other than Ernst Stavro Blofeld and Irma Bunt! Bond makes the swim one night and explores the eerie garden. He eventually breaks into the castle, but falls into an oubliette. Blofeld and Bunt recognize Bond and take him to the "Question Room," which consists of a throne directly above an active geyser which spurts every fifteen minutes. Bond manages to avoid being killed by the geyser and attacks the couple with a staff. He knocks Bunt unconscious and finally strangles Blofeld to death. He then rigs the geyser to explode, and escapes from the castle via a huge helium-filled weather balloon. A piece of debris hits Bond in the head, and he falls into the ocean. Kissy rescues him, but Bond has lost his memory. The agent lives with the girl for a year until he notices the name of a Russian city in a newspaper; he decides he must travel to Russia in search of his true identity. One golden morning, Kissy, who hasn't informed Bond that she is pregnant with his child, gives him some money and sends the agent on his way to Russia.

□ STYLE AND THEMES

The structure of YOU ONLY LIVE TWICE basically follows the same formula Fleming has generally used. The opening chapter is a scene which takes place after the story has begun: Bond is at a geisha party with Tiger Tanaka. This is followed by flashback chapters which eventually lead the reader to the point at which the story began. The action of the book doesn't really begin, though, until two-thirds into the novel. This lengthy first section is mostly travelogue material; it's Fleming at his journalistic best, describing the sights, sounds, and textures of Japan. Much of this material, though entertaining and sometimes very funny (it contains some of Fleming's most humorous writing), is unnecessary. Kingsley Amis complained that it "gets in the way" of the story. While this is not entirely true, since some of the information contributes to the development of the story, much of it is superfluous. For example, the sightseeing sequences (at the Kobe beef restaurant or *ninja* training school) are not needed. The long and detailed report on poisonous plants is completely dispensable; but one must suppose Fleming felt it necessary to embellish the story with realistic technical data. One favorable aspect of the travelogue material is Bond's reaction to it all; he is usually humorous and sarcastic in playing Tiger Tanaka's game throughout the story.

Once Bond is on Kuro Island and prepares to venture to Dr. Shatterhand's castle, the book incorporates a new style. Fleming's writing becomes allegorical and almost *epic* in its use of Bond as the symbol of Good, and Blofeld as the symbol of Evil. Fleming's imagery in the last third of the novel is horrific, dreamlike, and surrealistic. James Bond, in YOU ONLY LIVE TWICE, journeys to hell and back.

The St. George and the dragon theme is played to the hilt here. Even Tiger Tanaka makes the analogy:

"Bondo-san, does it not amuse you to think of that foolish dragon dozing all unsuspecting in his castle while St. George comes silently riding towards his lair across the waves? It would make the subject for a most entertaining Japanese print."

(YOU ONLY LIVE TWICE, Chapter 13)

Another strong theme in the novel is that of revenge. Once Bond is aware that Dr. Shatterhand is none other than Ernst Stavro Blofeld, his attitude toward his mission changes. He becomes determined, serious, and hardened—in contrast to the stoical, casual Bond of the first half of the story. And when Bond achieves his revenge, it is most explosive.

Another theme is stated by Dikko Henderson, relating a Japanese custom he calls an ON. An ON is an obligation to repay a favor.

"When you have an ON, you're not very happy until you've discharged it *honourably*, if you'll pardon the bad pun. And if a man makes you a present of a salmon, you mustn't repay him with a shrimp. It's got to be with an equally large salmon—larger, if possible—so that then you've jumped the man, and now he has an ON with regard to you, and you're quids in morally, socially, and spiritually—and the last one's the most important."

(YOU ONLY LIVE TWICE, Chapter 4)

Tiger Tanaka uses this custom to force Bond into agreeing to assassinate Dr. Shatterhand. Tanaka will turn over Magic 44 to Bond only if the agent repays the favor by performing this ugly task.

But the most important theme in the novel is that of rebirth. This theme underlies the *haiku* which Bond creates for Tiger:

You only live twice;
Once when you're born,
Once when you look death in the face.

In this story, Bond completes a cycle in his life. Ever since the death of Vesper Lynd in CASINO ROYALE, Bond has hardened himself to relationships. Vesper was the first girl he truly wanted to marry, and losing her hurt him deeply. Ten years later, Bond met Tracy and fell in love. Bond, revitalized toward love and marriage, proposed to Tracy; but their dreams were shattered when she was shot by Blofeld. After her death, in the beginning of YOU ONLY LIVE TWICE, Bond is in limbo, so to speak. He is falling apart, with no purpose in life. He simply doesn't care. But once he learns that Dr. Shatterhand is Blofeld, his mission becomes one of revenge. Suddenly, his life has a purpose again—to avenge the death of his wife. Bond achieves his revenge and completes the cycle, a changed man. At the end of YOU ONLY LIVE TWICE, he is no longer James Bond—he is Taro Todoroki (his cover name among the Japanese). He has been reborn because he looked death (Blofeld) in the face. Bond has made a journey to hell (the Garden of Death), which could be interpreted as being the opposite of the Garden of Eden, or the Garden of Life.

Fleming's preoccupation with death further segregates YOU ONLY LIVE TWICE from the other novels. The Japanese people and their customs fascinated Fleming, but he found their beliefs in suicide the most intriguing.

Bond shares Fleming's awe at this way of life when Tiger Tanaka explains why suicide is an honorable way of dying in Japan. A young university student failed his examination for the second time and brought dishonor on his parents. The youth walked to a nearby construction site and quickly placed his head underneath a piledriver. But the boy, and his family, "gained great face in their neighbourhood." (Bond's comment is, "You can't gain face from strawberry jam.") Tanaka continues to explain that:

"Dishonour must be expunged—according to those of us who remain what you would describe as old-fashioned. There is no apology more sincere than the offering up of your own life. It is literally all you have to give."

(YOU ONLY LIVE TWICE, Chapter 8)

Tanaka tells Bond that twenty-five thousand Japanese people commit suicide every year. Only the bureaucrats regard suicide as a shameful practice. And the more fantastic and spectacular the suicide, the more warmly it is approved by the community.

With this background stimulating his imagination, Fleming came up with the perfect vehicle for its exploitation. The Garden of Evil is the most haunting image Fleming created in the entire Bond series. It is a world in which James Bond's emotions run the gamut—he is at once horrified and fascinated by what he sees in the garden. It is the place where he will become a new man.

□ **CHARACTERS**
James Bond's condition at the beginning of YOU ONLY LIVE TWICE is neatly summed up in Chapter 2:

The state of your health, the state of the weather, the wonders of nature—these are things that rarely occupy the average man's mind until he reaches the middle thirties. It is only on the threshold of middle-age that you don't take them all for granted, just part of an unremarkable background to more urgent, more interesting things.

The truth of the matter is that Bond, in M's words, is "going to pieces." The death of Tracy, after eight months, still has Bond in shock. M complains to Sir James Molony, the famous neurologist assigned to the Service, that Bond is constantly late for work, making mistakes, drinking too much, and losing a lot of money at a casino. M may have to fire 007 because the agent is becoming a security risk. But thanks to Molony, M gives Bond one more chance to redeem himself. Assigning Bond to what M calls "an impossible mission" seems to be just what the doctor ordered. Bond perks up, takes a new interest in his work, and genuinely attempts to do the job well.

It is now that Bond's sense of humor surfaces more than ever before. Perhaps Fleming was influenced by the James Bond character of the films in production at this time—the literary character now has a more easy-going, nonchalant attitude toward life. Whatever the reason, Bond is wonderful in YOU ONLY LIVE TWICE. His sense of humor is not necessarily witty, but is full of pleasant sarcasm. Throughout his adventures with Tiger Tanaka, Bond is constantly throwing out wisecracks about the food they are eating, the customs he is learning, etc. For example, when Tanaka explains there are no swear words in Japan, not even dirty sex words, Bond says,

"Well I'm . . . I mean, well, I'm astonished! A violent people without a violent language! I must write a learned paper on this. No wonder you have nothing left but to commit suicide when you fail an exam, or cut your girl friend's head off when she annoys you."

(YOU ONLY LIVE TWICE, Chapter 9)

Then there is the comment Bond makes to Blofeld, finally revealing his identity to his archenemy. Blofeld has just forced Bond to sit on a throne with a hole in the seat which is positioned over an active geyser; Bond has stood and avoided the geyser's spray in the nick of time:

Bond turned and faced the couple under the clock. He said cheerfully, "Well, Blofeld, you mad bastard. I'll admit that your effects man down below knows his stuff. Now bring on the twelve she-devils, and if they're all as beautiful as Fraulein Bunt, we'll get Noël Coward to put it to music and have it on Broadway by Christmas. How about it?"

(YOU ONLY LIVE TWICE, Chapter 19)

But the most revealing facts about Bond in this novel are in the form of an obituary that M writes for *The Times* when Bond is presumed dead. The obituary, for the first time, sketches out Bond's early life, his schooling, and even gives the only hint to his birthdate.

At the end of the novel, Bond is a new man. He has lost his memory, and Kissy Suzuki talks him into believing he is Taro Todoroki and that he lives with her on Kuro Island. Bond stays with Kissy for many months until he finds a Russian newspaper which jars his memory. Bond takes off for Russia at the novel's end in search of his true identity. But he is unaware that he leaves an heir, which, sadly, is never mentioned again in the series.

Tiger Tanaka is an extremely colorful character and ally. He is immediately likable, and most of the novel's humor is derived from his conversations with Bond. Fleming has created mannerisms and patterns of speech that make Tanaka vivid and believable. He is a "big, square figure," with glittering eyes and long dark lashes that are almost feminine. Tanaka, head of the Japanese Secret Service, hides his headquarters behind a front called the Bureau of All-Asian Folkways, a kind of historical documentation society for the East. Behind closed doors, however, is a Secret Service which seems much more advanced than the British Service. At least the Japanese are in control of Magic 44, the secret deciphering formula which the British need. Tanaka is resourceful, pleasant, but, true to his *samurai* heritage, he can be a very tough character if he chooses.

Kissy Suzuki is a most appealing heroine. Kissy, an Ama girl, has "almond eyes and a rosy-tinted skin on a golden background." She is healthy and strong. Kissy was once chosen to make a film in Hollywood because of her great beauty. There, she learned English and a few Western customs, but she disliked Hollywood and returned home to Kuro Island after the film was completed. She says that the only man she liked in Hollywood was David Niven (who happened to be a friend of Ian Fleming), after whom she named her pet cormorant. Kissy is a little selfish—she wants to keep Bond for herself when she realizes he has lost his memory at the story's end. She plots with the local priest to allow Bond to stay on the island until he wishes to leave on his own accord. And she doesn't reveal to Bond what she knows about his past. Kissy, who apparently loves Bond very much, does finally give in when he wishes to leave at the end. She is intelligent, warm, and a far more interesting woman than many of Fleming's other female characters.

Richard "Dikko" Henderson, who is based on Fleming's true-life Australian friend Richard Hughes, is another amusing character who appears briefly in the book. Henderson, another ally, is always drinking and cursing. When he arrives at Bond's hotel one morning to accompany Bond to Tanaka's headquarters, the first thing Henderson does is order a drink at the bar. Henderson is like a middle-aged prize fighter who has retired and taken to the bottle. He has a craggy, sympathetic face, blue eyes, and a badly broken nose. He is a man who is "always sweating," and who barges his way through a crowd. The conversations the man has with Bond are amusing and informative.

The M/Bond scene in the novel is a classic. M does his best to control his temper, as well as to hide the fact that he's practically given up on Bond. M's bluffing about the assignment covers what he really feels—that the mission actually *is* impossible, and that Bond had better get his act together. When Bond offers his resignation, M explodes:

M did something Bond had never seen him do before. He lifted his right fist and brought it crashing down on the desk. "Who the devil do you think you're talking to? Who the devil d'you think's running this show? God in Heaven! I send for you to give you promotion and the most important job of your career and you talk to me about resignation! Pig-headed young fool!"

Bond was dumbfounded. A great surge of excitement ran through him. What in hell was all this about? He said, "I'm terribly sorry, sir. I thought I'd been letting the side down lately."

"I'll soon tell you when you're letting the side down." M. thumped the desk for a second time, but less hard.

(YOU ONLY LIVE TWICE, Chapter 3)

Throughout the scene, one can sense the tension underneath M's bravado, and the Admiral's concern for Bond. M doesn't want to lose his best agent, or be forced to fire him.

Last but not least are the villains, Ernst Blofeld, aka Dr. Shatterhand, and his "wife," Irma Bunt. Blofeld takes on the role of "the root of all evil" here. The man even admits to Bond that he is mad:

"So was Frederick the Great, so was Nietzsche, so was Van Gogh. We are in good, in illustrious company, Mister Bond. On the other hand, what are you? You are a common thug, a blunt instrument wielded by dolts in high places. Having done what you are told to do, out of some mistaken idea of duty or patriotism, you satisfy your brutish instincts with alcohol, nicotine, and sex while waiting to be dispatched on the next misbegotten foray. Twice before, your chief has sent you to do battle with me, Mister Bond, and by a combination of luck and brute force, you were successful in destroying two projects of my genius. You and your government would categorize these projects as crimes against humanity, and various authorities still seek to bring me to book for them. But try and summon such wits as you possess, Mister Bond, and see them in a realistic light and in the higher realm of my own thinking."

(YOU ONLY LIVE TWICE, Chapter 20)

Blofeld goes on to say that he is providing public services with his projects. For example, his suicide program is only a convenient way for the Japanese to commit suicide in pleasant surroundings. Indeed, the man is mad, and egocentric. Like the other major villains before him, his attitude toward Bond is one of father to son, and he is correcting the son for disagreeing with his omnipotent authority.

□ **HIGHLIGHTS AND OTHER INGREDIENTS**

Besides the M/Bond scene, other highlights include almost everything that happens after Bond arrives on Kuro Island. But one thrilling moment previous to this occurs when Bond discovers the true identity of Dr. Shatterhand. Bond experiences an emotional explosion when he sees Blofeld's photograph:

The superintendent went to the bottom of his file, extracted what looked like a blown-up copy of Doctor Guntram Shatterhand's passport photograph, and handed it over.

Bond took it nonchalantly. Then his whole body stiffened. He said to himself, *God Almighty! God Almighty!* Yes. There was no doubt, no doubt at all! He had grown a drooping black moustache. He had had the syphilitic nose repaired. There was a gold-capped tooth among the upper frontals, but there could be no doubt. Bond looked up. He said, "Have you got one of the woman?"

Startled by the look of controlled venom on Bond's face, and by the pallor that showed through the walnut dye, the superintendent bowed energetically and scrabbled through his file.

Yes, there she was, the bitch—the flat ugly wardress face, the dull eyes, the scraped-back bun of hair.

Bond held the pictures, not looking at them, thinking. Ernst Stavro Blofeld. Irma Bunt. So this was where they had come to hide! And the long strong gut of fate had lassoed him to them! They of all people! He of all people! A taxi-ride down the coast in this remote corner of Japan. Could they smell him coming? Had the dead spy got hold of his name and told them? Unlikely. The power and prestige of Tiger would have protected him. Privacy, discretion, are the heartbeat of Japanese inns. But would they know that an enemy was on his way? That fate had arranged this appointment in Samarra? Bond looked up from the pictures. He was in cold control of himself. This was now a private matter. It had nothing to do with Tiger or Japan. It had nothing to do with MAGIC 44. It was an ancient feud.

(YOU ONLY LIVE TWICE, Chapter 12)

Additionally, all of the sequences in the Garden of Death are eerie, full of frightening imagery. The last third of the book takes on a nightmarish quality that is unusual for Fleming. The final battle with Blofeld is excruciatingly intense. When Bond has Blofeld's throat in his hands and is screaming, "Die, Blofeld, die!" the effect is exhilarating.

And finally, a major highlight is Bond's obituary, which M writes for *The Times*. There is even a brief moment of self-parody within the obit:

The inevitable publicity, particularly in the foreign press, accorded some of these adventures, made him, much against his will, something of a public figure, with the inevitable result that a series of popular books came to be written around him by a personal friend and former colleague of James Bond. If the quality of these books, or their degree of veracity, had been any higher, the author would certainly have been prosecuted under the Official Secrets Act. It is a measure of the disdain in which these fictions are held at the ministry that action has not yet—I emphasize the qualification—been taken against the author and publisher of these high-flown and romanticized caricatures of episodes in the career of an outstanding public servant.

(YOU ONLY LIVE TWICE, Chapter 21)

This paragraph only shows that Fleming's tongue has always been in his cheek. Fleming considered the Bond novels particularly funny himself; although for the most part, they are serious on the surface. The obit also contains the proposed epitaph for James Bond, put forth by Mary Goodnight, which can be applied to Fleming himself: "I shall not waste my days in trying to prolong them. I shall use my time."

YOU ONLY LIVE TWICE is an Ian Fleming masterpiece. It's also an incredibly appropriate final work with its exploration of attitudes toward death and rebirth— Bond comes to terms with death and begins a personal voyage of rediscovery and re-evaluation which should lead to a new James Bond, able to reaffirm the value of life.

THE MAN WITH THE GOLDEN GUN (1965)

The last James Bond novel by Ian Fleming is a major disappointment and is the weakest book in the series. It is not the author's fault. He died before he could revise, polish, and add the rich detail he always incorporated after he had completed the first draft. Glidrose Productions finished the book for him, and released it posthumously in 1965. Likewise, Glidrose cannot be blamed for the weak book; they were obligated to

publish the book because Fleming's fans were entitled to learn what happens to their hero, since YOU ONLY LIVE TWICE ends with a cliffhanger. The series simply couldn't end with James Bond waltzing off to Russia with no idea who he was! But sadly, the novel is extremely sketchy; it lacks detail, suspense, an adequate villain, an adequate girl, and an adequate plot. Only a couple of passages capture the excitement and thrills one expects from the series.

The story opens with James Bond arriving in London after being found in Vladivostock. Bond was brainwashed there, and is now requesting permission to see M. Once alone in the familiar office, 007 attempts to assassinate his chief, but the ever-ready M presses a button on his chair and a bullet-proof glass sheet falls in front of the desk from a slit in the ceiling. After six months of "de-brainwashing," Bond is himself again and ready to tackle his latest assignment. A certain "Pistols" Scaramanga, a freelance assassin under KGB control in Cuba, the Caribbean, and Central America, has been responsible for the deaths of many Secret Service men. Scaramanga is known as The Man With the Golden Gun because he uses a gold-plated Colt .45. Bond is sent to Jamaica to find him and terminate his activities. Through a lead found at the airport, Bond locates Scaramanga at a house of prostitution. There, Bond introduces himself as Mark Hazard, and strikes up a conversation with the killer. Scaramanga is impressed with Hazard, and offers him a job for the weekend as bodyguard at a conference at his hotel. The conference is a hoods' convention. As time goes by, Bond learns that Scaramanga's group is responsible for the recent sugarcane fires which will benefit Castro's regime; that the KGB is involved with the Group; that the Group is planning extensive drug smuggling into America; that they plan to sabotage Jamaica's bauxite industry; and that Bond's identity has been discovered. Later, a gun battle erupts on a train ride after Scaramanga fools Bond into believing that heroine Mary Goodnight is tied to the railroad tracks ahead. But Felix Leiter, who has been hiding on the train, wounds Scaramanga. Bond, Leiter, and Scaramanga jump from the train before it is derailed by an explosion prepared earlier by Leiter. Bond locates Scaramanga lying in a swamp, where they have a final duel.

☐ STYLE AND THEMES

THE MAN WITH THE GOLDEN GUN is a short novel (only sixteen chapters), but each chapter is fairly dense with material. The story begins with a bang: James Bond has been brainwashed by the KGB and sent to assassinate M. After this terrific and unusual opening, the novel reverts to a familiar formula: a dossier on the villain (Scaramanga) is presented; Bond is sent after the adversary; a flashback explains the events which lead Bond to the villain; and Bond finally establishes contact with Scaramanga.

The Fleming Sweep, thankfully, is intact. This is one stylistic element that was inherent in Fleming's first drafts. The novel is never boring; it moves just as quickly as the others. But sometimes it moves too quickly. The opening two chapters, which deal with the assassination attempt on M, are over far too soon. It's almost as if this sequence were tacked on after the main story had been written. The explanation in Chapter 4 that reveals how Bond recovered from his ordeal with psychiatrists and the de-brainwashing procedure is not satisfactory. It might have been far more interesting had the author illustrated the procedure in one or two additional chapters. To say, "after six months Bond was cured," excludes the reader from an important part of the story.

But, the opening assassination attempt does begin the novel explosively; in fact, the book never quite regains this energy level. It is certainly an offbeat opening, and had Fleming been able to flesh it out fully, it might have been one of the best novels of the series.

Several key elements are missing from THE MAN WITH THE GOLDEN GUN—not only the rich detail and descriptions that were always worked into the second draft, but also that distinctive inner voice of the author which permeates the other novels. For once, it doesn't seem as if one is experiencing Fleming's world through Bond, as is usually the case. This time, the narrative voice speaks more often in the third person. Gone is the identification with the character which succeeded in giving Bond the well-rounded traits that had become so familiar. The novel is simply too stiff; it comes off as what it is—a first draft.

Another curious aspect of the novel is its use of cruder language and more violent deaths. Vulgarities are used for the first time in a Fleming novel (e.g., "screwing"), and the descriptions of the shootout on the train are overly gory. One wonders if this is Fleming's writing or Glidrose Productions' embellishments.

Many critics complained that the story contained several reworkings of old devices. For example, The Group (the shareholders) having a weekend conference is a direct steal from the hoods' congress in GOLD-

FINGER. The train sequence, although much more exciting here, is a reworking of the railroad scene in DIAMONDS ARE FOREVER. The plot is too thin: Bond poses as Mark Hazard, who is inspecting the sugar cane fires. Scaramanga is impressed with Hazard's bravado and offers him a job as his bodyguard for the conference. This is unbelievable, considering Scaramanga is the highest paid assassin in the Western Hemisphere—why should he even *need* a bodyguard? And how did he happen to be stupid enough to hire Felix Leiter and Nick Nicholson as hotel managers? There are a few moments in the novel that promise to lead to something original but never pan out. For example, it is revealed that Scaramanga has a third nipple as a distinguishing mark. Nothing is ever made of this. We are also told that Scaramanga is sexually impotent, which is one reason why he releases his frustrations by murdering people. Again, nothing is ever made of this. And finally, the moment in which Bond removes a bullet from Scaramanga's gun promises a tense scene to come, presumably involving a showdown between Bond and Scaramanga. But it never occurs. Scaramanga carelessly fires the empty chamber into the air at the train station. The only result is Bond's amusement at Scaramanga's confusion. This device could have been used more deftly in the actual final showdown between Bond and the villain.

The gambling theme is present again. Bond constantly takes chances throughout the story. He pretends he is someone he's not, and risks being discovered several times. Even when Bond learns that Hendriks and Scaramanga know his true identity, Bond keeps up the gamble and decides to wait and see what happens. He even overhears their plot to kill him on the train ride. But Bond, almost enthusiastically, tags along to discover how they plan to murder him.

Bond was told to get in the back of the car. They set off. Once again that offered neck! Crazy not to take him now! But it was open country with no cover and there were five guns riding behind. The odds simply weren't good enough. What was the plan for his removal? During the "hunting" presumably. James Bond smiled grimly to himself. He was feeling happy. He wouldn't have been able to explain the emotion. It was a feeling of being keyed up, wound taut. It was the moment, after twenty passes, when you got a hand you could bet on—not necessarily win, but bet on. He had been after this man for over six weeks. Today, this morning perhaps, was to come the payoff he had been ordered to bring about. It was win or lose. The odds? Foreknowledge was playing for him.

(THE MAN WITH THE GOLDEN GUN, Chapter 13)

Other gambles include Bond removing the bullet from Scaramanga's gun; his allowing Mary Goodnight to enter his hotel room despite the danger of being discovered; and the blowing of his cover when the train is about to run over the mannequin tied to the railroad tracks (whom he believes to be Mary).

□ CHARACTERS

James Bond is robotlike in this novel. He's simply not the same man as in the previous books. Is this because Fleming was unable to finish the novel, or was it the author's intention to make Bond a "new man" since his ordeal with amnesia and brainwashing? If the latter is the case, the experiment does not work. Bond, in THE MAN WITH THE GOLDEN GUN, has lost the sense of humor he gained in the preceding books; he is colder, more emotionless than he has been of late (it's almost as if he's been thrown back to the Bond of CASINO ROYALE); and he is, in general, simply carrying out the action of the plot with no feelings one way or the other toward his mission. He does, however, have a moment of doubt when he is face to face with Scaramanga at the novel's end. Scaramanga is lying wounded in the swamp, supposedly helpless, as Bond prepares to execute him in cold blood. But Bond has trouble carrying out his assignment. Bond has always had trouble killing in cold blood, and in this instance, the prospect of doing so impedes his reflexes and better judgment. This hesitation proves to be near fatal for Bond.

Another interesting revelation about Bond's character, which hasn't been discussed before, is his feeling toward his Scottish heritage. When the prime minister offers to grant Bond a knighthood, Bond refuses on the grounds that he "is a Scottish peasant, and will always be a Scottish peasant." The image of being Sir James Bond is not attractive to the agent at all. Fleming seems to be going to great pains to emphasize that Bond is only a civil servant doing his duty, and that the glory and glamor of the job is a secondary benefit (or nuisance).

"Pistols" Scaramanga is hardly adequate for a Bond villain. He's a second-rate, smalltime crook who happens to have gotten lucky with his shooting. After making a reputation for himself in the Caribbean as a crackshot assassin, Scaramanga has become a cocky, egotistical hood who thinks he's better than he really is. Scaramanga, in fact, is very low in intelligence. All the other Bond villains are extremely intelligent, if somewhat mad, individuals. A Bond villain with no brains

is no villain at all; hence, Scaramanga is more a henchman, comparable to Oddjob or Wint or Kidd, than an interesting adversary.

A major fault in the novel is that Scaramanga's prowess with a gun is never demonstrated. We are *told* that Scaramanga is a deadly shot. But the only instances in which he uses the gun are to shoot two birds, a defenseless hood during a meeting, and a few animals. From Scaramanga's dossier, one comes to expect some kind of classic gunfight between Bond and the villain, but it never happens. The duel in the swamp is flawed because Scaramanga is lying on his back, wounded. His hidden derringer ploy is too predictable to satisfy the promises the novel makes early on.

Felix Leiter seems to be the same old amiable character. Although there is no traditional drinking scene between Bond and Felix (a disappointing first), the sequences in which the Texan appears are good. As usual, Leiter pops up in the nick of time at the novel's end, clearing the way for Bond to clean up the business at hand. And again, as usual, Leiter is hurt and can't participate in the final battle. Leiter escapes this adventure by breaking his one good leg, and reveals somewhat mixed feelings as he leaves the hospital on crutches. He tells Mary Goodnight:

"Okay, Miss Goodnight. Tell matron to take him off the danger list. And tell him to keep away from me for a week or two. Every time I see him a piece of me gets broken off. I don't fancy myself as The Vanishing Man." Again he raised his only hand in Bond's direction and limped out.

(THE MAN WITH THE GOLDEN GUN, Chapter 15)

But generally, Leiter's appearances provide the usual breath of fresh air.

Mary Goodnight hardly qualifies as a Bond heroine since her appearances in the story are so brief and inconsequential. She has nothing to do with the plot, and seems to have been included as an afterthought. It is nice to know that she still exists, after the building up of her character in the previous two novels. (It's a little odd that she began her role in the series with dark hair and ends it with blond.) But her eagerness to help and her bubbly manner (her only defined characteristics) do add a little brightness to an otherwise stale story.

Some new information about M is revealed in THE MAN WITH THE GOLDEN GUN. It is learned that M is Sir Miles Messervy, for one thing. One curious aspect is the compassion M shows Bond after the foiled assassination attempt. This seems entirely out of character for M and is almost unbelievable. It is more likely that if an agent had just attempted to murder him, the old chief would immediately terminate the agent's employment, as well as press charges. After all, M was ready to fire Bond at the beginning of YOU ONLY LIVE TWICE because the agent had adopted a few bad habits since the death of Tracy. Now, with Bond an ever greater security risk, M is content with de-brainwashing Bond with the help of Sir James Molony, and immediately placing the agent back into the system with a tough assignment. M's reacceptance of Bond is sudden, and like the rest of the assassination sequence, too hurried.

☐ HIGHLIGHTS AND OTHER INGREDIENTS

The meager highlights of THE MAN WITH THE GOLDEN GUN include the assassination sequence simply for its originality and offbeat premise; and the resolution to the previous novel's cliffhanger, which is necessary and interesting.

The train shootout is practically the only other exciting passage. The biggest thrill comes when a "naked, pink body" is seen tied to the railroad tracks in the distance, and Scaramanga announces to the passengers that the woman up ahead is Mary Goodnight. This is pure Fleming, and is the only real shot in the arm in the entire novel. The subsequent gun battle is over very quickly, and the death of Scaramanga is somehow unsatisfying. It's too bad that Fleming's last novel, as published, did not reach the standard the author had set for himself and the series. One can only wonder how differently the book might have turned out if Fleming had lived long enough to finish it properly.

OCTOPUSSY (1966)

OCTOPUSSY is a collection of short stories by Ian Fleming published posthumously in 1966. The original hardcover consisted of two stories, "Octopussy," and "The Living Daylights." The subsequent paperback edition included a third story, "The Property of a Lady," originally written for Sotheby's. All three stories are typical of the Fleming mold, but none of them are as successful as those in FOR YOUR EYES ONLY.

☐ "OCTOPUSSY"

The story concerns James Bond's investigation of Major Dexter Smythe, a fifty-four-year-old retired Serviceman. Bond visits Smythe in Jamaica to question him about his work during World War II. Bond is aware that Smythe has committed a crime, and he gives the man ten minutes to think about confessing. The narrative flashes back to Germany in 1945. Smythe has discovered details of a Nazi treasure hidden on a mountain. Smythe arrests an innocent guide, Hannes Oberhauser, and forces him to lead him up the mountain. Once at the designated spot, Smythe shoots the guide. After a great deal of work, Smythe finds the gold and transports it back to his camp. Years later, Smythe has been able to sell bits of his gold and has become a wealthy man. But his paradise disappears when James Bond comes inquiring. Smythe finally confesses. After Bond leaves, Smythe swims out to visit his pet octopus, whom he has affectionately named "Octopussy." He finds a scorpionfish and wonders if the octopus will eat it. But the fish stings Smythe in the belly. Rather than submit to a courtmartial, he elects to remain in the water until the scorpionfish's poison takes effect.

"Octopussy" is a marginally interesting story concerning the actions of Major Dexter Smythe, whom James Bond entices to commit suicide rather than face life imprisonment for murder and robbery. It contains no real excitement or thrills, and Bond is merely a supporting character in what is basically a morality tale. Bond acts only as a catalyst to force Smythe into remembering the details of his crime, which in a flashback, are the only highlights of the story.

The style here seems more fleshed out than in THE MAN WITH THE GOLDEN GUN; therefore, one may presume that the story was written before the last novel in the series. There is some semblance of the Fleming Sweep—the story manages to move quickly despite the absence of action sequences. The usual rich detail, missing from GOLDEN GUN, is present in "Octopussy," and saves the story from failing totally. The tale's structure relies on the flashback technique of which Fleming was so fond: the story begins with Major Smythe remembering his meeting with Bond earlier that morning (presented in a flashback); a further flashback details the events of Major Smythe's crime.

"Octopussy" is similar to "Quantum of Solace" in that it is a morality tale of sorts. In "Octopussy," Fleming seems to be saying that greed will ultimately bring one misfortune—a minor variation on an age-old theme.

James Bond does not play a major role in "Octopussy," and seems a little out of place. What is Bond doing investigating the twenty-year-old death of a mountain guide? Bond says Oberhauser was his friend, which is why he is interested in the case; but this kind of work seems out of line for a top member of the Double-0 Section. Nothing new is learned about Bond's character. He is very businesslike and official. In fact, the character is viewed objectively from Smythe's point of view as another Service official doing his job.

It is curious that Bond would hint for Smythe to commit suicide. Bond, as learned in YOU ONLY LIVE TWICE, feels that suicide is cowardly. Therefore, what Bond suggests is a contradiction to his beliefs. Perhaps he feels that suicide would be the best thing for a man like Smythe; a lengthy and damaging trial might kill him anyway.

Dexter Smythe is the protagonist of the story, and "Octopussy" is his tale. Smythe is a weak man with big ideas. His mistake is that he truly believed he could get away with the crime he committed. Smythe is not an evil man at all. Stealing gold belonging to Hitler's army might not have seemed a crime to him; the ugly crime, of course, is his murder of the mountain guide Oberhauser.

Octopussy, the affectionately named pet that Smythe feeds daily, could be a symbol of the treasure which is just beyond reach. Smythe teases the animal with a scorpionfish at the story's end, and the octopus grabs Smythe instead of the fish. The treasure has backfired and attacked the hunter, perhaps because this particular treasure should have been left untouched. (Major Smythe's plot to find and steal the Reich's gold also backfired—the "Devil" came to collect Smythe's dues years later.)

The flashback sequence on the mountain is the only real highlight of the story, and the murder of Oberhauser comes as a surprise. But otherwise, "Octopussy" is a limp fish.

□ **"THE LIVING DAYLIGHTS"**

In this story, Bond is assigned to cover the escape of a British agent from East Berlin by assassinating a Russian executioner named Trigger before the killer can shoot the British agent. Bond stations himself in a building overlooking the no-man's land between East and West, armed with a .308 caliber Winchester rifle. Trigger will presumably attempt to fire at the British agent from the opposite building. While watching the street, Bond is struck by the beauty of a blond girl carrying a cello case. Finally, on the third evening, the British agent appears on the street. Bond takes aim at the window from which Trigger's gun is now pointing. As the agent runs, Trigger leans out of the window to shoot. The executioner is none other than the blond cellist. After a second's hesitation, Bond fires, wounding Trigger rather than killing her. The British agent makes it across to safety.

"The Living Daylights" is by far the best story in the collection, and is similar to the short stories of FOR YOUR EYES ONLY in that it has a good plot, plenty of action, good characterizations, and Fleming's choice stylistic elements.

The plot is straightforward. The Fleming Sweep takes the reader through the tale at a quick pace; it is compressed and intensely written. The usual rich detail abounds: descriptions of the shooting range at the story's opening, sights of Berlin, and the assassination attempt are vivid. The story is further enhanced by a surprise ending.

Thematically, the story deals with the dirty side of Bond's profession. Bond has never liked killing as an assignment; but do his duty he must. Bond questions the morality of the job at one point. Captain Sender, the Serviceman in West Berlin, gives Bond a bit of trouble:

Bond narrowly averted a row with Captain Sender because, that evening, Bond took a stiff drink of the whiskey before he donned the hideous cowl that now stank of his sweat. Captain Sender had tried to prevent him, and when he failed, had threatened to call up Head of Station and report Bond for breaking training.

"Look, my friend," said Bond wearily, "I've got to commit a murder tonight. Not you. Me. So be a good chap and stuff it, will you? You can tell Tanqueray anything you like when it's over. Think I like this job? Having a Double-0 number and so on? I'd be quite happy for you to get me sacked from the Double-0 Section. Then I could settle down and make a snug nest of papers as an ordinary staffer. Right?" Bond drank down his whiskey, reached for his thriller—now arriving at an appalling climax—and threw himself on the bed.

("The Living Daylights," OCTOPUSSY)

Bond's attitude is what makes the story interesting and involving. Of course, Bond really doesn't believe what he is saying. He would go crazy in a soft desk job. But this passage reveals that even Bond can succumb to feelings of distaste for his particular line of work.

The agent is at his toughest in this story. He is hard,

determined, and intent on accomplishing the job, whether he likes it or not. Nevertheless, his weakness for women almost causes him to fail. Throughout the three days of waiting for the moment of execution, Bond watches, from a distance, a pretty blond who plays with a women's orchestra on the other side of the border. When this blond is revealed to be Trigger, the Russian hit woman, Bond hesitates before shooting his rifle. When Sender chastises Bond for only wounding Trigger, Bond shrugs it off, saying, "Okay. With any luck it will cost me my Double-0 number." At this point, Bond doesn't care. Complacency is a new trait for James Bond!

The story also reveals M's attitude toward this kind of work. Whenever M sends Bond on a nasty assignment such as the execution of someone, he hardens and is brusque with Bond:

The clear blue eyes remained cold as ice. But Bond knew that they remained so only with an effort of will. M didn't like sending any man to a killing. But, when it had to be done, he always put on this fierce, cold act of command. Bond knew why. It was to take some of the pressure, some of the guilt, off the killer's shoulders.

("The Living Daylights," OCTOPUSSY)

Highlights of the story include the Bond/M scene and the actual shooting sequence. The story builds to a tense climax as the third night of watching for Agent Number 272 approaches. The surprise ending, when Trigger is revealed as the blond cellist, is a nice twist. All in all, "The Living Daylights" equals most of Fleming's better works.

□ "THE PROPERTY OF A LADY"

In this story, a double agent working for the KGB, Maria Freudenstein, has been planted in the heart of the British Secret Service. The Service is aware of her double agent status, and has been giving her false information to pass on to the Russians for the past three years. Now, however, it seems that the famous Russian jeweler Fabergé once made a valuable emerald sphere for Freudenstein's grandfather, and the jewel has just been sent to her from Russia. M informs Bond that Freudenstein is soon holding an auction at Sotheby's. He suspects that the Russians are paying Freudenstein for a job well done by sending the artifact and allowing her to auction it at a high price. Bond suggests that the Russians may have a plant at the

auction to bid up the price so that Freudenstein can sell the piece for the maximum amount. It's also very possible that this plant could be the resident director of KGB operations in London—the identity of whom the Service has been after for quite some time. Bond proposes to attend the auction and attempt to identify this person so that an arrest can be made. As the bidding begins, Bond watches the auctioneer carefully, attempting to determine the identity of the unseen bidder. Someone keeps pushing up the bid, until it finally exceeds 150,000 pounds. When Bond's contact at Sotheby's bids a maximum 155,000 pounds, Bond notices a man in the back of the room removing his dark glasses—which must be a signal to the auctioneer that the bidder is finished. Bond follows the man from the room and tails his car, not surprisingly, to the Soviet Embassy. His hunch, then, was correct.

The addition of "The Property of a Lady" to OCTOPUSSY seems to have been an afterthought. It is hardly worth the effort, for this story is perhaps the weakest one Fleming ever wrote. Written in 1963, the suspenseless plot is resolved with little effort on Bond's part.

The premise of the story is rather farfetched. For three years, a double agent named Maria Freudenstein has been fed false information by the British to pass on to the Russians; only a handful of people in the Service know this fact. It seems that if Freudenstein had been working on the inside of the service for three years, she would have picked up reliable information on her own—unless, of course, she's extraordinarily stupid.

The story does manage to move quickly, but spends unnecessary time explaining auction methods and the history of rare jewelry. There is absolutely no suspense in the story, and the mystery of the identity of the resident director from the KGB is solved so quickly and easily that there is no climax in the narrative.

Nothing new is learned about James Bond. The story opens with Bond in a foul mood, doing routine office paperwork, and basically complaining of that familiar malaise: boredom. If "The Property of a Lady" is an example of one of Bond's routine assignments, Bond must lead a dull life indeed when he's not pursuing someone like Ernst Blofeld or Auric Goldfinger (which only occurs once a year in a major novel).

M shows that he, too, is susceptible to the fear of boredom. When Bond is summoned to M's office, he unexpectedly finds M with a stranger, a Dr. Fanshawe, who is an expert on jewelry.

Bond wished that M. had given him some kind of a brief, hadn't got this puckish, rather childishly malign desire to surprise—to spring the jack-in-the-box on his staff. But Bond, remembering his own boredom of ten minutes ago, and putting himself in M's place, had the intuition to realize that M. himself might have been subject to the same June heat, the same oppressive vacuum in his duties, and, faced by the unexpected relief of an emergency, a small one perhaps, had decided to extract the maximum effect, the maximum drama, out of it to relieve his own tedium.

("The Property of a Lady," OCTOPUSSY)

The story picks up a little once Bond arrives at the auction, but the entire incident is over so quickly it is hardly worth one's time. Of course, one must remember that "The Property of a Lady" was originally commissioned by Sotheby's to be included in their publication, *The Ivory Hammer: The Year at Sotheby's.* Perhaps this explains its thinness.

As a whole, OCTOPUSSY is not a grand finale to the Fleming Bond saga. It's too bad that his *oeuvre* ends with the two weakest books in the series. But, as Glidrose Productions probably assumed, weak Fleming is better than no Fleming.

The James Bond saga entered a hiatus after OCTOPUSSY was published in 1966. It was not until 1968 that Kingsley Amis (under the pseudonym Robert Markham), took the reins and resurrected Bond from literary inactivity.

THE NON-FLEMING NOVELS: COLONEL SUN (1968)

COLONEL SUN, by Robert Markham (Kingsley Amis), continues the Bond saga and is a worthy successor to the Ian Fleming novels. It is not totally faithful to the Fleming books, but it would be foolish to expect a new author to mirror Fleming's style completely. It is important, however, to maintain the continuity of Bond's character and the events that have a direct bearing on Bond's life. COLONEL SUN achieves this. Despite a slow middle and an overly complicated plot, COLONEL SUN contains several exciting passages, good characterizations, and the rich detail that typify Fleming's work.

The story concerns Bond's attempts to rescue M, who has been kidnapped by Red Chinese forces belonging to one Colonel Sun Liang-tan. Colonel Sun hopes to lure Bond into his clutches so that both the famous agent and his chief can be killed. An important Russian summit conference is scheduled to take place in Greece; Sun plans to bomb the conference with a mortar gun and leave the two Englishmen's bodies at the site to implicate their guilt in the crime. 007 teams up with Russian agent Ariadne Alexandrou and her Greek friend, Niko Litsas, to combat Colonel Sun and his henchman, an ex-Nazi named Von Richter. The allies are eventually captured by the villains; Bond is severely tortured but is saved by a prostitute staying with Sun. The girl's intervention gives 007 the advantage over his enemies, and he and his confederates overcome Sun and succeed in rescuing M.

□ STYLE AND THEMES

COLONEL SUN begins and ends with explosive events. The main problem with the book is the middle, which is slow-moving and sometimes a little boring. At the beginning of the story, M is kidnapped by terrorists working for Red China; the Hammonds, who take care of M and his home, Quarterdeck, are murdered.

This is one of the most frightening and suspenseful openings to any of the James Bond books. Finding M in a helpless state—drugged and immobile—is a very disturbing image and it stamps the novel with a dark, foreboding mood which persists throughout the story. COLONEL SUN is the most violent, the sexiest, and one of the most unsettling of all the Bond books. The climax is extremely bloody, and James Bond undergoes perhaps the worst torture he has ever experienced.

One of the problems with COLONEL SUN is the lack of the Fleming Sweep. This is the one stylistic element which Amis has failed to duplicate in the series. The book is sometimes tedious, and this is not helped by the fact that the author has used an extremely complicated political plot. It is a lengthy book, and each chapter is dense with information and detail. Although there are a few tense passages in the middle of the book (the gun battle in the streets of Greece before Ariadne takes Bond to meet Litsas; the sea battle in which Bond sinks the enemy ship), the slow overall pace of the novel is a flaw.

Amis manages to create an adequate semblance of Fleming's penchant for rich detail, eloquently describing locations, characters, and events. He is also much more daring than Fleming in chronicling the sex act:

Within seconds they stood flesh to flesh. She shuddered briefly and moaned; her arms tightened round his neck, her loins thrust against his and he felt the strength of her as well as the softness. As if they had become one creature with a single will, the two bodies sank to the bed. No preliminaries were needed. The man and the woman were joined immediately, with almost savage exultation. She leapt and strained in his grip, her movements as violent as his. The pace was too hot for their strivings to be prolonged. Their voices blended in the cry of joy that sounds so oddly akin to the inarticulate language of despair.

(COLONEL SUN, Chapter 8)

Though tame by today's standards, this is more explicit than anything Fleming wrote.

COLONEL SUN marks James Bond's first important involvement with politics. It is also Bond's first encounter with the Red Chinese as adversaries. A strong theme in the novel is that of keeping the peace between nations, especially Britain and Russia. Until Bond realizes that his adversaries are the Chinese, he of course believes them to be Russian. It seems that Amis is making a point that the Russians are no longer enemies of the British Empire as they were portrayed in the earlier Fleming novels. The ending of the story is ironic, as a Russian official thanks and offers James Bond a medal for defending Russia. Amis is extremely successful in maintaining the tension between the Russian official and Bond. Although nothing is said of Bond's past encounters with the Soviet government, there is a definite subtext underlying their conversation. The Russian chooses his words carefully, not quite apologizing for his government's treatment of Bond in the past, but rather approving the valiant efforts Bond has made on their behalf. Even M agrees that it was appropriate for the British Secret Service, this time, to help Russia in a common fight against Red China.

Another theme of the novel deals with Bond's permanent tie to his profession. The last few lines of the book present the two spies from opposite sides, Bond and Ariadne, reaching for each other's companionship; but deep down they both know a union would be impossible:

Bond said, "Come to London with me, Ariadne. Just for a little while. I know they'll give you leave."

"I want to come with you, just as you don't want to go. But I can't. I knew you'd ask me and I was all set to say yes. Then I saw it somehow wouldn't be right. . . . I'm still stuck with my middle-class respectability. Does that sound silly?"

"No. But it makes me feel sad."

"Me too. It all comes from our job. People think it must be wonderful and free and everything. But we're not free, are we?"

"No," said Bond again. "We're prisoners. But let's enjoy our captivity when we can."

(COLONEL SUN, Chapter 21)

What Bond means is that he and Ariadne are both prisoners of their professions. In a way, this is a flashback to the same feeling Fleming brought to the end of MOONRAKER with the allusion to James Bond as a "man without a silhouette." Bond is trapped in his profession—there will never be an escape. This was underscored with the deaths of Vesper Lynd and Tracy di Vicenzo, the only women he admitted truly loving, as well as by his devotion to rescuing M from his abductors in COLONEL SUN.

Finally, the other strong theme in the novel is that of revenge. James Bond is intent on avenging the deaths of the Hammonds and the kidnapping of M. Bond is particularly brutal in achieving his goal:

Bond just had time to notice the deep parallel scratches on the gunman's left cheek before Litsas grabbed him and clapped a large hand over his mouth. Bond stepped forward and looked into the dilated eyes. "This is for the Hammonds," he hissed, and drove the knife in. De Graaf's body gave one great throe, as if he had touched a live terminal, then went totally limp.

(COLONEL SUN, Chapter 20)

The revenge is very satisfying. This is Bond at his toughest. Amis has not forgotten that Bond is primarily an executioner—a prime element in the make-up of his character.

□ CHARACTERS

Luckily, Amis has not tampered with the character of Bond. He is the same darkly handsome man first introduced in CASINO ROYALE. At the book's opening, Bond is troubled by the familiar malaise—boredom and complacency. The agent also seems to be much more hardened since YOU ONLY LIVE TWICE. It's almost as if Amis has brought back the humorless Bond of the early novels. Perhaps the agent has built new walls around himself since his traumatic ordeals of the past five years. The death of Tracy; the fight with Blofeld in Japan; the loss of memory and subsequent year of living with Kissy Suzuki; the brainwashing ordeal in Russia; the assassination attempt on M; and the fight against death after Scaramanga's poison-tipped bullet almost eliminated the agent forever—all have had a toll on Bond. He is in a new cycle of his life. Now it's only the job that matters. He is as grim and determined as before, but with a renewed strength. This is illustrated in the scene at Colonel Sun's house in which Bond sees M for the first time in weeks. When his chief orders Bond to leave him behind if there is a chance for the agent to escape, Bond flatly refuses. Bond's loyalty to his job and chief are stronger than ever in COLONEL SUN.

Ariadne Alexandrou is a very appealing heroine and a creation of whom Fleming would be proud. She is beautiful—a Greek, but unlike the "overrated, beaky, 'classical' look one associates with old coins." She has skin with soft tints of tan and white and olive and rose. Her eyes are tan-colored, and she has "tobacco-blonde hair." Ariadne is tough, intelligent, and resourceful. In many ways, she is superior to most Fleming heroines in that she has strong beliefs and ideals for which she is fighting. She is extremely independent (a common Bond-heroine trait), and can hold her own in a fight. Bond is impressed by her ability to knock down a thug twice her size, as well as by her sexual magnetism.

Colonel Sun Liang-tan is a cruel, methodical villain, and very worthy of inclusion in the Bond saga. He is tall for a Chinese (nearly six foot) and is big-boned and long-headed. His skin color is the usual flat light yellow, his hair is blue-black and dead straight, and the "epicanthic eye-fold is notably conspicuous." One immediately compares him with Dr. No, not only because of the doctor's half-Chinese origin, but also because of his manner of speech and the control with which he holds himself. His methods and philosophies of torture, presented in the obligatory lecture scene, reveal Sun's demoniacal inclinations:

"In the divine Marquis de Sade's great work *Justine* there's a character who says to his victim: 'Heaven has decreed that it is your part to endure these sufferings, just as it is my part to inflict them.' That's the kind of relationship you and I are entering into, James. . . ."

"You must understand that I'm not the slightest bit interested in studying resistance to pain or any such pseudo-scientific claptrap. I just want to torture people. But—this is the point—not for any selfish reason, unless you call a saint or a martyr selfish. As de Sade explains in *The Philosopher in the Boudoir,* through cruelty one rises to heights of superhuman awareness, of sensitivity to new modes of being, that can't be attained by any other method. And the victim—you too, James, will be spiritually illuminated in the way so many Christian authorities describe as uplifting to the soul: through suffering. Side by side you and I will explore the heights."

(COLONEL SUN, Chapter 19)

Sun's words are chilling, and the subsequent torture Bond undergoes is excruciating for the reader as well as for the hero. Sun proceeds to probe the orifices of Bond's head with extremely thin wires which reach into his brain. Sun's words reveal the sick mind of the villain, and this impression is further refined at the end when Bond corners the wounded madman. Prepared to die at the hands of Bond, Sun welcomes his angel of death and pathetically attempts to apologize for the cruel treatment he has visited upon Bond. Also chilling is his use of "James" instead of the usual "Mister Bond." Sun's "Goodbye, James," as Bond plunges a knife into his heart, is the final plea for absolution.

Niko Litsas is an admirable Bond ally along the lines of Darko Kerim and Colombo. In his mid-forties, Litsas is a World War II hero and an excellent sailor. He is tanned a rich brown after years of sun and salt air, and is remarkably handsome. Bond puts him down as a loyal friend and a totally implacable and ruthless enemy. He "trusts him on sight." His obvious similarities to Kerim and Colombo prevent him from becoming an outstanding Bond ally, but he is certainly more interesting than the Felix Leiter of THE MAN WITH THE GOLDEN GUN. Litsas shows tremendous bravery and fortitude throughout the story, and his character is an integral part of the plot.

A different side of M is revealed in COLONEL SUN. The opening scene presents a catatonic, zombielike Admiral, a condition which frightens Bond and intensifies his determination to rescue his chief. M, for the first time, is seen in a helpless, defenseless state. He is reduced to dealing with violence on the same level as Bond. The image of the great Admiral for whom Bond holds "his deepest respect" in such a state cannot help but evoke an emotional response from the reader.

☐ HIGHLIGHTS AND OTHER INGREDIENTS

Among the outstanding moments in the novel one must include the Quarterdeck scene at the opening. It is explosive, highly dramatic, and immediately sets the book's peculiar, foreboding tone. The action scenes in the first half of the book are somewhat flawed by the fact that the plot, which is extremely complicated and sometimes confusing, has not yet been fully explained. For example, it is sometimes difficult to tell the two different houses on the islet apart, as well as distinguish who inhabits which house. It may have been a mistake on Amis' part not to reveal the implications of the Russians' summit conference until very late in the book.

Once Bond is captured by Colonel Sun, the book never lets up in excitement. The torture scene is particularly unsettling, and the subsequent fight with Sun and his men is bloody and violent in a way Fleming never attempted to picture.

Despite the slow patches, COLONEL SUN is a worthy successor to the Fleming *oeuvre*. It is too bad Kingsley Amis was not interested in continuing the series. COLONEL SUN would be the last James Bond novel for another thirteen years. Weak in the middle but terrific at both ends, COLONEL SUN is just as important to the Bond saga as the Fleming books, and should not be ignored by the serious Bond reader.

THE JOHN GARDNER BOOKS

The summer of 1981 was significant for James Bond fans: the first in a new series of novels was published. British mystery writer John Gardner was approached by Glidrose to resurrect Bond from literary limbo, and the result was LICENSE RENEWED. This was followed by FOR SPECIAL SERVICES (1982), and ICEBREAKER (1983). Gardner has since been signed to write additional 007 novels.

The books are controversial among Bond fans in that they make many changes in Bond's world. Gardner's writing style is dissimilar to Fleming's, and Gardner/Glidrose have elected to update Bond's environment; basically, the character has been picked up and placed unchanged in the eighties. This change may be disconcerting to some fans who desire a continuity with the Fleming series. In 1981, the "real" James Bond would be in his late fifties; the Bond of the Gardner novels is still fairly young—perhaps in his forties (there is a little grey showing in his black hair). Another striking stylistic element of the books is that they resemble the film scripts more than the original Fleming novels. Gadgets abound in the books, and LICENSE RENEWED especially borrows ingredients from the film versions of GOLDFINGER, THUNDERBALL, and ON HER MAJESTY'S SECRET SERVICE. But, despite these disconcerting changes, all three Gardner efforts are fast reading, slick, and entertaining.

LICENSE RENEWED concerns James Bond's investigation of Anton Murik, the Laird of Murcaldy. Murik was a top nuclear scientist who had developed plans for a "perfectly safe" nuclear reactor. But his col-

leagues at the International Atomic Energy Research Commission would not approve his plan; Murik resigned and began making plans to hire terrorists to infiltrate six major nuclear plants around the world in order to cause meltdowns unless he is allowed to build his own reactor.

FOR SPECIAL SERVICES, the most engaging of the three books, involves a new SPECTRE organization controlled by an offspring of Ernst Stavro Blofeld. Clues have pointed to a wealthy Texan named Markus Bismaquer, an entrepreneur working out of a huge ranch. Bond teams up with Cedar Leiter, daughter of his friend Felix, and together they uncover SPECTRE's plot to drug the personnel of NORAD headquarters in Colorado with specially prepared ice cream. Once the personnel are at the mercy of SPECTRE, a disguised team of military personnel will infiltrate the headquarters and steal the computer tapes controlling the Space Wolves, the new laser-equipped satellites which can monopolize the arms race.

ICEBREAKER, the weakest of the trio of novels, concerns Bond's attempts to destroy a terrorist organization called the National Socialist Action Army (NSAA), whose objective is to rid the world of communism. The NSAA is revealed to be an extreme fascist group controlled by ex-Nazi Count Konrad von Glöda. In Finland, Bond teams up with KGB agent Kolya Mosolov, CIA agent Brad Tirpitz, and an agent from the Mossad of Israel, the beautiful Rivke Ingber. After a series of mistaken-identity situations, Bond and a girlfriend working for Finnish Intelligence, Paula Vacker, thwart von Glöda's plans to recreate the Third Reich.

□ STYLE AND THEMES

The obvious element missing from Gardner's writing is Fleming's journalistic flair for detail. Gardner *is* descriptive—he takes pains to describe foods, gadgets, locales—but his writing is simply not as colorful as that of Fleming. It doesn't have that distinctive elite tone—the original author's inner voice—which heightened the early novels. Gardner seems to be injecting detail into the story simply because it is expected in a James Bond novel. Whereas Fleming managed to weave technical and descriptive detail into his tales with exceptional believability, the "Gardner Effect" only calls attention to itself.

There is a semblance of a "sweep," however. The books undeniably move very quickly and generate a fair amount of suspense. Gardner is no amateur. He manages to manipulate and involve the reader in the story, and he uses a plot structure similar to Fleming's in order to do so. But in a way, the novels move *too* quickly. They can be read easily and digested without much thought. The Gardner books might be termed "fast-food" James Bond. As an analogy, if Fleming's works were savored at Sardi's, then Gardner's efforts would be munched at McDonald's.

LICENSE RENEWED has plotline problems mainly because they ring too familiar with readers who have seen many of the James Bond films. Listed below are instances in the book which correspond to similar moments in the films:

1. Bond assumes a cover to infiltrate Murik's castle. The door to Bond's room locks automatically from the outside. (*On Her Majesty's Secret Service*—the film *and* the novel.)

2. Bond spies on Murik's castle at night and is discovered by the guards; this is followed by a car chase, and Bond is eventually captured. (*Goldfinger.*)

3. Murik plans to blackmail Western governments with a nuclear threat. (*Thunderball.*)

4. Caber, Murik's henchman, is ejected from an airplane via an airlock. (*Goldfinger.*)

5. There is a street festival in Perpignan, creating a crowd in which Bond can hide from Murik's guards. (*Thunderball.*)

6. Murik claims he is the heir to the Murcaldy clan. (*On Her Majesty's Secret Service.*)

7. Murik has an evil mistress who attempts to seduce Bond. (*Thunderball.*)

The novel is also heavily inspired by the plot of the film *The China Syndrome*. Bond even remembers the title of this Jane Fonda vehicle when he learns of Murik's plot to cause meltdowns in nuclear power plants around the world.

On the other hand, FOR SPECIAL SERVICES has a good, if implausible, story. The Space Wolf satellites of which SPECTRE is attempting to gain control, Gardner claims, actually *exist* even though no government will admit the fact. The Space Wolves are laser-equipped and can be launched into orbit at a moment's notice when unidentified objects fly into friendly air space. When the object is deemed harmless, the Space Wolves can be recalled to base. These machines sound like they're from a James Bond *film,* but somehow Gard-

ner makes the notion acceptable. In 1961, THUNDERBALL seemed far-fetched. Today, the plot of that novel is quite credible.

Of course, the most interesting aspect of FOR SPECIAL SERVICES is the fact that the new leader of SPECTRE is named Blofeld. The true identity of this person is not revealed until the novel's end, but it doesn't take much intelligence to see through the ploy and determine early in the story that Blofeld is a woman. She is, in fact, the daughter of Ernst Blofeld, and possesses the same perverse qualities which characterized her father. Because Blofeld Sr. murdered Bond's wife, the mere name of the villain painfully jars Bond's memory. The reader is sympathetic to 007's feelings here, and this helps make the Bond character more human than he is in LICENSE RENEWED or ICEBREAKER. That's a secret to the appeal of the earlier novels—Fleming made James Bond believable as a man, as opposed to an indestructible superman.

Another successful element in FOR SPECIAL SERVICES is its irony. For instance, Bond goes to bed with Blofeld's daughter before he learns her true identity. In fact, he is quite taken with her. When he learns the truth, the shock leaves him speechless. Had Nena Blofeld acted a little quicker, she might have been able to destroy Bond in his moment of frozen horror.

ICEBREAKER contains enough ingredients for a potentially good Bond adventure: new and exciting locations, a plot involving a new terrorist group with political objectives, and plenty of action scenes. But unfortunately, the novel is weak because the Bond formula is so obviously recognizable in the structure. In addition, the plot advances in spite of Bond—nothing he does in the book has much effect on the outcome of most of the story. The character isn't even involved in the final battle—it is the Russian army that attacks von Glöda's Ice Palace. Because 007's actions seem peripheral to the story, ICEBREAKER's plot development becomes forced and mechanical; the events all begin to seem ridiculously contrived. There are so many instances of mistaken identity it verges on the absurd. For example:

1. At the beginning of the story Paula Vacker is simply an old girlfriend of Bond's. Suddenly she is a Nazi and works for Konrad von Glöda. In a moment of convenience (plotwise), she is revealed to be in reality a SUPO agent doubling *against* von Glöda.

2. Konrad von Glöda is really Aarne Tudeer, a wanted Nazi official.

3. Rivke Ingber is in reality Anni Tudeer, the daughter of von Glöda. She masquerades through the novel as a Mossad agent working against her father; but in the end it is revealed that she is in cahoots with the former Nazi.

4. Kolya Mosolov is supposedly on Bond's side, but in reality he is working with von Glöda in an attempt to trap Bond inside Russia. After this is accomplished, Kolya doublecrosses von Glöda and turns against him.

5. Brad Tirpitz of the CIA suddenly becomes Hans Buchtman, von Glöda's right-hand man. But in a convenient *deus ex machina*, Buchtman turns out to be CIA agent Brad Tirpitz after all!

Throughout the story, Bond is bombarded by these sudden, unrealistic changes of identity and dramatic objectives; as a result, 007 is kept confused and bewildered as he is bounced from plot device to plot device. These devices are finally so implausible that the story loses any suspense that may have been created.

Probably the weakest element of ICEBREAKER is its lack of character development, not only of all the supporting characters, but of Bond as well. Gardner has made the super sleuth a cardboard character. The reason for the implausibility of the many shifts in supporting character identities is the fact that the reader is unable to grasp who these people are *before* the deception occurs. Gardner never gives the characters in ICEBREAKER a chance to make a first impression.

Thematically, the novels hold nothing new. There is a moment when Bond reminds himself of his job's political implications:

In the old blood-and-thunder novels of his adolescence, Bond had read time and again of mad professors, or masterminds, whose aim was to dominate the world. At the time, the young Bond had wondered what the mad, or bad, villains would do with the world once it was in their power. Now he knew. SPECTRE, and other organizations like it—with close links to Russia and the Communist ideology—were dedicated to placing all mankind slowly under the heel of a society dominated by the state: a state which controlled the individual's every action and thought, down to what kind of music could be heard and what books read.

In crushing SPECTRE, James Bond would be striking a blow for true democracy—not the wishy-washy, half-hearted ideals that, of late, seemed to permeate the West.

(FOR SPECIAL SERVICES, Chapter 8)

So the ever-unchanging mission of James Bond is to act as St. George against the Dragon, no matter what disguise the animal may don. It's an age-old theme, but one that works.

☐ CHARACTERS

The eighties have brought a few changes in James Bond's possessions. He no longer drives the beloved Mark II Continental Bentley. He now sports a Saab 900 Turbo, complete with accessories from Q Branch. These accessories are not totally revealed in the first Gardner effort—each successive novel uncovers more of the Saab's secrets. Bond also owns, in addition to his flat off King's Road, a small country retreat some five miles out of Haslemere. He still uses Guerlain's Imperial Cologne and dresses in white Sea Island cotton shirts and navy slacks. And Bond basically looks the same:

. . . the bronzed good-looking face, with rather long dark eyebrows above the wide, level blue eyes; the three-inch scar which just showed down his right cheek; the long, very straight nose, and the fine, though cruel, mouth. Minute flecks of gray had just started to show in the dark hair, which still retained its boyish black comma above the right eye. As yet, no plumpness had appeared around the jowls, and the line of the jaw was as straight and firm as ever.

(LICENSE RENEWED, Chapter 2)

But there have been changes in the Service since the sixties. The Double-O Section has been abolished, but M still insists on calling Bond "007." M tells him:

"As far as I'm concerned, 007, you will remain 007. I shall take full responsibility for you, and you will, as ever, accept orders and assignments only from me. There are moments when this country needs a troubleshooter—a blunt instrument—and by heaven it's going to have one. They can issue their pieces of bumf and abolish the Double-0 section. We can simply change its name. It will now be the Special Section, and *you* are it. Understand, 007?"

(LICENSE RENEWED, Chapter 2)

To keep up with the times, Bond is watching his health more than usual. He continues his morning habit of pushups, as well as a rigorous workout of leg-raising, arm-flexing, and breathing exercises. He takes a refresher course on combat and silent kills once a month, and practices shooting weekly at the electronic range below Regent Park's headquarters. He has curtailed his alcohol intake, and arranged for Morlands of Grosvenor Street to create a special cigarette with a tar content slightly lower than any currently available on the market. In FOR SPECIAL SERVICES, Bond changes brands: his cigarettes are made especially for him by H. Simmons of Burlington Arcade, which is the earliest known cigarette manufacturer in London. He still carries the cigarettes, each with the distinctive gold bands, in his gunmetal case kept in his breast pocket.

In LICENSE RENEWED, Bond uses a Browning 9mm rather than the old Walther PPK. In addition, he secretly keeps an unauthorized Ruger Super Blackhawk .44 Magnum in a secret compartment in his Saab. The handgun is changed in FOR SPECIAL SERVICES to a Heckler & Koch VP70, a weapon which both M and Major Boothroyd insist will be carried by all officers in the Service. In ICEBREAKER, the model is changed again:

After some argument, mainly from Bond, the Armourer had agreed on Heckler & Koch's P7, "squeeze cocking" 9mm automatic in preference to the rather cumbersome VP70, with its long "double-action" pull for each single shot. The weapon was lighter and more like his old beloved Walther PPK, now banned by the Security Services.

(ICEBREAKER, Chapter 6)

The past continues to haunt Bond, and this is an aspect Gardner should emphasize more strongly, as it gives the agent realistic human qualities. When Q'ute, the girl from the Armoury, asks Bond about the white scar on his right hand, Bond becomes cold:

Bond glanced up sharply, his eyes suddenly losing their humor and turning to ice in a way that almost frightened Q'ute. "Someone tried to be clever a long time ago," he said slowly. In the back of his mind he remembered quite clearly all the circumstances which had led to the plastic surgery, that showed now only as a white blemish, after the Cyrillic letter *Ш*—standing for SH—had been carved into the back of his hand in an attempt by SMERSH to brand him as a spy. It was long ago, and very far away now, but clear as yesterday. He detected the break he had made in Q'ute's guard with his sharp cruelty. So long ago, he thought—the business with Le Chiffre at Royale-lex-Eaux, and a woman called Vesper—about the same age as this girl sitting on the workbench, showing off her shapely knees and calves—lying dead from an overdose, her body under the sheets like a stone effigy in a tomb.

The coldness in Bond's mien faded. He smiled at Q'ute, again looking down at his hand. "A small accident—carelessness on my part. Needed a bit of surgery, that's all."

(LICENSE RENEWED, Chapter 5)

Moments like these are a pleasure in the Gardner books, for they link the novels with Fleming's series. They serve to remind the reader that they are part of the same saga, even though times have changed and Bond is basically not much older than when he last appeared.

FOR SPECIAL SERVICES is most successful in humanizing Bond because the plotline involves memories of Blofeld and the murder of Tracy. Early in the story, Bond lies in bed with the sleeping Q'ute but daydreams about his dead wife.

Gardner regresses in ICEBREAKER, however. James Bond in this story never uses his wits or intelligence to solve anything. He walks blindly into traps and is fooled over and over again by false identities. The most unbelievable action on Bond's part is allowing Kolya Mosolov to lead him into Russia when 007 knows that the entire operation is a trap. He walks conveniently into the NSAA's arms as a result. Fleming's James Bond would have had better sense.

The villains are an interesting bunch. LICENSE RENEWED's Anton Murik is a typical Flemingesque villain, similar to Auric Goldfinger or Hugo Drax. He's a civilized, brilliant scientist who walks with the stride of a "Scottish chieftain." As usual, Murik is obsessed with proving his genius to the rest of the world, and it is soon clear that he is another megalomaniac out to demonstrate his superiority over the underlings on the globe. He is untrustworthy, even to his own men—he hires 007 to assassinate Franco, the man Murik used to train and organize the terrorists taking control of the power plants around the world. He even plans to kill his own ward, heroine Lavender Peacock, to prevent the girl from becoming the rightful heir to the Murcaldy title. Nena Bismaquer (later revealed to be Nena Blofeld) of FOR SPECIAL SERVICES is the most successful villain Gardner has created. She is a beautiful woman whose face gives a hint of sensuality Bond finds "more than engaging." But her eyes give her away: they burn with a hatred which Bond recognizes later as the same evil that lay in the black eyes of Ernst Stavro Blofeld. Nena Blofeld succeeds where many villains have failed, and that is to seduce Bond into trusting her completely. Bond makes love to her and he is completely taken off guard by the surprise revelation of her identity. There is another peculiarity which fits the perverse Blofeld mold: Nena has only one breast. The other is flat, like a boy's. ICEBREAKER's Konrad von Glöda, alias Aarne Tudeer, is an elderly but statuesque ex-Nazi official who is the leader of the NSAA. At one point in the story, Bond thinks that von Glöda may be his match. But there is nothing in the character development which might give Bond these thoughts. Compared to his previous adversaries, von Glöda is *nothing*. He is a cardboard villain without even a convincing obligatory "how I came into power" speech. Von Glöda is a plot device—nothing more.

Gardner's heroines are formidable. LICENSE RENEWED's Lavender Peacock looks like a "young Lauren Bacall." She is brave and intelligent, and thankfully possesses none of the neurotic tendencies which plagued some of the Fleming women such as Tiffany and Tracy. Mary Jane Mashkin, in the same book, seems to be a direct imitation of the Fiona character from the film *Thunderball*. She attempts to use her seductive charms on Bond, but fails miserably. From then on, she is an enemy; she gets even with Bond during the obligatory torture scene—this time with the use of a high-frequency sound-wave transmitter. FOR SPECIAL SERVICES introduces the reader to Felix Leiter's daughter, Cedar. It was never mentioned in previous novels that Felix was married or had children, but Bond here claims he knew that Leiter had a wife. Cedar is working for the CIA, undercover, and even her father does not know it. She proves herself to be quite useful—while in a New York hotel room, she and Bond are held at bay by four thugs. When Bond gives her the signal, she overcomes her opponent with skill and proficiency. But she is also typical of the Bond-girl mold: she falls for 007 early in the novel, providing a pleasurable romantic subplot to the story: Cedar wants Bond, but he resists on the grounds that she is the daughter of his best friend. Their constant byplay sometimes reminds one of a Rock Hudson/Doris Day comedy, but it's an interesting twist to the standard "Bond meets girl, girl sleeps with Bond" story. At the end of the novel, Cedar is blatantly making it clear that she wants to go to bed with him, while 007 remains gallantly impassive. He assumes a fatherly stance with her, and even calls her "daughter." At one point he threatens to "warm her pretty little backside" if she doesn't stop flirting with him. She replies, giggling, "Oh. Promises." ICEBREAKER's Paula Vacker, the character most easily labeled the heroine, is a beautiful blond from Finland with large "grey-flecked eyes," and lips "built for one purpose." This is about all one learns about Paula except that she manages to fool 007 a couple of times into believing she is one thing and then another. Paula's objectives in the story are very contrived; hence, she is unbelievable as a character.

M is practically ignored as a character in the first two Gardner efforts. Only in ICEBREAKER does the author provide a good Bond/M confrontation scene reminiscent of the old days. M is angry at 007 for stopping in Helsinki after the Service training exercise in the Arctic. This foolishness almost costs Bond his life as well as the security of Operation Icebreaker. But then M takes the responsibility for Bond's actions, explaining that he should have been more explicit with 007's instructions. At this point, Bond thinks M may be withholding information.

M remained silent for a full minute. Above him, Robert Taylor's original *Trafalgar* set the whole tone of M's determination and character. That painting had lasted two years. Before then there had been Cooper's *Cape St. Vincent,* on loan from the National Maritime Museum, and before that . . . Bond could not recall, but they were always paintings of Britain's naval victories. M was the possessor of that essential arrogance which put allegiance to country first, and a firm belief in the invincibility of Britain's fighting forces, no matter what the odds, or how long it took

(ICEBREAKER, Chapter 4)

This passage is the most descriptive Gardner has written about Bond's stodgy old boss—and it's a good one.

Recurring characters still appear: Bill Tanner, the Chief of Staff, the reliable Miss Moneypenny, and even Felix Leiter himself makes a brief entrance in FOR SPECIAL SERVICES. One new character Gardner has created is the previously-mentioned assistant in Q Branch. Ann Reilly, nicknamed Q'ute, becomes good friends with Bond after a shaky start, and it appears that the couple are occasional lovers.

□ HIGHLIGHTS AND OTHER INGREDIENTS

There is an overabundance of gadgetry in all three Gardner efforts. In LICENSE RENEWED, the best is perhaps the cigarette lighter filled with a knockout gas, which Bond uses to put away Murik's henchman Caber during a wrestling match. In ICEBREAKER, Bond is equipped with a customized briefcase containing two Sykes Fairbairn commando knives (all screened so that they do not appear on airport X-ray machines). 007's most handy device in this story is the "VL34," a so-called "Privacy Protector," a small, advanced electronic bug for detecting listening devices planted in hotel rooms. The Saab 900 Turbo contains hidden compartments, a bright light attached to the rear bumper for blinding tailing drivers, a handy communications phone hidden in the dashboard, and a clever fire-extinguishing system which automatically douses any flames. This last item figures prominently during one highlight of FOR SPECIAL SERVICES in which Bond is challenged to a Grand Prix-style race by one of Markus Bismaquer's henchmen.

Of torture scenes, ICEBREAKER provides the most interesting one. Bond is hung naked in igloo-like surroundings and is repeatedly dipped into freezing water.

All things considered, how do the Gardner books compare with the Fleming series? Although the updating of the character and his world takes some getting used to, James Bond is still basically the same man he was in the sixties. Gardner lacks the elaborate command of the English language so distinctive in Fleming; but the new author's stories are fast-moving and engaging narratives. Though all are weak in plausibility and detail, they valiantly attempt to recapture the spirit of the original series. FOR SPECIAL SERVICES is by far the most successful of the three books, and ICEBREAKER is definitely the weakest. Gardner will be continuing the series with three more books. One must acknowledge the fact that he had a truly difficult task to perform—following in Ian Fleming's footsteps. Despite the faults of the new series, Gardner must be credited with having guts to continue the Bond saga at all; and, as the sales of the books attest, he must be congratulated for pulling it off.

□ FIVE □
The Films

THE JAMES BOND FILMS BY EON PRODUCTIONS

TITLE	PLACES	GIRL(S)	VILLAIN & EMPLOYER	VILLAIN'S PROJECT
Dr. No (1962)	London; Jamaica; Crab Key	Honey Ryder; Sylvia Trench	Dr. No/SPECTRE	To topple U.S. missiles with beaming device
From Russia With Love (1963)	Venice; London; Istanbul; Orient Express; Mediterranean	Tatiana Romanova; Sylvia Trench	Blofeld/SPECTRE; Red Grant; Rosa Klebb	To steal Lektor machine from Russians and kill Bond
Goldfinger (1964)	South America; Miami; London; Switzerland; Kentucky	Pussy Galore; Jill Masterson; Tilly Masterson	Auric Goldfinger/Red China	To detonate atomic bomb in Ft. Knox, thereby increasing worth of his own supply
Thunderball (1965)	France; Kent; Bahamas	Domino Vitali; Patricia Fearing	Blofeld/SPECTRE; Emilio Largo	To blackmail U.S. and Britain with nuclear threat
You Only Live Twice (1967)	Outer Space; Hong Kong; Japan	Aki; Kissy Suzuki	Blofeld/SPECTRE	To hijack space capsules in orbit and begin WWIII
On Her Majesty's Secret Service (1969)	France; London; Portugal; Swiss Alps	Tracy di Vicenzo; Ruby Windsor	Blofeld/SPECTRE	To infect Britain with crop and livestock pests
Diamonds Are Forever (1971)	London; Africa; Amsterdam; L.A.; Las Vegas	Tiffany Case; Plenty O'Toole	Blofeld/SPECTRE	To threaten major powers w/ diamond-powered laser satellite
Live and Let Die (1973)	London; New York; New Orleans; San Monique	Solitaire; Rosie Carver	Kananga (Mr. Big)/Self	To push heroin into the U.S.
The Man With the Golden Gun (1974)	London; Hong Kong; Thailand; Phuket	Mary Goodnight; Andrea Anders	Scaramanga/Red China	To perfect solar energy weapon and sell to highest bidder
The Spy Who Loved Me (1977)	Asgard; London; Egypt; Sardinia	Anya Amasova	Karl Stromberg/Self	To hijack nuclear submarines and threaten major powers
Moonraker (1979)	London; L.A.; Venice; Rio de Janeiro; Outer Space	Holly Goodhead; Corinne Dufour	Hugo Drax/Self	To begin "master race" in space and destroy the world
For Your Eyes Only (1981)	London; Madrid; Greece; Italy	Melina Havelock; Bibi; Contessa Lisl	Kristatos/USSR	To obtain ATAC system and sell to Russians
Octopussy (1983)	Cuba; East and West Germany; London; India	Octopussy; Magda	Kamal Khan/General Orlov	To smuggle atomic bomb onto NATO air base and detonate it

Key to symbols under "Remarks":

* = The villain's headquarters explode at the film's end.
+ = The film's plot has something to do with outer space.
# = The film contains scenes filmed underwater.

"OBLIGATORY SACRIFICIAL LAMB"	MINOR VILLAIN(S)	BOND'S FRIENDS	GADGETS	REMARKS
Quarrel	Prof. Dent; Miss Taro; Three Blind Mice	Quarrel; Felix Leiter	None	Most violent and toughest of the films; Connery at his best * +
Kerim Bey	Kronsteen; Krilencu	Kerim Bey	Attache case w/ sniperscope	Most realistic of the films; close to Fleming original; best ensemble acting of series
Jill Masterson; Tilly Masterson	Oddjob	Felix Leiter	Aston Martin w/ accessories	The blueprint of all Bond films; most consistently successful of all films; fast moving and exciting
Paula	Fiona Volpe; Count Lippe; Vargas; Janni	Felix Leiter; Paula	Aston Martin; jet pack; scuba tanks; Geiger watch & camera; 4-minute breathing device; homing pill; more	Spectacular in scope, but bogs down under its own weight; still better than '70s films #
Aki	Helga Brandt; Mr. Osata	Tiger Tanaka; Henderson	"Little Nelly" one-man helicopter; safe combination cracker	Most spectacular film visually; sets and locales steal show from outlandish plot * + #
Shaun Campbell	Irma Bunt	Marc-Ange Draco	Combination safe-cracker & Xerox duplicator	Closest to Fleming original; exciting and tough; would have been best film had Connery done it *
Plenty O'Toole	Wint & Kidd	Felix Leiter	Gun w/ cable and grappling hooks; pocket mousetrap; thumbprint	First injection of juvenile humor; Connery's return best part * +
Rosie Carver	Tee Hee; Whisper	Felix Leiter; Strutter; Quarrel Jr.	Wrist watch w/ magnet and sawblade; gas pellet gun	Fairly lame film built around locations; Moore plays Bond too lightly
Andrea Anders	Nick Nack; Hai Fat	Hip	False nipple	Stays on one level and is basically unexciting; locations nice visually *
Fekkesh; Max Kalba	Jaws; Sandor; Naomi	Hussain	Lotus; ski stick gun; wrist watch	Basically a remake of "You Only Live Twice"; sprawling production * #
Corinne Dufour	Jaws; Chang	Holly Goodhead	Wrist dart gun; gondola w/ accessories; speedboat w/ accessories	Most juvenile of all films; outlandish and ridiculous * +
Ferrara; Contessa Lisl	Emile Locque; Eric Kriegler; Gonzales	Columbo; Ferrara	Rope gun w/climbing pegs; two-man sub	Best film since "OHMSS"; a return to original format; terrific stunts #
Vijay	Gobinda; Twin Knife Throwers	Vijay	*AcroStar* Bede jet; combination fountain pen & wristwatch homing device	Intriguing plot marred by lapses into humor; style fluctuates too much between an "early" film and a "later" film

Oddjob "blows a fuse." The late Harold Sakata as the Korean bodyguard in Goldfinger. (Photo by Loomis Dean, Life Magazine. © Copyright 1964 by Time, Inc.)

INTRODUCTION

Title credits designer Maurice Binder told a Museum of Modern Art audience in 1979 that he had fifteen minutes before a conference to come up with a design for the opening of the first James Bond film, *Dr. No.* He scribbled down his ideas and rushed to the meeting. The result was the famous gun-barrel logo which begins every 007 picture in the Eon Productions series. First, the United Artists logo silently appears on the screen. Next the audience hears (very loudly) the John Barry orchestra blasting out "The James Bond Theme," as two white circles roll onto the screen from the left, dancing about until they converge. The circle enlarges and suddenly the audience is looking through a gun barrel. From the right walks James Bond, who turns and fires a gun at the camera. The action freezes and a red wash flows down from the top of the screen. The figure fades out to a white circle again. The circle moves around the screen as if it's searching for a place to settle; when it finally stops, the circle disappears and we are at some exotic location. Following this sequence, another traditional element—the pre-credits sequence—is played out until the main title credits appear and the theme song of the picture is heard.

Adherence to a traditional formula created by the films' producers, Albert R. Broccoli and Harry Saltzman, is a major reason for the success of the Bond series. This formula has proven that James Bond is a very marketable item, and Eon Productions, Ltd., formed by Broccoli and Saltzman back in 1961 to make the films, is one of the most successful operations in the history of cinema. To date, there have been thirteen James Bond films (excluding *Casino Royale,* produced by Charles K. Feldman in 1967, and *Never Say Never Again,* produced by Jack Schwartzman with Kevin McClory as executive producer in 1983) and each has made money. The only film that was not a runaway hit was *On Her Majesty's Secret Service* (1969), but it has since proven to be financially successful. This film fell short precisely because it broke several traditions, especially in its concept.

The formula fundamentally follows this outline: James Bond (played by a star that audiences admire) goes to investigate mysterious goings-on involving international security; finds a villain (usually with a super-strong henchman/sidekick) in his own super-technological headquarters; infiltrates the headquarters and eventually blows it up with the help of gadgetry, a military force of good guys and/or his own resourcefulness. The formula, begun in the first film, *Dr. No,* was more or less repeated in *Goldfinger, Thunderball, You Only Live Twice, Diamonds Are Forever, Live and Let Die, The Man With the Golden Gun, The Spy Who Loved Me, Moonraker,* and *Octopussy.*

John Brosnan in *James Bond in the Cinema* considers *Goldfinger* the best film in the series, which was at its peak at the time, with all the elements of the formula working in top form. After *Goldfinger,* Brosnan notes, the producers were faced with the problem of topping it and were forced to repeat the formula, disguised by bigger budgets, more exotic locations and set-pieces, more gadgets, more slapstick comedy, and more special effects.

☐ THE PRODUCERS

Albert R. Broccoli was born in New York in 1909 and spent the early part of his life working for relatives in a number of different jobs, including one as an assistant undertaker (which explains the profusion of coffin/undertaker jokes in the Bond films). He became a tea boy at 20th Century-Fox studios and rose in the ranks to assistant director. After World War II he cofounded Warwick Films and coproduced such features as *The Red Beret* and *Zarak* (both directed by Terence Young), *Hell Below Zero* (written by Richard Maibaum), *The Black Knight, Cockleshell Heroes,* and *The Man Inside,* all in the 1950s. Broccoli became interested in the James Bond novels, but when he inquired about purchasing film options, he discovered that Harry Saltzman had already done so.

Saltzman was born in Quebec in 1915 and had an early vaudeville and circus background. He lived in France for quite a while, working in theatrical circles. After World War II, he moved to the United States and found work in television. Saltzman successfully coproduced John Osborne's *Look Back in Anger* on

Broadway, ultimately coproducing the film as well. Forming a partnership with John Osborne and director Tony Richardson, Saltzman made two more superb British films, *The Entertainer* and *Saturday Night and Sunday Morning*. After the latter, Saltzman left the partnership, discovered the Bond novels, approached Ian Fleming and bought the rights to the entire series, excepting only CASINO ROYALE (which had already been sold and was then owned by Charles K. Feldman), and THUNDERBALL (which came under litigation as soon it was published in 1961). Shortly before the option on the books ran out, Saltzman met Broccoli and they formed Eon Productions, Ltd. *Dr. No* was their first James Bond film.

From the very beginning Broccoli and Saltzman had total control over the Bond pictures. They dictated to what degree the screenplay should reflect the novel, decided what elements should go into the film and approved final casting. It was their decision to make the films more humorous than the novels. It took a couple of films to find the right mixture of seriousness and humor to suit them, but once they did, the formula was set. Convincing Broccoli and Saltzman to depart from the formula would be no easy task for a director or script writer.

Broccoli and Saltzman also dictate the amount of sex and violence in the films. *Dr. No,* the most violent of the pictures, featured the first and only instance in which 007 shoots a man in cold blood. After *Dr. No,* the violence was toned down considerably, and by the time *Goldfinger* rolled around, action scenes were stylized and bloodless. Audiences are never asked to watch gory bloodletting in the Bond films. The same applies to sex. The first three films offered several seduction scenes, and Bond was certainly something of a male chauvinist by today's standards. After *Goldfinger,* however, sex in the films became basically voyeuristic, limited to shots of lovely women in scanty bikinis or evening gowns; the camera almost always fades out as Bond's seduction of the heroine begins. The Bond films are *family* films, Saltzman liked to stress.

Broccoli and Saltzman's formula envelops the idea of making the films *total* cinema, i.e., high standards of production, lots of action and breathtaking stunts, on-location shooting in exotic places around the world, exaggerated sound effects, and exhilarating musical scores. John Brosnan points out that the films are actually several miniature films (with beginnings, middles, and ends) strung together as set-pieces (Broccoli calls them "bumps") to create the overall whole. For instance, in *Dr. No,* we have the London sequence, the

The Bond films producer Albert R. "Cubby" Broccoli, at a recent press conference in New York. Ever since co-producer Harry Saltzman left Eon Productions in 1974, Broccoli has held the reins of the films alone. (Photo by Richard Schenkman.)

Kingston sequences (including the scenes with Miss Taro and Professor Dent), the Crab Key sequence, and the scenes in Dr. No's laboratory. The later films begin to lose the overall continuity between these set-pieces, and by *Moonraker* (1979), it is very difficult to follow the storyline, which gets lost in the shuffle. Perhaps the producers didn't care at this point whether the total movie made sense or not—it was the set-piece formula that had always worked before, and that is what they would continue to use.

☐ THE SCREENPLAYS

The man responsible for most of the Bond screenplays is Richard Maibaum. Maibaum was born in New York, like Broccoli, in 1909. He began to study law, but became a writer for radio. His play *The Tree* was produced in New York in 1932, and he acted in several productions of the New York Shakespeare Repertory Theatre. His play *Sweet Mystery of Life* was produced on Broadway in 1935, after which he moved to Hollywood, where he wrote *They Gave Me a Gun* and *I Wanted Wings* for MGM. After World War II, he

Roger Moore with co-producer Harry Saltzman on the set of Live and Let Die *in New Orleans. (UPI Photo.)*

worked for Paramount and wrote the screenplay for the 1949 film of *The Great Gatsby*, among others. In 1954, he wrote *Hell Below Zero* for producer Albert R. Broccoli.

When Broccoli first approached him about doing a Bond film, reportedly Maibaum felt that the Fleming novels were too violent and sexy to adapt to the screen. Even Fleming's biographer, John Pearson, agreed that the books were dead serious, and lacked humor. Sean Connery, who played James Bond in six of the films, has said that his wife at the time, Diane Cilento, read the first screenplay and advised Connery not to take the role unless some humor was added. Although the producers, along with director Terence Young, certainly deserve a share of the credit, Maibaum is probably the man most responsible for lacing the Bond screenplays with humor. Herein lies the major difference between the novels and the films—the latter are played for laughs. The humor in the early pictures was subtle and tongue-in-cheek; but it grew over the years to broad farce. John Brosnan calls *Moonraker* the "most expensive slapstick movie since *It's a Mad, Mad, Mad, Mad World.*"

The films also differ from the novels in plot details. The early movies tend to follow Fleming's original storylines for the most part; but the fifth film, *You Only Live Twice,* is nothing like the novel. Written by Roald Dahl, it is virtually a remake of *Dr. No* on a much grander scale. *The Spy Who Loved Me* is easily discernible as a remake of *You Only Live Twice;* and all of the films since *Goldfinger* contain sequences that rehash scenes from earlier efforts.

Two films have screenplays that are fairly close to the Fleming originals: *From Russia With Love* and *On Her Majesty's Secret Service (OHMSS)*. Not surprisingly, these are two of the best films in the series. *OHMSS* adheres almost perfectly to the novel, even daring to include the tragic ending—Bond's new bride is shot to death by archenemy Blofeld. As mentioned before, this is the only film that was not a runaway success. But *From Russia With Love,* the second film in the series, was very successful. Only a couple of departures from the original plot were made, i.e., changing the criminal organization from SMERSH to SPECTRE, and adding the Blofeld character.

Maibaum collaborated on ten of the thirteen Bond films (he wrote *OHMSS* alone). His cowriters included Berkley Mather, Johanna Harwood, Paul Dehn, John Hopkins, Tom Mankiewicz, Christopher Wood, George MacDonald Fraser, and Michael G. Wilson. This impressive track record can only indicate that Maibaum's work is an important element in the successful Bond formula.

□ THE DIRECTORS

Departing from the modern tradition of *auteurism,* which emphasizes directorial control of all creative aspects of a film, the producers of the 007 series have forced their directors to work within strict artistic boundaries. But certain stylistic differences can be discerned among the chief directors of the Bonds, and play a subtle yet important part in the success or failure of the films.

Terence Young directed three of the best Bond films: *Dr. No, From Russia With Love,* and *Thunderball.* Born in 1915, Young has had a fairly active career, having directed a number of films including *Corridor of Mirrors* (1948), *The Red Beret* and *Zarak* (1953 and 1956, respectively, both for producer Albert R. Broccoli), and *Too Hot to Handle* (1960). Since making the Bond films he achieved acclaim for directing *Wait Until Dark* (1967), and has gone on to direct other films such as *Red Sun* (1971).

Young's directorial style is the most realistic of all

Terence Young, the man who directed Dr. No, From Russia With Love, *and* Thunderball. *(Photo by Richard Schenkman.)*

the Bond helmsmen. He maintains a stricter balance between seriousness and humor than others have; thus his films manage to avoid silliness. By the same token, his films move slower in contrast with most of the others and dynamic levels are kept more in the midrange. This helps as well as hinders the effectiveness of his efforts. *Thunderball* is the weakest of the three films in terms of excitement and suspense; but it is impressive visually. Violence is more pervasive in Young's films than in the others: there is the cold-blooded murder of Professor Dent and the breaking of the flash bulb on Quarrel's cheek in *Dr. No;* the gypsy girl fight and the brutal battle between Bond and Red Grant in *From Russia With Love;* and the murder of Domino's brother and the execution of Largo's henchman by throwing him to the sharks in *Thunderball.* All of these violent acts are presented with a high degree of realism—more blood, genuine fright on the part of the victims, and a cold point of view toward the act. Young also tends to pull strong performances from his actors—*From Russia With Love* features perhaps the best ensemble acting of all the Bond films.

Guy Hamilton, director of *Goldfinger, Diamonds Are Forever, Live and Let Die,* and *The Man With the Golden Gun,* was born in 1922 and was once an as-

sistant to veteran director Carol Reed. Among his film credits are *An Inspector Calls* (1954), *The Man in the Middle* (1964), *Funeral in Berlin* (1965), and *The Battle of Britain* (1969). Hamilton's style incorporates quick editing, a faster pace, and a much more humorous approach to the material. This new style works extremely well in *Goldfinger,* works for the most part in *Diamonds Are Forever,* but backfires in his two later films. Hamilton's direction of *Goldfinger* was inspired and fresh, and ranks as the most trend-setting directorial job of all the films.

Lewis Gilbert, the director of *You Only Live Twice, The Spy Who Loved Me,* and *Moonraker,* was born in 1920 and has had a career as both a writer and director. His directorial efforts include *Albert RN* (1953), *The Good Die Young* (1954), *Reach for the Sky* (1956), *Sink the Bismarck* (1960), and *Alfie* (1966). He was nominated for an Academy Award for his direction of the last film. The most obvious stylistic element common to all three Gilbert-directed Bond films is that all are big productions. These films are the most expensive of the series (*Moonraker* holds the record with a budget of $30,000,000); and all, unfortunately, are basically variations of the same film. *You Only Live Twice* goes as far as the producers possibly can in terms of lavish sets, exotic locations, and far-out gadgets. The other two films repeat all this—only locations and hardware have been changed. Gilbert also uses a faster cutting style than Hamilton or Young. Gilbert's films move from one set-piece to another so rapidly that the audience barely has time to comprehend the change of locale. As a result, these three films suffer from overkill to the point that James Bond as a character scarcely exists. He is like a pinball in these films, bouncing around from place to place, getting in and out of predicaments—the action is so unrealistic that the films could be labelled science fiction comedy-fantasies. *Moonraker* in particular suffers from this flaw: it is so unrealistic as to be absurd—but this may be due more to the screenplay than the direction.

The other two directors, Peter Hunt (*On Her Majesty's Secret Service*) and John Glen (*For Your Eyes Only* and *Octopussy*), made impressive directorial debuts with their Bond films. Both men were Bond film veterans—Hunt was the editor and second unit director for previous Bond films, as was Glen. Their work will be discussed with their respective films.

□ ACTORS AND CHARACTERS

When the producers received the go-ahead from United

Artists to make the first Bond film, the big question was: Who was going to play James Bond? Many names were tossed around, including David Niven (who would play Sir James Bond in the 007 spoof, *Casino Royale*), Richard Burton, and, believe it or not, James Stewart. But because *Dr. No* had a relatively small budget, Broccoli and Saltzman were forced to go with an unknown. After many interviews and auditions, the producers came up with a handful of names. Reportedly, second on the list was Roger Moore. First on the list, as we have seen already, was Sean Connery.

Born in Edinburgh in 1930, Thomas Sean Connery was the son of a truck driver. He held many jobs, including newspaper boy, milkman, coffin polisher, cement mixer, and merchant seaman. He landed a chorus part in the British production of *South Pacific,* which led him to films. Before making *Dr. No,* Connery starred in four forgettable films: *Another Time, Another Place* (1958), Walt Disney's *Darby O'Gill and the Little People* (1959), *Tarzan's Greatest Adventure* (1959), and *Frightened City* (1960). It was the role of James Bond that made Sean Connery a star. By the mid-sixties he was the number one box-office draw the world over, and it wasn't because of his non-Bond films such as Hitchcock's *Marnie* or Sidney Lumet's *The Hill.* Connery became so identified with the character of James Bond that it was hard for audiences to accept anyone else in the part. The ad campaign for *You Only Live Twice* read: "Sean Connery *Is* James Bond in Ian Fleming's *You Only Live Twice.*" Inevitably, this alterego complex became too much for Connery, and he tried more than once to leave the Bond series. His boredom with the role is quite evident in *You Only Live Twice,* after which he quit, but he was persuaded to return once more four years later in *Diamonds Are Forever.*

George Lazenby, who replaced Connery in *On Her Majesty's Secret Service,* was an unknown Australian model. He had worked in TV commercials, but had no previous film acting experience. Lazenby had been a car salesman before switching to modeling. He was certainly handsome and dapper, but these modeling qualities did not create a plausible James Bond; audiences and critics alike gave him the unanimous thumbs down. In retrospect, Lazenby's performance is quite sincere, and he probably could have grown into the role with subsequent films. Lazenby has gone on to make other movies, such as Peter Bogdanovich's *Saint Jack.*

Connery was enticed to play Bond again in *Diamonds Are Forever,* having been lured back by the

Sean Connery, the actor who became famous playing James Bond. (Photo by Arthur Evans, Wide World Photo.)

George Lazenby portrayed James Bond one time in the 1969-released On Her Majesty's Secret Service. *(Photo by Terry O'Neil, Globe Photos.)*

The new 007. Roger Moore takes over the role in the 1973-released Live and Let Die. *(Wide World Photo.)*

Since *Live and Let Die* was released in 1973, Moore has been accepted as and has remained James Bond in the Eon Productions series.

The most puzzling feature common to all three actors cast as 007 over the years is their uniform lack of suitability for the role. None of them really resembles Bond as Fleming intended him. When the author first saw Sean Connery, he was reportedly aghast and claimed that the actor was "totally wrong." But after seeing Connery in character, Fleming changed his mind, and even gave the literary James Bond a Scottish heritage in subsequent novels. But the cinematic James Bond remains quite different from the man in the books. Connery could have played Bond as Fleming had written him had the screenplays allowed. But the film scripts put the accent on humor; and Bond in the movies was dapper, witty, and extremely nonchalant. Connery did play a tougher Bond than Moore, and his dry delivery of gag lines somehow fit the sardonic detachment with which the literary Bond regarded life. Moore, on the other hand, is quite bland in the role. The directors and scenarists of the later pictures require the actor to embody a James Bond who stands idly by with a twinkle in his eye while frantic action explodes harmlessly around him. Moore's Bond is simply too nice and well mannered to be a James Bond of any real substance.

very lucrative deal with United Artists recounted earlier. After *Diamonds Are Forever,* Connery insisted that he would never play Bond again, so the producers had to search for a new leading man once more. (Fortunately for Connery's fans, the actor played Bond once again in the non-Eon Productions film, *Never Say Never Again,* released in 1983.) Broccoli and Saltzman settled on their original second choice, Roger Moore.

Moore was born in 1927 and had his first break as an extra in *Caesar and Cleopatra* (1945). He understudied David Tomlinson in the London stage production of *The Little Hut,* which brought him a certain amount of recognition. This brought interest from Hollywood, where he made films such as *The Last Time I Saw Paris* (1954), *Interrupted Melody* and *The King's Thief* (both 1955), and starred opposite Lana Turner in *Diane* (also 1955). Moore became very successful in the British TV series, *Ivanhoe,* and went on to international fame as TV's Simon Templar in *The Saint* and in a recurring role in *Maverick.*

The late Bernard Lee appeared as a character actor in more than 100 films. He was best known for portraying Bond's Chief, M. (UPI Photo.)

Three other British actors have been important to the series: the late Bernard Lee, who portrayed M in eleven of the films; Lois Maxwell, who still plays Miss Moneypenny; and Desmond Llewelyn, who has brought to life the role of Q, the Armourer.

Lee was born in 1908 and played character roles in many films, including *The Fallen Idol* (1948), *The Third Man* (1949), *Father Brown* (1954), and *Whistle Down the Wind* (1961); but he was best known to audiences around the world as Bond's crusty boss. Lee passed away after *Moonraker* was released, and his role was replaced by the characters of the Minister of Defense and Chief of Staff Bill Tanner in *For Your Eyes Only*. Veteran actor Robert Brown took over the role in *Octopussy*. Lee perfectly embodied the M of the novels in his aloofness toward Bond, although he tended to become comically perturbed at Bond's addiction to a wild life (women, fast cars, etc.). But Lee exhibited M's paternalism and wisdom quite well. He will be missed.

Lois Maxwell was born Lois Hooker in Canada in 1927. After a brief Hollywood career, she settled in England, where she made several films, including *Corridor of Mirrors* (1948, directed by Terence Young), *The Woman's Angle* (1952), *Kill Me Tomorrow* (1957), and Stanley Kubrick's *Lolita* (1962). She is probably best known as Miss Moneypenny, M's faithful secretary with a lifelong crush on James Bond. The short flirtatious scenes between Moneypenny and Bond in the films range from pleasant and refreshing to trite and maudlin. But Maxwell exhibits the requisite charm for Moneypenny, and does quite well in the role. (It's interesting to note that the character was given quite a bit more to do in the films than in the novels.) Maxwell, incidentally, is the only other person besides producer Broccoli to have been associated with each Bond film.

Q (in the novels and first couple of films he is called Major Boothroyd) is the head of the weapons branch and is always turning up in the films with some new gimmick for Bond to use. In the first film, *Dr. No* (in which Boothroyd was portrayed by Peter Burton), all he presents to Bond is a new pistol. Desmond Llewelyn took the role in *From Russia With Love* and issues Bond an attaché case with all kinds of clever devices. In *Goldfinger,* Bond acquires the famous Aston Martin equipped with a veritable arsenal. From then on, each successive film features a more impressive type of weapon than the last. Llewelyn's Q shares the cinematic M's disgust at the way Bond treats his equipment, women, etc. As the films progress, Q becomes more

Lois Maxwell, as the ever-faithful Miss Moneypenny. (Wide World Photo.)

and more sarcastic, and the Q/Bond scenes function as comic relief. Llewelyn, having made a career as a character actor in a number of British films, is fine in the role.

Other actors will be discussed in relation to the particular films in which they appear.

☐ OTHER ASPECTS

All the Bond films, particularly those with larger budgets, are impressive visually. They all feature lavish photography, beautiful sets, and believable special effects. Sound is an important part of all the films—usually recorded at an exaggerated volume. Fight scenes are accompanied by a resounding "CRRRRAAASSHHH" when a fist meets a jaw, and gunshots and explosions are deafening. Cinematography is usually very beautiful—*Thunderball* features some impressive underwater photography never before attempted, and *You Only Live Twice* provides panoramic views of Japan. But the artistic ingredients that figure most prominently in the Broccoli/Saltzman formula are the production designs and musical scores.

The man responsible for the unmistakable look of a Bond film is Ken Adam, a German-born designer who has worked on a number of distinguished films, including *Queen of Spades* (1948), *Around the World in Eighty Days* (1956), *Dr. Strangelove* (1964), *Sleuth* (1972), and many others. He won an Academy Award for art direction for Stanley Kubrick's *Barry Lyndon* (1975). Inspired by classic German cinema design, Adam

Designer Ken Adam in front of his fabulous Fort Knox set for Goldfinger. *(Photo by Loomis Dean, Life Magazine. © Copyright 1964 by Time, Inc.)*

brought an expressionistic look to his settings—surreal angles, sloping ceilings, and sharp changes of line direction. He designed all but five of the pictures, and must be considered a major contributor to the Bond film formula.

Syd Cain, the art director who took over for Ken Adam on *From Russia With Love, On Her Majesty's Secret Service,* and *Live and Let Die,* took a more realistic approach to his designs. *From Russia With Love* featured no fantastic designs except for SPECTRE's training camp. *Live and Let Die,* however, did tend to copy Adam's expressionistic designs a little, especially in Dr. Kananga's laboratory at the film's end.

Peter Murton designed *The Man With the Golden Gun,* which recalls Ken Adam's work; but this film was enhanced by the special effects and model work of Derek Meddings, who has been special effects supervisor for each Bond film since 1974. Meddings' work is good, and he is well known in the field, along with Douglas Trumbull, John Stears, and John Dykstra. Meddings was nominated for an Academy Award for his work on *Moonraker.* (He won the Oscar in 1978 for *Superman.*) Another man in the special effects field who has been with the Bond films since the beginning is John Stears, who won an Academy Award for visual effects for *Thunderball.* His work is outstanding in each film. Peter Lamont, an art director from previous Bond films, made an impressive debut as production designer on *For Your Eyes Only,* and his work will be discussed in that section.

The other artistic element of the formula that always helps make or break a 007 film is the musical score. Usually, one man's name is synonymous with James Bond music: John Barry.

Barry was born in 1933, and is one of the most respected names in film scoring today. He has won two Academy Awards (*Born Free,* 1966, and *The Lion in Winter,* 1968), and has composed music for many films, including *The L-Shaped Room* (1962), *The Ipcress File* (1965), *Midnight Cowboy* (1969), *The Day of the Locust* (1975), and *The Black Hole* (1979). He scored all but four of the Bond pictures.

Barry's music for the Bond films is stirring and dynamic. Most of it consists of a big-band jazz sound with electrical instruments (especially guitars), a bit of brass, and, often, exotic instruments such as gongs and harps. Each Bond film features a title tune, all but two of them with lyrics. The title songs for *Goldfinger* and *You Only Live Twice* were both hits, as were three non-Barry efforts: *Live and Let Die* (by Paul and Linda McCartney), "Nobody Does It Better" from *The Spy Who Loved Me* (by Marvin Hamlisch and Carole Bayer Sager), and *For Your Eyes Only* (by Bill Conti and Michael Leeson). The songs accompany the main title designs, usually the work of Maurice Binder, and the union is beautiful to the eyes and ears. Usually featured with the main titles are silhouetted nudes, as well as gun and spy motifs.

Soundtrack albums of the Bond films have sold well too, which is further proof that the music is an important ingredient in their success. John Barry became famous as a result of the Bond music (though, surprisingly, he has never been nominated for an Oscar for a Bond score). Each soundtrack will be discussed in the appropriate film's section.

DR. NO (1962)

☐ PRODUCTION

The first James Bond film was produced for only a million dollars, and is one of the best of the series. It is simple, compared to the rest of the films, and this is the main reason for its success. There is no gadgetry in the film—007 relies on his wits and strength to accomplish his mission. Characters are well drawn and the plot is tight and moves quickly. The film is rough, tough, and exciting, with what is probably Sean Connery's most accomplished and sincere performance as James Bond.

Sean Connery takes a breather and grins for the cameras on location in Jamaica for the filming of Dr. No. *He's wearing James Bond's "Sea Island" cotton shirt. (UPI Photo.)*

Interiors were shot at Pinewood Studios in England, while location shooting took place in Jamaica. Broccoli's idea of the set-piece format is immediately apparent in the first few scenes. First, we see the sequence in Kingston in which Strangways and his secretary are murdered by the three-blind-mice henchmen. Then there is a cut to London, where we see the communications network of the Secret Service. The scene moves from there to a casino where we first meet James Bond. The "bumps" in *Dr. No* follow a logical cause-and-effect sequence (not always true in later films), and the editing prowess of Peter Hunt keeps the film moving with suspense.

Dr. No is the most violent, and one of the most realistic of the films. Save for the science fiction elements of Dr. No's laboratory and his plan to topple U.S. missiles, the bulk of the film is based in reality. The fight scenes, coordinated by Bob Simmons, are tough and believable. There is one scene which captures the essence of Bond's profession as a killer, something that has been largely ignored in subsequent films. Bond is waiting at Miss Taro's house for the arrival of would-be assassin Professor Dent. (Dent and Taro are a pair of Dr. No's underlings—characters created for the film.) Bond is sitting behind the bedroom door after having stuffed the bed full of pillows to resemble a body. Dent opens the door quietly and empties his gun into the shape in the bed. Bond then makes his presence known and orders Dent to drop the gun. After asking Dent a few questions, 007 calmly shoots the man in cold blood. He even fires a superfluous bullet into the fallen man's back! Bond then removes the silencer from his gun and nonchalantly blows the smoke away. The scene fades out quietly.

The above sequence is one of the most effective moments in the entire James Bond film series, yet it caused considerable controversy at the time of release. Director Terence Young fought hard for the scene to remain intact, insisting that Bond "is an executioner—we must not forget that." It is a scene that captures Fleming's Bond perfectly, and Connery plays it with ruthlessness. Unfortunately, this was to be the only sequence of its kind in the series. In each of the following films, the violence is toned down considerably, and Bond would never kill anyone with such methodical coldness again.

Humor in *Dr. No* takes the form of tongue-in-cheek innuendos and one-liner asides. The humor is subtle and avoids the juvenile, an achievement which eludes the later Bond films.

Ursula Andress, playing the first screen Bond-girl, Honeychile Rider, adjusts her costume before shooting a scene in Dr. NO. (UPI Photo.)

☐ **SCREENPLAY**

As would be the case with all the James Bond films, the screenplay departed in several instances from the Ian Fleming novel (although compared to some of the later films, *Dr. No* seems extremely faithful). The novel's premise seems fairly improbable. The decision was made to discard some of Fleming's more fantastic elements and attempt to create a more believable chain of events. But in doing so, a great deal was lost as well. The alterations in *Dr. No* are not as extreme as in some of the later films, in which Fleming's plot is sometimes *completely* jettisoned.

Screenwriter Richard Maibaum (with the aid of Johanna Harwood and Berkley Mather) added a lengthy midsection to the story involving Professor Dent and Miss Taro. These sequences add weight to the middle of the film and are actually improvements over Fleming's original story. Other changes include the introduction of SPECTRE, mainly because the producers knew this criminal organization would figure prominently in later films. (Maibaum had worked on a screenplay for *Thunderball* before the decision was made to start the series with *Dr. No.* SPECTRE was originally created for *Thunderball.* Maibaum was perhaps influenced by this story as well.) SPECTRE is only mentioned briefly by Dr. No in the film, as a hint of things to come. Another addition is the inclusion of the Felix Leiter character. Bond's CIA friend appears in several of the novels, but not DOCTOR NO; apparently Maibaum felt that the Bond ally in this story, Quarrel, was not a strong enough character. But frankly, the addition of Leiter is extraneous to the dramatic action; the character doesn't serve any major function.

A disappointing change from the novel is the substitution of a tarantula for the centipede which crawls on Bond's body while he's in bed. The producers probably felt that audiences wouldn't realize that a centipede is lethal. Tarantulas are creatures everyone can recognize. Unfortunately, the filming of this scene isn't as successful as it probably looked on paper. Due to clumsy camera work and special effects, it is embarrassingly apparent that there is a sheet of glass between Connery's arm and the spider.

The most important change is in the last reel, beginning with the obstacle course sequence. In the novel, the ventilation shaft through which Bond makes his escape is a planned-out gauntlet containing all sorts of horrors, ending with a drop into a lagoon containing a man-eating giant squid. In the film, the shaft is not an obstacle course, but merely a harrowing means of escape from the cell. Bond is shot by some unidentified gun which only causes him some pain and doesn't seriously harm him. Next he encounters hot metal around the chute, as in the novel, but gone are the cage of spiders and the giant squid. The film's climax takes place in Dr. No's laboratory, where Bond foils the madman's plans to topple a U.S. missile. Dr. No's death in the nuclear reactor pool is more believable cinematically than his death beneath a pile of bird guano might have been. This is an improvement over the novel's ending. The final shots of *Dr. No* feature what would become standard operating procedure for the series: the villain's establishment is spectacularly blown up, as Bond and his girl (in this case, Honey) barely escape by boat.

☐ DIRECTION

It is difficult, in a Bond film, to determine if a particular sequence's success is the work of the director, the actor, the scriptwriter, or the editor. Broccoli insists that the films are collaborative efforts, and that no one person should receive credit for a film's success. But it would be unfair to underestimate the contribution Terence Young made to the James Bond films. In an interview for *Bondage* magazine, Young claims that he originated the style of the series:

Well, without being arrogant, that was established very simply, on the floor, by me. I knew what I wanted. I didn't think the picture was going to be anywhere near as popular as it was. I thought it was going to be a thing for rather highbrow tastes. I thought an awful lot of the jokes were going to be in-jokes. I think it caught on very well . . .

When you analyze it, and this is no disrespect to Ian, they (the books) were very sophisticated "B"-picture movie plots. If someone tells you, "a James Bond film," you'd say, "My God, that's for Monogram," or Republic Pictures, who used to be around in those days. You would have never thought of it for a serious "A" film. But it had considerable sophistication, and this was very consciously put in by Ian . . .

One wanted the films to have a very slick quality. We wanted to make them as sophisticated as we could, and above all I gave the picture an enormous sense of tempo, in fact, it changed styles of filmmaking.

(From "The Terence Young Interview" by Richard Schenkman, *Bondage* Number 10)

Young and editor Peter Hunt worked hand in hand to create this tempo and it's a style that stuck throughout the series. At first, Young remembers, Hunt was mortified by the cuts he was asked to make. But after a screening of a rough cut, Hunt was very enthusiastic, and on *From Russia With Love,* the editor was cutting the film with an outrageous extroverted zeal. According to Young, the head of the Cinémathèque in France declared that *Dr. No* was "one of the great innovative films. Years from now, all films will be made like this." Television action films especially adopted the editing style of *Dr. No.*

Young's style tends to be slightly more realistic than that of other Bond directors. All of the more violent scenes in Young's efforts are presented with a hard-edged seriousness, save for the exaggerated sound effects. The murders of Strangways and his secretary

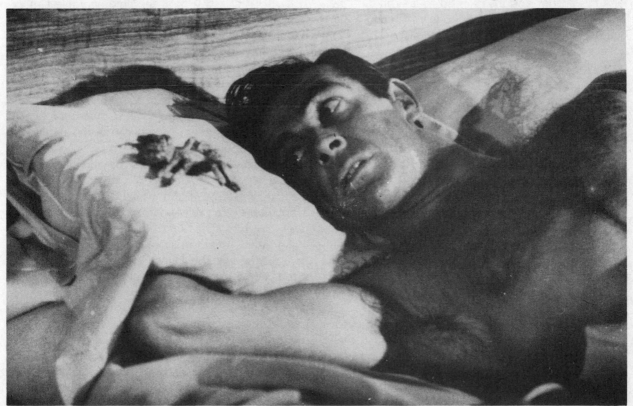

James Bond's bedside companion this time isn't very friendly! On the set of Dr. No. *(UPI Photo.)*

at the beginning of *Dr. No* may be the bloodiest scenes in all of the films. The sequence in which Quarrel's face is slashed by a broken flash cube is unnerving. Because this violence is portrayed with some degree of realism, the humor in the film comes as a pleasant surprise. This element boosted the series' success: the audience is released from a tense action scene by a witty one-liner from Bond. The juxtaposition of gravity with levity was probably Terence Young's idea (with the aid of Connery's ad libs), and it is what makes the Bond films so much fun to watch. Unfortunately, the later films lost touch with this key element, and began to play the serious action scenes for laughs as well.

Although Young was successful in establishing an original style for the films, his efforts tend to be a little sloppy technically. Of course, budgets were smaller in those days. There are continuity problems in all three of Young's Bond pictures, and there are instances in which Young's *mise en scène* does not focus our attention on the appropriate action. For instance, when Bond is leaving the Kingston airport in *Dr. No,* a black female snaps Bond's photograph. Because the camera has placed her in a corner of the frame, it is easy to miss this action (and it's referred to later in the film). But the atmosphere and moods of Young's films override any technical problems that may exist. His three pictures are definitely among the best of the series.

☐ ACTORS AND CHARACTERS

Sean Connery's first appearance as James Bond, based loosely on Paul Muni's entrance in the film *Juarez,* is a marvelous sequence. The camera does not reveal Bond's face until a key moment. We first discover Bond in a casino in London, playing *chemin de fer* with an attractive woman. We see only his shoulders, the back of his head, and his hands. The woman loses to Bond twice before she looks hard at him and says, "I admire your luck, Mr., er . . ." The camera finally reveals Connery; he lights a cigarette and replies with that now-famous phrase and with absolutely *no warmth*: "Bond. James Bond." The "James Bond Theme" fades up on the soundtrack, and we have ourselves a piece of classic cinema.

Sean Connery is wonderful as Bond in *Dr. No,* although readers of the novels would recognize that he is not quite the image that is painted by Fleming. But Connery embodies a ruggedness and an intense screen presence which transcends any preconceived notions

about the character. With *Dr. No,* Sean Connery *became* James Bond and was quite unable to escape the image until recently.

The James Bond of the films, as mentioned earlier, is a little different from the character in the novels. The Bond in the books is 99 percent humorless; the film Bond is witty and has the perfect *double entendre* for every occasion. It was probably a wise choice on the filmmakers' part to create a Bond with a sense of humor. The novels contain humor, to be sure, but the fact that Bond is so serious about everything he does helps create that humor. It might not have worked as such on the screen; therefore we have Fleming's Bond, and we have Bond as created by United Artists.

Connery probably gives his most professional and sincere performance as Bond in *Dr. No.* Although his Scottish burr comes through stronger in this film than in any of the others, Connery portrays Bond with an assured toughness that epitomizes the machismo male. Exuding coldness, Connery portrays Bond as the hardened, dedicated civil servant Fleming created; yet the darkly handsome Connery is also able to turn on a charm that captivated his female audience.

Ursula Andress, who at the time had little film experience, was chosen to play the first Bond movie heroine, Honeychile Rider (in the film her name is Honey Ryder). Andress is adequate in the role, and certainly attractive. Her entrance in *Dr. No,* like Connery's, is a special moment. The camera catches her emerging from the sea onto the beach dressed in a skimpy white bikini (in the novel she was naked). Andress benefits from having a well-written role; Honey in the film is able to relate some of her past history (direct from the novel), which is something later Bond heroines are denied. Andress' foreign accent helps emphasize Honey's lack of a formal education—her delivery comes off as slightly childlike, which works perfectly.

A veteran American stage actor, Joseph Wiseman, portrays the evil Dr. Julius No. Although he doesn't resemble the Dr. No of the novel, he conveys many of the literary character's qualities. Wiseman achieves Dr. No's "gliding" effect in movement, as well as the monotonous and sinister voice which hints ever so slightly at impending doom. (Wiseman was employed later in *Thunderball* to provide the voice of the unseen Ernst Stavro Blofeld.) The film Dr. No also does not have mechanical pincers for hands—instead, he has metal hands that look like black gloves, which, although not as perverse as pincers, work well enough on the screen. These metal hands are the primary cause of Dr. No's death in the film—he is unable to grip a slippery steel girder and pull himself out of the nuclear reactor pool.

Jack Lord was cast as Felix Leiter, Bond's CIA friend. This character has been a continuing source of frustration for Bond fans, for he has never been portrayed successfully on film. No fewer than six actors have been cast as Leiter, and only one comes close to being right for the role. Jack Lord is one of the weakest of the five Leiters. Felix Leiter is supposed to be buoyant, jovial, and above all, a friendly Texan. Jack Lord comes across as wooden, humorless, and a little boring. Add to this the fact that the character is unnecessary to this script, and the part of Felix Leiter must count as one of *Dr. No*'s few failures.

John Kitzmiller, on the other hand, is very effective as Quarrel, the Cayman Islander who meets his death on Dr. No's island. The script treats Quarrel as comic relief by using the character's superstitions as the basis for a laugh or two, which comes off as somewhat derogatory. But Kitzmiller is able to play the warmth and good nature of the character, which is what made him so appealing in the book.

Quarrel in the film also becomes the first in a series of what John Brosnan, in *James Bond in the Cinema*, calls the "Obligatory Sacrificial Lambs." In every Bond film, at least one good character is killed by the enemy. Quarrel meets his death by being burned alive, in a graphic sequence, by Dr. No's "dragon" tank. The Obligatory Sacrificial Lamb not only serves to give the villains some credibility, but it also allows James Bond a moment to show a little emotion (but not much).

The Bond film veterans, Bernard Lee and Lois Maxwell, make their first appearances as M and Miss Moneypenny in *Dr. No*. Lee's scene with Connery is one of the best M/Bond sequences in the series, allowing the actor to show several sides of M's character—testiness, authority, and paternalism. The first of the Bond/Moneypenny flirtation scenes features a moment of verbal volleyball between the two characters. This is something created by the filmmakers—these scenes never existed in the Fleming novels.

Other actors/characters in *Dr. No* worth mentioning are Anthony Dawson as Professor Dent, Zena Marshall as Miss Taro, and Eunice Gayson as Sylvia Trench. Dawson (who also attempts to strangle Grace Kelly in Hitchcock's *Dial M for Murder*) is good as the shifty hireling who attempts to kill Bond three times. Zena Marshall, an attractive Oriental actress, exudes the wanton seductive qualities common to all female villains in the series. Variations on this type of character recur in almost all of the remaining films. Sylvia Trench was to be a continuing character in the series, but appeared only in the first two films. She was to have taken part in a running joke involving Bond being repeatedly called away on assignments as Sylvia and he are on the verge of making love. Eunice Gayson is able to portray a somewhat comic sexuality; it is too bad the character was discontinued when director Terence Young left the series (Sylvia had been his idea).

□ **OTHER ASPECTS**

The distinctive look of a Bond film began in *Dr. No* with Ken Adam's marvelous design for Dr. No's laboratory. Although many of his designs for the films look very 1960s today, they established a pattern that would be copied in other spy films throughout the decade. The first of his expressionistic designs is the room where Professor Dent is instructed to place a tarantula in Bond's bed. It's an eerie room with a sloping ceiling containing a large circular grille for illumination; it is the setting for the audience's first glimpse of Dr. No's world. Dr. No's dining room is also an impressive set, containing a wall-size aquarium. It was co-scriptwriter Johanna Harwood who suggested including a recently stolen Goya painting, "The Duke of Wellington," in Dr. No's dining room—an in-joke that received favorable critical reaction when the film was released. (Audiences who did not realize the painting had been missing when the film opened might not have grasped the significance of Bond's double take when he sees the painting.)

Ted Moore begins his long reign as cinematographer for the Bond films with *Dr. No*. His work in the film is admirable, especially in the outdoor location sequences. Peter Hunt's editing prowess helps establish the pace and rhythm of the film, and his quick cuts in fight sequences are especially noteworthy. It is almost impossible to perceive the cuts between the real actors and stuntmen during a Peter Hunt–edited fight scene. The special effects work in the film is performed by Frank George, whose model of Dr. No's fortress looks convincingly real when it is blown up at the film's end.

Monty Norman, a British composer whose other credits include the music for *Irma La Douce*, composed the score for *Dr. No*. The music features several Jamaican calypso songs which are performed on-screen by Byron Lee's all-Chinese band. The importance and appeal of the Bond films' musical scores were established with the first film—not only was "The James Bond Theme" an enormously successful hit, but other songs like "Under the Mango Tree" and "Jamaica Jump-Up" were published in sheet music. Steven Rubin, in his book *The James Bond Films,* claims that John Barry (whose orchestra performs "The James Bond Theme" for the film) actually composed the song. The story goes that Broccoli and Saltzman were unhappy with Monty Norman's theme and at the last minute asked Barry to compose one. Adapting a couple of tunes he had written for his jazz band, The John Barry Seven, the composer whipped up the famous theme in a few hours without having seen the film. Due to contractual obligations, Monty Norman has always received the credit for the Bond theme. But the producers made it up to Barry by hiring him to score no fewer than nine of the remaining Bond films.

Produced on a small budget but relying on the creative talents of a selected team of individuals, Cubby Broccoli and Harry Saltzman produced, in *Dr. No,* the beginning of a cinematic phenomenon. The film was surprisingly successful in England when it was released in October, 1962, and did very well in America when it was released there seven months later. James Bond's future in the cinema seemed confirmed at this point.

FROM RUSSIA WITH LOVE (1963)

□ PRODUCTION

With *Dr. No* a surprise hit, United Artists gave the go-ahead for Broccoli and Saltzman to make the next James Bond film. *From Russia With Love* was chosen for a number of reasons: it was one of Fleming's best novels; it had well-drawn characters and an exotic location (Istanbul) and it was a familiar title to the public. John F. Kennedy, you will recall, had listed this novel as one of his ten favorite books a year before production began.

The producers used most of the same production people who made *Dr. No,* and the result is again one of the best in the series. Many fans consider it *the* best Bond film simply because it is close to Fleming's original story. But as John Brosnan points out in his study of the films, *From Russia With Love* is out of step with the rest of the series. The formula, which is perfected in the third film, is noticeably absent in *From Russia With Love.* Missing are Ken Adam's futuristic, expressionistic sets, as well as the science fiction aspects that would dominate most of the Bond films. *From Russia With Love* tells a straight spy story, keeping well

On location in Istanbul for the gypsy girl fight in From Russia With Love. *(UPI Photo.)*

Sean Connery with co-star Daniela Bianchi in Istanbul for the filming of From Russia With Love. *(Wide World Photo.)*

within the bounds of realism. The film is also very well cast, with strong performances by theater veterans Robert Shaw and Lotte Lenya, as well as a good performance by Connery.

With a larger budget than was allowed on *Dr. No,* production of the second James Bond film began in 1962. Location filming took place in Istanbul, where the crew encountered many problems. The outdoor boat chase sequence caused innumerable difficulties, and the scene was finally reshot near England after two tries on location. Actor Pedro Armendariz, who portrayed Kerim Bey, was very ill during shooting; it was soon discovered he had a terminal disease. When Terence Young learned this, he rearranged the shooting schedule so that all of Armendariz's scenes could be shot immediately, and a stand-in could be used later if needed. (Armendariz reportedly killed himself in the hospital soon after shooting had been completed, rather than submit to a long and painful illness.)

The remainder of the film was shot near Pinewood Studios in England. For instance, the SPECTRE training camp was set up on the studio lawn. *From Russia With Love* was released in England in October of 1963, and was released six months later in the United States.

From Russia With Love begins with a pre-credits sequence which, from this point on, would become a continuing device in the series. It was reportedly Harry Saltzman who came up with this idea, which other filmmakers began to copy. TV action series began using pre-credits sequences as well. Many times the Bond pre-credits scenes have nothing to do with the main body of the films; but in *From Russia With Love,* the sequence is not only related, but serves as a foreshadowing of things to come.

Saltzman's idea was to have the film, which involved a plot to assassinate James Bond, begin with the actual assassination—only it wouldn't really be Bond! The scene shows Red Grant, the SPECTRE assassin, stalking James Bond through a moonlit garden (Young supposedly based the scene on one in Alain Resnais' *Last Year at Marienbad*) and eventually strangling the British agent with a garroting wire. But a SPECTRE official walks up to the dead body and removes a mask, revealing the agent to be someone else entirely. The scene is effective, and immediately creates a mysterious atmosphere that pervades the entire film. From this point on, the dangerous presence of Red Grant is emphasized by the memory of this scene.

Another important decision the producers made affecting the film and the ones that followed was the creation of James Bond gadgetry. Q Branch, the Armoury of the Secret Service, comes into its own in *From Russia With Love* and provides James Bond with a black attaché case containing all sorts of weaponry and devices. The early films' use of gadgetry, for the most part, was clever and amusing; but beginning with *Thunderball,* these contraptions began to dominate the screen and reduce the characters and the stories to simple manipulators of machinery.

The attaché case was actually based on Fleming's original idea. In the novel, the case contained a secret compartment and a flat throwing knife hidden in the lining. The film adds a sniperscope (with infra-red lens), ammunition, hidden gold sovereigns, and a tear gas cartridge which can be triggered only by using a trick method of opening the case. All of these devices come into play at crucial times during the film, and unlike the use of such implements in other Bond films, 007 must here rely on his wits and quick thinking to activate them.

□ SCREENPLAY

From Russia With Love is one of Richard Maibaum's most successful Bond screenplays mainly because of his faithful adaptation (with the help of Johanna Harwood) of the Fleming novel.

The most obvious difference in the story is the inclusion of SPECTRE. Continuing where he left off in *Dr. No,* Maibaum took Fleming's lead and changed the villain's organization from SMERSH (the Russians) to SPECTRE. In the novel, SMERSH is conducting a personal vendetta against James Bond. In the film, SPECTRE is playing both ends against the middle, as they pit the Russians against the British. SPECTRE's plot is to steal the Lektor coding machine (changed from Fleming's Spektor coding machine for obvious reasons) from the Russians and hand it over to James Bond through the actions of an innocent Russian girl. Their next step is to murder Bond in an embarrassing fashion and repossess the Lektor for resale to the Russians. The addition of SPECTRE complicates the plot somewhat, but not enough to do any real damage to the action of the story. The Russian girl, Tatiana Romanova, is still ordered by Rosa Klebb (who in the film retains her status in SMERSH but is secretly a member of SPECTRE) to seduce Bond and allow him to take the Lektor machine from the Russian Consulate in Istanbul. Red Grant, now a SPECTRE assassin rather than an employee of SMERSH, still stalks Bond throughout the story until the final confrontation aboard the Orient Express.

Other changes include a shortening of the assassination planning which took up a lengthy section of the novel. Maibaum's script capsulizes the plotting into a few scenes that total about fifteen minutes of screen time. There is also an additional well-written scene between Bond and Tania aboard the Orient Express in which Bond confronts the girl with Kerim's death. This scene took place off-screen in the novel; its inclusion in the film adds a moment of authentic dramatic conflict between the two characters (a kind of scene that rarely occurs in a James Bond film).

Finally, the producers told Maibaum to add two outdoor chase sequences toward the end of the film, perhaps feeling that the film would be claustrophobic up to this point. Although unnecessary, these scenes are exciting and do open up the film visually. Fans of the novel will also find that the ending is different. In the book, Rosa Klebb kicks Bond with the poison-tipped shoe, leaving him to crash "headlong to the wine-red floor." The film version couldn't end this way, so Rosa Klebb receives her just reward in the final scene. It is a nice touch having Tania, rather than Bond, shoot the woman.

Otherwise, almost everything else in the novel remains intact in the film. The gypsy camp battle, the assassination of Krilencu (although the actress' face on the billboard was changed from Marilyn Monroe to Anita Ekberg), and the Orient Express sequences all translate wonderfully to the screen.

□ DIRECTION

Terence Young is back at the helm for his second James Bond film. Much of the same stylistic qualities which made *Dr. No* a success are present in the new film: a fast tempo, hard-edged action scenes ending with moments of humor, and lively editing. But there is also a more sophisticated feeling in *From Russia With Love.* More attention has been paid to the story-telling (due largely to the fine script by Maibaum and the excellent ensemble acting by the cast), and the transitions between set-pieces are smoother. Moreover, Young has made the film as realistic as possible. *Dr. No* had its flights into fantasy, but *From Russia With Love* is for the most part believable throughout. The events in Fleming's story were not that far removed from things that could actually happen in the world of espionage, and Young managed to keep the action credible.

The film appears a little sloppy when compared to later Bond films. Young blames this on the "frantic shooting schedule" associated with the Bond films. The director told an interesting story to *Bondage* magazine about Pedro Armendariz's best scene as Kerim Bey having to be cut because it featured a character who had been killed in an earlier scene. There was to have been a scene before Bond's rendezvous with Tania on the ferry in which Bond is followed by the Bulgar with the glasses. Bond's taxi stops by a curb, and the Bulgar's car pulls up bumper-to-bumper behind it. Another car pulls up behind the Bulgar's car, blocking it between the two cars. When the Bulgar steps out to chew out the driver of the third car, he finds none other than Kerim Bey at the wheel. Another car pulls up beside Bond's taxi—he immediately enters it and is driven away, leaving the Bulgar pinned against the curb. Kerim, flicking a long ash from his cigar, says to the Bulgar, "My friend, that is life." When the rough cut of the film was screened, someone's son pointed out that the Bulgar was the same man killed earlier in the St. Sophia mosque, and the scene had to be eliminated.

☐ ACTORS AND CHARACTERS

Sean Connery delivers another fine performance in *From Russia With Love.* He seems more relaxed and confident than he did in *Dr. No,* although one misses the hard edges that were present only in that first film. But Connery, at this point, was growing into the role; he adds more sophistication to the way Bond carries himself. The character also shows a side that never appeared in any of the Fleming novels. This is during the new scene aboard the Orient Express, in which he confronts Tania with Kerim's death. James Bond actually slaps Tania, and spits out his questions with spite. One can hardly blame him, since his best friend has just died and he now believes that the girl, whom he has trusted all this time, has been lying to him. When Tania tearfully claims that she loves him, Bond mutters, "I'm sure you do," and walks into the next compartment. Connery plays the scene beautifully, and one can sense the harsh anger that emerges from within when he's crossed.

Daniela Bianchi makes an impressive film debut in *From Russia With Love* as Tatiana Romanova. Even though her role is boosted considerably by the fine script, Bianchi is convincing in presenting the essential qualities of her character—innocence, intelligence, and romantic idealism. Yet Tania is also a dedicated citizen of the Soviet Union, and when she is ordered by Rosa Klebb to accept the unusual assignment on behalf of the State, she doesn't hesitate. Bianchi, an extremely beautiful actress, exhibits all of these desires and internal conflicts between heart and mind; it is a shame she hasn't been seen in too many other films. One scene that stands out particularly is when she is trying on the new nightgowns Bond has bought for her. Through her playful attitude, one realizes that she is no longer pretending her love for him. She has warmed to her role of romantic spy and is playing it with conviction.

Bond's friend and ally in Turkey, Kerim Bey, is played by the late Pedro Armendariz, a fine character actor. The role is well cast, and Armendariz manages to flood the screen with the warmth and good nature of the character. It is Kerim who is the Obligatory Sacrificial Lamb of this picture, and it is truly a blow when he is murdered. Most of Fleming's descriptions of the man apply, although not enough time is spent on the character's interesting background.

The film contains two strong performances by its main villains: the late Robert Shaw as the killer, Red Grant; and Lotte Lenya as the evil Rosa Klebb. Shaw, noted at the time of the film mainly for his stage work, underwent a body-building course which transformed him into the muscular SPECTRE assassin. It was wise on the scriptwriter's part to keep the Grant character silent until Bond finally meets him as Captain Nash aboard the Orient Express. Up to this point, Grant appears several times in the film, watching and waiting for the appropriate time for the killing. This helps build suspense, and when Grant finally speaks to Bond, the effect is even more frightening. Shaw delivers a cold, menacing, brilliant performance.

The late Lotte Lenya, widow of the composer Kurt Weill and once a member of Bertolt Brecht's famous ensemble in Germany (she created the role of Jenny in *The Threepenny Opera*), might have seemed too glamorous for the role of an ugly, evil Russian murderess. But casting Lenya was a brilliant ploy on the producers' part. She delivers perfectly the "toad-like" qualities of the character, as well as the "perverse" aspects. The character's Lesbianism is even vaguely hinted at in the film. During the briefing with Tania, Lenya circles the girl like a cat ready to pounce on its prey. At one point, Klebb lays her hand momentarily on Tania's knee, causing a quick shock of negative electricity between the two characters. The audience feels the shock as well, which is a tribute to Lenya's acting ability.

Another well-cast character is that of Kronsteen, the master planner for SPECTRE. Played by Vladek Sheybal, Kronsteen is portrayed just as Fleming created him—cold, methodical, and confident.

This brings us to the problem of SPECTRE's leader, Ernst Stavro Blofeld, aka No. 1. In *From Russia With Love,* all we see of Blofeld are his shoulders and hands. Blofeld remains faceless until the fifth film, *You Only Live Twice,* which was a clever idea on the filmmakers' part. Blofeld is also associated with a long-haired white cat, which constantly sits in his lap receiving attention. The animal is purely an invention of the filmmakers, for the Blofeld of the novels never showed an affectation for pets. This was fine until Blofeld's face was revealed in the films, since the image didn't live up to expectation. The part of Blofeld has never been cast successfully, which is another source of frustration for Bond fans. But in *From Russia With Love* Blofeld serves his function and lends a certain mystery to the SPECTRE conception. The uncredited actor playing the role in this film was Anthony Dawson (who played Professor Dent in *Dr. No*), but the voice was dubbed by Eric Pohlman (also uncredited).

Desmond Llewelyn makes his first appearance as Major Boothroyd (or Q, as he will be called in subsequent films) in *From Russia With Love.* Usually a source of laughs, the Q Branch scenes (in which Q shows Bond the newest set of weapons and how they work) began rather simply but in later films have gone overboard, as have the gadgets themselves, in attempting the most outrageous visual jokes. Llewelyn has managed to make something of the character, and delivers his weapons lectures with a straight British face which is always amusing.

Bernard Lee and Lois Maxwell, as usual, deliver crisp performances as M and Miss Moneypenny. There is one amusing moment when Bond first enters the office and flings his hat across the room to the hat rack. He proclaims, "For my next miracle . . ." but suddenly realizes M is standing behind him. Bond shuffles his feet a moment, looks embarrassed, and walks on into M's office. M glances at Moneypenny, rolls his eyes, and follows Bond.

OTHER ASPECTS

As mentioned earlier, Ken Adam did not design this film. Instead, the previous film's art director, Syd Cain, is in charge. Cain's work in the film primarily utilizes existing locations. Some interiors were built, such as the cabin of the Orient Express, but the realism of the story was emphasized by the authentic locations.

Peter Hunt is editor again, and continues his fine work in keeping the pace and action moving. His editing of the gypsy camp attack is an especially well-constructed sequence and of course, his work on stunts is still a marvel. There is one flaw in the Bond/Grant fight scene, however; we don't see the tear gas cartridge explode in Grant's face when he opens the attaché case. Instead, the editor chose a reaction shot from Bond and a quick cut to Grant in a cloud of smoke. This doesn't quite work, but the editing of the fisticuffs that follow more than makes up for it. Peter Perkins choreographed the now-famous fight. It's certainly one of the longest screen scuffles ever staged, and it's quite brutal. Bob Simmons doubled for Connery, but it's impossible to tell when the cuts are made between Connery and Simmons, as well as between Shaw and his double. The fight is less bloody than the Fleming version, but it's made more interesting by the use of the gadgets inside the attaché case. (A word of

warning to television viewers: ABC edited the scene drastically. In fact, ABC did a poor job of editing *all* of the early 007 films for television.)

Ted Moore's cinematography seems more colorful than before, and the special effects, created by John Stears and Frank George and consisting mainly of helicopters and boats exploding, are well executed. Jocelyn Rickards' costume designs are worth mentioning simply because of their believability in period and locale.

John Barry composed, arranged, and conducted the score for the film, save for the title track. The sound of the score is quite different from that of *Dr. No,* (except for "The James Bond Theme") in that Barry uses a full orchestra, emphasizing brass and percussion. The *From Russia With Love* score is serious and moody, with many levels of dynamics. Barry likes to emphasize fight scenes with sudden increases of volume and syncopation. One tune, entitled "007," is featured during the gypsy camp battle and the raid on the Russian consulate. This highly syncopated piece has become a standard tune in most of the Barry-scored Bond films. Lionel Bart's title theme is lush and romantic, and works well as the first of the Bond vocal tunes. *From Russia With Love* features Matt Monroe crooning the main theme at the film's end.

From Russia With Love received even more critical and popular attention that its predecessor. Knowing that they now had a valuable investment on their hands, Cubby Broccoli and Harry Saltzman added an announcement to the end credits of the film, stating that "James Bond will return . . . in *Goldfinger.*" This was to become another standard device in the films—the announcement of the next one.

This film was the last one that Ian Fleming saw. Luckily, it is one of the best in the series, and something of which he could be proud.

GOLDFINGER (1964)

□ PRODUCTION

Goldfinger represents the peak of the series. It is the most perfectly realized of all the films with hardly a wrong step made throughout its length. It moves at a fast and furious pace, but the plot holds together logically enough (more logically than the book) and is a perfect blend of the real and the fantastic.

(John Brosnan, *James Bond in the Cinema*)

Sean Connery and the gold-painted Shirley Eaton on the set of Goldfinger. (UPI Photo.)

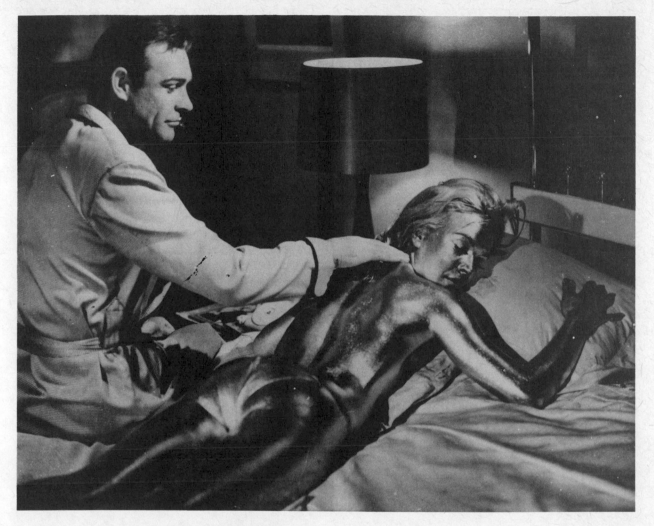

I agree totally with this statement. *Goldfinger* is the representative film of the James Bond series. It's also an excellent action/adventure picture on its own: it has suspense, sex, and satire. It is the first Bond film to actually poke fun at itself, but it never loses sight of the central character. The Broccoli and Saltzman formula was perfected with this, their third film. The remaining pictures simply are slight variations on the formula.

One and a quarter million pounds were spent on the making of *Goldfinger,* almost four times the amount spent on *Dr. No.* United Artists also spent more money promoting the new film, and the resulting publicity made James Bond a household name. Released in December of 1964, *Goldfinger* was a blockbuster hit, and the catalyst of the big spy movie boom in the sixties.

Goldfinger differs from its predecessors in that a new director is at the helm, bringing the film a tighter, wittier style without diminishing the level of suspense. As Steven Jay Rubin points out in his book *The James Bond Films,* a sequence like the Aston Martin car chase around Auric Enterprises is fun and amusing. Then suddenly—Oddjob's hat kills Tilly Masterson, and the mood abruptly switches to one of foreboding. There are also more fantastic elements in *Goldfinger* than in the first two Bond films. This is due mainly to Ken Adam's designs for the film, and also to the swarm of gadgets. This was a time of fascination with "gee whiz" technology. The film is the first to include a realistically presented laser. An atomic bomb features prominently in the plot. The audience is given a glimpse of the test center for Q Branch, where employees experiment with the latest in exploding parking meters, bulletproof vests, and other gadgets of the spy trade. Here, Bond is issued the ultimate company car. James Bond's now-famous Aston Martin DB-V was actually made by the Aston Martin plant in Newport Pagnall. By using a control box inside an arm rest, Bond could release a smoke screen, an oil slick, raise a bulletproof shield, or slash another car's tires. The car has a radar homing device, as in the novel, but it also comes equipped with machine guns behind the front and rear parking lights. And the *coup de grace* is an ejector seat, controlled by a red button located in the stick shift. At the time of the film's release, the Aston Martin was a fantastic, outrageous put-on; yet audiences all over the world wanted to believe it was real. The ideas behind the car are not that far from reality—the car *could* exist. This is precisely why the gadgetry in *Goldfinger* works, but doesn't in some of the later films. Though the simulated technology of the film places it in a genre resembling science fiction, the gadgetry is believable.

Goldfinger is also significant in that it is the last Bond film to actually attempt to be erotic. Bond's scenes with Jill Masterson early in the film are the most sugges-tive of any Bond film, as is Shirley Eaton's near nudity. There has never been nudity in a Bond film; we see a flash of leg here, a glimpse of back there, but nothing beyond the titillation level. Miss Eaton's role was a departure from those constraints, and the Bonds have never been the same since. Additionally, the film is probably the most sexist of them all. When Bond slaps the masseuse, Dink, on the rear after sending her away because he and Felix Leiter must perform "man talk," the situation is embarrassingly chauvinistic.

☐ **SCREENPLAY**

Steven Rubin calls the Richard Maibaum/Paul Dehn script for *Goldfinger* the "key script" which became the "blueprint" for future Bonds. This is very true. One can easily pinpoint the elements from the screenplay that have been repeated in later films: a car chase; Bond's seduction of a female enemy to gain an ally; a climax featuring two "armies" battling it out; a countdown which must be stopped to save the world; a villain employing a super-strong henchman; and a final

Honor Blackman (as Pussy Galore) practices her judo on stuntman Bob Simmons in preparation for a scene in Goldfinger. (Photo by Loomis Dean, Life Magazine. © Copyright 1964 by Time, Inc.)

scene with a "sting"—just when the audience has been led to believe Bond's danger is past, the peril resumes.

The Maibaum/Dehn script is very clever. It is full of ingenious plot twists and witty dialogue. I feel it's the only film in the series to *improve* on Fleming's original story. There are several reasons why this is so. First, the script calls for Bond to *discover* Jill Masterson's gold-painted, dead body. In the novel, Bond leaves Jill early in the story and learns about her death second-hand in the middle of the book. The screen version is far more effective—we actually *see* the body. It's an eerie, ghostly scene. Bond has been knocked unconscious by Oddjob, and wakes to find Jill lying face down on the bed. Her body seems to radiate in the bronze-colored room, and the music takes on a sombre tone. The scene captures perfectly the serious side of the James Bond films. There's certainly nothing amusing about it.

A second improvement over the Fleming original is the elimination of Tilly Masterson early in the film. In the novel, Tilly becomes a major character, and is with Bond all the way through the raid on Fort Knox. There, she finally meets her death by Oddjob's bowler hat. Her presence in the novel is gratuitous after we learn that she is Jill Masterson's sister, and this is corrected in the film. Tilly is killed in the first half of the story, which makes more sense. Goldfinger would have killed her anyway, once he had found out she was Jill's sister. His failure to do so in the book is implausible.

Third, as John Brosnan mentions, the script improved on the novel by having Goldfinger take Bond to America as a prisoner rather than as an employee. Abruptly deciding to spare Bond's life (as well as Tilly's) and hire him as a secretary is unbelievable. In the film, Goldfinger keeps Bond alive and in his sight, simply to keep anyone who may be observing (such as Felix Leiter) from thinking Bond is in any danger. Goldfinger orders Pussy Galore to dress more seductively and openly show Bond around the stud farm "as a guest." And of course, Goldfinger can't resist the temptation of handcuffing Bond to the atomic bomb inside Fort Knox—something he probably planned when he made the decision to keep Bond alive.

Fourth, the script changes Goldfinger's intention. In the novel, his plan is simply to *rob* Fort Knox. In the film, he plans to detonate an atomic bomb inside the vault, thereby contaminating the U.S. gold supply for the next fifty-eight years or so. Not only would this cause economic disaster for America, it would also increase the value of Goldfinger's own supply of bul-

lion ten-fold. It's a more ingenious plot, for which Maibaum and Dehn share the credit.

Finally, there is a change in the cause of death for both Oddjob and Goldfinger. In the book, Oddjob is sucked out of the airplane window when Bond smashes it with a throwing-knife. Goldfinger dies by Bond's own hands, strangled to death. In the film, Oddjob meets his death in a more spectacular way during the climax of the film. He is electrocuted, thanks to Bond's quick thinking, inside the vault of Fort Knox. And it's Goldfinger who is sucked out of the airplane window, after a gun has been fired in the cabin. This reworking of the ending is more logical in terms of structure, and is ultimately more satisfying.

As usual, there are a couple of sequences that don't quite work. For example, there is the scene in which Goldfinger explains Operation Grand Slam to a room full of gangsters. He promises them one million dollars today if they'd like, or ten million tomorrow if they stay and hear him out. All but one stay and listen to the plan to raid Fort Knox, about which they all seem enthusiastic. But Goldfinger then leaves the room and gives an order for the gangsters to be killed with nerve gas. Why he does this is never explained. Perhaps Goldfinger just wanted to express his megalomanic desires to this group of top American gangsters, then decided he didn't need them after all.

The script contains some awfully funny lines. In one scene, a radio is blaring out that the president is "completely satisfied." Bond's hand turns the radio off at this point, and we see him in bed with Jill Masterson. "That makes two of us," he says with a contented sigh. A little later, as he's taking a bottle of champagne from the refrigerator, Bond tells her that "drinking Dom Perignon '53 at a temperature above thirty-eight degrees Farenheit is like listening to the Beatles without ear-muffs." One of my favorite lines in the film occurs when Bond is strapped down, watching a laser beam inch closer and closer toward his groin. "You expect me to talk?" he asks Goldfinger. "No, Mr. Bond," Goldfinger replies, "I expect you to die!"

□ DIRECTION

Terence Young began preproduction work on *Goldfinger* before deciding to direct *The Amorous Adventures of Moll Flanders* instead. To replace him, Broccoli and Saltzman turned to Guy Hamilton, one of their original choices for *Dr. No.*

Hamilton brought to the series a fresher, tighter style.

Hamilton has a special flare for comedy as well, which is evident in the Bond films he directed (Hamilton holds the record—four Bond films). Unfortunately, the other three Hamilton efforts are low on the totem pole as far as the series is concerned, mainly due to his leanings toward comedy. Too often, the comedy is downright silly. But in *Goldfinger,* the humor is witty and sharp. The visual jokes are a pleasure, and not offensive at all.

Hamilton brought an even faster pace to the rhythm of the film. *Goldfinger* moves rapidly, effecting changes of location so quickly that one can understand why Broccoli calls them "bumps." Less than two hours long, *Goldfinger* is the shortest Bond film in the series, yet there is nothing missing in terms of plot development. Hamilton makes sure that all information is emphasized and heard, and his *mise en scène* is controlled and sophisticated. The only sloppiness in *Goldfinger* is during the raid on Fort Knox, in which the soldiers do not die convincingly, and at the film's end, when the wires holding the model airplane can be seen.

Hamilton's overall style is nowhere more evident than in the brilliant pre-credits sequence. It's the best of the series, and could stand on its own as a short subject. The scene begins with a visual joke: we see a duck in the water, which is revealed to be a rubber decoy attached to James Bond's head! Bond climbs out of the water, dressed in a rubber suit, and scales a wall surrounding a factory in South America. After disposing of a guard, Bond sets a timed explosive inside a strange room filled with heroin poppies. (This sequence is vaguely alluded to in the novel.) Bond then leaves the premises and discards the rubber suit to reveal a fresh white tuxedo underneath. A red carnation is added to the lapel, which provokes another laugh. Bond then visits a nearby nightclub, where he meets a dancer in her dressing room. Bond hangs his shoulder holster near the bathtub and embraces the girl, who is draped only in a towel. But she has set him up—in her eye, Bond sees the reflection of a man approaching him from behind. Bond whirls the girl around to catch the man's blow, and a very tough fight sequence ensues. Bond succeeds in throwing the man into the bathtub. The man grabs for Bond's gun hanging nearby, but Bond tosses an electric heater into the tub. The man is electrocuted instantly. Bond mutters, "Shocking. Positively shocking." It is said with a straight face, and with an inflection containing no amusement. The effect, however, brings the house down. Bond silently leaves the room and shuts the door.

This opening sequence is a terrific exercise in style—there is humor, intrigue, eroticism, violence, sophistication—and Hamilton manages to keep it up for the remainder of the film.

☐ ACTORS AND CHARACTERS

Richard Maibaum, in an article appearing in *Playboy* magazine, said that Guy Hamilton "evoked from (Sean) Connery an even surer, brisker, more sardonic Bond than in the earlier films. The effect was to make him more perversely attractive." This is definitely true. Sean Connery gives a performance that is a pleasure to watch. He personifies the meaning of "cool" in this film—he is totally relaxed, yet able to take command of any situation. He retains the tough persona but reveals an even more sophisticated wit than Bond has had in previous films. This is especially true during the golf game with Goldfinger. Connery succeeds in giving Bond an innocent exterior while the character is secretly conning Goldfinger out of five thousand pounds. Pussy Galore is an enemy, and Bond later realizes the value of having the woman as an ally. After relying on an arsenal of gadgets throughout the film, Bond must now trust his ultimate weapon—himself—to use on Pussy. Needless to say, Pussy's tomboy tendencies are vanquished.

Gert Frobe takes the top prize as best villain in a Bond film. This German actor fits Fleming's description perfectly: he is short, round, and redheaded. It is claimed that Frobe's voice was dubbed for the film, but it certainly doesn't appear so. Frobe exhibits Goldfinger's controlled madness superbly, and his obsession for gold is quite believable. The look on Frobe's face when Bond tosses the gold brick down next to Goldfinger's ball on the putting green is priceless. Another great moment is when Goldfinger's gin rummy ploy has been wrecked by Bond. The camera moves in for a huge close-up of Goldfinger's red face after losing, and it is shaking with anger.

Honor Blackman, who became a star playing Cathy Gale in the TV series, *The Avengers,* before the program was shown in America, portrays Pussy Galore. In the film, Pussy Galore is Goldfinger's employee and works as his personal pilot. In the novel, she was just another one of the hoods' congress members who became more actively involved in Operation Grand Slam. Blackman is good in the role, displaying the appropriate "butch" quality required for the character. In the novel, Pussy Galore is a Lesbian, and makes no bones about it until Bond comes along. In the film, these qualities are vaguely hinted at, but at the most, Pussy comes off as just a tough tomboy. Blackman is especially good with the stunts, doing most of her own work without a stand-in. Already experienced in the martial arts from her TV series, Blackman seems to be a natural at judo.

The beautiful Shirley Eaton portrays the doomed Jill Masterson, one of this film's two Obligatory Sacrificial Lambs. Though her role is brief, it is memorable. One can scarcely forget the many pictures of the "golden girl" used in the film's advertising campaign. She was even featured on the cover of *Life*. Eaton was convincing as an English "party girl," and it's a shame her role wasn't larger.

The late Harold Sakata (also known as Tosh Togo) became an overnight sensation with his portrayal of the first in a long line of villains' super-strong henchmen. Variations on this character would be created for subsequent Bond films, but none of them have been as successful as the immortal Oddjob. Short, but built like an ox, Sakata is perfect as Goldfinger's Korean bodyguard and chauffeur. The character's dialogue, as in the book, only consists of grunts and inarticulate sounds, but the actor makes these sounds enormously expressive. He has a deadly smile, too. When he beckons to Bond before their massive fight inside the vault of Fort Knox, his accompanying grin makes us laugh and shiver at the same time.

Tania Mallet gives an adequate performance as Tilly Masterson, who is *Goldfinger*'s second Obligatory Sacrificial Lamb. In the novel, she too, is a Lesbian, but nothing is made of this in the film. Instead, Tilly is portrayed as a very independent woman who is out for revenge. She is a little reckless, and at one point almost shoots Bond accidentally. She is also stubborn and uncooperative; it is her fault primarily that she and Bond are caught spying on Auric Enterprises. But Miss Mallet's performance still manages to evoke sympathy when Tilly is killed by Oddjob's bowler hat.

Felix Leiter is miscast once again, and this time the unlucky actor is Cec Linder, a Canadian. Linder is too old for the role—he looks like Bond's uncle rather than his best friend. Linder (and the script) depict Leiter as a terrifically nice guy, but a bit short on brains. This character, once again, has been misrepresented in the script and on the screen. And what's Felix Leiter doing relaying instructions from M to Bond? Leiter works for the CIA, not the British Secret Service. Apparently the two organizations have the same Q Branch too, for

Leiter's car is also equipped with a radar homing screen.

Bernard Lee, Lois Maxwell, and Desmond Llewelyn all return for the third Bond outing, and give their usual impeccable performances. Llewelyn, especially, has his moment of glory when explaining the Aston Martin's features to Bond. After a wonderful set-up by Connery ("Ejector seat? You're joking!"), Q delivers a perfectly deadpan line to the camera: "I *never* joke about my work, 007."

□ OTHER ASPECTS

Ken Adam is back as production designer for *Goldfinger,* and the film is one of his finest pieces of work. Fresh from designing Stanley Kubrick's *Dr. Strangelove,* Adam places his unmistakable stamp on *Goldfinger* with several fantastic, ultramodern sets. The pre-credits sequence features two interesting settings, including the weird room full of heroin poppies. The test center for Q Branch, Goldfinger's laser room, and Goldfinger's study are all unusual, expressionistic designs. But Adam's most breathtaking accomplishment in the film is the conception of the interior of Fort Knox. After having been denied admittance to the real Fort Knox, Adam was forced to design the vault according to his imagination. The result, in his own words, is "what we *want* the inside of Fort Knox to be like." It is a huge room of several stories, surrounded on all sides by jail-like bars housing piles of gold bricks. The set glitters and glows in the lights and is beautiful to look at. It also serves as a wonderful stage for the fight between Bond and Oddjob. With the help of art director Peter Murton, Adam has established a gold motif underlying the film's designs. As John Brosnan notes, the color seems to saturate every scene in the movie. It is one of Adam's best efforts. Ted Moore's cinematography also benefits from the illustrious designs. *Goldfinger,* as a result, is one of the most attractive films of its genre.

The picture won the series' first Academy Award for best achievement in sound effects. The work of sound recordists Dudley Messenger and Gordon McCullum established a norm for the rest of the series, emphasizing exaggerated effects (especially in fight scenes).

Peter Hunt once again shows his expertise at editing a fast-paced action film. His work on the Bond/Oddjob fight must count as one of his finest achievements. The same can be said for stunt arranger Bob Simmons. The Bond/Oddjob battle is certainly the best in any Bond film, and must surely stand as one of the great cinematic combats. During the fight, Oddjob plays with Bond like a cat plays with a mouse. Bond is thrown against walls, slammed in the chest, and sent hurtling across the floor. (Connery was even hurt during the filming of the scene.) Maibaum and Dehn again must share some of the credit, for the details of the fight are ingenious. When Oddjob's metal-rimmed bowler hat is stuck between the bars of the vault, Bond tricks the Korean into walking over to retrieve it. It is then that Bond uses a previously severed electrical cable to cause Oddjob to (as Bond puts it later) "blow a fuse."

John Barry's musical score is tops, and like the other production elements, serves as a groundplan for future scores. Shirley Bassey's rendition of the *Goldfinger* theme (with lyrics by Anthony Newley and Leslie Bricusse) is explosive and exciting. The song became a familiar tune connected with the series, and was the first Bond musical hit. The song is featured over the film's main title credits, which are designed by Robert Brownjohn. Similar to the credits of *From Russia With Love,* the sequence features projections on the body of a gold-painted girl.

Barry's score is brassy and raunchy. It has a sassy sexiness to it, personified by muted horns and tuned percussion. In 1964, John Barry was just reaching his prime. His scores for the rest of the series, as well as for other films in the mid- to late sixties, feature his best work.

The producers achieved a remarkable degree of originality and freshness in *Goldfinger* (and in the first two films, for that matter). Unfortunately, this was the peak, and although there would be some exciting and interesting moments in future Bond films, none would equal *Goldfinger* or its two predecessors.

THUNDERBALL (1965)

□ PRODUCTION

Thunderball, you will recall, is based on an original story by Kevin McClory, Jack Whittingham, and Ian Fleming. McClory won the film rights to THUNDERBALL in 1963, after a two-year court battle with Fleming and Ivar Bryce, while Fleming retained the rights to his published novel. Meanwhile, during the filming of *Goldfinger,* Cubby Broccoli and Harry Saltzman were planning the next Bond film (which was to be *On Her Majesty's Secret Service*). But these plans were dropped when McClory was approached by the producers with a deal to coproduce *Thunderball.*

McClory proved to be invaluable to Broccoli and Saltzman in the making of the film. An avid water sportsman, McClory lent his expertise in scuba diving to the production. His many contacts in this field were helpful, and the coproduction was a success.

The producers decided to make *Thunderball* even more larger than life than *Goldfinger.* Allotted a budget of two and a half million pounds, the film emphasizes exaggeration. There are more gadgets, and the technology of the film takes the starring role. As a result, *Thunderball* is spectacular visually, but this approach has its detrimental effects as well. Beginning with *Thunderball,* Eon Productions began to lose sight of the James Bond character, as well as the special world created by Ian Fleming. James Bond became a character with no motivation—a man simply manipulated by the technology filling the screen. Credibility also began to go out the window; the James Bond films became something resembling science fiction.

Thunderball, however, is still better than any of the Bond films produced after 1970. It manages to retain some of the hard edges found in the earlier films. This is most likely due to the film's director, Terence Young, who is back after a one-picture absence. But even Young was dissatisfied with the film; he admits that it "is not his favorite by a long shot." *Thunderball* tends to bog down under the weight of its own bigness. Parts of the film are extremely slow moving, the plot is over-complicated, and the film is too lengthy. Assets of the film include impressive visual effects; underwater photography; a fairly good cast; the most exotic locations yet; a fine John Barry score; and a few moments here and there which stand out as pure Bond.

The film was made on location in the Bahamas and interiors were shot, as usual, at Pinewood Studios in England. In terms of box office receipts, *Thunderball* was a phenomenal success.

□ SCREENPLAY

Richard Maibaum wrote a screenplay based on the novel THUNDERBALL in 1961 when it was considered for the first of Eon Productions' series. These plans were dropped when the title went into litigation, and *Dr. No* was substituted. In 1964, Maibaum wrote a new screenplay with John Hopkins. The final version of the script is fairly faithful to Fleming's novel, with a few variations.

Sean Connery with Claudine Auger as Domino on location in the Bahamas for the filming of Thunderball. (Wide World Photo.)

SPECTRE is back, as is Ernst Stavro Blofeld. As in the novel, the SPECTRE headquarters are in Paris and its cover identity is an organization that locates missing members of the French Resistance, which is credible enough. But SPECTRE would become comparable to a *Fortune* 500 conglomerate in later films. In *From Russia With Love,* SPECTRE's headquarters were aboard a yacht near Venice. In *Thunderball,* Ken Adam's futuristic design of SPECTRE's conference room tends to ultramodernize Fleming's original conception. The script includes the execution of a SPECTRE agent who has been embezzling funds. He is electrocuted in his chair during the meeting. As John Brosnan notes, this is basically a rehash of the execution of Kronsteen in *From Russia With Love.* (Since the electrocution occurred in Fleming's novel, perhaps the scene in *Russia* was inspired by the *Thunderball* execution.) Variations of this type of execution scene would appear in subsequent films.

Maibaum and Hopkins have needlessly complicated SPECTRE's plot to hijack two atomic bombs. In the novel, SPECTRE hires a NATO pilot named Petacchi

to crash-land the *Vulcan* near the Bahamas. In the film, SPECTRE hires a man named Angelo to first undergo plastic surgery in order to *impersonate* the pilot of the *Vulcan,* who is named Derval. In the novel, Petacchi is Domino's brother. In the film, it is the original pilot, Derval, who is Domino's brother. Derval is murdered early in the film by Angelo, and from then on, the hijack operation takes the same course it does in the novel. It is unnecessary to introduce this additional plot device, and it isn't all that clear what's going on during the shifting around of bodies at Shrublands Health Spa, where the dead Derval is ultimately deposited. As a result, the first half hour of *Thunderball* is confusing.

One well-written scene takes place at the casino in Nassau where Bond challenges Emilio Largo to a game of *chemin de fer.* This is one of the more successful sequences in the novel as well, and the film manages to capture the scene intact. Although the scene isn't as tense as it should have been, the dialogue works very well. The scene that follows in the Café Martinique is also quite good. This is when Domino begins to become enchanted by Bond, and lets him know she would like to get away from Largo. It's one of the more romantic scenes in any of the Bond films.

The scriptwriters have also created a new character for the film. She is Fiona Volpe, a beautiful SPECTRE agent who first seduces Bond, then attempts to kill him. She is basically a variation of the Miss Taro character from *Dr. No,* and there would be more variations on this character in subsequent films. Fiona, however, is the most successful of all these female villains. The scene in which Bond is taken captive after their love-making in his hotel room contains the film's only remnants of Fleming's James Bond character. When he realizes he has not won Fiona to his side with his amorous assets, he tells her with spite, "You don't think I *enjoyed* what we did this evening, do you? What I did tonight was for Queen and country!" This statement causes Fiona to fume. It's an effective scene.

The film also adds a spectacular foot chase through the famous Junkanoo Parade which takes place in Nassau every year. The parade was staged for filming, since it was the wrong season for the actual event. It's one of the film's more exciting sequences, and the subsequent action at the Kiss Kiss Club is also interesting. Bond hides there from the SPECTRE agents by mixing with some dancers. Fiona, however, finds him and cuts in. Though it smacks of the pre-credits sequence in *Goldfinger,* the death of Fiona is a high-

Adolfo Celi as Emilio Largo, addressing a group of SPECTRE frogmen in Thunderball. *(Photo by Loomis Dean,* Life Magazine. *© Copyright 1965 by Time, Inc.)*

light of the film. Bond sees that one of the SPECTRE men is aiming a gun at him from behind the band. He whirls Fiona around to receive the bullet, after which he sets her in a chair at a crowded table. "Can my wife sit here?" he asks innocently. "She's just dead."

The remainder of the film basically follows the novel, except that Bond and Leiter do not tail the *Disco Volante* in a submarine. Instead, Bond disposes of a SPECTRE agent and impersonates the man in order to infiltrate the *Disco* (which is the same thing he did to gain entrance to Dr. No's laboratory in that film). But Bond is discovered, and Largo's men manage to trap him in a cave. Thanks to a homing pill provided by Q Branch, Leiter is able to track Bond down. Bond then joins the NATO team of paratroopers who attack the SPECTRE diving force. The ending is a little different, too. In the novel, Largo meets his death underwater during the big battle. In the film, Largo escapes the battle and boards the *Disco Volante* for a getaway. Bond pursues him and a final climactic fight (which doesn't quite work) occurs on the boat. It is here that

Domino shoots Largo in the back with a spear gun, just as Largo is aiming a pistol at Bond. (Shades of the Klebb/Romanova/Bond final scene in *From Russia With Love.*)

The script does contain some of the series' best one-liners. Bond is equipped with more funny asides than he is with Q's weaponry—and many of them are just as deadly! Some of the better ones: Q, explaining the new equipment to Bond, commands, "I want you to keep this flare on you day and night." Bond says, "I resent that remark." Later, as Largo is showing Bond around his home, Palmyra, Bond picks up a rifle. "Lady's gun, isn't it?" Bond asks. "Oh, do you know a lot about guns?" Largo asks. "No," Bond replies, "but I know a little bit about women."

□ DIRECTION

With the return of the original Bond director, Terence Young, *Thunderball* lacks the exceptionally fast pace that *Goldfinger* had. It is most damaging in this case, for if anything, *Thunderball* needs to move faster. Young blames this on other problems!

To my mind all that underwater stuff was anti–James Bond, because it was slow motion. People swim slowly and you couldn't have them going very fast; we undercranked some of the shots and they looked ridiculous—the water was wobbling around so much it suddenly became stupid.

(From "The Terence Young Interview," by Richard Schenkman, *Bondage* 10)

Young also disagreed with the direction in which the producers wanted *Thunderball* to go, although he reluctantly admitted it was probably commercially viable to load it with gadgetry.

I thought if we were going to make this underwater stuff we've got to put in, like I said (one of my old lines in the picture) "He's wearing everything including the Kitchen Sink." I really meant that. I thought if we're going to go with this, let's do it properly, and they did. They piled in as much as they could, and that's why I said after *Thunderball,* "I think you don't want a director anymore, you want an MIT graduate to handle all the machines."

(*Bondage, Ibid.*)

Thunderball does recapture the more realistic style of the earlier films in relation to action scenes. All of the fight sequences are tough (the pre-credits fight between Bond and the widow is terrific) and the violence is hard edged. The instance in which a SPECTRE agent is thrown into Largo's shark pool is particularly graphic, even though we don't really see him being eaten alive. But the scene is one of the bloodier sequences in any Bond film.

Young's staging of the Junkanoo Parade is masterful. The director instructed his several assistant directors to weave in and out of the parade, with strict orders not to stop the procession. Peter Hunt's editing again takes center stage here, as many different shots are composed to create the big chase.

There are still continuity problems in *Thunderball.* The most obvious mistake is during the big underwater battle, when Bond's blue face mask is pulled off by Largo. Bond reaches down and pulls a *black* mask off of a dead SPECTRE frogman. In the very next shot, Bond is wearing the *blue* mask again. Young and Hunt both attribute this to the furious shooting schedules of the Bond films. The important thing, they feel, is to keep the action moving and not give the audience time to ask questions until they're on the way home from the theater.

Thunderball was Young's last Bond film. It's too bad, for Young is the man who originated the style of the series and attempted to keep some semblance of Ian Fleming's original concepts intact. Young told *Bondage* magazine that he would be willing to return to the series, if asked, only to direct the last film.

The *"Disco Volante"* in Thunderball. (Photo by Loomis Dean, Life Magazine. © Copyright 1965 by Time, Inc.)

□ ACTORS AND CHARACTERS

Sean Connery gives another confident performance as James Bond, but his character is minimized by the production. Aside from a few moments of real drama (such as the scene with Fiona), Connery is not given much of a chance to display the James Bond qualities of the early films. The script has given him some terrific one-liners, and these he delivers with a subtlety that works very well. His toying with Emilio Largo while lunching with the villain at Palmyra is especially amusing.

Claudine Auger, a former Miss France, makes her film debut as the spoiled Italian beauty, Domino Vitali. The script unfortunately does not make use of the character as well as it could have. Miss Auger is well cast, and displays the "rich bitch" qualities of the character effectively (until charmed by Bond), but she isn't given the chance to explore the role fully. Domino is one of Fleming's more successful female characters, but the film script reduces her to just another cardboard Bond-girl. The actress is attractive, and adequate to the film's demands.

Noted Brazilian actor and director Adolfo Celi portrays the rugged SPECTRE villain, Emilio Largo. Celi is well cast also, although his voice is dubbed. The actor faces the same problem that Miss Auger does, i.e., the script does not do justice to Fleming's character. Celi does manage to create a menacing villain nonetheless, wearing a black eyepatch that adds a great deal to Largo's screen presence. The white hair, the black patch, and Celi's thin lips create a truly powerful image. His best scene occurs during the *chemin de fer* sequence, when he begins to suspect Bond of being an enemy agent. Accusing the Englishman of putting the evil eye on his cards, Largo returns the gesture by making the old Italian curse sign of outstretched second and fifth fingers. The rising anger in Largo is portrayed vividly in Celi's eye and shoulders.

Luciana Paluzzi portrays Fiona Volpe, the red-headed SPECTRE beauty. Miss Paluzzi is quite good, and for once, we believe the actress when she throws Bond's sexual prowess back into his face. She is a most effective *femme fatale,* and her character is one of the most successful elements in the film. Paluzzi possesses the good looks and catlike sexual aggressiveness necessary to make the role credible.

Felix Leiter is portrayed by yet a third actor, Rik Van Nutter. This is by far the most successful casting of the CIA agent to date. Nutter is lean, blond, and boyish. The script, however, does not give the char-

acter any real depth. Leiter comes off as Bond's side-kick—he is always there to say, "Gee whiz, James, do you think that's the right thing to do?" or something to that effect. He doesn't seem to have any independence. And the filmmakers still resist featuring Leiter with a hook and a wooden leg. Therefore, despite the good casting, Nutter suffers in a mediocre role.

The film's Obligatory Sacrificial Lamb is Martine Beswick as Paula. This is Miss Beswick's second James Bond film, for she appeared in *From Russia With Love* as one of the gypsy girls who fights for the love of Vavra's son. Paula is the Secret Service's agent in the Bahamas, and appears to be around only to aid Bond and look attractive. Her character, created for the film, never does anything particularly useful, and she basically serves as just another Bond beauty included to provide glamour. Paula is kidnapped by Fiona's hoodlums, and swallows a cyanide pill to avoid torture. Another Bond-girl in the film (this one's loaded with them) is Molly Peters as Patricia Fearing. Patricia, a nurse at the Shrublands Health Spa, is a character right out of the novel. Her role is relatively small, but serves the function of providing Bond with female attention for the first two reels. Miss Peters displays the good looks necessary for the part.

Count Lippe is a disappointment in the film. The novel creates an interesting character who, because of his eccentricities, first gives Bond suspicions that something wicked is afoot. Lippe's actions in the film are taken practically verbatim from the novel, but somehow the casting of Guy Doleman (who hasn't much screen presence) does not fit the bill. More successful, however, are the casting of Philip Locke and Michael Brennan as two of Largo's slimy henchmen, Vargas and Janni.

Blofeld is again hidden from the camera in this film. His voice, however, is dubbed by Joseph Wiseman, who played Dr. No in the first film. Still petting that silly white cat, Blofeld sits up in an isolated booth overlooking the SPECTRE conference room. Venetian blinds discreetly cover the actor's face, whoever it may be. Wiseman's "voice of doom" cannot help but evoke snickers from the audience—he sounds so sinister that it's a wonder his own men trust him. (Who'd want to be in SPECTRE anyway? One foul-up and you either get kicked with a poisoned shoe, electrocuted in your own chair, or blown up on the highway!)

Bernard Lee has a wonderful moment as M. Bond is late for an important meeting of the entire Secret Service staff. When he finally arrives, M begins the meeting by giving 007 a dirty look and saying, "Now that we're all *here* . . ." And later, during his private briefing, Bond shows M the photograph of Domino and her brother. "You think she's worth going after?" M inquires. Bond blinks and replies, "Well, I wouldn't put it quite *that* way, sir."

Lois Maxwell and Desmond Llewelyn respectively give their usual flirtatious and authoritative performances, although it's becoming obvious that the filmmakers are running out of fresh ideas for these traditional scenes.

☐ OTHER ASPECTS

The film *is* stunning visually. Ted Moore's cinematography captures the beauty of the locations, and gives the film the most open and colorful look yet. Ivan Tors Underwater Studios, Ltd., was hired to film the underwater scenes. Underwater cameraman Lamar Boren does a splendid job, especially during the hijack operation. This is the film's most striking scene, in which SPECTRE frogmen extract the two atomic bombs from the sunken *Vulcan* and load them onto their underwater "chariot." Other underwater scenes include Bond's reconaissance of the *Disco Volante*'s hull, his discovery of the Vulcan, and the final, climactic battle between the NATO paratroopers and the SPECTRE team. This last scene drags a bit (due to the slow movements in the water) and does not build to a higher level of excitement. This is an unfortunate problem in submarine filming.

Ken Adam is designing again, but because the film is heavy on outdoor locations, Adam's duties are restricted to a few interiors and the many gadgets that flood the film. Among these items are Bond's jet-pack; a Geiger counter camera and wristwatch (the only gadgets inspired by the novel); a four-minute "breather" which Bond uses twice in the film; jet-propelled scuba tanks that look as if they weigh a ton (they come equipped with CO_2 guns and a smoke screen sprayer); a motorcycle able to fire rockets; and the film's pride and joy, Largo's *Disco Volante*. The yacht cost two hundred thousand pounds to build, and all of its features are real. The *Disco* can eject its rear outer shell, allowing a smaller hydrofoil to emerge for a fast getaway. Though it took the production crew at least six times to get it right, the scene in which this happens is thrilling.

John Stears won the series' second Academy Award for his work in *Thunderball*. Though the term "visual effects" implies spaceships and the like, Stears' work consists of the many incendiary action scenes (such as the execution of Count Lippe with the rocket-firing motorcycle), Bond's flight with a jet-pack, and other similar passages which fall properly under the visual effects heading.

Maurice Binder returns as main title designer with *Thunderball,* after having designed the titles for *Dr. No* and the gun-barrel logo. Binder would design the main titles for all the subsequent Bonds, traditionally featuring a vivid montage of silhouetted nudes and psychedelic patterns.

John Barry's score for *Thunderball* is low-key and basically serious in atmosphere. His "underwater" music is particularly effective in evoking a ghostly, other-worldly ambience. Barry also brings back his "007" theme for the Junkanoo chase and the climactic frogman battle. Another fine tune, "Mr. Kiss Kiss Bang Bang," was specially arranged and recorded for the soundtrack album, but only appears in the film in a lesser arrangement. The main title theme, sung with bravura by Tom Jones, is unusually unmelodic. But its real problem is Don Black's inane lyrics. Black would pen two more Bond song lyrics; neither of them are particularly memorable. The instrumental versions of the *Thunderball* tune, on the contrary, are lush and quite nice.

Thunderball, all things considered, is another turning point. With the emphasis now going to bigger sets, bigger locations, and bigger budgets, the Bonds became exercises in film technology. The public ate it up.

YOU ONLY LIVE TWICE (1967)

☐ PRODUCTION

While *Thunderball* was in the making, plans were dropped to film *On Her Majesty's Secret Service* as the next Bond film because it was felt that the plots were too similar (they aren't). Instead, *You Only Live Twice* was chosen, probably because it was a recent bestselling title. It also provided the filmmakers an opportunity to travel to Japan, the most exotic location yet for a Bond film.

With the huge financial success of *Thunderball* behind them, Cubby Broccoli and Harry Saltzman received a three-million-pound budget from United Artists to film the fifth James Bond epic. And an epic it is, for *You Only Live Twice* is an even bigger production than its predecessor, and the most spectacular of all the films—it is a visual achievement that few action/adventure films have surpassed. Why it wasn't nominated for an Academy Award in art direction is a mystery. The film may have had a smaller budget than the later Bond films of the seventies, but it remains the most visually impressive. Unfortunately, this aspect, along with John Barry's memorable score, are among the few redeemable elements of the film.

You Only Live Twice marks the first film in which the producers totally discarded Fleming's story. As John Brosnan says, "The title was the same but the plot had been changed to protect the box office." It's a shame this was done, for *You Only Live Twice* is one of Fleming's most interesting books. You will recall that in the novel Bond seeks revenge for the murder of his wife, Tracy, and finally finds Ernst Stavro Blofeld in an isolated castle in Japan. There, he strangles Blofeld

with his bare hands. Since the producers decided to reverse the order of the stories by filming *On Her Majesty's Secret Service* after *You Only Live Twice*, this important segment of the James Bond Saga is lost.

Another problem with the film is that Sean Connery's boredom with the role of Bond is obvious. Connery was released from his picture-a-year contract and was signed to do *You Only Live Twice* as a one-picture deal. The producers hoped he would do the same for a subsequent film. But Connery began to make it very clear that this would be the last James Bond film he would make. One can hardly blame him. The character of Bond, especially in this film, had become a superficial caricature. Very little of the Ian Fleming creation can be seen on the screen.

This does not mean that *You Only Live Twice* is a particularly bad film. In many ways, it is more entertaining than *Thunderball.* It certainly moves faster, thanks to the work of a new director, Lewis Gilbert. The plot, outrageous as it is, is taken more seriously than those

Ken Adam's spectacular set for SPECTRE's volcano headquarters in You Only Live Twice. *(Wide World Photo.)*

of the seventies. And it contains some of the best technical work in the entire series. It's simply a matter of taste. *You Only Live Twice* is not a James Bond film, but a spy-adventure-cum-science-fiction extravaganza.

There are several new talents working on the film, including a new scriptwriter. Apparently, Richard Maibaum was not available to do the screenplay, so the producers turned to Roald Dahl. Dahl, who had been friends with Fleming, was not an experienced screenplay writer; he was, however, a respected author, especially of children's literature. There is also a new cinematographer on the film—Freddie Young, who had just won an Academy Award for *Doctor Zhivago*.

Editor Peter Hunt had hoped to direct the film, but was instead offered the job of second unit director with the promise of directing the next film. Thelma Connell replaced Hunt as supervising editor, while he was busy filming the action scenes and stunts. Hunt was persuaded, however, to resume responsibility for the editing when it became apparent that Ms. Connell couldn't handle the film alone.

You Only Live Twice had a troubled production history, all of which is recounted by Steven Rubin in his book, *The James Bond Films*. Tragedy occurred when John Jordan, a cameraman specializing in aerial photography, lost a foot while shooting the spectacular helicopter battle. A blade of a SPECTRE copter's propeller sliced it off when an updraft swung the vehicle into Jordan's copter. His life was saved, but the leg had to be amputated three months later in England. Tony Brown replaced Jordan as aerial photographer. There were other delays, causing the production to go weeks over schedule, and the film finally wrapped only three months prior to its release date.

□ SCREENPLAY

When Cubby Broccoli was touring Japan scouting locations, he was unable to find a suitable castle to fit Fleming's story. But at one point during the trip, Broccoli spotted a huge volcano with a lake in its crater. This gave him the idea to abandon Fleming's setting and place the SPECTRE hideout inside an ancient volcano.

This was all Roald Dahl had to go on in creating his unusual screenplay. The producers also imposed artistic restrictions to make Dahl conform to the Bond Formula. Dahl relates what the producers told him in their initial meeting, in this excerpt from an amusing *Playboy* article:

"You can come up with anything you like so far as the story goes," they told me, "but there are two things you mustn't mess about with. The first is the character of Bond. That's fixed. The second is the girl formula. That is also fixed."

"What's the girl formula?" I asked.

"There's nothing to it. You use three different girls and Bond has them all."

"Separately or en masse?"

One of them took a deep breath and let it out slowly. "How many Bond films have you seen?" he asked.

"Just one. The one with the crazy motorcar."

"You'd better see the others right away. We'll send them out to your house with a projector and someone to work it." This was the first small hint I was to get of the swift, efficient expansive way in which the Bond producers operated. Nobody else does things quite like them.

"So you put in three girls. No more and no less. Girl number one is pro-Bond. She stays around roughly through the first reel of the picture. Then she is bumped off by the enemy, preferably in Bond's arms."

"In bed or not in bed?" I asked.

"Wherever you like, so long as it's in good taste. Girl number two is anti-Bond. She works for the enemy and stays around throughout the middle third of the picture. She must capture Bond, and Bond must save himself by bowling her over with sheer sexual magnetism. This girl should also be bumped off, preferably in an original fashion."

"There aren't many of those left," I said.

Sean Connery and co-star Akiko Wakabayashi (as Aki) relaxing between takes on location in Japan for You Only Live Twice. *(UPI Photo.)*

"We'll find one," they answered. "Girl number three is violently pro-Bond. She occupies the final third of the picture, and she must on no account be killed. Nor must she permit Bond to take any lecherous liberties with her until the very end of the story. We keep that for the fade-out."

("007's Oriental Eyefuls," from *Playboy*, June 1967)

Although Dahl may have been a little facetious in his telling of the story, there's a lot of truth in it. One can see how the girl formula was established in *Dr. No*, and perfected in *Thunderball*.

Dahl created a science fiction plot in which SPECTRE, led by our friend Ernst Stavro Blofeld, is being paid by the Red Chinese to cause World War III between America and Russia. Blofeld means to do this by hijacking space capsules from both the United States and the Soviets, and making it appear as if the other country is doing the dirty work. SPECTRE is now hiding inside a huge, hollow volcano, which is completely equipped with a launching pad, the hijacking missile, monorails, thousands of employees, tunnels, cells, and a suite where Blofeld resides. Inside the suite is a piranha pool covered by a small bridge which can be dropped at the touch of a button (Blofeld's latest method for disposing of unsuccessful subordinates). When the United States or the Soviets launch a space capsule, SPECTRE launches their intercepting rocket. In orbit, the rocket approaches the space capsule; its nose opens like a flower, swallowing the capsule; and the rocket returns to the SPECTRE volcano with its prisoners.

In 1967, outer space was a viable commercial commodity. Kubrick's *2001* was in the making, as well as *Planet of the Apes.* America's space program was approaching a zenith; man had recently walked in space. Therefore, Dahl's outer space idea was enthusiastically approved by the producers. But, as John Brosnan notes, this plot is basically a rehash of the science fiction plot of *Dr. No.* The enemy is causing havoc with a major power's space program. Bond investigates and discovers a hidden headquarters; Bond alters the villain's plans in a countdown climax; and finally the villain's establishment is blown up spectacularly. Just where SPECTRE found the funds to build themselves a super complex inside a volcano is not mentioned. It seems that after the failure of Plan Omega in *Thunderball,* Blofeld would have a little trouble obtaining backers. But this is a James Bond film—who needs credibility?

The title of the film gains significance in a pre-credits sequence involving a staged murder of James Bond. Apparently, the British fake the murder in Hong Kong so that Bond's enemies will leave him alone and free him to work openly on the space capsule case. This sequence is a little contrived, and as a result, it lacks the excitement of pre-credits scenes of previous films.

Besides using Bond, Blofeld, Tiger Tanaka, Kissy Suzuki, and Dikko Henderson (the major characters of the novel), Dahl creates some additional characters. Aki is "girl number one," and the major female role of the film. She is working for the Japanese Secret Service until she becomes the film's Obligatory Sacrificial Lamb. Helga Brandt is "girl number two," and, like Fiona in *Thunderball,* works for SPECTRE. Helga's boss is Mr. Osata, who runs the chemical and engineering front for SPECTRE.

You Only Live Twice combines all of the elements associated with the Bond film series: outer space; underwater scenes; a few good fight scenes; lavish surroundings and set-pieces; beautiful women; gadgets; and a climactic demolition of the villain's headquarters at the film's end. The screenplay has its moments of flash, but ultimately it serves as a mere vehicle for the overpowering set-pieces.

☐ DIRECTION

Lewis Gilbert joins the Bond team to direct *You Only Live Twice.* One suspects that Gilbert didn't have too much say in the actual production planning of the film. The producers knew in what direction they wanted their series to go, and Gilbert was hired only to maintain control of the massive undertaking the film became. All things considered, Gilbert does an impressive job. There are extremely large crowds to contend with, as well as huge sets on which to plot action. Gilbert proved adept at handling a big picture, and he would be hired again later in the series to direct two more Bond films.

Gilbert's style incorporates the fastest tempo yet in a Bond film. This is an improvement over *Thunderball*—the new picture really moves. Gilbert also has a good eye for composition, helped immensely by the work of cinematographer Freddie Young.

Gilbert is less successful bringing out adequate performances from the cast. Connery, especially, seems unmotivated and uninspired. And Gilbert could not overcome the serious miscasting of Donald Pleasence as Blofeld. The Japanese actors all do competent jobs, but there are no scenes requiring any serious dramatic interplay.

One particular scene is successful in generating a sombre mood, and that is the death of Aki. Bond and Aki are asleep in bed. A SPECTRE assassin sneaks into the rafters above them and hangs a thread above Bond's mouth. The assassin carefully pours a couple of drops of poison onto the thread; they slowly inch their way down. But Bond shifts his body in his sleep, and Aki moves with him. The poison drops fall into her mouth instead. This scene is suspenseful and eerie.

Another marvelous sequence is the Kobe dock fight. Bond and Aki have been spying on the shipping vessel *Ning-Po,* and are caught by SPECTRE dock workers. (It seems that everybody in Japan either works for SPECTRE or the Japanese Secret Service!) Bond is chased across a rooftop, and there's a magnificent aerial shot of him knocking off his attackers one by one. This shot, combined with John Barry's vigorous music, produces an exhilarating effect.

Gilbert is also successful in creating a bit of Fleming "travelogue" for the film. There is one sequence in which Bond is "married" to Kissy Suzuki for the purposes of cover. A traditional Japanese wedding is set up, and the audience is treated to a display of Oriental costume and ritual. Sequences such as this make *You Only Live Twice* an interesting film.

*   *   *

□ ACTORS AND CHARACTERS

Another example of how radically the film series has changed James Bond from the Ian Fleming original is summed up in one line. Miss Moneypenny throws Bond a Japanese phrase book as he is exiting for his mission. Bond tosses it back, saying that she has forgotten he "took a first in Oriental languages at Cambridge." Well, James Bond never attended Cambridge. Or Oxford for that matter.

Sean Connery, in his fifth appearance as James Bond, looks weary and bored with the entire goings-on. He is overweight, slow-moving, and doesn't seem to be trying to create a credible character. What is amazing is that despite this, Connery here still radiates more screen presence than Roger Moore or George Lazenby. Halfway through the film, Bond is transformed into a Japanese man. Bikini-clad Japanese women perform an elaborate operation, depilating him, slanting his eyes, and changing his hair style. As Brosnan notes, the result is unconvincing, and Connery looks a little ridiculous slouching around with his head down in stereotypical Japanese humility.

Jan Werich was originally cast as Blofeld, but the actor became very ill before his scenes were shot. Acting hastily, the producers cast Donald Pleasence as Bond's archenemy. Pleasence is a terrific actor, and is especially good at character roles; but in this case, he is seriously miscast. This film marks the first appearance of Blofeld's face on screen (yes, he's still petting that damned white cat), and Pleasence is a disappointment. He is a small man with a voice that in no way resembles the Blofeld voices used in *From Russia With Love* or *Thunderball*. Although Blofeld's features alter from novel to novel, he always remains physically large and mentally methodical. Pleasence's Blofeld resembles a rash, hyperactive Dr. Frankenstein. Pleasence's makeup includes an ugly scar down the right side of his face, and his characterization suggests an ugly, spoiled child who throws a tantrum when he doesn't get his way. As a result, Blofeld is unintentionally comical. My favorite line in the film comes from Blofeld when he orders Mr. Osata to "Kill Bond—NOW!" The delivery is maniacally funny.

Blofeld comes equipped with a superstrong bodyguard named Hans. Hans doesn't say anything through the entire film, and is basically a variation of Oddjob. Bond quickly disposes of him during one of the film's weaker fight scenes.

Akiko Wakabayashi portrays Aki, the beautiful Japanese girl who befriends Bond in the first half of the picture. Miss Wakabayashi is very good in the role, and gives the most accomplished performance in the film. Aki is very independent, intelligent, and resourceful. She also happens to show up in the nick of time repeatedly to save Bond from danger. Aki is unfortunately the film's Obligatory Sacrificial Lamb, and meets her death in the previously mentioned bedroom scene.

Tetsuro Tamba portrays the wise Tiger Tanaka, head of the Japanese Secret Service. Fleming's Tanaka is one of his most developed and entertaining characters, but Tanaka in the film has been written down. Also, Tamba is not particularly engaging in the role. Though he speaks with the wisdom and authority required of the character, he appears too young and a little mechanical.

Lovely Mie Hama is Kissy Suzuki, whom Bond "marries" on Kuro Island. Miss Hama, like Akiko Wakabayashi, is well cast and does a very competent job in portraying the Ama diving girl with an American education. Although her role has been changed considerably from the original story (in the film, she's a trained agent skilled in the martial arts, working for the Japanese Secret Service), Miss Hama displays an innocent charm that is appealing.

German actress Karin Dor is cast as Helga Brandt, the SPECTRE agent who first uses Bond sexually for her own purposes, then attempts to kill him. The character is basically Fiona Volpe revisited, and is not nearly as successful. Dor displays adequate sexual appeal for the role, but is not nearly as villainous as Luciana Paluzzi. Helga Brandt meets her death in another of the now-famous SPECTRE executions for failure. This time, Blofeld terminates her employment by feeding her to his pet piranhas.

A Japanese actor with a face familiar to American audiences, Teru Shimada, portrays Mr. Osata, the man who owns the chemical and engineering front for SPECTRE. Shimada isn't given much to do, but performs his tasks with conviction, nonetheless. He, too, is killed by Blofeld for failing to eliminate Bond. (Blofeld here chooses a simpler method: he pulls out a pistol and shoots Osata at point-blank range.)

Another interesting character from the novel is short-changed in the film. This is Dikko Henderson, the British agent working at the Tokyo Station. Charles Gray (who later returns to the series to contribute his own version of Blofeld) portrays Henderson, but he isn't given much screen time. He's interrupted in the middle of perhaps his third speech by a knife in the back (this didn't happen in the book). Henderson also has a

Sean Connery and Mie Hama (Kissy Suzuki) on a Japanese mountain in You Only Live Twice. A SPECTRE helicopter will soon interrupt the picnic. (UPI Photo.)

wooden leg in the film—a handicap not suffered by the original character.

It's obvious the filmmakers are running out of ideas for original M/Miss Moneypenny scenes. In *You Only Live Twice,* Bond reports to headquarters aboard M's private submarine (!) which happens to be stationed near Japan. It's the first time we see the Service personnel (including Bond and M) in full Naval attire, but the notion is ridiculous. Q makes his usual appearance on location in Japan to instruct Bond in operating "Little Nellie," the latest in Q Branch technology.

□ **OTHER ASPECTS**

As mentioned earlier, *You Only Live Twice* is the most visually attractive movie of the entire series. Freddie Young's cinematography is gorgeous, especially in the panoramic views of the Japanese countryside. Young has done a splendid job capturing the beauty and color of the East.

But the film's look belongs to Ken Adam. *You Only Live Twice* contains his most impressive work. It's no wonder, for Adam was allotted at least half of the film's total budget to create the many interiors for the film.

Among these are Osata's office, where Bond fights a heavy Sumo wrestler; Tanaka's Secret Service headquarters, filled with TV screens and sleek, metal walls; M's submarine office; Blofeld's suite, complete with piranha pool and bridge; and several Japanese houses. But the most outstanding set is the SPECTRE volcano. At a cost of one million dollars, the huge set was built on the back-lot of Pinewood Studios, and could be seen at least three miles away. It was the largest and most expensive set ever built for a motion picture. Everything inside worked—monorails, elevators, and motor vehicles. A helicopter could actually descend through the opening in the ceiling and land on the launching pad. This set epitomizes the bigness of the Bond films, and it's worth the price of admission just to see it.

The film contains as many gadgets (if not more) than *Thunderball.* Among these are the thousands of television screens and radio transmitters that everyone in the film seems to carry; a handy little safecracker Bond happens to have on his person which, after a few seconds of waiting, reveals a safe's combination to its user; and various items used by the *ninjas,* such as cigarettes containing explosive projectiles. But the star gadget is the "Little Nellie," a gyro-helicopter for one passenger, which actually works, and was flown in the film by Nellie's designer and owner, Ken Wallis. It is in effect a flying Aston Martin, for it comes equipped with machine guns, a smokescreen sprayer, rockets, a mine field launcher, and two heat-seeking missiles which practically steal the film during Bond's aerial battle with four SPECTRE helicopters.

Bob Simmons is in charge of the stunts again, with assistance from George Leech. Their work is especially impressive during the climactic battle in the volcano between the SPECTRE forces and Tanaka's *ninjas.* Over 120 stuntmen were employed for the scene, and it's a magnificent display of panoramic acrobatics. There is one particular *ninja* who, during the training camp sequence, is given his own moment of glory when he displays his swordsmanship in a whirlwind tour de force. The sequence is repeated against enemy SPECTRE agents during the climactic battle, and it almost always receives a round of applause from the audiences with which I've seen the film. The actor performing this role was also one of Kurosawa's original *Seven Samurai.*

John Stears is once again in charge of special effects, and does his usual explosive job with pyrotechnics. His work on the outer space sequences is less successful, but one must remember that this was before the advent of Kubrick's *2001,* which changed the norm of special effects work in space films.

Eileen Sullivan, as wardrobe mistress, deserves a mention for the Japanese costumes and *ninja* outfits. The design aspects of the film all blend well to create the most visually consistent of all the Bond films.

John Barry deserves special mention for his beautiful score for the film, which is truly one of his best. Nancy Sinatra's rendition of the title song (with lyrics by Leslie Bricusse) was a hit single, and is one of the best main themes. It has a haunting melody which is difficult to forget. Barry also created a unique sound with strings for the outer space segments. Again, the overall mood is haunting and awe-inspiring. Barry is also given a chance to compose music with an Oriental flavor for the wedding scene and the bits in Tanaka's home. It's a truly lovely score, and is one of the film's greatest assets.

Finally, Maurice Binder does it again with his main title design, this time employing Oriental motifs and semi-clad geisha girls. As usual, it's a feast for the eyes, and, blended with Barry's title theme, it launches *You Only Live Twice* most promisingly.

ON HER MAJESTY'S SECRET SERVICE (1969)

☐ PRODUCTION

When Sean Connery made it absolutely clear that he was not going to play James Bond in the next film, Eon Productions decided to hold a massive talent search to cast a new 007. The resulting choice was an unusual one—Australian model George Lazenby. What won him the part, supposedly, were his test fight scenes. Grilled by stuntman George Leech, Lazenby proved his prowess in displaying the tough aspects of Bond. It was finally announced that George Lazenby would be the next James Bond in *On Her Majesty's Secret Service.*

The sixth James Bond film is extraordinary for several reasons, and it is usually a fond favorite among Bond fans. But it has been forgotten by the general public. First of all, the obvious element separating it from the rest of the series is the casting of Lazenby. Second, the film departs from the direction established by the series' formula. The film's director, Peter Hunt (in his debut), wanted to make the film as close to the

Mr. and Mrs. James Bond. Actually it's Diana Rigg as Tracy and George Lazenby as 007. On the set of On Her Majesty's Secret Service *for the filming of the famous wedding. (Wide World Photo.)*

Fleming original as possible. This meant the script had to concentrate more on character and plot than on art direction and gadgetry. You will recall that *On Her Majesty's Secret Service* is the novel in which James Bond falls in love and marries Tracy di Vicenzo, only to have her murdered at the story's end by Ernst Stavro Blofeld. Hunt wanted to make the film more like the early pictures and he finally succeeded in persuading the producers to see it his way. Commercially, the gambit didn't pay off. Critics blamed George Lazenby. The producers blamed the departure from the established formula *and* George Lazenby. *On Her Majesty's Secret Service* did make a good deal of money, but it was two years after its initial release that it finally recouped its costs.

It's unfortunate that the film wasn't an immediate financial success because it is undoubtedly an artistic triumph. I agree with John Brosnan, who believes that *On Her Majesty's Secret Service* might have been the best James Bond film in the series had Sean Connery performed the leading role. The film, like *From Russia With Love,* follows the novel very closely, with a few minor changes. It even ends sadly with the death of Tracy. And George Lazenby isn't all that bad, either. More on him later.

There is limited gadgetry in the film. Bond depends on his wits and courage to get him through the dangers he faces. In the pre-credits sequence, we see Q experimenting with radioactive lint, which, when planted on someone, makes him easy to track. M simply shakes his head and wonders how to keep track of 007. This dismissal of Q's idea, Brosnan believes, perhaps underlines Peter Hunt's attitude toward the series' penchant for gadgets. The only other such apparatus in the film

Piz Gloria, the Swiss Alp headquarters of Ernst Stavro Blofeld in On Her Majesty's Secret Service. *Art director Syd Cain turned this revolving restaurant into the SPECTRE hideout. (Piz Gloria publicity photo.)*

is a clever combination safecracker and xerox duplicator, which Bond uses when he breaks into a lawyer's office to obtain information leading to the whereabouts of Blofeld. The large and heavy mechanism is supplied to him once he's inside the office by a friendly agent operating a crane in the construction site behind the building. The machine is delivered through the window, Bond sets it up, and it performs the work while the lawyer is out to lunch. Bond simply sits and reads *Playboy* magazine while he waits. This is another touch of humor at the expense of improbable gadgetry.

Gone, too, are Ken Adam's futuristic designs. Syd Cain, who designed *From Russia With Love,* is back, and creates a more realistic look for the film. The cast, aside from Bond, is well chosen for the most part, and Richard Maibaum supplies a faithful and engaging script. Filmed on location in Switzerland and Portugal, *On Her Majesty's Secret Service* contains beautiful scenery and tough action scenes. It is pure Bond. And it's certainly a better film than *Thunderball* or *You Only Live Twice.*

Steven Rubin recounts many of the production problems that were faced while making the film in his book, *The James Bond Films.* The British press especially exploited the disagreements between George Lazenby and the filmmakers. Lazenby's biggest mistake was that he announced, prior to the release of the film, that he would not be making any more James Bond films. This comment particularly alienated the producers.

Prolonged bad weather was another obstacle, delaying the shooting schedule by several weeks. The cold temperature was hazardous to the cast and crew, and the thin air created difficulties for the stuntmen. Problems notwithstanding, *On Her Majesty's Secret Service* is an interesting adventure film and one of the best of the series.

☐ SCREENPLAY

Richard Maibaum takes the screenplay credit alone this time, and his work is splendid. He has remained faithful to Fleming's intention, and has even improved certain sections with an additional scene or two.

The circumstances in which Bond meets Tracy have been slightly altered. In the novel, the opening beach sequence occurs in the present, as Bond and Tracy are abducted by Draco's men. The next two chapters then flash back to the events leading up to the first chapter. In the film, the latter sequences are not flashbacks, but continuous action. Bond *meets* Tracy on the beach in the pre-credits sequence, and the scene works very well as a prologue. Maibaum creates a clever device for easing Lazenby into the role of James Bond. After Bond has vanquished Draco's thugs and Tracy (whom he has rescued from attempted suicide) has run away, Bond picks up one of her dropped slippers and mutters, "This never happened to the other fellow." (Maurice Binder even contributed to this device by inserting shots from previous Bond films, *sans* Connery, into his main title design.)

The events at Royale-les-Eaux are practically verbatim from the novel, and contain good dialogue. There is a scene in which Bond unexpectedly finds Tracy in his hotel suite (this wasn't in the novel) that has shades of the confrontation scene aboard the Orient Express in *From Russia With Love*. Bond treats Tracy pretty roughly and even slaps her (it's the second time Bond has struck a woman onscreen). There is authentic dramatic tension here, and it's primarily due to Maibaum's fine script.

There are other dissimilarities between film and novel. In the book, Bond is sick and tired of Operation Bedlam (the search for Blofeld) and mentally drafts a letter of resignation from the service. In the film, it's just the opposite. M wants to take Bond off Operation Bedlam, and Bond is adamant about sticking with it and finding Blofeld. M curtly makes his order final and dismisses Bond (it's a terrific Bond/M scene). Angrily, Bond steps into the outer office and actually *dictates* a letter of resignation to a shocked Miss Moneypenny. Bond then storms to his own office (the first and only time we see it in the films), and begins to empty his desk. Maibaum throws in more references to the past as Bond goes through the desk's contents, which include Honey's belt and knife from *Dr. No,* Grant's garroting wrist watch in *From Russia With Love,* and the four-minute breather from *Thunderball*. M then calls Bond back into his office, and without looking up, says, "Request granted." Stunned by the cold dismissal, Bond slowly walks out to face Moneypenny. But she reveals that she changed Bond's letter of resignation to a request for two weeks' leave. This entire sequence is one of the best of the obligatory office scenes.

Another new sequence is the previously mentioned safe-cracking scene in which Bond learns Blofeld's whereabouts. Draco knows that a lawyer named Gumbold has been corresponding with Blofeld. The trick is to break into Gumbold's office and safe, find correspondence from Blofeld, and duplicate the letters. Maibaum builds great suspense with this scene, with John Glen's editing contributing to its effectiveness.

There is one flaw in the script that disturbs the continuity of the film series. In the novel, Bond and Blofeld have never met before they encounter each other at Piz Gloria, the new headquarters for SPECTRE in the Swiss Alps. In the films, Bond had already met Blofeld in *You Only Live Twice;* but in this film Blofeld does not recognize Bond and they haven't ever met. Of course, Bond *is* disguised (slightly) as Sir Hilary Bray.

Also, in the film, Bond is caught by Blofeld before he can escape Piz Gloria on skis. Bond is placed in a strange room that houses the cable car mechanism, from which he escapes by climbing onto the huge gears and inching out by hand onto the cable. He hitches a ride on an approaching cable car, and then drops to the snow when the ground is close enough. The scene is suspenseful and required impressive stunt work, but it seems a little silly that Blofeld would place Bond in such an escapable prison.

The final change occurs after Bond has escaped and found Tracy in the village. The morning after Bond proposes to her, Tracy is captured by Blofeld after she and Bond are buried by a SPECTRE-made avalanche. Thus, Bond's mission becomes twofold: stopping Blofeld's bacterial warfare plot (straight from the novel), and rescuing Tracy. This overcomes one of the main criticisms of the novel—that the book's two plots (the pursuit of Blofeld and the romance with Tracy) weren't related. By involving Tracy in Bond's pursuit of Blofeld, Maibaum has solved this problem.

The remainder of the film follows the novel closely, down to the last line spoken by Bond as he is cradling the dead Tracy in his arms: "We have all the time in the world."

Despite the return to a more serious format, *On Her Majesty's Secret Service* still contains a good deal of humor. The jokes sneak up on us, such as when Blofeld delivers one of my favorite lines during the exciting ski chase: "We'll head him off at the precipice!"

□ **DIRECTION**

Editor-turned-director Peter Hunt makes an impressive debut with *On Her Majesty's Secret Service*. The film has style, pace, and conviction. There are a couple of scenes that don't quite work, and there *are* moments when the acting is flat, but this is true of the cast as a whole, not just George Lazenby. What carries the film are the spectacular action sequences, stunts, fights, and the pictorial beauty of the surroundings. Above all, Hunt is a good storyteller, and the film doesn't seem built around a series of set-pieces.

The pre-credits sequence is unique in the series. Rather than providing an up-tempo beginning for the movie, the prologue is melancholic and dark and remains so until Lazenby's last line. Hunt's shots of Tracy walking into the ocean and her subsequent rescue by Bond are not only beautiful to behold, but are tense and haunting. Michael Reed's photography and John Barry's score stand out here. The sky has an eerie blue-green glow about it, as the sun is rising, that perfectly captures Fleming's description of the scene: "Seascape with Figures."

Hunt injects his own contributions to the film's comic relief. While Bond is led through a warehouse (at gunpoint) to meet Marc-Ange Draco (Tracy's father), we see a midget janitor sweeping the floor. Bond film fans recognize that he's whistling the theme from *Goldfinger*.

Hunt directed half of the action scenes in the picture, while second unit director/editor John Glen took control of the other half. The fight sequences are among the toughest in the series. The tumble with the large black man in Tracy's hotel room near the beginning of the picture is especially explosive.

The only scene that mars the film takes place during Bond and Tracy's courtship. After showing up at Draco's birthday party (at Draco's insistence) simply to see Tracy again, Bond begins to fall for her. Once this feeling has become mutual, there is one of those corny, romantic montage sequences where we see the man and woman walking along the beach (or in a field, or riding horses)—underscored by a passionate love song. The number happens to be a very lovely tune by Barry called "We Have All the Time in the World," with lyrics by Hal David. The problem is that the late Louis Armstrong's rendition of the song seems more out of place than the sequence itself. The effect of seeing James Bond and a woman in a Harlequin Romance setting with the raspy, deep voice of Armstrong crooning along is, well, laughable.

Another bit that doesn't work too well is the scene in which Bond witnesses the "treatment" of Ruby in her room at Piz Gloria. Ruby is one of the ten "allergy" patients at the supposed clinic, but in reality her treatment is nothing but a brainwashing by Blofeld. Bond and Ruby have just finished making love, when suddenly Blofeld's reverberating voice crackles from a hidden speaker as the lights flicker and change colors. Bond watches with confusion as Ruby falls asleep while listening to Blofeld say, "You love chickens . . . you like their feathers . . ." etc. It's one of the series' best (unintentionally) silly sequences.

The film is played straight overall, and exhibits a great deal of sophistication. The casino scene, and all the sequences with Tracy, evince a certain elegance which is missing from the later Eon offerings. Hunt has succeeded, perhaps more than any other Bond director, in closely capturing Fleming's world.

□ ACTORS AND CHARACTERS

George Lazenby is introduced to us as Bond in a manner similar to that used for Connery. The first few shots of Bond are only of his shoulders, the back of his head, his hands, etc. He is driving his Aston Martin down a highway in Portugal and is passed recklessly by Tracy. "The James Bond Theme" is heard with an unusual arrangement as Bond shifts gears and speeds after her. He follows her to the beach, spies on her with the telescopic sight from his attache case, and realizes she is attempting to drown herself. We see the figure exit the car, remove his jacket, and run down the dune to rescue her. Bond carries her out of the water, lays her down on the sand, and revives her. "I don't think we've been properly introduced," he says. Then there is a shot of this new face, looking fresh and a bit young for Bond. "The name's Bond. James Bond." The voice is pleasant, with a slight Australian accent.

Once one gets over the shock of a different actor saying those words, it is not difficult to accept Lazenby as Bond. In many ways he more closely resembles the Ian Fleming version of Bond than either of the other two actors. He is dark, with a thin face. He is handsome, yet his looks have a hard edge. At times Lazenby does seem a little young for the role, but his physical abilities overcome this problem. He is terrific in the fight scenes, and handles the love scenes with surprising confidence. He's most awkward in lengthy conversation scenes, such as the first meeting with Marc-Ange Draco. Lazenby's handling of the romantic interchanges with Tracy (such as the proposal) is admirable for a beginning actor. Unfortunately, the actor's ultimate downfall was his lack of a powerful, charismatic screen presence akin to an actor such as Sean Connery. The critics were too harsh on Lazenby. His performance is the most honest and sincere of any of the actors who have played Bond.

Distinguished British actress Diana Rigg, known to

Americans for her role in *The Avengers* on television, portrays Teresa di Vicenzo, the only woman *ever* to be Mrs. James Bond. Since Bond was being played by an unknown, the producers felt that perhaps this time the heroine should be someone with more experience. Miss Rigg is very good in the role, although she portrays a slightly different Tracy from the one in the novel. She plays the contessa image to the hilt, sometimes coming off a little haughty. And although Tracy in the novel is rich and spoiled, she retains a helplessness for which Bond is the cure. We never believe the film Tracy needs James Bond. But we do believe she loves him, and this is important. The film Tracy also has a bit of Emma Peel (the character Rigg portrayed in *The Avengers*) in her make-up. She knows judo and handles being kidnapped by the villain reasonably well. Had she been kidnapped in the novel, I doubt that Tracy would have remained calm. Rigg is particularly effective in the scenes at Draco's birthday party. When she discovers that her father has invited Bond to his house on her behalf, we see some emotions rarely displayed by a Bond-girl onscreen. The proposal scene in the barn is effective, too. When Bond finally pops the question, Miss Rigg's face assumes the perfect expression of disbelief. Even Tracy di Vicenzo finds it hard to believe that *the* James Bond has actually proposed to a woman, and it happens to be her.

Ernst Stavro Blofeld is miscast again, but the error is not as grave as in the preceding film. Telly Savalas plays the SPECTRE leader, still attached to that white cat. He's bald, as was Pleasence's Blofeld, but he has lost the ugly scar. Only Blofeld's ear lobes are missing, because the character is passing himself as the Count de Bleuville. Savalas is too energetic and too snide to be Blofeld. He seems more like a New York gangster. There is none of Blofeld's wisdom or methodical probing in Savalas' characterization. He is successful at bringing out the man's villainy—his obligatory "spilling the beans" scene is one of the best. Blofeld plans to launch biological warfare on England by hypnotizing ten beautiful girls (supposedly allergy victims) and ordering them to do his bidding. The girls will go out into the land and poison livestock and crops. Blofeld's demands for stopping the virus attack are complete amnesty from all governments with a price on his head, and recognition of his title of Count. This makes sense, considering what hell he's caused in the past: knocking down American test flights, stealing government cipher machines, blackmailing governments with atomic bombs and so forth. Another oddity of Savalas' Blofeld is that he takes part in the ski chase after Bond escapes from

Piz Gloria. The real Blofeld would have had more dignity.

The most successful casting in the film is that of Ilse Steppat as Irma Bunt. Though her character appeared in the novel *You Only Live Twice,* she isn't in the film. Her character is important here, and she is used faithfully. The casting of Miss Steppat reminds one of the casting of Lotte Lenya as Rosa Klebb. Steppat is a matronly middle-aged actress who fits Fleming's description of Bunt perfectly. Actually, Irma Bunt comes off more menacing than Blofeld in this picture. The audience is given quite a jolt when Bond sneaks into Ruby's room a second time at Piz Gloria, only to find Irma Bunt in bed where Ruby should be.

Italian actor Gabriele Ferzetti plays Marc-Ange Draco, the head of the Union Corse, and briefly, Bond's father-in-law. This is also a good piece of casting. It is said that Draco's voice was dubbed, though this isn't noticeable (the dubbing in Bond films has always been surprisingly good), and Ferzetti displays a good deal of the charm required for the part. An element which is missing until the final showdown at Piz Gloria is the fact that Draco can be a tough customer. After all, he *is* the head of the most powerful crime syndicate in France. Ferzetti seems a little too nice at times. But during the big battle, he proves he can hold his own in a dangerous situation. There is one funny moment showcasing Ferzetti: Draco is trying to convince Tracy to get inside the helicopter so they can escape from the alp. Piz Gloria will blow up any second, but Bond is still inside. Draco is finally forced to punch her in the jaw, knocking her unconscious. He shrugs at a companion and says, "Spare the rod, spoil the child," and lifts her into the copter.

Cute Angela Scoular giggles her way through the role of Ruby, one of the ten allergy patients who is lucky enough to have an affair with James Bond. In the book, she is the only one who gets to know Bond in the biblical sense, but in the film, Bond also makes love to a girl named Nancy (played by Catherine Von Schell), and it's implied that he woos a Chinese girl.

The film's Obligatory Sacrificial Lamb is the Swiss agent Shaun Campbell from Station Z. His role is small, but his presence is emphasized in key scenes. Played by Bernard Horsfall, he is the agent who oversees the crane operation that delivers the safecracker/duplicator through Gumbold's office window to Bond. He also painfully follows Bond on his journey to Piz Gloria, making the trip the hard way—mostly on foot. Campbell meets his end by being strung up by his feet over a cliff after he is caught spying. (A little more dignified than past SPECTRE killings. It's also interesting that the film is missing the usual SPECTRE execution of one of its own members, even though there is one of these scenes in the book.)

As mentioned earlier, Bernard Lee and Lois Maxwell have rare moments with their characterizations of M and Miss Moneypenny, respectively. The resignation scene captures the M/Bond relationship very well, and the subsequent saving-of-the-day by Moneypenny lends her character a depth never suggested in the novels. There is also the scene at Quarterdeck, M's home. We meet Chief Petty Officer Hammond (much younger than expected) and we find M playing with a butterfly collection (his hobby in the book was watercolors). Desmond Llewelyn makes brief appearances in the film; once at the beginning, explaining his radioactive lint, and again in the wedding sequence. Referring to Tracy, Bond tells Q as he's leaving for his honeymoon that this time *he* has the gadgets, and that he "knows how to use them."

□ OTHER ASPECTS

The look of the film is picturesque. The location photography of the Swiss Alps provides a colorful and awesome backdrop for the film. Snow is everywhere and the picture's Christmas timeframe gives it a very seasonal atmosphere.

Syd Cain designs his second Bond feature and does a splendid job. Most impressive is his work on Piz Gloria. Piz Gloria is actually a revolving restaurant atop the Schilthorn Mountain ("Magic Mountain"), some 6900 feet above the Lauterbrunnen valley near Murren. The restaurant was nearing completion when Eon Productions discovered its existence and began negotiating to use the site for filming. The final agreement was that Eon Productions would furnish interior designs and execute them, as well as build a heliport outside in exchange for use of the building. The restaurant was even renamed Piz Gloria permanently.

Michael Reed's photography has a sharpness not previously seen in Bond films, which gives the film a chic look. John Jordan, unimpeded by an artificial leg, is back to film the aerial sequences, and his work is as impressive as ever. Jordan was tragically killed later the same year working on *Catch-22*. The stunning ski chases and bobsled scene were filmed by skiing champion Willy Bogner, Jr., who reportedly performed all kinds of daredevil tricks to obtain certain shots. These sequences were directed by second unit man John Glen, who would direct future Bond films. Glen also

serves as the film's editor, and he follows Peter Hunt's footsteps in continuing the latter's fast-paced style.

John Stears returns at the special effects helm, and his model of Piz Gloria (which explodes, as usual, at the film's end) looks authentic. George Leech choreographed the action sequences, and succeeds in creating tough fight scenes and exciting chases. Anthony Squire directed the wonderful stock car chase in which Bond and Tracy escape a SPECTRE Rolls by joining a rally in progress. This scene is a variation of the "fork left to hell" scene in the novel, in which Bond sends the SPECTRE car over a cliff by reversing a KEEP RIGHT road sign. Marjory Cornelius deserves mention for her wardrobe designs, especially for the ten allergy patients at Piz Gloria. Bond's baronet outfit is amusing and all of Tracy's clothes are alluring and appealing.

OHMSS contains perhaps the best score of the series. John Barry outdoes himself with an innovative sound for the film. The Bond scores have always had a modern feel to them, but this one is raunchy and jazzy. The theme is instrumental, with an upbeat, driving tempo. The use of a fuzz-box on the guitar is prominent, creating a gritty texture. There are also several beautiful lyrical sections, such as the backgrounds to the prologue, the journey to Blofeld's hideaway, and the helicopter approach to Piz Gloria at the film's climax. "We Have All the Time in the World" is a lovely melody, and is used wistfully at the film's end when Bond realizes Tracy is dead. Like the film itself, the score is unique in the series. John Barry gambled with this one, as did Peter Hunt and the producers. *On Her Majesty's Secret Service* may not be the best Bond film, but it just might be the most admirable.

DIAMONDS ARE FOREVER (1971)

□ PRODUCTION

Sean Connery returned to the series on a one-time basis to play Bond in *Diamonds Are Forever*. Since *On Her Majesty's Secret Service* had not been as successful as the preceding films, the producers decided to revert back to the standard Bond formula. Connery was back, and the fantasy elements would be played up again. Ken Adam also returned to design more of his futuristic, sparkling sets. ·

Sean Connery's back and Jill St. John's got him in the 1971-released Diamonds Are Forever. (UPI Photo.)

Diamonds Are Forever also marks a new direction in the series. Humor began to play an increasingly important role in the films beginning in the seventies. Although *Diamonds* still has its share of thrills and some suspense, much of it is played strictly for laughs. Tom Mankiewicz, co-scriptwriter for the film, explained his theory on why the Bond films changed in the seventies in an interview for *Bondage* magazine:

Well, I think what turned the Bond pictures around, in my opinion—and long before I got on them—was that car in *Goldfinger*. I think the minute Sean pressed the button on the ejector seat, and the audience roared, the series turned around. The audiences saw outlandish things they had never seen before, and the natural response of anybody—a writer, a filmmaker—is to give them more; more of what they want. And there's constant pressure as the films gross a great deal of money to make each one bigger, and "more" than the last.

Let's take *You Only Live Twice*. Once you have a helicopter come by with a giant magnet and pick a car up off the road, and dump it out in the ocean—it's a staggering thing to look at. Once you say to an audience, "All's fair;

we can do that," it's awful tough to keep a serious plot line going. You have so many tools available, so many outlandish things which an audience is not only used to, but they want to see, they got indoctrinated into it, and that's when I say Bond became Disney, in a certain way. It became an entertainment; it became an afternoon out, where for two hours you were going to see stuff you never saw before . . . The feeling of the studio (I mean United Artists and Cubby) was that if you pulled your horns in, and made a smaller picture, they (the audience) would be disappointed.

(From "The Tom Mankiewicz Interview,"
by Richard Schenkman,
Bondage, Number 8)

Mankiewicz's theory makes sense, and explains the mentality of the producers. Granted, Ian Fleming's lesser novels, such as DIAMONDS ARE FOREVER, might not translate well into cinematic material. One can understand why the filmmakers opted to go this route.

The general public isn't made up of James Bond purists. The people who flock to the Bond films are going to be entertained, as Mankiewicz states. The Bond purists, who have continually objected to the way James Bond has been handled on the screen since 1970, are relatively small in number. Mankiewicz told *Bondage* that he is a fan of Fleming's Bond, but believes that the change in the character for the films was necessary both commercially and cinematically. The Bond films, starting with *Diamonds,* became "romps," (to use Mankiewicz's word), and this, in part, explains their artistic decline in the seventies. Ironically, these movies made even more money than had the previous six. James Bond, apparently, is a successful commodity in almost any form.

Diamonds Are Forever employed both European and American crews. Locations were shot in Amsterdam and England with one group, and in Los Angeles and Las Vegas with the other. The production was completed in under eighteen weeks, so United Artists escaped having to pay Connery the $10,000-per-week-over-schedule salary guaranteed in his contract.

The film was enormously successful when it was released in December of 1971—it appeared that the picture would outgross all the previous Bonds. The film *is* entertaining, without a doubt, with fast-paced action and spectacular settings. The dialogue is sometimes very funny, containing a few terrific one-liners. Guy Hamilton is back at the helm, giving the film the speed and polish that enhanced *Goldfinger.* But the prime asset of the film is Sean Connery's return as James Bond. This was proven in theaters around the world, when audiences cheered at Connery's first appearance on the screen saying those famous words: "The name is Bond. James Bond."

□ SCREENPLAY

Much of the screenplay was written by committee, as usual, with a lot of input from Broccoli and Saltzman, as well as Hamilton. Richard Maibaum wrote the first draft, and Tom Mankiewicz was brought in later for a rewrite.

The film differs a great deal from the novel. There are a few similar scenes in the first quarter of the film, but they are in an entirely different context. The plot now involves SPECTRE, rather than the syndicate known as the Spangled Mob. Good old Ernst Stavro Blofeld is in control once more (in the novel the villains are Mafia-style gangsters named Jack and Seraffimo Spang). The film harks back to the science fiction aspects of *Dr. No* and *You Only Live Twice,* involving the creation of a laser-equipped satellite which SPECTRE will use to blackmail (as usual) major government powers. The laser gun is powered by diamonds which have been smuggled from a mine in South Africa owned by the British. At the beginning of the film, the British know that the diamonds are being smuggled but are mystified because the gems are not appearing on the black market. Someone is apparently stockpiling them, and it's up to James Bond to infiltrate the smuggling pipeline and find out who the culprit is. Blofeld and SPECTRE were brought into the plot, apparently, to maintain a semblance of continuity in the cinematic saga. Bond would naturally be seeking revenge for the murder of his wife in the previous film. Therefore, in the pre-credits sequence, we see Bond attacking various people in different locations, demanding to know the whereabouts of Blofeld. Bond finally locates him in the act of creating duplicates of himself by means of plastic surgery. Bond breaks into the futuristic operating room and kills Blofeld (at least he *thinks* it's Blofeld). We learn later in the film that it was only one of Blofeld's duplicates, and the real villain is alive and well and threatening governments again.

This pre-credits sequence is very confusing and is over before the audience can fully comprehend what has happened. In a way, this is a problem with the entire film. The plot itself is overcomplicated, and several scenes cut in the final editing probably explained a great deal that seems missing from the released version. For instance, it's not totally clear that it is SPECTRE that is running the smuggling pipeline. It seems that a different organization is behind the operation, and

Bond (Sean Connery) and Tiffany Case (Jill St. John) congratulate each other on a good day's work on location in Las Vegas for Diamonds Are Forever. *(UPI Photo.)*

SPECTRE has interfered and begun sidetracking the pipeline into their own coffers. After a couple of viewings, it becomes clear that the links in the pipeline—the dentist in South Africa, the elderly schoolteacher in Amsterdam, Peter Franks, and Tiffany Case—do not know they're working for SPECTRE. Wint and Kidd, the two homosexual SPECTRE assassins, begin killing the pipeline links; it's not clear until later that SPECTRE intended to close the operation once they had obtained all the diamonds needed to complete the satellite project.

A scene from the novel that appears in the film almost intact depicts Bond's impersonation of Peter Franks and his visit to Tiffany Case's hotel room. She is dressed in her underwear, as in the novel, but her character is written differently.

A few characters from the novel were retained—Tiffany, Felix Leiter, Wint and Kidd, Shady Tree—but new ones were created as well: Willard Whyte (the Howard Hughes–like character whom Blofeld impersonates for his new front), Plenty O'Toole (just another Bond-girl), and Burt Saxby (one of Blofeld's underlings who manages the Las Vegas hotel where Bond stays).

The script does contain some funny lines, probably thanks to the wit of Tom Mankiewicz. Some of these lines were a little too witty for Broccoli's taste, but the dialogue remains in the film anyway. One example occurs when Leiter is looking for the diamonds hidden inside the dead body of Peter Franks. "Where are they?" he asks Bond. Bond replies with a smile, "Alimentary, Dr. Leiter." Connery's delivery of these lines is wry. Another funny moment is when Miss O'Toole introduces herself to Bond at the casino. "Hi, I'm Plenty," she says. Bond looks her up and down and replies, "Of course you are." "No," she says, "Plenty O'Toole!" Bond then says, "Named after your father, no doubt."

□ DIRECTION

Guy Hamilton is back for his second Bond film, to which he brings much of the same slick style of *Goldfinger*. But the touch is lighter this time. *Diamonds* emphasizes wit and high camp at the expense of suspense and danger. The film moves so rapidly that one can barely follow the storyline. The action speeds recklessly from set-piece to set-piece, never giving the audience time to ask, "Now, why did *that* happen?" It seems to be a strategy on the part of the filmmakers for covering weak plot details: move over them *fast* if they don't make sense.

This doesn't mean that *Diamonds Are Forever* isn't stylish. The opening scenes revealing the diamond pipeline are moody, thanks to John Barry's eerie score. The scene in which Bond is trapped inside a coffin loaded into a crematorium creates a good deal of suspense, but his rescue by Shady Tree is a cop-out. The most atmospheric and Bondian scene in the film is when 007 rides the elevator to the top of the Whyte House in order to break into the penthouse. Using a gun that fires a cable and grappling hooks, Bond dangles in midair over Las Vegas for a few minutes as he pulls himself up. The music, the night sky, and the shadowy photography create a breathtaking effect.

The film's highlights are the two chases: one involving a moon buggy from the satellite space laboratory, and the other pitting Bond and Tiffany's Mustang against the Las Vegas police. This latter sequence is full of thrills and is really the high point of the film, even though it's markedly similar to the Aston Martin car chase in *Goldfinger*. Over twenty automobiles were totalled for the filming of this scene.

The main problem with Hamilton's direction is that he takes many of the characters too lightly, Blofeld in particular. In *You Only Live Twice*, Blofeld seems a raving lunatic. In *Diamonds*, Blofeld is British (a mistake) and very charming. He has as much style and elegance as Bond himself. The treatment of Wint and Kidd is especially annoying. In the novel, the homo-

sexual couple are extremely dangerous characters. In the film, they are simply silly. Much of the picture's humor is derived from these two. Finally, the character of James Bond himself is treated with levity. Connery still manages to bring a certain amount of macho ruggedness to the role, but the character seems to be floating through this assignment on a breeze. It's all too easy for him. Connery's performance aside, one can easily see that the Bond character as written here would easily harmonize with Roger Moore's personality for future films.

□ ACTORS AND CHARACTERS

Sean Connery's performance brings the film a cut above the other Bonds made in the seventies. Connery has that certain presence and charisma which one associates with Bond. His performance in *Diamonds* is much more sincere than that of *You Only Live Twice*. It's obvious that Connery had a good time while filming the movie. He seems to be enjoying himself in the role, and thus, gives the most relaxed and confident performance as Bond since *Goldfinger*. He looks quite a bit older than when we last saw him—he's at least twenty pounds heavier, and he's beginning to grey at the temples. Some fans complained that he looked horrible, but in many ways, he looks that much more worldly. Connery also adds a touch of self-parody to the character that works well in the context of the lighter direction the film takes. After the fight with Peter Franks in the elevator, Bond switches wallets with the man before Tiffany can examine him. She looks at Franks' wallet and exclaims, "You've just killed James Bond!" Wide-eyed, but with a hint of mischievousness, Connery delivers the line, "Is *that* who it was? Well, it just goes to show you that no one's indestructible!"

Jill St. John gives what may be the performance of her career as Tiffany Case. This character bears little resemblance to Fleming's original. The literary Tiffany is very neurotic, and has eccentricities that made her a much more interesting person than the cocky, self-confident Tiffany of the film. But Miss St. John turns in a masterful portrayal of the character as rewritten. She's one of the sexiest Bond heroines ever, and dressed in costumes by Donfeld, she creates an alluring foil for 007. Miss St. John has been typecast in similar roles throughout her career, but none of them have displayed her strengths as well.

Charles Gray is miscast as Blofeld, the third infuriating time the character has been misrepresented. Gray is a fine actor with a polished delivery, but Blofeld should never be British. It's also strange that the film-makers would cast someone with hair this time, since the two previous Blofelds were bald. The main problem with Gray's Blofeld is that he is not at all menacing. He's much too charming and poised. This is a serious flaw in the film. The white cat is used in an interesting way, for once. When Bond discovers two different Blofelds in Willard Whyte's penthouse, he decides to gamble. When the white cat enters the room, Bond kicks it. Bond then quickly shoots the Blofeld whose arms the cat jumps into. But immediately after doing this, *another* white cat enters the room (this one wears a diamond collar) and strolls to the real Blofeld. "Right idea, 007," muses Blofeld. "But wrong pussy," laments Bond.

The death of Blofeld is also unsatisfying, if indeed it is a death. Bond's archenemy is attempting to escape his oil rig headquarters at Baja in a one-man submarine which is being hoisted to the water by a crane. Bond gains control of the crane, and begins toying with the sub as if it were a yo-yo. Bond finally evacuates the area and the entire rig explodes. We never learn whether Blofeld escapes from the sub or is destroyed in the explosion. Since he doesn't return in subsequent films (except for a confusing appearance in *For Your Eyes Only* ten years later), we must presume he is dead. But it seems that a James Bond intent on revenge would have made sure of this fact.

Lana Wood (Natalie's younger sister) plays Plenty O'Toole, an extra Bond-girl created for the film. Plenty's presence is gratuitous, especially since most of her scenes were cut from the final print. She is the film's Obligatory Sacrificial Lamb, but her death hardly makes sense. She is found floating in Tiffany's swimming pool at her house near Las Vegas. Just why she happened to be at Tiffany's is unexplained. Apparently, the excised scenes told a more complete story. After she is rudely evicted from Bond's hotel suite by Slumber Inc.'s hoods (they throw her out the window into a swimming pool), she supposedly returns, dripping wet. There, she overhears Bond and Tiffany in his bedroom. Plenty then rifles Tiffany's purse, finds her keys and address, and decides to go there. And that's where Wint and Kidd catch up with her, thinking that she is Tiffany. (Why she *wants* to go to Tiffany's house is beyond me.)

Felix Leiter is miscast for the fourth time. Norman Burton, a middle-aged American actor, emphasizes the joviality of the character, but he doesn't look the part at all. Burton is overweight and too old for the role. And again, there is no indication of Leiter's handicaps.

Leiter serves basic plot functions here, but no more.

Jimmy Dean gives an admirable performance as Willard Whyte, the billionaire kidnapped by Blofeld. His country twang is comical, and he provides a good deal of the film's humor in the latter third. There's one terrific moment when he is shot at by his employee, Burt Saxby. One of Leiter's men takes aim and kills Saxby on the spot. They tell Whyte it was Saxby who shot at him. "Saxby?" he exclaims. "Tell him he's fired!"

Wint and Kidd are played by Bruce Glover and Putter Smith, respectively They are a bizarre-looking couple, but they lose their menacing qualities immediately when they are seen holding hands and walking into the distance. From then on, their characters are jokes and they are never again able to produce a threatening effect.

Acrobats Donna Garratt and Trina Parks portray Bambi and Thumper, two SPECTRE martial arts experts guarding Willard Whyte. Bond has a fairly well-staged fight with these two, but after battling the likes of Red Grant, Oddjob, and a Sumo wrestler, Bond hardly seems endangered. They gain the upper hand at first, but it's hard to believe. Bond finally calms them down by dunking them into a swimming pool and holding their heads underwater. Too easy.

The obligatory M/Moneypenny/Q scenes all occur separately this time. Bond shares the usual banter with M at the beginning of the film; the scene is played with mutual contempt. Apparently, the filmmakers intend the conflict between Bond and M to be funny, but it rarely works. They never poke fun at each other in the novels as they do in this scene. Moneypenny appears where she never should—impersonating a customs official near Holland. And Q is seen briefly at Q Branch, where in the background we see a lot of rockets loaded into the front end of Bond's Aston Martin. This visual joke is humorous if you're lucky enough to notice it. Q later appears on location in Las Vegas, experimenting with a gadget that automatically wins jackpots when it's attached to a slot machine. The attempts at humor at the expense of these three characters are becoming ludicrous.

□ **OTHER ASPECTS**

Ken Adam is back as production designer, but after the tour de force of *You Only Live Twice*, the sets do not seem as impressive. In fact, they're beginning to resemble each other by now. Blofeld's penthouse (actually Willard Whyte's) looks very much like the suite used in *You Only Live Twice.* The operating room/lab in the pre-credits sequence is a rehash of Dr. No's surroundings. But all the sets seem to glitter, a quality tying in very well with the diamond theme. Ted Moore is back as cinematographer after a two-film absence, and he gives the picture a very professional, glitzy look. Coupled with Adam's designs, the visual properties of the film, though they have a *déjà vu* quality, are chic.

The editing work is by Bert Bates and John W. Holmes, and they created a tight, speedy action film. The trouble is that too many explanatory scenes were edited from the picture. But their work on the car chase, the moon buggy chase, and especially the fight scene in the elevator between Bond and Peter Franks is impressive.

Bob Simmons is back choreographing the fight scenes, with the help of Paul Baxley. Though *Diamonds* doesn't feature many action sequences, the one in the elevator is exciting. With such a small, cramped space to work with, one wouldn't think that an interesting fight could be choreographed. But Simmons and his assistant come up with a tense and tough minute or two that is reminiscent of the old Bond battles.

John Barry's score for the film is disappointing. He uses sounds and themes similar to those heard in previous films, and the entire score is ultimately very predictable. The "007" theme is heard again at the film's climactic battle on the oil rig—something we've seen and heard too many times before. The main title theme, once again featuring Shirley Bassey, is particularly disappointing due once more to Don Black's expendable lyrics. The song comes off as corny. Even Maurice Binder's title design is beginning to look like the same old palette of silhouetted nudes, emphasizing the fact that the filmmakers are running out of fresh ideas.

Diamonds Are Forever, then, is a very mixed bag. Connery's return as Bond, of course, is the best thing the film has going for it. The picture has a witty script by Maibaum and Mankiewicz, but *everything* is played for laughs now. The missing element of authentic suspense is the picture's main flaw, and as one will see, this is not corrected in subsequent films. The matter is only made worse.

LIVE AND LET DIE (1973)

□ PRODUCTION

The huge financial success of *Diamonds Are Forever* assured Eon Productions that there would be another James Bond film, with or without Sean Connery. The producers began yet another talent search to cast James Bond for their next project, *Live and Let Die.* Again Burt Reynolds was considered, but Cubby Broccoli insisted Bond must be played by an Englishman. Their final choice was the man who was reportedly second on the list when they were casting *Dr. No:* Roger Moore.

Moore seemed to be a good choice—he had sophistication, experience, good looks, and would not be an unknown face outside of England. Audiences accepted him in the role of James Bond, although he plays it quite differently from his predecessors.

Moore arrived on the scene just as the direction in the Bond films began veering towards comedy. Since Moore's forte *is* light comedy, he fit right in. From *Live and Let Die* on, the scriptwriters tailored the screenplays to fit Roger Moore's personality. As a result, James Bond lost much of the *machismo* image which was so prominent in the sixties. It seems Bond never gets hurt in any of the subsequent films—the Roger Moore Bond uses his wits rather than fists to escape dangerous situations. One-liners are geared to Moore's brand of delivery (such as adding "darling" when he's speaking to a woman). The Roger Moore Bond sails effortlessly through his adventures—which reflects the work of the scriptwriters and directors more than the actor.

Once Roger Moore was cast, United Artists immediately launched a heavy publicity campaign to sell him as Bond. The producers told the press that Roger Moore was closer to Ian Fleming's original conception of Bond than Sean Connery—straight British, old Etonian dropout, etc. This is, in fact, untrue. Fleming certainly never conceived Bond as an old Etonian dropout (he was *kicked* out)—if anything, Bond looks back on his school years with a great deal of cynicism. And Fleming's Bond is Scottish. Nevertheless, by the time *Live and Let Die* was released in the summer of 1973, the public had been well conditioned to accept Roger Moore as the new James Bond.

The second decade of James Bond films is certainly a different batch from the first. The trend toward comedy initiated in *Diamonds* progressed until the Bond films became something of a mixture of *Smokey and the Bandit* and *Star Wars.* They were all successful, but 007 was lost on the screen. None of the seventies' scripts resemble Fleming's stories, and the standard Bond formula became embarrassingly repetitious. Inevitably, the Bond films attracted a younger and younger audience.

Live and Let Die contains moments of spectacle, as does every Bond film, but the "bumps" formula weak-

THE FILMS □ 207

ens the narrative. When a script is written around a series of locations already chosen for the film, one can't expect a plot to make a whole lot of sense. The first Roger Moore vehicle is admirable in a few ways: it's attractive to look at, there are some funny bits, the locations are interesting, and the cast is fairly good. What mars the film are its digressions into the absurd.

One ingredient critics attacked when the film was released was its all-black villainous organization. The film happened to be released during the peak of the black film boom of 1972 and 1973. *Sounder* had been nominated for Academy Awards that spring, as had *Lady Sings the Blues. Shaft* was becoming a cult hero. Eon Productions was accused of exploiting blacks just because there was a current boom in black films. These attacks were unwarranted, for Fleming's original novel also features an all-black villainous organization. If anything, the filmmakers created a much more sophisticated group than Fleming had.

Location shooting took place in New Orleans, Jamaica, and New York; interiors were shot, as usual, at Pinewood Studios in England. Guy Hamilton was in charge of his third Bond film, and the future of James Bond fell into the hands of Roger Moore.

□ SCREENPLAY

For the second time in the series, Richard Maibaum's name is missing from the screenplay credit. Tom Mankiewicz is the sole author.

Mankiewicz told *Bondage* magazine that he had written the script before he knew Roger Moore was going to play Bond. He had been told by the producers and United Artists president David Picker that the new film must be an entertaining, action-packed film, no matter *who* was going to play Bond. Therefore, Mankiewicz injected the set-piece formula into the script in such a way that the film basically jumps from stunt to stunt.

As usual, Fleming's original story was thrown out. Because it was felt that the novel's treatment of blacks was patronizing, the filmmakers decided to create a high-class criminal organization as opposed to Fleming's group of second-rate crooks. The result was a SPECTRE-like organization operating from the Caribbean island of San Monique. The prime minister of the island, Dr. Kananga, is attempting to smuggle heroin into the states via a chain of restaurants in New Orleans and New York. While in New York, Dr. Kananga masquerades as Mr. Big in order to instill fear in his underlings. Gone is Bloody Morgan's pirate hoard,

as well as the fascinating character of Mr. Big himself. Kananga's Mr. Big is inconsequential.

Mankiewicz does retain some of the original elements and characters: Solitaire, the Bond-girl with telepathic powers; Felix Leiter; Tee-Hee, one of the black hoods; and Baron Samedi, the Prince of Darkness. The voodoo motifs are also used in the film, as well as a deck of tarot cards which becomes the design metaphor for the picture. Several new characters are created: Rosie Carver, a black CIA agent helping Bond in the Caribbean; J. W. Pepper, comic relief in the form of a redneck Southern sheriff; and other assorted black hoodlums. Samedi is made an actual character who also serves as a visual metaphor in the film.

The *Live and Let Die* script is witty and entertaining, but not very original. When compared to the novel, it is second-rate. Fleming's story is one of his best, and it is preposterous that the filmmakers discarded the superior plot of the book. Several of Fleming's scenes would have translated wonderfully to the screen: Bond and Leiter's barhopping in Harlem; Bond and Solitaire's train ride to Florida (this location was changed to New Orleans in the film); the loss of Leiter's hand and leg; the fight in the fish warehouse; Bond's swim through Shark Bay; and several others. Granted, changing the villains' operation to smuggling heroin is more timely, but that would have worked in the context of the original story. As it is, *Live and Let Die* operated on a totally visual level—full of stunts, exotic locales, and a hell of a lot of destruction of public property. As a story, though, the film is limp.

The pre-credits sequence does not even feature James Bond. Usually, this traditional device tells a complete story in itself, whether it is related to the main plot or not. In *Live and Let Die,* we see three British men murdered by blacks—one at the United Nations, one on a New Orleans street corner, and one on the island of San Monique. The scenes do not grab the audience, and this pre-credits sequence is therefore the weakest of the series.

The opening scene of the film proper takes place at James Bond's flat. We see him in bed with a girl, where he is rudely awakened by none other than M at his front door. The scene provides a few laughs, especially when Miss Moneypenny catches the semi-clad girl attempting to hide in Bond's closet. But in the past, Bond has always been *summoned* to the office in a matter of emergency. Why would M and/or Miss Moneypenny bother to travel to Bond's house so early in the morning? The idea is ridiculous. But if one forgets this, the scene is one of the more enjoyable in the film.

Roger Moore as Bond rescues Solitaire (Jane Seymour) from a voodoo ritual in Live and Let Die. *(UPI Photo.)*

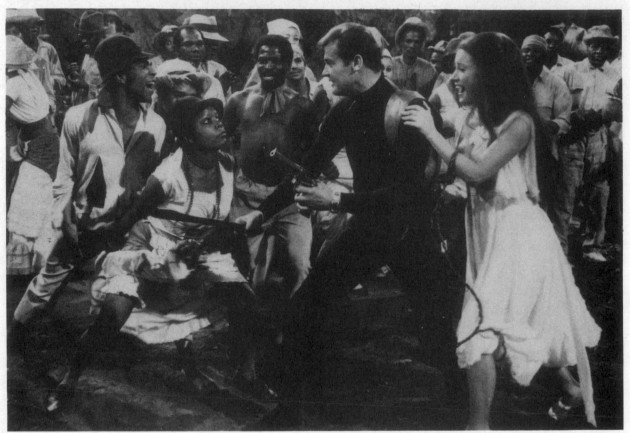

None of the characters is particularly well written. Most disappointing is the development of Solitaire, who could have been used to much greater advantage. The Kananga/Mr. Big confusion doesn't work, and the Rosie Carver business is just another variation on the female villain ploy. Moore is provided with some funny lines, but isn't given ample opportunity to show any depth of character. *Live and Let Die* is a situation comedy with several outdoor action scenes.

□ **DIRECTION**

Guy Hamilton is in charge again, and lends his usual fast-paced, light touch to the proceedings. But this time there is no bite to the film.

Hamilton's tarot card motif does give the film visual unity. Throughout the picture, especially when Bond is traveling from one country to another, Solitaire's voice is dubbed over the action. We see her hands turning over tarot cards superimposed on the screen, as she explains what the future will bring. Additionally,

Hamilton and Mankiewicz gave several characters representative tarot cards: Solitaire is "The High Priestess," Rosie Carver is "The Queen of Cups," and Bond himself is "The Fool." The image of Baron Samedi in appearances throughout the film also gives the story a symbolic continuity. Samedi represents death, and he appears several times in bizarre costume and makeup. One particularly striking image is the shot of Samedi, in rags, sitting by a tombstone in a cemetery playing a wooden flute. The final image of the film is that of Samedi, riding on the back of the train carrying Bond and Solitaire to New York. With his demonic laugh filling the theater, the image reminds us that death will always be following close behind wherever we go.

One sequence does manage to deliver some impact. Bond is sitting in a New Orleans nightclub when his table drops through the floor and into the room below (this scene is similar to the one in the novel at Table Z). Tee-Hee, who in the film has a mechanical pincer in place of one arm, is ordered to snap off Bond's little finger if Solitaire cannot correctly name the serial number on the back of Bond's watch. (Kananga suspects that Solitaire has lost her telepathic powers as a result of losing her virginity to Bond.) There is a tense moment as Solitaire makes a wild guess, and Bond is released. He is taken away, and it is then revealed that Solitaire was wrong about the number. As Kananga chastises her, Baron Samedi sits in the corner of the room, laughing and overturning tarot cards. Hamilton has provided this scene with a bit of tension.

The most annoying aspect of the film is its leaning toward juvenile humor. The introduction of Sheriff J. W. Pepper is the first in what would grow to be a very damaging element of the series. Basically a variation on the redneck Las Vegas sheriff in *Diamonds Are Forever,* Louisiana Sheriff Pepper joins the speedboat chase in order to catch Bond; he is unaware that Bond is a British secret agent. Though the boat stunts are spectacular, this section of the film regresses to Three Stooges–style violence and absurdity. What could have been a truly exciting boat chase is undercut by this so-called humor.

Finally, the film stays on one level throughout. The climax is flat and predictable, and the death of Kananga is particularly silly. Bond shoves a gas pellet from a shark gun into Kananga's mouth. Kananga inflates like a balloon, floats to the ceiling, and bursts. Bond purists the world over surely hid their heads in embarrassment during this sequence.

□ ACTORS AND CHARACTERS

Roger Moore has always approached the role of James Bond with a light and humorous attitude, emphasizing the sophistication and intelligence of the character, relying on his smooth voice, agile charm, and good looks to carry him through. The actor's *James Bond Diary,* written during the filming of *Live and Let Die,* reveals how Moore perceives his role. He constantly refers to the character as "Jimmy" Bond, and enjoys telling the story of how he attempted looking mean for several days.

In a press conference held when *For Your Eyes Only* was released, Moore admitted what little preparation he does for the character:

Q: How much Fleming do you need to read to keep in touch with the character?
Moore: It's very difficult to get in touch with the character by reading Fleming, because there's very little about Bond—about the person that he is, only what he's doing.
Q: But, even when you started back in '73 . . .

Moore: Ah, yes, I sort of did a quick sifting through all the books to try and find out what he was like. I only found one thing and that was that he had a scar on his cheek and looked like Hoagy Carmichael. And the only other key to the character was that he had come back from Mexico where he had eliminated somebody. He didn't particularly like killing, but he took pride in doing his job well. That was the only thing I could find out about Bond.
Q: So you based your characterization on those two facts.
Moore: Yes. I don't like killing, but I'm pleased that I do it well.

(From "The For Your Eyes Only Press Conference," by Richard Schenkman; *Bondage,* Number 11)

Apparently, the producers' direction and Roger Moore's approach toward his role blended smoothly to create what could be called the "James Bond Comedies."

Actually, Roger Moore's performance in *Live and Let Die* is in an experimental stage. There are moments when Moore attempts a bit of cynicism. He's very convincing in the scene with Rosie Carver in the jungle of San Monique. Stopping for a picnic, they spread a blanket, rest from their search for Kananga's hideout, and make love. Afterwards, Bond pries her for information. (He had received a warning that Rosie is a traitor.) Rosie, shocked when Bond threatens her, asks, "You mean you'd kill me after . . .?" To which Bond (with Moore being as nasty as possible) replies, "You don't think I'd kill you before, do you?"

In the final analysis, Roger Moore's main problem with playing Bond is a lack of dynamics. A tough side essential to the character is missing.

Yaphet Kotto portrays Dr. Kananga/Mr. Big. Why Mankiewicz chose to confuse the issue by having the villain masquerade as another one is unclear. Kotto's makeup is unconvincing and looks rather silly, but he is a fine actor. He approaches the role seriously and exudes power in his speeches. It's too bad the material he has to work with creates a totally unbelievable character.

Jane Seymour, as Solitaire, is lovely to look at and is an extremely talented actress who has gone on to an illustrious career since her debut in *Live and Let Die.* But her character, too, suffers from a poor script. In the novel, Solitaire is mysterious, frightened and vulnerable, but also proud. There is an attempt on Miss Seymour's part to communicate these traits, but the script provides her nothing with which to work. As a result, Solitaire comes off as an unintelligent little girl.

Felix Leiter is given a fair characterization, for once,

by David Hedison, an American actor familiar to television audiences via *Voyage to the Bottom of the Sea*. He's miscast, and the character is totally wrong, but he's the best Leiter next to Rik Van Nutter. If more humor had been injected into *his* character rather than Bond's, we might have had something. Another disappointment.

Gloria Hendry gives an impressive performance as Rosie Carver, a double agent working for the CIA. The sections involving her character do not advance the plot much; they simply provide another Obligatory Sacrificial Lamb. She has been ordered by Kananga to kill Bond; she falls for him instead, and fails her task. She is then shot by a voodoo scarecrow in the jungle while fleeing from the angry Bond. Her character is unbelievable—why would the CIA send Bond a girl who seems so obviously inexperienced?

Since the Quarrel character was killed by the dragon in *Dr. No,* the filmmakers created an improbably adult Quarrel Jr. for *Live and Let Die*. Played by Roy Stewart, Quarrel Jr. has little dialogue, and is included only for plot mechanics. He pitches in by setting the explosives at Kananga's poppy field.

Kananga's gang of black crooks include Baron Samedi, a weirdo who uses costume and makeup to become the evil Prince of Darkness. Played by Geoffrey Holder (who also choreographed the dance sequences), Samedi is one of the most successful characters in the film. Holder gives an electric performance, and practically steals the show. Mostly, Samedi is seen in various locations, hovering over the action. Holder's volcanic laugh is terrific, and his extremely tall frame is godlike.

Julius Harris as Tee-Hee makes a good superhenchman. Of course, Tee-Hee is a reincarnation of Oddjob, but with a strong mechanical pincer for an arm. Harris manages to play the character with enough variation to maintain interest. His grin is contagious, and it's particularly effective in the alligator farm sequence. Earl Jolly Brown plays a grossly fat henchman who constantly whispers. This character is too humorous to be menacing. His name is, appropriately, Whisper.

Then there is J. W. Pepper, played by an extremely funny actor, Clifton James. The trouble is that this type of character has no business being in a James Bond film. Sheriff Pepper is simply a caricature of a Southern lawman—a redneck, short on brains. The character produces laughs, but he seems an arbitrary and pointless addition to the cast. The character returns for an even less successful encore in the next film, *The Man*

with the Golden Gun. The idea of laughs at the expense of a dumb lawman is trite.

Bernard Lee and Lois Maxwell perform with their usual alacrity. (Q is missing from this film.) Lee is given a particularly good line. Bond is explaining that his new wristwatch contains a magnet powerful enough to deflect a bullet. M says, "I'm tempted to test that theory right now."

☐ OTHER ASPECTS

Syd Cain is production designer for his third Bond film. There aren't many interiors in the picture. It is primarily an outdoor film, like *Dr. No*. Kananga's laboratory at the end of the movie is Ken Adam influenced, and Bond's flat has a certain excessiveness akin to Adam's work. But the outdoor locations are marvelous and extremely colorful. That's one thing about the Bond films that will always be attractive—well-photographed views of a foreign land. In this case, the film captures the flavor of the South and Ted Moore's usual fine work shines in the bayou sequences.

Editors Bert Bates, Raymond Poulton, and John Shirley put together a tight film and their work on the boat chase sequences is amazing. Costumes, by Julie Harris, are exceptionally colorful, and help create the thematic unity of tarot cards and mysticism. Solitaire's clothes have the ceremonial quality of a high priestess' garments.

Derek Meddings joins Eon Productions as special effects man with *Live and Let Die*. Meddings is a fine craftsman, and his work in the series is superb. His contribution to *Live and Let Die* is minimal, however. He built ramps and whatnot for the boat stunts, and created a miniature (his specialty) of the poppy field to blow up. His best work for the Bonds will be seen later.

The stuntwork in the film is one of the few highlights. Coordinated by Bob Simmons, Eddie Smith, Bill Bennot, Ross Kananga, Joey Chitwood, Jerry Comeaux, and Maurice Patchett, the stunts are originals performed by their creators. The most outrageous stunt and a classic in the series occurs when Bond steps over the backs of alligators to escape from a small island surrounded by the reptiles. There's a fascinating story behind this scene. Originally, Mankiewicz had Bond being taken by Tee-Hee to a coffee granulator. While Mankiewicz and Hamilton were scouting locations, they came upon the actual sign which appears in the film reading TRESPASSERS WILL BE EATEN. It was an alligator farm, owned by a man named (believe it or not) Ross Kananga. Kananga was enthusiastic about the prospect of a Bond film being shot on his farm and gladly participated in the stuntwork. In fact, it was Kananga who suggested that Bond use the alligators' backs as stepping stones to escape from the island. The film-makers were dubious about getting someone to do the stunt. Kananga said he would, if the animals' legs were tied down first. That's what they did, and it's a wonderful moment.

Maurice Patchett, a London bus driver, performed the double-decker bus stunt, in which the entire upper deck is knocked off by a low bridge. Actually, the upper deck was previously sawn off and placed on rollers, but still. . . . The action on the airfield smashing up airplanes is amusing but becomes tiresome after a while. There is also one of those out-of-place characters present: a middle-aged woman waiting for her flying lesson who is unwittingly kidnapped by a fleeing Bond.

The film's main highlight is the boat chase, orchestrated by Jerry Comeaux and Joey Chitwood. Boats fly onto land, over roads, into cars, through weddings, and almost anywhere but the water. The sequence is fun but is rife with misplaced humor. Still, the boats themselves, and their captains, are first rate.

Bond's gadget in this film is a fancy wristwatch that contains a powerful magnet strong enough to grab something from across the room. Pretty outlandish. It also has a feature we aren't told about, which, as John Brosnan accuses, "breaks the Bondian rules." It isn't fair that the watch becomes a buzz saw at the end of the film when Bond is tied with Solitaire in a hoist above the shark pool. We didn't know it could do that.

John Barry is absent this time, and the Beatles' producer, George Martin, is in charge of the score for *Live and Let Die.* But his work is entirely overshadowed by Paul and Linda McCartney's main title song. Performed by Wings, "Live and Let Die" is a bizarre song, especially for a Bond film. But it works beautifully, and remains one of the best main titles of the series. (It was nominated for an Academy Award.) It's energetic, loud, and powerful. Martin's score is admirable, with a couple of catchy tunes such as "San Monique." His version of "The James Bond Theme" is overproduced, but on the whole, the score moves with the film.

Live and Let Die, successful as it was financially, is a mediocre film. There is no real excitement because it's very predictable. It marks a period of unrest at Eon Productions. The James Bond films were in a state of confusion, and it would take three more attempts before Eon Productions would decide to return to the original style of the sixties' pictures.

THE MAN WITH THE GOLDEN GUN (1974)

□ PRODUCTION

The ninth James Bond film marks the end of Harry Saltzman's association with Eon Productions. Relations between Saltzman and Broccoli had become strained, and the producers took turns producing *Live and Let Die* and the new film, *The Man With the Golden Gun.*

It was Saltzman who had always wanted to go on location in Hong Kong and Thailand, and these locations are the highlights of *Golden Gun.* Otherwise, the ninth James Bond entry is weak, even lower in quality than *Live and Let Die.* The main problem is that the film stays on one dynamic level throughout and is played entirely too lightly. Guy Hamilton must take the blame for the failure of *Golden Gun,* although its script, by Richard Maibaum and Tom Mankiewicz, is none too thrilling. The set-piece formula is again apparent, creating the effect that the plot was built around the film's locations. There are a few good moments in the picture, but as a whole, it lacks unity.

Golden Gun was shot in Hong Kong; in and around Bangkok, Thailand; and near the resort island of Phuket. Production designer Peter Murton found an unusual set of islands near Phuket, and one of these, Kao Ping-Kan, was used as the headquarters of Francisco Scaramanga. The site is otherworldly and exotic.

□ SCREENPLAY

Tom Mankiewicz wrote the initial draft of *The Man With the Golden Gun* before resigning from the project due to reported disagreements with Guy Hamilton. As usual, the Fleming original was completely thrown out. Granted, Fleming's novel is probably his weakest, but it contains enough good elements to serve as a departure point for a screenplay. Instead, Mankiewicz created a new story involving not a second-rate Cuban assassin like Fleming's Scaramanga, but a super-villain of the stature of Bond himself. Scaramanga is equipped with his own island headquarters which resembles Crab Key in *Dr. No.* Mankiewicz's original idea for the story was to involve a duel between the two best shots in the world—Bond and Scaramanga. Supposedly, Mankiewicz wanted the film to be more serious, opposing Hamilton's wishes.

Richard Maibaum was hired to rewrite the script. Maibaum added a "MacGuffin" (Hitchcock's term for

Roger Moore with co-star Britt Ekland (as Mary Goodnight) in The Man With the Golden Gun. *(UPI Photo)*

an item that is basically meaningless but serves as the villains' objective in order to motivate the action, such as the Lektor coding machine in *From Russia With Love*). Maibaum's MacGuffin is a solex agitator, a device which will convert radiation from the sun into pure energy. In the film, Scaramanga and the British Secret Service are both searching for the agitator, which is in the possession of a traitorous British agent in Hong Kong. Scaramanga is employed by the Red Chinese through a rich merchant named Hai Fat, who resides in Bangkok. A subplot is inaugurated when Scaramanga sends a golden bullet (his trademark) to Universal Export with the number 007 engraved on it. M presumes this means that someone has paid Scaramanga his one million dollar fee to assassinate Bond. Therefore, Bond must somehow find Scaramanga before the killer finds Bond.

On paper, the script probably looked pretty good, but on the screen the story is flat. There are too many sections that lack credibility, and Hamilton's direction evokes no excitement. Juvenile humor, such as a scene involving J. W. Pepper (the Louisiana Sheriff from *Live and Let Die*), adds nothing to the plot.

There *is* one scene in which the James Bond character is presented in a harsher light. When Bond visits Scaramanga's girl friend, Andrea Anders, in her hotel room, he treats her roughly. He attempts to find out where Scaramanga is, and slaps Andrea in the process. This is the third time Bond has slapped a woman on-screen. I don't endorse the mistreatment of women, but this is the best scene in the film. There is authentic dramatic conflict here.

The script also makes use of Scaramanga's congenital oddity, a third nipple. Fleming mentions the birthmark in the novel, but nothing is ever made of it. In the film, Bond impersonates Scaramanga at one point, and thanks to Q Branch, a third nipple is added to Bond's chest. This is a clever idea that might have been used even more effectively.

The duel at the end of the film is quite unsatisfying. Apparently, some footage was cut between the beach duel and the cat and mouse game in Scaramanga's "fun house." The fun house is Scaramanga's playpen for stalking practice victims. There is no build-up to Scaramanga's death scene, and it basically repeats the limp pre-credits scene, in which Scaramanga stalks a gangster through the fun house as a form of target practice. Once again, James Bond does not appear in the pre-credits sequence except in the form of a wax dummy that Scaramanga has placed in his fun house.

The concept of the fun house doesn't work at all; it seems childish for a man of Scaramanga's stature to be playing around with such carnival trappings.

□ DIRECTION

Guy Hamilton, in his fourth Bond effort, creates a film that could be subtitled "James Bond Visits the Jungle Ride at Disneyland." Like its predecessor, *The Man with the Golden Gun* is played much too lightly. It's all fun and games, and most of it isn't particularly fun. The film is a predictable amusement park ride.

There is no threat in the film. Christopher Lee, who portrays Scaramanga, has said that Guy Hamilton kept telling him to play the character lightly. During the final scenes on Scaramanga's island, Hamilton ordered Moore and Lee to "enjoy it more—to have fun." As John Brosnan notes, the actors had too much fun, and as a result, there is no tension in the encounter. The characters are simply too polite to each other.

Hamilton's storytelling is often obscure as well. The plot is confusing, and there are several times when things aren't clear. For example, the details concerning the solex agitator are inadequately explained until far too late. The merging of the two plots (the search for the agitator and the duel between Scaramanga and Bond) is not smooth.

Another criticism of the film is that Hamilton does not make sufficient use of Peter Murton's admirable sets. Again, Brosnan points out that Scaramanga's lab is especially ignored, with only *one* technician overseeing the mess.

Perhaps I'm being too hard on Hamilton. The Bond films have always been collaborative efforts. The producers have just as much say in the direction the film takes as the director himself. To put it bluntly, the collaborative effort created an exercise in blandness in the case of *Golden Gun*.

□ ACTORS AND CHARACTERS

Roger Moore, in his second performance as James Bond, makes fewer attempts to toughen the character than he did in *Live and Let Die*. Hamilton's direction naturally released Moore's easy-going mannerisms. Even in the scene in which Moore slaps Anders, his harshness is contradictory. It's difficult to accept Roger Moore slapping anyone, much less a pretty girl. There is one funny line, though, when Bond is visiting Mr. Lazar in Thailand. (Lazar provides Scaramanga with his golden bullets.) Bond points a rifle at Lazar's crotch in an attempt to learn the whereabouts of Scaramanga. "Speak now or forever hold your peace," Bond warns, taking aim. A terrific Moore-ism.

Horror-film veteran Christopher Lee portrays Francisco Scaramanga (the "Pistols" nickname from the novel has been dropped). Lee is a distant cousin of Ian Fleming and was once told by the author that he would have made a good Dr. No. Lee is finally able to play a Bond villain, and it could have been one of the best characterizations of the series. Unfortunately, the script and direction reduce Scaramanga to an almost harmless entity. Lee's Scaramanga is much too charming and elegant to be evil. He isn't frightening in the least; in fact, he tends to evoke sympathy when the audience is told of Scaramanga's past and his tragedy with a pet elephant (one of the few Fleming elements transferred to the screen). Scaramanga, as a boy, shot a policeman who killed the elephant when it went berserk. The incident gives the villain an excuse. But there is one striking image when Scaramanga is escaping from Hong Kong with Andrea and Nick Nack on his fishing vessel. As he and Andrea stand on the deck watching the Hong Kong skyline, he caresses her face with his golden gun. Though a little obvious symbolically, it's an image that works.

Britt Ekland portrays Mary Goodnight, Bond's aide in the East. In the novels, she is Bond's second secretary, but in the film she is merely working for the Service's station in Hong Kong. Miss Ekland has been directed to play the character as a dumb blond. Apparently, the intention was to make a comic character, which is a little patronizing to both the actress and Ian Fleming. As a result, Mary Goodnight is nothing but a clumsy fool, getting herself kidnapped or finding herself stuck in a closet. Ms. Ekland does an adequate job and provides the audience with a few good laughs, but the character, though attractive, is basically an idiot.

The exotic model Maud Adams portrays Andrea Anders, Scaramanga's girl friend. It is she who sends the golden bullet engraved with "007" to Universal Export. Andrea is attempting to contact Bond so that he will rescue her from Scaramanga's clutches. Why she doesn't reveal this during the first meeting with Bond is confusing, since she's so desperate. Andrea is the film's Obligatory Sacrificial Lamb, killed by Scaramanga himself in a boxing ring in Bangkok. Miss Adams's role is the most sophisticated in the story.

Herve Villechaize (of TV's *Fantasy Island*) portrays Nick Nack, Scaramanga's midget manservant and

bodyguard. Nick Nack is simply another version of Oddjob, although his small size and high intelligence create an interesting variation. Unfortunately, the direction of the film makes Nick Nack a figure of fun (he's even accompanied by a humorous musical theme), thereby depriving Bond of any true menace. The final battle aboard Scaramanga's vessel with Nick Nack is embarrassing—as is the way Bond punishes the character. Bond scoops up Nick Nack in a suitcase, and hoists him to the top of the ship's masthead!

Clifton James appears in another cameo in this film as J. W. Pepper. The big question, though, is what is Sheriff Pepper doing on vacation in Thailand? And furthermore, why is he considering buying a new car in Bangkok? Bond accidentally runs into him first on the floating market in Bangkok during a boat chase. Pepper becomes so excited about seeing Bond again that he is knocked into the canal by an elephant (which just happens to be standing next to him). This sequence might have been funny to anyone under twelve years old. Next we see Pepper with his wife in a new car showroom, where Bond steals a car in order to chase Scaramanga. Pepper happens to be in the passenger seat of the car when Bond hops in and drives it through the showroom window. The scene is too ludicrous for words.

M and Miss Moneypenny, as well as Q, appear on location in the Orient again. This time their headquarters is inside the sunken Queen Elizabeth, which is still sitting on its side in Hong Kong harbor. There are shades of *The Poseidon Adventure* when Bond visits the headquarters: the rooms slant awkwardly, but new, horizontal walkways have been built to accommodate the staff. For once, Q doesn't supply Bond with any gadgets to speak of. The only real gadget in the film, besides the false third nipple that Bond uses, is Scaramanga's golden gun, which is assembled from ordinary items such as a ballpoint pen, cigarette lighter, etc. The gun was designed and built by Colibri Lighters.

☐ OTHER ASPECTS

Peter Murton, the film's production designer, had worked on previous Bond films as art director. His sets are very good, even though they smack of Ken Adam influences. As mentioned before, the only problem with the sets is that they are underused. But Scaramanga's dining room is especially attractive, and looks similar to Dr. No's dining room. Ted Moore's cinematography is among his best work for the series, and puts the only polished touch on the film's proceedings.

Supervising editor John Shirley and his assistant, Ray Poulton, give the film the usual tight, fast-paced tempo. Their work is especially effective during the film's main set-pieces: the boat chase around the floating market and the car chase outside of Bangkok.

The car chase features a very impressive stunt which was created by the film's stunt coordinator, W. J. Milligan, Jr. At one point, Bond decides to drive his car onto a collapsed bridge, hoping to leap over the water and land on the other side. The two sections of broken bridge are curved, so that the car does a 360-degree turn in mid-air before landing on the second bridge. The stunt, performed by Milligan, is breathtaking. Each Bond film, no matter how weak it may be, features some kind of spectacular stunt that somehow makes it all seem worthwhile.

The martial arts school fight is another highlight of the film, featuring some of the best in kung-fu and karate action sequences. Bond plays it a bit nasty when he kicks one opponent in the head during the customary bow. The sequence is fun to watch, but it lacks the flash of the *ninjas* in *You Only Live Twice*. The sequence lapses into incredibility when Hip (Bond's Chinese ally) and his two teenage nieces help Bond vanquish the entire martial arts school. And why do Hip and his nieces drive away in their car, abandoning Bond to use a motorboat to make his escape?

Derek Meddings' miniatures are impressive. A model was built of Scaramanga's lab, as well as a section of the island itself, for the incredible explosion at the film's end. Scaramanga's auto-plane is also a model. This outlandish gimmick features a car that becomes an airplane.

John Barry is back to score the film. Unfortunately, Don Black is also back doing the inane lyrics for the title song. "He has a powerful weapon, he charges a million a shot; an assassin that's second to none—the man with the golden gun." The song should have been an instrumental. Performed with exaggerated zeal by Lulu, the main title theme must rank as the series' worst. The rest of the Barry score, though, is quite good. The Far Eastern setting provided him with another opportunity to create exotic Oriental music, which is successful in capturing the flavor of the locations. There are sections, though, where the music takes on a humorous quality, complementing the action on the screen.

The Man With the Golden Gun, then, represents a low point in the series. It was no financial blockbuster either, and some time elapsed before work began on the next film, mainly due to Harry Saltzman's departure. But when a new Bond film finally was scheduled, with Cubby Broccoli in total control, the series struck back with the most lavish production yet.

THE SPY WHO LOVED ME (1977)

☐ PRODUCTION

Since Cubby Broccoli was going it alone, he enlisted the help of his stepson, Michael G. Wilson, who has been actively involved with Eon Productions ever since as an associate producer. *The Spy Who Loved Me* was chosen as the next title in the Bond film series, and plans were made for a splashy comeback after the lukewarm reception of *The Man With the Golden Gun.*

Ian Fleming had put some strange restrictions on the use of this particular novel. When Fleming sold the rights to the novel to Broccoli and Saltzman, he specified that only the title could be used. A new story would have to be written for the film. After clearing the rights with the Fleming estate, which proved to be a very involved process, writers were called in to begin a screenplay.

Since Eon Productions was already experienced in throwing out Fleming stories, the producers probably anticipated few difficulties in preparing a new *Spy*. But as Steven Rubin documents in his book, *The James Bond Films,* the screenplay for the film went through many changes and authors, most of them uncredited. Among the writers who contributed were Tom Mankiewicz, Ronald Hardy, Anthony Barwick, Derek Marlowe, Sterling Silliphant, John Landis, and even Anthony Burgess. But it was Richard Maibaum who was called back to complete an initial draft. Christopher Wood was brought in later by director Lewis Gilbert for a rewrite, and it is Maibaum and Wood who share the screenplay credit.

With a script finally in hand, production began in 1976. As reported by both John Brosnan and Steve Rubin, the story involved a typical formulized plot with Ernst Stavro Blofeld and SPECTRE back in action again after a two-picture absence. But legal problems began when Kevin McClory claimed that the screenplay was similar to one that he, Len Deighton, and Sean Connery had written, entitled *Warhead*. The issue of McClory owning the rights to the character of Blofeld and the SPECTRE organization, since they were originally created for *Thunderball*, was deep in legal controversy.

Broccoli decided to avoid a confrontation with McClory and ordered Christopher Wood to extract any references to SPECTRE and Blofeld from *The Spy Who Loved Me*. So Blofeld became Karl Stromberg, but his set-up is still very SPECTRE-like, even featuring an efficient method of disposing of unsuccessful underlings.

The Spy Who Loved Me was allotted the biggest budget yet for a Bond film—thirteen and one-half million dollars. The result is a very lavish production. There have been several articles in *Bondage* magazine and other publications claiming that *The Spy Who Loved Me* is similar to, and is in essence, a remake of *You Only Live Twice*. John Brosnan has this to say about the film:

The Spy Who Loved Me is basically an anthology of all the Bond films that have gone before. It's as if Broccoli and his team deliberately set out to take a number of the more memorable set-pieces and remake them, even bigger and more spectacular. The pre-credits sequence, with its skiing scenes, for instance, comes from *On Her Majesty's Secret Service;* the fight on the train comes from *From Russia With Love* and *Live and Let Die;* the scene involving the motorcycle assassin and his rocket-powered sidecar is obviously inspired by the similar scene in *Thunderball;* the car chase with the gimmicked-up Lotus is a repeat of the one in *Gold-*

finger with the Aston Martin; the underwater battles are from *Thunderball;* and the basic plot, together with the final climactic scenes in the tanker are, as we've mentioned before, from *You Only Live Twice*.

(John Brosnan, *James Bond in the Cinema*)

Despite the *déjà vu* of many of the sequences, *The Spy Who Loved Me,* surprisingly, turns out to be a very high-class film. Humor is still emphasized, and the science fiction formula returns; but the quality of the production, the spectacular stunts, and even Roger Moore's performance are all better than ever. Technically, the film is beautiful to look at—the huge budget can be seen in all areas of production. Even Ken Adam is back, designing dazzling and spectacular sets.

More locations were used in the filming of *The Spy Who Loved Me* than ever before. Interiors, as usual, were shot at Pinewood Studios in England, and primary locations were shot in Sardinia and Egypt. Additional footage was shot in the Bahamas, Baffin Island in Canada, Scotland, and Switzerland.

The film was released in the summer of 1977, and although it was competing with *Star Wars,* it was a blockbuster and the biggest grosser since *Thunderball*.

☐ SCREENPLAY

The Spy Who Loved Me is basically *You Only Live Twice* using submarines instead of space capsules. In an interesting article from *Bondage* magazine, Saul Fischer made a list of the similarities between the two films, totalling *forty-six* entries. A few of these similarities follow:

YOU ONLY LIVE TWICE	THE SPY WHO LOVED ME
The plot concerns villain's ship destroying Russia and America by capturing crafts of each to bring about a nuclear confrontation between them, which is eventually destroyed by Bond.	The plot concerns villain's ship destroying Russia and America by capturing crafts of each to bring about a nuclear confrontation between them, which is eventually destroyed by Bond.
M and Miss Moneypenny pop up later in the film on location where Bond is.	M and Miss Moneypenny pop up later in the film on location where Bond is.
The film opens with an American craft being captured by the villain's ship. The U.S. crew doesn't see it coming up from astern while the ship's forward section opens like a steel mouth, swallowing the craft, and rendering all communications dead.	The film opens with a British craft being captured by the villain's ship. The U.K. crew doesn't see it coming up from astern while the ship's forward section opens like a steel mouth, swallowing the craft, and rendering all communications dead.

The villain's main establishment is an elaborate plush drawing room where TV screens abound, filled with long colonial tables, expensive furniture, and religious Old Master paintings. Here we are introduced to the tall silent henchman, Hans. Two businessmen appear, who are then shocked when the villain kills his secretary by letting her fall into a piranha pool.	The villain's main establishment is an elaborate plush drawing room where TV screens abound, filled with long colonial tables, expensive furniture, and religious Old Master paintings. Here we are introduced to the tall, silent henchman, Jaws. Two businessmen appear, who are then shocked when the villain kills his secretary by letting her fall into a shark pool.
Bond makes his earliest contact in the audience at the Sumo wrestling arena where he first sees the female agent he will eventually join forces with.	Bond makes his earliest contact in the audience at the Egyptian pyramids where he first sees the female agent he will eventually join forces with.
Osata Chemical & Engineering Co. is the villain's front.	Stromberg Shipping Lines is the villain's front.
The villain uses a tanker, the *Ning Po,* in his power for world domination.	The villain uses a tanker, the *Liparus,* in his power for world domination.
Bond, with Aki, uses a white sports car equipped with TV monitor, for a big chase involving a black car with armed henchmen, and a helicopter which forces the enemy's car into the sea.	Bond, with Anya, uses a white sports car equipped with TV monitor, for a big chase involving a car with armed henchmen, and a black helicopter which forces Bond's car into the sea.
Bond pretends to be a legitimate businessman who, under the alias of being "Mr. Fisher," is accepted to Osata's establishment.	Bond pretends to be a legitimate marine biologist who, under the alias of being an expert on fish, is accepted to Stromberg's establishment.
Blofeld's hidden base is a huge, silver, circular docking port, complete with fuel tanks, catwalks, Russian and American prisoners, and a monorail encircling the perimeter. Huge silver shutters separate the base from Blofeld's control room.	Stromberg's hidden base is a huge, silver, circular docking port, complete with fuel tanks, catwalks, Russian and British prisoners, and a monorail encircling the perimeter. Huge silver shutters separate the base from Stromberg's control room.
The big battle between Blofeld's men and the *ninja* soldiers at the film's climax occurs in Blofeld's secret base.	The big battle between Stromberg's men and the submarine crews at the film's climax occurs in Stromberg's secret base.
Bond and the men attack the Blofeld base, going in the docking port first before entering the more heavily guarded control room.	Bond and the men attack the Stromberg base, going in the docking port first before entering the more heavily guarded control room.
When Bond enters the control room, he destroys the enemy ship before the villain's mission has been accomplished.	When Bond enters the control room, he destroys the enemy ship before the villain's mission has been accomplished.

(From "The Spy Who Lived Twice," by Saul Fischer, *Bondage* Number 7)

An interesting sidelight to all this is that when Cubby Broccoli was asked about the similarity between the two films at a public press conference held at the Museum of Modern Art in 1979, he replied that he didn't think the films were similar at all, and seemed confused that the question was even asked.

There is an attempt in the film to make the Bond character a little tougher, in contrast to Roger Moore's earlier approach. There are a few more fight scenes than in the two previous Moore efforts. But he still emerges from the battles basically unscratched. The fight with Jaws at the Egyptian ruins confirms Roger Moore's "brains before brawn" characterization of Bond. Jaws has accidentally knocked over a support beam while attempting to hit Bond, and the entire structure falls down on top of the giant. Bond walks away from the ordeal briskly wiping his hands, as if he had just swatted a fly.

The comic emphases are still present. Jaws, the new Oddjob, is a terrific character and might have been the best henchman of the series. But the script makes him absolutely indestructible; therefore, the character's increasing frustration at being outsmarted by Bond is intended to be funny. (It's like the notion behind the coyote character in the "Road Runner" cartoons.) Jaws is subjected to all kinds of punishment: electric shocks, toppling ruins, and the prospect of drowning in the ocean off the coast of Sardinia—but he seems always to come out unharmed. More on him later.

Christopher Wood supposedly added quite a few of these comic elements to the script. This theory is further supported by the fact that Wood alone wrote the screenplay to the most juvenile of the films, *Moonraker*.

Unlike the three previous Bond films, *The Spy Who Loved Me* at least holds together as a story. The set-piece formula, though executed with overindulgence, does not seem so obvious. There is a natural progression from location to location, and there are even some sections with genuine suspense. It is, without a doubt, the best Bond screenplay of the seventies.

☐ DIRECTION

Lewis Gilbert is back for his second Bond film. Significantly, he was the man who directed *You Only Live Twice*, the film that the new one so closely resembles. And like the previous film, *The Spy Who Loved Me* is full of big action scenes involving hundreds of extras and massive sets. Gilbert is a very good logistical director. His *mise en scène* captures the panorama of large picturizations with remarkable ease and control. The film moves with a brisk pace, never letting the audience catch its breath. But this speed hampers the picture in some ways. First, the plot information is communicated in extremely brief dialogue scenes, and

the rest of the film consists of fast-moving set-pieces. Second, the comic elements of the movie tend to feed on the fast pace.

This is where Gilbert gets into trouble. He often allows the humor in the film to lapse into comic-book material. For instance, Bond is attempting to rescue Anya from Stromberg's establishment, Atlantis, before it is torpedoed by the *U.S.S. Wayne*. He comes upon the gargantuan Jaws, and a tense fight ensues. It looks as if it's going to recall the good old Oddjob days, as their grapplings take them into the room containing a shark pool. But the action then regresses into pure silliness when Bond maneuvers some kind of magnet attached to a line running above the pool over Jaws' head (what it's *supposed* to be used for is not explained). Bond gives a very Moore-ish grin at Jaws, causing the killer to smile. The magnet pulls Jaws up by his steel teeth. Unable to free himself, Jaws is then maneuvered by Bond over the shark pool. When he's in the right spot, Bond releases the magnet and runs to find Anya. Jaws falls into the shark pool. But he isn't eaten, of course. *He* eats the *shark* and climbs out of the pool!

There is also an embarrassing moment as Bond and Anya are walking across the desert after their van breaks down. The soundtrack plays the theme of *Lawrence of Arabia*. This is too cute. James Bond films should be anything but *cute*.

Gilbert also does not do much with the couple of good dramatic scenes the scriptwriters have provided. During the scene in which Anya discovers that it was Bond who killed her lover in Asgard, Roger Moore is surprisingly good and Barbara Bach is embarrassingly bad. Miss Bach is a competent actress, and has much presence throughout most of the film; but here, she is like cardboard. Gilbert could have shot more life into this flaccid, and important, scene.

The action passages, though, are very good. The final battle in the super tanker *Liparus* is quite a spectacle. Though it is entirely too reminiscent of the attack on Blofeld's volcano fortress (and Piz Gloria, *and* the oil rig in Baja), it is fun to watch. There is one good moment of suspense when Bond decides to extract a detonator from a nuclear missile and use it to blow their way into the fortified control room. After a few seconds of concentration and worry from the witnesses, Bond removes the device. He then rides atop a roving security camera attached to the ceiling across the area to the control booth window. He attaches the explosive to the wall, and the moving camera begins its retreat. But the controls are switched off from inside so that the technicians may focus the camera on something. Bond is stuck ten feet away from the explosive. And he's at least fifty feet from the floor! After a moment of seat-clutching tension, the camera's belt is switched on again, and Bond makes it to a safe distance just as the detonator explodes.

There is one moment which seems out of place because of its violent realism. When Bond finally kills Karl Stromberg, the actor has been directed to convulse horribly for a second or two; and there is more blood than usual in a Bond film. There hasn't been a death this ugly since *Thunderball.*

Gilbert seems to have a confused sense of directorial judgment. There are sequences that stand out jarringly in the film. The humor undermines most of the suspense or tension in the story. What Gilbert has handled well is the overpowering spectacle of it all; and this is the picture's primary asset.

☐ ACTORS AND CHARACTERS
Roger Moore is his usual suave, sophisticated self, but there are moments when flashes of a tougher character come through. The filmmakers seem intent on emphasizing their belief that Moore is the ideal Bond ac-

Roger Moore's leading lady in The Spy Who Loved Me *was lovely Barbara Bach as Russian agent Anya Amasova. (Wide World Photo.)*

cording to Fleming's picture of the character. At one point in the film. Bond visits a sheikh named Hussain. Hussain was an Etonian classmate of Bond's, and they refer to this in their conversation. But the "real" Bond would be disinclined to talk about his days at Eton, since his attitude toward his school tie is very cynical, so the filmmakers are distorting Bond's character with this ploy.

Moore is better in the fight sequences, though. There is one terrific fight on a rooftop with Sandor, one of Stromberg's henchmen. At one point in the battle, Sandor almost falls off the roof backwards, but saves himself by grabbing hold of Bond's tie. All Bond has to do is knock Sandor's hand away and the man will fall to his death. Bond asks where he can find Fekkesh, a man in possession of a microfilm containing plans of Stromberg's submarine tracker. Sandor, fearing for his life, answers Bond quickly. And then, Moore calmly chops the man's hand and Sandor falls. This is more like something the Sean Connery Bond would have done—it's somewhat out of character for the Roger Moore Bond. It's a moment that stands out.

There's another interesting instance when Bond first speaks with Anya at the Mojave Club. She seems to know all about him, and begins to relate his past and biographical facts to his face. Bond is slightly amused until she begins talking about his marriage. Immediately, we see Bond stiffen, and a dark cloud passes over his face. He cuts her off and abruptly rises from his seat. This is the first reference to Tracy since *On Her Majesty's Secret Service*. Moments like this tend to make Bond a little more human, and they are a pleasure to see. Moore is quite effective here.

Barbara Bach, an extremely attractive actress and model, portrays the "Me" of *The Spy Who Loved Me*. But Vivienne Michel she isn't. She is Major Anya Amasova, Agent XXX of the Soviet Union. Apparently, Broccoli thought it would be a classic situation for Bond to join forces with a Russian female counterpart. Therefore, Anya serves not only as the Bond-girl in the film, but also as the ally. Miss Bach is adequate in the role, but there are certain dramatic scenes in which she lacks dynamics. In the previously mentioned scene in which she swears to kill Bond once their mission is completed, she displays no emotion at all. But in the more romantic sequences, such as when she and Bond have hitched a ride in a peasant's boat up the Nile to Cairo, Miss Bach is very effective. She's a beautiful woman with a strong screen presence that is missing in some Bond-girls.

The late veteran German actor Curt Jurgens por-

trays Karl Stromberg, and his performance is disappointing. Stromberg is a man in love with the sea, hoping to build a new city of followers in Atlantis, his underwater fortress. He is attempting to destroy life on land to make this possible. It's obvious that Stromberg was Blofeld in an early script, because his mannerisms, speech, and environment all reflect that character. The only thing missing is the white cat. Jurgens is a fine actor, but he plays the role on one level. He speaks slowly, and there is no energy in his delivery. To put it bluntly, Karl Stromberg is a dull villain. We've heard and seen it all before.

More interesting, however, is his super-henchman, Jaws. Played by the over-seven-foot-tall Richard Kiel, this character was an immediate hit with younger audiences. The response to the character was so great that the producers decided to bring Jaws back in the next film, *Moonraker*. An indestructible giant of a man, equipped with sharp, steel teeth, Jaws disposes of his victims by biting them in the neck, Dracula-style. Jaws has no dialogue, but he makes his intentions known through facial expression. The character is fun and proves to be quite menacing in certain sections. But the filmmakers insist on using the character for comic effect. The situation would worsen in *Moonraker*. Kiel, however, performs his role with vigor and conviction.

A familiar face from fantasy films (such as the Sinbad series), Caroline Munro, portrays Stromberg's mistress and helicopter pilot, Naomi. Miss Munro is also an extremely attractive actress, and for once, uses her seductive qualities for an evil character. The shame is that her role isn't larger. Miss Munro creates an unusual female villain type (à la Fiona in *Thunderball*) but the script gives her nothing to do. She meets her death soon after her first appearance when Bond's Lotus fires a missile at her helicopter.

Vernon Dobtcheff and Nadim Sawalha portray the film's two Obligatory Sacrificial Lambs, but they barely qualify. The characters are Max Kalba and Fekkesh, respectively. They are contacts in Egypt who lead Bond to the stolen microfilm containing the plans for Stromberg's submarine tracker. Both characters meet their death early in the film, not giving us much chance to develop any sympathy for them.

Walter Gotell, who played the SPECTRE training camp commander in *From Russia With Love*, portrays General Gogol of the KGB, who becomes a regular character in the series from this point. In this film, Gogol joins forces with M, since the search for the microfilm is in the best interest of both countries. Geoffrey Keen makes an appearance as the Minister of Defense, who also becomes a running character in the series. Basically another M, this character adds more comedy in the form of an authority figure's constant exasperation with Bond's actions.

M, Moneypenny, and Q all show up on location in Egypt, as well as on a huge battleship off Sardinia at the film's end. There is even a special Egyptian Q Branch, where Q is developing items such as a hookah with guns in the hoses. These obligatory sequences are becoming increasingly egregious.

□ OTHER ASPECTS

Ken Adam does it again, designing monstrous, spectacular sets for the film. The notable achievement this time is that Adam allotted at least a million dollars of his budget to build an entirely new soundstage at Pinewood Studios. It is the largest soundstage in the world, measuring 374 feet long, 160 feet wide, and 53 feet high. The building has been named Number 007 and will be used for subsequent Bond films as well as other pictures. For *The Spy Who Loved Me,* the soundstage was used as the inside of the *Liparus* tanker, where replicas of nuclear submarines are held in troughs. It is here that the final climactic battle between Stromberg's forces and the submarine crews takes place. The set is sleek, workable, and beautiful to look at.

Cinematography in the film is by Claude Renoir, whose grandfather was the brilliant painter, Pierre Auguste Renoir, and whose uncle was the great filmmaker, Jean Renoir. His work is impressive, giving the film a polished and exotic look that is a cut above the rest of the series, except for perhaps *You Only Live Twice.* Lamar Boren, who photographed the underwater scenes in *Thunderball* and *You Only Live Twice,* filmed the many ocean sequences.

Editor and second unit director John Glen makes his mark in the series with *The Spy Who Loved Me.* Glen had been second unit director/editor for *On Her Majesty's Secret Service,* and his filming of the pre-credits scene of the new picture recalls the former one. Ski champion Willy Bogner, Jr. is again the camera operator for the ski scenes, and the entire sequence is thrilling. In fact, the pre-credits scene in this film is the best one since *Goldfinger.* It contains the most outrageous and spectacular stunt of the entire series. As Bond is chased on skis by a Russian hit team, he shoots the leader with a ski-stick gun, and then skis straight off a ledge. We see Bond falling and falling into the abyss, losing his skis and turning somersaults. The de-

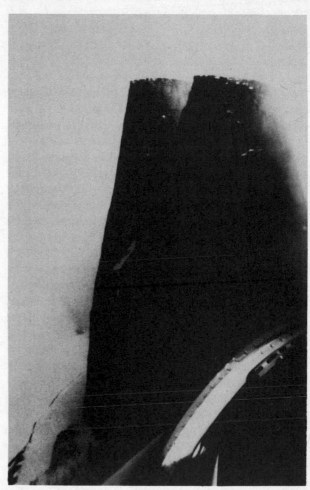

The 3,000 foot Asgard peak off of which stuntman Rick Sylvester skied in the spectacular pre-credits scene in The Spy Who Loved Me. *(Photo by Rick Sylvester, courtesy of Steven Jay Rubin.)*

scent seems to go on forever as the audience wonders where in the world they filmed this sequence. Finally, we see a parachute, decorated with the Union Jack, open and carry Bond to safety.

This magnificent stunt was performed by ski champion Rick Sylvester (for which I hope he received a great deal of money). Weather conditions had to be completely perfect for Sylvester to do the jump. The location was the three-thousand-foot-high Asgard peak in Auquittuq National Park on Canada's Baffin Island. Naturally, the jump had to be shot in one take, so several cameras were set up in key locations, only one of which was successful in capturing the stunt. John Glen supervised the sequence.

Bob Simmons, as usual, handled the remaining stunt work, including the fights with Jaws. And thanks to

John Glen's editing, it is impossible to tell whether it's Moore fighting, or Simmons doubling Moore.

The big gadget in the film is the updated Aston Martin—the Lotus Esprit. On land, it's basically like its predecessor (it contains a paint sprayer in its tail end rather than an oil slick); but its most impressive feature is the fact that it can become a submarine. Lotus provided Eon Productions with several bodies for the car, and Perry Submarines and Oceanographics built the rest of "Wet Nellie," as it is called. The car is actually a submersible, which means that the driver must wear a skindiving suit and oxygen tanks. When it's underwater, the Lotus can fire CO_2 guns, launch mines, and perform the usual assortment of tricks associated with a Q Branch creation. Much of the success of the Lotus sequence is attributed to special effects supervisor Derek Meddings. His model work for the film is state of the art. Many of the Lotus shots feature models, and the shots of Stromberg's tanker, the *Liparus,* also incorporate a model. The *Liparus* model was over seventy feet long, and was actually exploded for the final scene.

John Barry is absent from the film, and popular composer Marvin Hamlisch scores *The Spy Who Loved Me.* Hamlisch does a marvelous job, for which he received two Oscar nominations: one for best score and the other for best song. The main title song is "Nobody Does It Better," with lyrics by Carole Bayer Sager. Carly Simon performs the song in the film, and it subsequently became a hit single. Maurice Binder's main title design incorporates images of Roger Moore behind this song, the first time that the actor playing Bond has been used here. The rest of Hamlisch's score is very modern; his version of "The James Bond Theme" (called "Bond 77" on the soundtrack album) has the semblance of a disco beat. His underwater music accompanying the Lotus is beautiful, and his work with arranger/composer Paul Buckmaster on the cabaret and nightclub scenes is also unique.

MOONRAKER (1979)

□ PRODUCTION

The eleventh James Bond film was originally announced to be *For Your Eyes Only,* but the success of *Star Wars* and *Close Encounters of the Third Kind* encouraged Cubby Broccoli to change his mind. *Moonraker,* the only available Fleming title that could

possibly incorporate an outer space theme, was chosen as the next adventure. But therein lies the rub—the entire concept behind choosing *Moonraker* for the next film emphasizes the Bond series' inability to maintain its originality. The new opus would simply be an imitation not only of *Star Wars* and the like, but of the Bond series itself.

As a result, *Moonraker* must rank as the least artistically successful film in the series. Ironically, *Moonraker* is now the biggest grosser to date for Eon Productions. Diehard Bond fans who complained about the direction the series has taken since *On Her Majesty's Secret Service* were few in number, and it was the new generation of adolescents at which *Moonraker* was aimed. The film contains the most absurd and ridiculous slapstick humor of all the films, and the character of James Bond functions merely as a focal point for a series of outlandish set-pieces. And even the set-pieces are recycled from previous films.

With Michael G. Wilson now executive producer, Broccoli was forced to join forces with a French production company due to Britain's tight tax laws. Therefore, only the special effects in *Moonraker* were shot at Pinewood Studios in England. All interiors were built and shot in France. Locations chosen for the film were Los Angeles, Venice, and South America. The film was the most expensive in the series, mainly due to the elaborate special effects, but also because of the relocation of the interior scenes. *Moonraker* cost thirty million dollars to make, which is thirty times the cost of *Dr. No,* and twice that of *The Spy Who Loved Me.*

The film was widely advertised as being "scientifically accurate." Broccoli went on record to say that everything in the film was "science fact, not fiction." With the help of NASA in an advisory capacity, the concepts behind the space shuttle in the film are truly believable; but the latter half of the film—dealing with space stations and laser battles between two armies of astronauts—is ridiculous. James Bond almost became an astronaut in *You Only Live Twice* but was stopped before he could enter the SPECTRE rocket. This is acceptable, to a certain extent; but actually putting Bond into space is another thing altogether. Ian Fleming's James Bond, despite rigorous training in Naval Intelligence and expertise in a number of fields, was never qualified for space travel. It's just another example of how little care is taken in developing the Bond character for the films.

□ SCREENPLAY

Tom Mankiewicz did initial work on the script of *Moonraker,* but is uncredited. Christopher Wood penned the final shooting script, as well as the novelizations for both *The Spy Who Loved Me* and *Moonraker.* The two plots are basically the same, and almost nothing remains from the original MOONRAKER novel (which, although somewhat dated, remains a very good story). Instead of planning to destroy London with an experimental rocket, Hugo Drax is plotting to destroy all human life on earth and breed a new generation of perfect mortals under his rule in a space station orbiting around the globe. Some difference! (And wasn't Karl Stromberg attempting to do the very same thing, only underwater?)

Jaws is back, but attempts are made to make him seem more human, and even lovable. At one point, Jaws emerges from a pile of wreckage to spy a small, freckle-faced, dumb, bespectacled, blond girl. Her name is Dolly, and it's love at first sight. Jaws grins, his steel teeth sparkling, and he takes Dolly's hand. Together they walk away from the debris as the music becomes tender. The series has never dipped so low into kitsch. At a crucial moment during the film's climax, Bond convinces Jaws that Drax intends to destroy the giant and his girlfriend because they are not considered perfect. Jaws ponders this, and then becomes a good guy and helps Bond defeat the evil Hugo Drax. It seems that the filmmakers intended Jaws to become some kind of hero, too, so that he could become a recurring character. But it is obvious that the plan failed, because most of Jaws' scenes in *Moonraker* are embarrassing. Any threat Jaws might have been to Bond is completely thrown out the window; he is simply a cartoon character who is in no danger of actually getting hurt. *Moonraker* is the first maudlin James Bond picture.

Several sequences recall similar events in previous films. For instance, the scene in which Bond is trapped inside a centrifuge machine is strikingly comparable to the "rack" scene in *Thunderball.* The street carnival in Rio recalls the junkanoo in the same film. The gondola boat chase is a rehash of the dong chase through the floating market in *The Man With the Golden Gun.* The boat chase in the Brazilian jungle is similar to the flotilla chase in *From Russia With Love.* And the final climactic battle between the NASA astronauts and Drax's army recalls the underwater battle from *Thunderball;* the assault on SPECTRE's volcano in *You Only Live Twice;* the raid on Piz Gloria in *On Her Majesty's Secret*

Service; the bombing of SPECTRE's oil rig in *Diamonds Are Forever;* and the battle between the submarine crews and Stromberg's men in *The Spy Who Loved Me.* The repetitiveness of the Bond series is most apparent in *Moonraker.*

There are a few funny lines, and most of them are given to Drax. "You appear with the inevitability of an unloved season," he tells Bond on their third encounter. But my favorite is when he turns to Chang, his manservant, and says, perfectly seriously, "Look after Mr. Bond. See that some harm comes to him." But many lines, unfortunately, are groaners. Holly Goodhead's last line in the film, as she and Bond make love in orbit above the earth, is, "Oh James, take me around the world one more time."

□ DIRECTION

Lewis Gilbert is back for his third Bond effort. His usual slick, fast tempo is applied to *Moonraker,* but the progression of events in the film is so contrived that it is difficult to detect any semblance of a story line. It seems that Bond simply hops from one country to another; it's not quite clear *why* he is doing so. Unless one's ears are pricked to catch every word, one might miss the fact that Bond travels to Venice to spy on a certain glass factory mentioned in one of the papers he found in Drax's safe in Los Angeles.

Gilbert's penchant for juvenile humor gets in the way quite a bit in *Moonraker.* The pre-credits sequence itself sets up the overall mood of the film. It begins with impressive model work by Derek Meddings, showing the hijacking of a Moonraker shuttle from the back of a 747. Next, we cut to a private airplane, where Bond is embracing a flight attendant. But she pulls a gun on him, and threatens to bail out of the plane with the pilot. Bond overpowers her and attacks the pilot. But the pilot jumps out of the plane. Then, Jaws suddenly appears from nowhere and tosses Bond out of the plane, without a parachute. What follows is literally breathtaking. Freefalling, Bond straightens his body like a spear and dives through the air to catch up with the pilot. He grabs the pilot and wrestles off the parachute. The pilot falls to his death as Bond puts the parachute on himself. If the filmmakers had ended the sequence here, it would have worked beautifully; but the tendency in *Moonraker* is toward overkill. Not far behind Bond is Jaws, now wearing a parachute. Jaws attempts the same trick of holding his body like a spear, and eventually catches Bond. Bond escapes by opening his parachute. Jaws attempts to open his chute, too, but the rip cord snaps. Jaws plummets into the middle of a circus tent, and of course, lives to chase Bond again later.

The skydiving scenes were difficult to film, requiring that stuntmen and cameramen make several jumps Second unit director/editor John Glen supervised the sequence, and visually it's stupendous. But the subsequent regression from excitement to cartoonish cat-and-mouse games is an error in judgment.

One of the sillier sequences in the film occurs when Bond is in Venice, and his gondola proves to be a floating arsenal from Q Branch. It might not have been so bad if we had been told beforehand that the craft was capable of making this transformation. But as it is, Bond simply hops into a gondola, is taken down a canal, and is attacked by a passing "funeral" lorry. A man rises from the exposed coffin and throws a knife at the agent. But Bond throws the knife back at the man, killing him. Then, the gondola becomes a high-speed launch as Bond and his gondolier are chased through the canals. To top it off, the gondola becomes a hovercraft and moves onto the Piazza San Marco. At this point, there are several shots of incredulous tourists, doing double takes and suspiciously eyeing their drinks; animals squawking; and people falling into the water. The sequence is so dumb that one wonders at what age group the film was really aimed.

Other unnecessary attempts for laughs include some topical references, such as the door leading to Drax's lab in Venice. It can only be opened by pressing touch-tones which play the tune of *Close Encounters of the Third Kind.* Too silly. There's another sequence in which Bond, dressed as a *gaucho,* rides a horse toward the South American branch of the Secret Service. The music on the soundtrack plays "The Magnificent Seven." This is simply annoying.

Gilbert does manage to handle the huge sets and hundreds of extras with proficiency, but the film loses any impact it may have had through overindulgence in all this slapstick and buffoonery.

☐ ACTORS AND CHARACTERS

After the promising development of his characterization of Bond in *The Spy Who Loved Me,* Roger Moore reverts to a cardboard representation in the new film. But then, the script does not give him much opportunity to show any human qualities. In fact, in *Moon-*

raker, James Bond, too, is a cartoon figure, functioning only as the center of all the confusion. It seems that Moore's entire characterization consists of raising one eyebrow.

Texas actress Lois Chiles was cast as Moore's leading lady, but she isn't Gala Brand, Special Branch agent from Scotland Yard (from the book). In the film, her name is Holly Goodhead (a blatant attempt at copying Pussy Galore), which doesn't fit the character at all. Holly is a CIA agent working undercover as a NASA scientist employed by Drax. She is quite independent, and gives Bond a rather hard time with his seduction ploys. Many times, she comes across as haughty and self-reliant, much like the Gala Brand character in the novel. The name Holly Goodhead conjures up visions of a Plenty O'Toole–type character. At least Miss Chiles has some screen presence, is attractive, and plays her part with a sincere straightforwardness. As written, Holly Goodhead is very similar to the Anya Amasova character in *The Spy Who Loved Me:* she eventually joins forces, reluctantly, with Bond in order to vanquish the villain.

Michael Lonsdale portrays Hugo Drax, and the character is quite different from the novel's villain. Drax in the book is a loud, obnoxious braggart. Lonsdale portrays Drax as methodical, sardonic, and careful. It works for the most part, and Lonsdale is a definite improvement over Curt Jurgens' Karl Stromberg. Drax in the film is an American billionaire working out of a French châteaulike mansion near Los Angeles. It is he who is responsible for the hijacking of his own Moonraker shuttle at the beginning of the film. The one he was planning to use for his own purposes developed equipment failure. Drax's obligatory speech explaining his dastardly plan is one of the better ones in the series, and it reveals the archetypal megalomania present in all Bond villains. Drax's death in the film is not very original—he is sucked out of an air lock of his own space station. Shades of *Goldfinger!*

Richard Kiel returns as Jaws, the indestructible superman. He's working for Hugo Drax now, and always happens to turn up right when one expects him. Attempts to make Jaws a lovable character simply lower the quality of what began as an interesting and formidable minor villain. Blanche Ravalec had the misfortune of being cast as Dolly, the object of Jaws' affection. She's just too cute for words.

Lovely Corinne Clery portrays the Obligatory Sacrificial Lamb of the film, Corinne Dufour. Corinne works for Drax, but once Bond turns on the charm, she switches her allegiance, of course. Her just reward for doing so is to be fed to Drax's pet Doberman pinschers. The scene in which this happens could have been brutal and gripping; as photographed, it is lush and soft focused. It simply doesn't work.

Emily Bolton portrays Manuela, the Secret Service contact in Rio de Janeiro. She is merely another version of Paula from *Thunderball,* Rosie in *Live and Let Die,* and Mary Goodnight in *The Man With the Golden Gun.* Toshiro Suga portrays Chang, Drax's equivalent of Oddjob. Chang is disposed of early in the film during one of the more successful action sequences. Bond encounters Chang in a Venetian glass shop and their subsequent fight smashes every piece of glass in the showroom. (But again, the scene regresses into child's play when Chang is thrown off a bal-

cony and into a grand piano at an outdoor concert.)

Bernard Lee makes his last appearance as M in *Moonraker.* Looking quite a bit older than before (Lee was very ill at the time), his scenes contain the usual banter between 007 and his superior. He shares most of his scenes with Minister of Defense Frederick Gray, played by Geoffrey Keen again. One particularly amusing passage occurs when Bond escorts M and Gray to the secret lab Bond has discovered in Venice. Upon arriving at the lab, they find that all of the equipment has been removed; nothing is there except some furniture and Hugo Drax lounging in a chair. Bond, M, and Gray enter the room wearing gas masks (for fear of the virus Drax was developing in his lab), and all look rather silly. Drax comments, "Forgive me gentlemen, but not being English, I don't quite share your unique

Moonraker's stars Richard Kiel (as Jaws), Lois Chiles (as Holly Goodhead), and Roger Moore as 007. (Photo by Michel Ginfray/Gamma-Liaison Agency.)

sense of humor.'' Q and Miss Moneypenny also have their share of obligatory scenes. Q is featured in a Q Branch sequence in South America, where equipment such as exploding bolos is being developed. No comment.

☐ OTHER ASPECTS

Ken Adam has designed a multitude of expressionistic and futuristic sets again, most notable of which is the space station interior. Consisting of tubes, circular hallways, and sloping floors, the area resembles an optical illusion. Even though the filmmakers claim that the movie features scientific accuracy, there are problems with the space station. For instance, the gravitational pull would be toward the outer edges of the station, not the horizontal floor as presented in the film.

Jean Tournier is director of photography for this picture, and has succeeded in capturing beautiful location shots, especially in the mountains overlooking Rio de Janeiro. The locales are one of the few redeeming features of *Moonraker.*

Perhaps the most outstanding technical achievement in *Moonraker* is Derek Meddings' special visual effects. Meddings was nominated for an Academy Award for his work, but was beaten by *Alien.* Since *Moonraker* contained several scenes involving space travel, many miniatures were built. These included several space shuttles designed to NASA specifications. The space travel sequences equal the quality of effects that *Star Wars* and *Star Trek—The Motion Picture* brought to the screen.

The gadgets in the film are predictable and tired. Bond is presented with a wrist gun which can be fired with the slightest flick of the hand. It fires poisonous darts. The device is used by Bond to escape the centrifuge machine, and to shoot Drax. Bond also has a gadget on his person that is used to kill a giant python which he is forced to fight at Drax's Brazilian headquarters. It's some kind of poisoned ballpoint pen, which he stabs into the snake's head. We didn't know he had this device, so, as Brosnan notes, it's another example of the Bondian rules being broken. Other gadgets include the souped-up gondola, and a speedboat equipped with the usual Bond arsenal. The latter also has an extractable hang glider, which Bond miraculously engages to escape plunging down a waterfall when his boat goes over. The sequence is reminiscent of the hang glider moment in *Live and Let Die,* as well as the trick parachute ploy in the pre-credits sequence of *The Spy Who Loved Me.*

One of the best things in the film is John Barry's lovely, laid-back score. The main title theme, with lyrics by Hal David and sung by Shirley Bassey, is a haunting melody; it's full of major-seventh chords that give the song an exotic quality. The rest of the score is mellow and evocative of space travel, and Barry has escaped from his usual ''science fiction'' sound, which he used in *You Only Live Twice* and *Diamonds Are Forever.* It is quite easy to dismiss the score of this film because it seems lost in all the shenanigans, but it's certainly Barry's best Bond effort since *On Her Majesty's Secret Service.* Maurice Binder's accompanying title design is, as usual, the most erotic thing in the film.

Moonraker was extremely successful and broke all of Eon Productions' records. But apparently Broccoli received much criticism from Bond fans, especially in North America. As a result, rumors began flying that the next Bond film would revert to the original, simpler style. Indeed, *Moonraker* went as far as Broccoli could go with outlandishness. The only direction possible for the Bond films of the eighties was backwards. The science fiction boom of the late seventies was already beginning to wane, and with competition like the *Star Wars* series, Broccoli realized that the Bond films couldn't contend on a special effects level. Broccoli's ace-in-the-hole was that James Bond is a fascinating character, potentially capable of much more than gracing a special effects action film. This would be proven correct.

FOR YOUR EYES ONLY
(1981)

☐ PRODUCTION

When *For Your Eyes Only* was released in the summer of 1981, it appeared that the James Bond of the eighties would be more like the Bond of the sixties—certainly a change for the better. Broccoli and Michael G. Wilson steered the production back down to earth to present a James Bond film that concentrates on its characters and plot rather than set pieces. The intention was to make another *From Russia With Love* or *On Her Majesty's Secret Service* type of film, both of which are heavily inspired by Fleming's original material.

Ken Adam and his futuristic sets are gone, and so is the Jaws character. There are not many gadgets in the film. Most of the action takes place outdoors, providing opportunities for underwater and ski photography. The story is based in reality, and there is a good deal of suspense in the film. The characters are the most developed in a long while, and the humor is kept to a sophisticated, subtle level. And the picture contains one of the best collections of stunts and action scenes in the series. As a result, *For Your Eyes Only,* save for an out-of-place and disappointing pre-credits sequence, is the best Bond film since *On Her Majesty's Secret Service.* As a matter of fact, the new film is similar in mood and texture to the former. This is perhaps due to the work of new director John Glen. Glen, you will recall, was second unit director/editor for *On Her Majesty's Secret Service, The Spy Who Loved Me,* and *Moonraker.* It was he who supervised the thrilling ski and bobsled sequences from *On Her Majesty's Secret Service,* and the opening ski chase in *Spy.* There are similar exciting ski scenes in *For Your Eyes Only.*

The film is beautiful to look at, and is another globe-trotter incorporating new territory: Corfu, Cortina d'Ampezzo in Northern Italy, the Bahamas, the Meteora mountains in central Greece, and Pinewood Studios in England. One scene was shot in a six hundred-year-old Byzantine monastery high atop a slender mountain near the village of Kalambaka in Greece. Permission was granted Broccoli to film on the site by the abbot, but there were a couple of monks who severely protested. The monks did everything they could to ruin shots, such as hang their laundry outdoors to mar the scenes. But the shots were finally finished and this sequence is one of the film's most impressive.

Public reaction to *For Your Eyes Only* was good. Though it didn't rival *Moonraker* in terms of ticket sales, the film did phenomenal business. And it was much less expensive, with a budget of under twenty million dollars. The gamble paid off. Bond was just as successful as before.

□ SCREENPLAY

Veteran Richard Maibaum was hired again to pen the screenplay to *Eyes Only,* with the help of Michael G. Wilson. The inspiration for the script came from two Fleming short stories that appeared in the 1960 anthology, FOR YOUR EYES ONLY. And for the first time in quite a while, a Bond film is more or less faithful to the Fleming originals.

The title story of the collection provided Maibaum and Wilson with the heroine, Judy Havelock, who seeks revenge for the murder of her parents. James Bond encounters her in the woods surrounding the villain's hideout and joins forces with her. In the film, her name is Melina Havelock, and her assassination of the killer is taken almost verbatim from the story (but it's in a different context). The main plot of the film comes from the story, "Risico," which involves the rivalry between two Italian smugglers: Kristatos and Colombo. The film shifts the locale from Italy to Greece, and changes the spelling of the latter smuggler to Columbo. The script writers linked the two stories together by means of another Bondian MacGuffin: a typewriterlike computer known as the ATAC system, which can be used to override manual controls on Polaris submarines. At the beginning of the film, a British surveillance ship carrying an ATAC device is sunk off the Albanian coast. Both the British and the Russians want the ATAC, and they send their best men to retrieve it. The Havelock girl becomes involved because her parents, who are British undercover agents working in Greece, are assassinated after Mr. Havelock locates the sunken ship. The assassin is a man named Gonzales and is employed by Kristatos, the true villain of the film. Kristatos is a freelancer working for the Russians to retrieve the ATAC. Columbo becomes a Bond ally to seek revenge on Kristatos, an old rival from the war. This strong theme of revenge provides a unity to the film which the last several Bonds have lacked. The story is played straight. There are moments of humor, but they do not regress into slapstick.

The pre-credits sequence is the film's only problem, and it doesn't relate to the rest of the picture at all. The scene opens with Bond visiting his wife Tracy's grave in a small church cemetery. A helicopter from Universal Export arrives to fetch him, but it has been sabotaged. Once the copter is in the air, the pilot is electrocuted in his seat and the controls are operated by an unseen force. A voice on a speaker in the cockpit informs "Mr. Bond" that there is nothing he can do to save himself. Then we see who the culprit is. On a rooftop is a wheelchair containing a bald-headed man holding a white cat. The camera never reveals his face, but it appears to be Ernst Stavro Blofeld (along the lines of Donald Pleasence or Telly Savalas). He is sitting in front of some kind of control panel, maneuvering the helicopter with a joystick. We are then treated to some outstanding flight stunts with the copter, as it weaves in and out of the chimneys and smokestacks of the Becton Gasworks in London's East End. Bond eventually crawls out of the back seat of the copter onto the outside of the craft. He clambers into the cockpit and tosses the dead pilot from the vehicle. He finally locates and pulls the power cable responsible for the dirty work. Blofeld loses control of the aircraft. It is here that the only instance of silliness appears in the film. Bond flies the copter down to Blofeld and scoops up his wheelchair with the landing strut of the craft. There is some clumsy makeup here, because it's obvious that the stuntman in the wheelchair is wearing a rubber bald cap. Bond then proceeds to drop the wheelchair, Blofeld and all, down a smokestack.

First, the sequence makes no sense because it isn't revealed whether or not this villain is actually Blofeld. We don't know why he's tampering with the copter, or why he's in the wheelchair. We could *assume* that it's Blofeld (we're certainly *meant* to) and that he's in the wheelchair because he was hurt at the end of *Diamonds Are Forever*. Second, after the breathtaking helicopter stunts, the sequence is marred by the unbelievable scooping up of the wheelchair. One explanation for the sequence could be that it is a nightmare of Bond's. He has just been visiting his wife's grave— perhaps the memory of Blofeld is haunting him, and the entire incident with the copter is in Bond's imagination. But if this is the case, Bond should "awaken" from his nightmare at the end of the sequence—which would have worked well, silliness and all.

But after this disappointing pre-credits sequence, the remainder of the film is top-notch.

There is one particular scene in the film which is lifted almost directly from "Risico." In the short story, Bond meets Kristatos at a restaurant and observes Colombo at another table with Lisl Baum. But Colombo is recording their conversation by means of a machine planted in an extra chair at their table. In the film, the tape recorder is in the table candle rather than the chair, and Lisl Baum has become Contessa Lisl. But the dramatic action of the scene is the same, and it's one of the best sequences in the film. At this point, we do not yet know that it is Kristatos who is the villain and Columbo who is friendly. (Actually, Bond is suspicious of both.) It is a perfect onscreen example of a Fleming situation. Also lifted directly from the short story is the subsequent conversation aboard Columbo's fishing vessel in which the truth about Kristatos is explained to Bond. Columbo gains Bond's trust by returning Bond's Walther PPK which was taken from him earlier.

Another scene is from the novel LIVE AND LET DIE, but wasn't in that film. Bond and Melina Havelock have been captured by Kristatos and are tied together face to face. Kristatos then pulls them by rope through the water behind his boat. His intention is that the couple will scrape over the sharp coral and attract sharks. (In the novel, it is Solitaire who shares this plight with Bond.) But in the film, they escape when Bond uses the coral to cut the rope binding his wrists during a pause as Kristatos' boat turns around for another run over the coral. Melina has left some air tanks on the ocean floor earlier, so she and Bond swim to them. Kristatos believes the two are dead when he sees that the rope is free. In no other sequence has a Bond heroine shared such a fiendish ordeal with 007.

Even something of a political statement is made in the new film. At the end, when General Gogol of the KGB arrives by helicopter from Moscow to retrieve the ATAC from Kristatos, Bond throws the machine off the mountain. The ATAC shatters into a thousand pieces. "Now neither of us have it," Bond says to Gogol. "That's détente, comrade." Gogol, after a pause, finally smiles. (Do these gentlemen forget they became allies during *The Spy Who Loved Me?*) Gogol turns, and leaves in his helicopter. Bond hasn't been successful in retrieving the ATAC for Britain, but he has kept it out of the Russians' hands. This passage cunningly suggests the possibility that the entire arms race could be the foolish pursuit of a MacGuffin.

As usual, there are some funny one-liners. One of the most memorable is when Bond unexpectedly finds young Bibi in his hotel bed. Bibi is a teenage Olympic ice skating protégée, and the ward of Kristatos. Bond avoids her advances gallantly, and finally tells her, "Now get dressed and I'll buy you an ice cream."

□ **DIRECTION**

John Glen follows in Peter Hunt's footsteps by making a very impressive directorial debut with *For Your Eyes Only*. Glen is immediately a good storyteller, and the technical aspects of the film are flawless. Above all, *Eyes Only* is a good *action* picture. It contains the best collection of stunt work in the series. There is a unique car chase; an exciting ski pursuit followed by a bobsled/ski/motorcycle romp; a fight on an ice hockey field; and plenty of fist fights and underwater battles. There are even a few old-fashioned shoot-em-ups with men running about and guns blazing, like the gypsy camp battle in *From Russia With Love*.

Glen maintains a serious tone in the film, despite the usual gags that always pop up in a Bond picture.

The film *does* recall the feel of *From Russia With Love* and *On Her Majesty's Secret Service;* not only because of the outdoors look and the Fleming story, but because the characters treat everything seriously. It isn't only fantasy we're dealing with this time—the *people* are important.

This is especially true in Glen's handling of the Melina Havelock character. She is very serious about avenging the murder of her parents. There is a marvelous closeup of her teary-eyed face just after she has seen her parents murdered. The shot captures Melina's anger, sadness, and confusion in a swirling moment while dramatic music complements the beauty and rage in her face.

Deaths are presented more in the style of Terence Young—realistically. The Havelocks are shot down aboard their yacht by hit man Gonzales. Their bodies are riveted with bullets. Melina receives satisfaction when she shoots Gonzales in the back with an arrow just as he is diving into his swimming pool. A little more blood than usual is seen here. Contessa Lisl is hit by a jeep, and it certainly appears painful. But there is one moment of violence in the film which is extremely funny, and it's one of the best jokes. Bond, Columbo,

and party are sneaking up to the monastery where Kristatos is hiding. Melina has wounded a guard in the arm with an arrow. He is gagged and tied, but is moaning and making noise. Melina wants to stay and help the man; but Columbo tells her to go on with the others, and that the man will be fine. As soon as she exits, Columbo knocks the man out and says, "Sorry."

Glen's tempo is slightly slower than that of Gilbert or Hamilton, but it complements the mood of the story. Glen succeeds in drawing good performances from his cast, as well as from his designers and technicians. He does a very admirable job indeed.

□ ACTORS AND CHARACTERS

One of the best things about *For Your Eyes Only* is that we finally are able to see Roger Moore get knocked about a bit. Bond goes through all kinds of hell in this one: he must hang on for dear life to a berserk helicopter as it tries to shake him off like a bug; he must survive a car wreck in a small Citroën; he is abused by three ice hockey players in full uniform on an empty ice field; he is attacked by an extremely powerful ad-

Bond as human fly. Roger Moore climbs a steep cliff to the abandoned monastery used by Kristatos as a hideout in For Your Eyes Only. *(Photo by Rick Sylvester, courtesy of Steven Jay Rubin.)*

versary in a "JIM" diving suit while underwater; he is dragged over coral; and he is dropped fifty feet from a cliff only to be caught by a rope tied around his waist. And Moore, for once, means business. It's his best performance as Bond to date.

Moore told reporters at a press conference that he didn't particularly like the "toughening" of the character for this film. It is true that the film is devoid of many Moore-isms, and Bond relies on physical strength rather than gadgets and one-liners to overcome obstacles. But this is who Bond really is, and Moore is finally afforded an opportunity to *be* tough. There's a satisfying moment when Bond chases Emile Locque's car to the edge of a cliff. Earlier in the film, Locque (one of Kristatos' henchmen) killed Bond's friend Ferrara, and left Columbo's pin on the body in order to frame the Greek. Locque's car is balanced precariously on the edge of the cliff. Bond calmly walks to the car. Locque is shaking, for the slightest motion might upset the balance of the auto. Bond tosses Columbo's pin to Locque and says, "I believe this is yours." Moore delivers the line with contempt. He then kicks the car, and it falls over the cliff. Moore has never been meaner.

Additionally, Moore is looking his age in the film. (He's a little older than Sean Connery.) No attempts are made to cover this up, and it works very well. Bond in this film seems to be resigned to the fact that he's getting older. He appears more world-weary, and this accords neatly with the identity of the literary Bond. Sean Connery's Bond would probably have taken up Bibi's offer to hop into bed. But the new Bond resists the young girl's advances with fatherly amusement. It's almost as if we're finally seeing James Bond act his age.

Melina Havelock is played by the beautiful Carole Bouquet, who was "half" of Luis Bunuel's *That Obscure Object of Desire*. Miss Bouquet benefits from one of the best-written parts for a Bond heroine in quite a while. This time, she has a real purpose in the story, rather than acting as the sex object of the film. Melina is out for revenge, and her Greek background emphasizes this. Miss Bouquet's performance is one of conviction and strength. She is especially good with the dramatic scenes, such as the one in which Bond forces her to go home from Cortina and wait for him at her father's yacht. She knows he is right, but is fighting the will to continue her quest.

Kristatos, likewise, is the best-written villain in years, and Julian Glover's performance ranks with those of the early adversaries. Kristatos is not a megalomaniac hiding in a super headquarters with hordes of guards working for him. He is simply a rich crook. Glover plays Kristatos straight. The character is a human being, and a rational one at that. Again, the emphasis in the script on real characters has given the actor something to work with, and Glover creates a menacing adversary.

Topol's performance as Columbo equals that of Pedro Armendariz's portrayal of Kerim Bey. It's the same type of character—an ally with a heart of gold. Kristatos, at first, attempts to lead Bond to believe that Columbo is the real villain. But Columbo proves this wrong by first abducting Bond, then explaining the situation, and handing back Bond's gun and ammunition. This, to Bond, is the act of a trustworthy fellow. Topol brings warmth, joviality, intelligence, and much depth to the character. His performance is a joy.

Lynn-Holly Johnson is Bibi. Bibi's sponsor and guardian is Kristatos, with whom she lives, along with her instructor Miss Brink (played by Jill Bennett). Bibi is a beautiful, precocious nymphet who falls all over Bond; she soon reveals to him that she isn't the innocent, virginal young thing she appears to be. The character was apparently added for comedy, and this Miss Johnson accomplishes. Her enthusiasm is infectious, and she provides some of the film's more humorous moments. Miss Brink, on the other hand, is cold and domineering. But she turns out all right in the end.

There are three important minor villains in the film. The first is Emile Locque, played by Michael Gothard. He is employed by Kristatos to kill the Havelocks. Locque is nothing but an assassin, and Gothard gives an intense performance. The second is Eric Kriegler, a Russian agent working with Kristatos and Locque. Kriegler, played by John Wyman, is a champion skier and rifle marksman. He is the film's obligatory super-strong henchman, but his character never goes beyond believability. The character also provides added dramatic tension when he turns against Kristatos toward the film's end and orders him to hand over the ATAC. The third is Gonzales, the Cuban hit man who is hired by Emile Locque to kill the Havelocks. Gonzales is played by Stephen Kalipha, but he doesn't stay around very long. Melina Havelock shoots him with an arrow in the first half hour.

John Moreno plays Luigi Ferrara, Bond's contact in Cortina. Ferrara is the first of the film's two Obligatory Sacrificial Lambs. Ferrara isn't on screen long—he's bumped off in a parking lot while Bond is inside a skating rink visiting Bibi. The second and more important Obligatory Sacrificial Lamb is Contessa Lisl, played by Cassandra Harris. Lisl is some kind of rich society lady and a friend of Columbo. Columbo asks Lisl to persuade Bond to come home with her so that he can abduct him and explain that it is Kristatos who is the true enemy. Lisl succeeds in getting Bond home and in bed, but the next morning she's not so successful getting out of the way of Emile Locque's jeep. The woman is brutally run over on the beach before Bond can save her. It's a classic Bond situation: after a night of love-making with a woman he has just met, Bond witnesses her death at the hands of the villains.

And of course, the series' regulars all make their appearances. General Gogol makes a third appearance. Q doesn't supply Bond with a gadget, but shows him how to work an Identigraph machine. This is actually from the GOLDFINGER novel (in which it is called the "Identicast"). The Identigraph's screen can illustrate a person's facial features as they are described to the machine. This sequence is an interesting variation on the Q Branch scenes. Lois Maxwell's Miss Moneypenny explains that "M is on leave," when 007 shows up at the office. In M's place are Minister of Defense Frederick Gray and Chief of Staff Bill Tanner (played by James Villiers). Villiers does not quite fit the picture of Tanner that is painted in the novels—Tanner should be a more athletic type, like Bond. But supposedly, this substitution for M was made at the last minute. Bernard Lee passed away just before his scenes were to have been shot.

□ **OTHER ASPECTS**

Technically, *For Your Eyes Only* has a polished, slick look. Peter Lamont makes his debut as production designer after working for the series in many capacities since *Goldfinger,* mainly as art director. His location work is outstanding, and the interiors of the St. Cyril monastery are worth mentioning. A former Bond second unit cameraman, Alan Hume, is director of photography. His work yields one of the most colorful of all Bond films. John Grover edits the picture with a steady pace which gains momentum throughout.

The underwater photography by Al Giddings is especially beautiful. The film features two underwater fights in a row, and they are spectacular. The first is between Bond, in a deep sea diving suit, and a man wearing an armored "JIM" diving suit. The second is between Bond and Melina's two-man lockout submarine and an insectlike one-man Osel "Mantis" submersible with mechanical manipulators.

Remy Julienne orchestrated an interesting variation on the Bond car chase. This time, Bond has no souped-up car bristling with gadgets and weaponry. (In one of the movie's best humorous passages, Bond's "burglar-proof" Lotus Esprit explodes in the faces of two over-curious guards.) Bond and Melina are forced to escape Gonzales' guards in her buglike 1980 Citroën. A Citroën can withstand tremendous punishment, and this one crashes at least three times during the pursuit. The original element of this chase is that the small size of the car becomes an advantage on the winding, downhill road on which the sequence is filmed.

The fantastic ski scenes were again filmed by Willy Bogner, Jr. At one point, Bond, on skis, escapes from Kriegler's motorcyclists by jumping onto a bobsled run. He just happens to jump onto the run behind a speeding bobsled! Much to his chagrin, the motorcycle follows him onto the run. Thus, we are treated to some dangerous stuntwork as a bobsled, a man on skis, and a motorcycle tail each other at tremendously high speed on a winding, curving bobsled chute.

But the best stunt in the film belongs once again to Rick Sylvester, who performed the ski/parachute jump at the beginning of *The Spy Who Loved Me.* Bond is climbing the columnar mountain on which the St. Cyril monastery is perched. Using an elaborate set of ropes and stakes, Bond slowly makes his way up until a guard hears him. The guard begins extracting the stakes from the rock. When only one remains, Bond drops almost one hundred feet, jerking to an abrupt halt upon reaching the limit of the rope tied around his waist. Sylvester doubled Moore, using a special sandbag pully system to ease the impact of the fall. It could easily have broken his back.

The film features a new composer, Bill Conti. Conti's work is very brassy (witness *Rocky*). It is a different sound for a Bond film, but the score works because it is loud and energetic. The main title theme, with lyrics by Michael Leeson and sung by Sheena Easton, is terrific. It became a big hit single and was nominated for an Academy Award as well. Maurice Binder's accompanying credits design features Ms. Easton herself, swirling amidst the silhouetted female nudes and rotoscopes of Roger Moore. It is the first time the vocalist has been seen in the title design.

OCTOPUSSY (1983)

□ PRODUCTION

The thirteenth Bond film, released in June 1983, begins with an unfamiliar logo: that of the MGM lion. (MGM merged with United Artists in 1982.) But the United Artists logo immediately follows and the traditional gun-barrel sequence propels Roger Moore into his sixth outing as 007.

Advance word on the film had promised that it would follow the direction taken with *For Your Eyes Only,* i.e., a more serious approach akin to the early films. Director John Glen was quoted as saying that *From Russia With Love* was the style model. This all made sense, seeing that *Octopussy* would most likely be competing with the rival Bond picture, *Never Say Never Again* (which promised a "straight" approach), due to be released in the fall. For the most part, *Octopussy* delivers what was promised, but there are many moments in which the film regresses to the juvenile humor of the other Bond films of the seventies. As a result, *Octopussy* only captures the original essence of Fleming's Bond and/or the early films in scattered sections. *Octopussy* has nowhere near the merit of *For Your Eyes Only,* but it's much better than, say, *Live and Let Die* or *The Man With the Golden Gun.* One thing is certain, *Octopussy* contains even more variations on the ingredients which have made the series successful—hair-raising stunts, colorful locales, and beautiful women. Although producer Cubby Broccoli and executive producer Michael G. Wilson have given their audience nothing new, the crowds eat it up just the same.

India was chosen as the setting for *Octopussy.* Much of the film, including scenes at Octopussy's headquarters and Kamal Khan's Monsoon Palace, was shot at Udaipur, a bastioned city standing on the banks of Lake Pichola. Other locations included London; Checkpoint Charlie in West Berlin; the privately owned railway in the Nene Valley near Peterborough in Cambridgeshire; the United States Air Force base at Upper Heyford, Oxfordshire; and the Royal Air Base at Northolt, Middlesex. The Nene Valley Railway, a standard-gauge steam railway running five miles through Nene Park, between Wansford and Orton Mere, Peterborough, has many locomotives from different countries. A suitable one was selected to represent Germany. Reliable Pinewood Studios and the 007 Stage were used for the Monsoon Palace courtyard and helipad.

□ SCREENPLAY

Octopussy unfortunately does not contain as much Fleming material as did *For Your Eyes Only.* "Octopussy" was one of the short stories in the anthology, OCTOPUSSY AND THE LIVING DAYLIGHTS, published posthumously in 1966. The low-key tale involves a visit by James Bond to retired Major Dexter Smythe at his home in Jamaica. Smythe comitted a crime during World War II and the British Secret Service have only just learned about it. Bond is sent to arrest the man, but instead, 007 grants him a bit of time—time for Smythe to commit suicide rather than face dishonor and a courtmartial. The title comes from the Major's pet octopus, which he affectionately calls "Octopussy."

The short story is referred to fleetingly in the film by a human character named Octopussy. At one point, Octopussy tells James Bond that she is the daughter of Major Dexter Smythe. She becomes an ally because she has always wanted to thank the British agent for presenting her father with an honorable choice. This reference is meaningless to anyone who has not read the story.

The Sotheby's auction scene in the short story, "The Property of a Lady," inspires a similar sequence in *Octopussy.* In a way, it is more clever than Ian Fleming's scene. In the original, Bond is at Sotheby's only to identify the Russian plant who will push the bid for the Fabergé egg to the highest limit. In the film, the Russians suddenly need to retrieve the particular egg being auctioned and the representative is forced by Bond (this time it is *007* who pushes the bid to the highest limit) to buy the egg at an extremely high price.

Writers George MacDonald Fraser (author of the *Flashman* series), veteran Richard Maibaum, and Michael G. Wilson create another globe-hopping scenario incorporating the usual elements of the Bond formula: a Bondian MacGuffin, a female villain who is number two to the main adversary, a nuclear crisis, and a climactic battle of two opposing armies—this time the villains are against a bevy of *very tough,* beautiful women!

In *Octopussy,* a mad Russian General, Orlov, is stealing the state jewelry from the Kremlin Art Repository. High-class forgeries are replaced in the Repository and the originals are smuggled into Western Europe and sold by one Kamal Khan, a freelancer who employs a clever means of transporting the gems across the border. Khan is in cahoots with a mysterious, beautiful woman known as Octopussy, who is never without her band of Octopussy Girls. Octopussy and her troupe deal in a number of enterprises, but most notably they work as a traveling circus. Octopussy smuggles the jewelry for Khan on her private railway. But why is General Orlov committing such a huge crime against the Soviet Union? The smuggling act is in fact a *cover up* for the madman's actual scheme. At one point in the smuggling operation, Orlov and Khan doublecross Octopussy and secretly replace the jewelry with a nuclear bomb set to explode during a performance by Octopussy's Circus at a NATO base in West Berlin. The bomb's detonation, it is hoped, will appear to be an American nuclear accident. A call for an immediate disarmament of Western Europe will most likely ensue, leaving General Orlov free to strike with ground forces and ignite World War III.

British Intelligence is alerted at the beginning of the film when agent 009 arrives fatally wounded at the British Embassy in West Berlin. He is dressed as a circus clown and has stolen a forgery of a Fabergé egg from Octopussy. James Bond's assignment is called "Operation Trove"; the agent must find out why 009 was killed. After investigating the sale of an original Fabergé egg at Sotheby's, Bond is put on the trail of Kamal Khan.

As a basic plot, there is quite a bit of potential here. What goes wrong is that the action scenes, as has often been the case in the later Bond films, grow increasingly illogical. For example, it is painfully obvious that the filmmakers wanted to shoot a sequence involving a spectacular Indian tiger hunt, complete with elephants, Indians in turbans, and a zoo of jungle animals—so a scene was written to accommodate. It is unnecessary for the advancement of the plot—in fact, it's damaging. In the previous sequence, Bond escapes from his cell at Kamal Khan's headquarters by nightfall and eavesdrops on Khan and Orlov's meeting. Suddenly, Bond's absence is discovered, and Khan organizes a tiger hunt to track him down. There are editing problems in this sequence as well, for the jump in time to dawn is confusing and creates the illusion that the tiger hunt was organized in the middle of the night and the party was ready and waiting for 007 to make his escape from the castle.

Another unnecessary scene is the final attack on Khan's fortress by Octopussy's women. It is anticlimactic after the terrific sequences on the train and Bond's disarmament of the bomb at the circus. It seems to have been written in simply to deliver the traditional army clash at the picture's end. This particular instance

James Bond disguised as an Argentine officer. Roger Moore in the latest United Artists 007 picture, Octopussy. *(Wide World Photo.)*

Roger Moore with co-star Maud Adams on the set of Octopussy. *Maud plays the title role. She also appeared as Scaramanga's mistress in* The Man With the Golden Gun. *(Wide World Photo.)*

of the formula device is ludicrous—scantily clad women attack tough Indian guards with exotically choreographed gymnastic feats. And to top it off, James Bond and Q appear from nowhere in a hot air balloon (decorated with a Union Jack) to lend the women a helping hand. Such sequences mar the interesting and complex plot of *Octopussy*.

Two of the better scenes in the film incorporate good examples of a Fleming situation. The first is the Sotheby auction where Bond quickwittedly doublecrosses Kamal Khan in the bidding and also manages to switch the original Fabergé egg with a stolen forgery in front of the spectators. The second scene is when Bond challenges Khan to a game of backgammon. Although this sequence never existed in Fleming's work, it recalls the gambling scenes which the author was so fond of writing. Here, Khan is using a pair of loaded dice against an unsuspecting Englishman. Bond takes over for the Englishman, states the player's privilege rule, grabs the loaded dice from Khan, and proceeds to win the game using the villain's own trick. 007 then reveals his possession of the original Fabergé egg to Khan, thus igniting a moment of truly Flemingesque dramatic tension.

As usual, there are the many witty one-liners and asides (which have too often been sexually oriented in the Roger Moore films). For instance, when Bond asks Magda about the octopus tattoo on her back, she replies, "Why, that's my little octopussy." A running joke is established after Bond tells an eager female bellhop, "Later, perhaps." The joke is carried until Q himself says it to an exuberant member of Octopussy's army. One funny line is set up when Bond asks Magda for her proposition. She says, "The Fabergé egg for your life." Bond says innocently, "Well, I heard the price of eggs was going up, but don't you think that's a little high?"

□ DIRECTION

John Glen's handling of *Octopussy* does not exhibit the same unity of style present in *For Your Eyes Only*. Although many of the dramatic scenes and several action scenes are treated seriously, too often the film's tone shifts into comedy. As a result, believability is lost along with suspense. It would seem that the producers did not know what type of film Glen should make— a more serious, realistic picture like the early Bonds, or a slapstick-oriented action comedy like some of the later ones. This dichotomy runs throughout *Octopussy* and the result is a confused mixture of styles.

At times, the film moves with that familiar Bondian tone of unsuspecting danger (enhanced by John Barry's familiar stalking music), such as in the beginning scene in which 009 is murdered, and in the sequence in which Bond spies on General Orlov and Kamal Khan in the Monsoon Palace. But when camels begin doing double takes at leaping Indian taxicabs (which look like golf carts) during a chase through a crowded street, how can the plot be taken seriously? At one point, Bond's ally in India, Vijay (portrayed by tennis star Vijay Amritraj), fights an opponent with a tennis racket. During the previously mentioned tiger hunt, Bond swings on a vine à la Tarzan. Director Glen has chosen to accompany this image with an authentic Tarzan yell, pushing the sequence farther into burlesque.

The climax of the film is very exciting, though, and could be one of the best sequences in any of the later Bond films. Bond learns that Octopussy's train is carrying a nuclear bomb. Racing against time, he avoids General Orlov and his men; makes it onto the speeding train with daredevil acrobatics; fights with Khan's henchmen on the top of the train; steals an auto to speed to the NATO base where the circus is performing; dresses in a clown outfit to gain entry into the tent; and finally convinces the commanding officer and a shocked Octopussy that there is a bomb inside the Human Cannonball's fake cannon. Moore's performance here is particularly sincere, and for once we feel that there is indeed a danger. Glen's handling of this section is masterful and well-paced.

□ ACTORS AND CHARACTERS

Roger Moore shows his age even more in *Octopussy* than he did in *For Your Eyes Only*. His approach to the role is no different, although the tougher characterization established in the previous film is carried over into this one for the most part. The trouble here is that Moore seems to function only as an occasional stand-in for the stuntmen. Because of the weakness of the straight dialogue scenes, Moore is rarely given an opportunity to act at all. He does use the humorous parts of the film to advantage, something that has always been Moore's trademark in playing 007. At one incongruous (but funny) point during the tiger hunt, Bond impersonates Barbara Woodhouse and orders a Bengal tiger to sit like a dog (which it does). *Of course, only James Bond* could possess the charisma necessary to accomplish such a feat! Roger Moore does manage to create the illusion that the character does indeed possess such mastery of wild animals.

Beautiful Swedish actress Maud Adams portrays Octopussy (this is her second role in a Bond film, having played Andrea in *The Man With the Golden Gun*). The actress' striking good looks and statuesque bearing automatically give her a commanding presence in a role which is underwritten (as is usually the case with Bond film heroine parts). The character of Octopussy is especially undeveloped; we have no idea why she has such power, where she got it, and why the ruthless Kamal Khan respects and fears her. Octopussy is the leader of an all-woman band of brigands, apparently supported by the Russians. If the scriptwriters had given the character some background beyond the fleeting reference to her deceased father, Miss Adams might have had the opportunity to create a truly mysterious and engaging character. The film makers also erred in allowing Octopussy to become Bond's ally too early in the picture, thereby losing any dramatic conflict which might have occurred between the characters. The Bond/Octopussy seduction scene in her boudoir makes no sense whatsoever: Octopussy tells 007 that they're "two of a kind" and offers him a job with her circus. Bond refuses and she becomes angry. But never fear—all Bond has to do is tell her that they *are* two of a kind and kiss her, and they fall forthwith into bed. Of what kind are they two? What happened to logical cause-and-effect dialogue? Nevertheless, Maud Adams fills the screen with beauty and grace and further perpetuates the adage that Bond films exist only for looks and form, not content.

Kamal Khan is played by the suave Louis Jourdan, and it is his performance which gives the film much of its buzz. Jourdan's characterization is smooth, cunning, and funny as well. It certainly ranks with Julian Glover's Kristatos in *For Your Eyes Only.* The inflection in Jourdan's speech exhibits not only menace and intelligence, but a bit of self-parody as well. This self-parody never dips too low into broad comedy—Kamal Khan remains a *villain* throughout the film. The filmmakers have also endowed Khan with certain Flemingesque qualities. There is even a scene in which Bond is wined and dined by Khan, who promises that the meal will be followed by a painful method of extracting some answers from the agent. (But Bond escapes before what might have been a grisly torture scene using hallucinogenic truth serums.) During the meal, Khan cooly plucks the eyeball from a stuffed sheep's head and munches it as he speaks, not only nauseating Bond, but the audience as well. One of Jourdan's funniest moments is at the end, when he orders his henchman Gobinda to climb out of the cockpit of a small aircraft

and "get" Bond (who is hanging onto the plane for dear life). The incredulous look on Gobinda's face when he realizes that Khan is serious is priceless!

Gobinda is played by Kabir Bedi, a noted Indian actor. The character is another obligatory strongman/henchman typical of the series and offers nothing new. There is, in fact, one bit which is a direct steal from Oddjob in *Goldfinger*. After Bond has beaten Khan in backgammon, Gobinda grabs the pair of dice and crushes them with his bare hand, just as the Korean bodyguard did with the golf ball after 007 defeated Goldfinger on the course. But Bedi manages to appear threatening in most of the sequences, and is no more or less successful at the role than other actors playing this type of character in earlier films.

Lovely Swedish actress Kristina Wayborn plays Magda, a villainess in cahoots with Octopussy and Kamal Khan. A former track star, Wayborn possesses a sleek athletic build which comes in handy for the gymnastic feats the women in the film must perform. Wayborn has a striking screen presence which works well for the role, but her lack of screen time is disappointing. She also functions as an early sex interest for Bond. At one point, while Bond and Magda are in bed, she lifts her empty wine glass into view and tells him that she needs "refilling." Bond mischievously raises his eyebrow.

As mentioned earlier, Indian tennis star Vijay Amritraj portrays Bond's ally in India, and also becomes the film's Obligatory Sacrificial Lamb. Posing as a fisherman while staking out Octopussy's island, poor Vijay is murdered by one of Khan's thugs by an ingenious yo-yo-like contraption with a table-saw blade. Amritraj delivers the necessary good-humored qualities typical of all Bond-allies, and comes off quite well in the role.

General Orlov is played by Steven Berkoff, a talented writer, actor, and director who is the founder of the London Theatre Group. Orlov, who sits on the Soviets' security council, is reminiscent of George C. Scott's radically right-wing general in *Dr. Strangelove.* Orlov wants the council to forget about peace talks and launch a massive attack on Western Europe just to satisfy his lust for military power. Naturally most of his colleagues think he's crazy. Berkoff delivers a fine performance which is both intense and engaging. But the entire Russian security council is depicted, for the most part, as a bunch of buffoons.

M is portrayed by a new actor, Robert Brown, a fine British character player and a contemporary of the late Bernard Lee. Brown is an adequate replacement in the role. But in *Octopussy,* M is once again underwritten, and Brown is not allowed the opportunity to explore and reveal his character traits. For example, none of M's testiness, crabiness, or even his persona of uncontestable authority is seen here. We see only his fatherly side. The character is altogether too nice. M's disagreeable qualities appear to have been inherited by the Minister of Defense (Geoffrey Keen), who sits in the office with M during the scene with Bond and grunts his approval and/or disapproval.

The series' other regulars all return: Desmond Llewelyn does a bit more than usual as Q (he participates in the climactic battle at Khan's fortress); Walter Gotell as General Gogol exhibits the "good" qualities of a Soviet officer (he despises the antics of General Orlov); and Lois Maxwell displays her usual charms as Miss Moneypenny. An addition to the Bond/Moneypenny scene is the introduction of a new secretarial assistant, Penelope Smallbone (Michaela Clavell). In this amusing scene, Bond enters the office with a bouquet of flowers, prepared to hand it to Moneypenny. After seeing the pretty new secretary, Bond gives one flower to Moneypenny, but the bouquet to Penelope, saying, "Welcome to the office."

☐ OTHER ASPECTS

Octopussy is less gadgety than usual, but the film features one particular item in the pre-credits sequence that practically steals the entire picture. This is the AcroStar Bede Jet, one of only two such planes in existence. The AcroStar is a one-man "portable" jet, only twelve feet in length and five feet eight inches high. As the world's smallest jet, it can soar at a top speed of 310 m.p.h., a cruising speed of 160 m.p.h., and can reach 30,000 feet with a climbing rate of 2,800 feet per minute. The AcroStar is powered by a single jet engine, a Micro-turbo TRS-18. The jet is owned and piloted by "Corkey" Fornof of Louisiana.

The pre-credits sequence takes place in a country resembling Cuba. Bond arrives at an airbase with the intention of blowing up a particular hangar containing some kind of spy plane. Equestrian activities are taking place nearby, allowing Bond to drive a horse trailer onto the premises. With the help of a beautiful Latin contact named Bianca, Bond boards the AcroStar, which is hidden inside the horse trailer. Bond takes off in the jet, and the audience is treated to some magnificent aerial stuntwork as the aircraft dodges a heat-seeking missile in pursuit. Bond cleverly leads the missile into the target hangar and manages to fly out sideways through the small open space of the quickly closing hangar doors. Of course, the missile doesn't make it

out of the hangar and Bond's mission is accomplished. After his escape, the jet runs out of gas. Bond pulls the AcroStar up to a gas station, just like a car (the wings fold up), smiles and says, "Fill 'er up."

Other gadgets include a combination wristwatch/fountain pen/homing device and the usual assortment of gag gadgets at India's Q Branch including a coiled rope which rises like a pole up which a man may climb. Unfortunately, it bends in the middle. Bond taunts, "Having trouble keeping it up, Q?"

Peter Lamont must be credited with exotic settings and a colorful production design. Octopussy's boudoir and her bed, in particular, are magnificent. The bed, a huge circular monstrosity surrounded by what look like gold-plated tentacles, gets a big laugh from the audience. Alan Hume returns as cinematographer and gives the film the same slick look he gave to *For Your Eyes Only.* Costume designer Emma Porteous has created some gorgeous exotic Indian outfits, especially for the women.

The film abounds with stuntwork (the Bond films must surely prevent any unemployment in the stunt industry). Bob Simmons is back as supervisor. One breathtaking sequence involves the aerial team from *Moonraker,* directed by Philip Wrestler: Bond and Gobinda fight with knives on the outside of a small airplane—while it's flying!

John Barry returns to the series with a moderately successful score. The title song, "All Time High," with lyrics by Tim Rice, contains an elusive melody, and Rita Coolidge's rendition of it grows on one only after repeated listenings. Considering the subject of the lyrics, the song might have been more successful had it been transposed to a higher key for a soprano voice. Although a very fine singer with lovely alto voice, Miss Coolidge seems to have been the wrong choice. The rest of the score is quite reminiscent of the early Bond soundtracks, in particular *From Russia With Love* and *Thunderball.*

Most critics tended to favor *Octopussy* over *For Your Eyes Only,* probably because they were more accustomed to the style and flavor of the later Bond films. *Octopussy* fits more easily with the other Roger Moore pictures than does *Eyes Only,* despite the intentions of the filmmakers to inject more of the early films' style. The reliance on sight gags and outlandish humor categorizes *Octopussy* as another "James Bond action comedy" rather than a "James Bond thriller." The film is entertaining and fun, to be sure, but ultimately mediocre. Nevertheless, James Bond *will* return in *A View to a Kill* in 1985.

THE ''OTHER'' BONDS

☐ CASINO ROYALE (1967)

As mentioned earlier, Ian Fleming sold the film rights of his first novel to producer Gregory Ratoff in 1955. Ratoff sat on the property until his death, after which his widow sold the rights to Charles K. Feldman in 1960. Therefore, Albert R. Broccoli and Harry Saltzman were unable to obtain the rights to CASINO ROYALE when they bought the remaining Fleming titles.

Feldman sat on the property a long time, too. He became interested again when the Eon Productions James Bond series became a phenomenon. At first, Feldman considered making a serious Bond film; but he wanted Sean Connery to play the role. The only solution was to approach Broccoli and Saltzman with a deal. After considering the offer, the producers refused. Feldman then decided to make a different kind of James Bond film. He made a Bond spoof.

What might have begun as a great idea ends up a total mess. The film, *Casino Royale,* is a confused mixture of styles, plots, characters, designs; all with little humor and not much Bond.

The film had a budget of almost $8,000,000 (*You Only Live Twice,* released the same year, had a budget of roughly $6,000,000), which made it the most expensive "James Bond film" at the time. And although it made an enormous amount of money, it was not the box-office winner Charles K. Feldman had hoped it would be. Feldman had just had a commercial success with *What's New, Pussycat?,* and he patterned *Casino Royale* after that "mod comedy." Peter Sellers and Woody Allen, stars of the former film, were brought in to work on the project. More international stars were persuaded to join the cast at one time or another during the lengthy shooting period. Sometimes new scenes were written into the script simply because a new star had been signed.

Three scriptwriters are credited with the screenplay: Wolf Mankowitz, John Law, and Michael Sayers. But several other writers worked on the script uncredited, including Ben Hecht, Terry Southern, Billy Wilder, and Woody Allen. With so many writers having a hand in the project, no wonder the film is such a jumble. In addition, there are *five* directors credited: John Huston, Ken Hughes, Val Guest, Robert Parrish, and Joe McGrath, and thus, as many styles in the film. It is obvious that producer Charles K. Feldman didn't know what he wanted.

This doesn't mean that *Casino Royale* isn't funny.

Some of it is, primarily the scenes with Woody Allen. Peter Sellers also contributes some good comedic bits. But most of the jokes in the film fall flat and are simply too bizarre. For instance, when Sir James, Mata Bond, James "Cooper" Bond, and Miss Moneypenny are searching for the exit of FANG headquarters, they run into Frankenstein's monster. "Do you know the way out?" they ask him. The monster points, and they thank him and run off. Where did *that* come from?

There are, surprisingly, a few references to the Ian Fleming novel. There is a scene in which Evelyn "James Bond" Tremble (Sellers) plays a game of baccarat with Orson Welles' Le Chiffre. Le Chiffre wears dark glasses which reveal the faces of the cards. This invisible ink device was used by the Roumanian team at the casino in Monte Carlo, where James Bond's first assignment with the Service took place. He discovered the Roumanians' method of cheating, and proceeded to beat them at their game. Later in the film, Tremble is kidnapped by Le Chiffre and strapped into a chair with a hole in the seat. This is precisely what happens to Bond in the novel, except that Peter Sellers is clothed. There is even a carpet beater hanging behind the chair. But the prop isn't used, for Le Chiffre proceeds to torture Bond with hypnosis—"torture of the mind," he calls it. And finally, Le Chiffre is liquidated by SMERSH, as in the novel. But here the assassin speaks to Le Chiffre from a TV screen, warning him that SMERSH is unhappy. Then, as if he were inside the TV set, the assassin breaks through the screen and shoots Le Chiffre. This is one of the funnier jokes in the film. The remainder of the picture has nothing to do with the novel.

Even the characters are confused. Sir James Bond, the "real" James Bond, is played by David Niven, which is intelligent casting. But a "Sir" James Bond is a contradiction in terms. At the end of the novel THE MAN WITH THE GOLDEN GUN, James Bond refuses a knighthood on the grounds that he cannot stomach the social responsibilities such an honor prescribes.

Sir James lives in a huge country mansion with lions and other wild animals on the grounds. He seems to have acquired a bit more culture in his old age—he now adores Debussy and *plays the piano* daily. (The Fleming James Bond would *never* be able to play piano.)

When M is killed by a bomb blast at Sir James' home, Bond decides to emerge from retirement and replace his old chief. M, we learn, had a wife and many, many daughters, all of whom try to seduce Bond. Sir

James teams up with Miss Moneypenny's daughter, also called Miss Moneypenny (portrayed by Barbara Bouchet), and proceeds to create several new "James Bond 007" agents to confuse the enemy (and the audience). He enlists the help of that beautiful spy, Vesper Lynd (name sound familiar?—well, the character isn't!), played by Ursula Andress. The casting of Miss Andress, in itself, is a joke, since she was the first Bond-girl of the official series. Sir James dubs Vesper "Agent 007" and begins to look for additional potential James Bonds. Peter Sellers, as a card shark named Evelyn Tremble, is recruited by Vesper and renamed James Bond. An agent known as "Cooper," (played by Terence Cooper), is personally picked by Miss Moneypenny (through a selection process solely involving kissing). He, in turn, recruits the new "secret weapon": a beautiful female agent known as the Detainer. Also renamed "007," the Detainer is played by Daliah Lavi. Sir James' daughter (?), Mata Bond, was the result of his love affair with the famous spy, Mata Hari (??). She is persuaded to join the force as well (Joanna Pettet gives a fine performance in this role). The seventh and final James Bond in the film is the villain, Dr. Noah, who is revealed to be none other than little "Jimmy" Bond (Sir James' nephew). Jimmy Bond is played by Woody Allen, who steals the movie. (This was Allen's second film as an actor.) Jimmy Bond's evil scheme is to unleash a virus that will make all the women in the world beautiful and all the men shorter than he.

John Huston is a bizarre choice for a peculiar M who wears a toupée; Orson Welles makes an interesting but somehow ridiculous Le Chiffre; and there are cameos and guest appearances by Deborah Kerr, William Holden, Charles Boyer, George Raft, Jean-Paul Belmondo, Gabriella Licudi, Tracy Reed, Kurt Kasznar, and even a young Jacqueline Bisset (as Miss Goodthighs).

The episodic plot is impossible to follow. Although it actually bears some resemblance to the "bumps" formula of the Broccoli and Saltzman camp, the set-pieces lack any kind of unity. While watching the film, one gets the feeling the reels are out of sequence.

There are some obvious jabs at the United Artists series, such as the takeoff on Q Branch, where midgets are used as security guards. The final climactic scene is a classic battle sequence right out of the official Bonds, only it's quite absurd. It takes place at Casino Royale, but it involves not only all of the James Bonds in the film, but SMERSH, FANG, the CIA, the Foreign Legion, the United States Cavalry, a tribe of Wild West Indian paratroopers, and a few circus animals. (The ironic thing is that it isn't too far from what the official Bond films almost became in the seventies.)

There is some noteworthy work in the film, especially Nicolas Roeg's cinematography (this was before he had gone on to become a director), and Burt Bacharach's lively, catchy score. Herb Alpert and the Tijuana Brass performed the title song, which became a hit single and popular favorite. A later nightclub standard, "The Look of Love," was also written for the film and was performed by Dusty Springfield during one of the picture's more stylish sequences. Vesper Lynd 007 has invited Evelyn Tremble 007 to her home and proceeds to seduce him. The slow motion, the white-and-pink design motif, and the music blend to create an elegant, romantic mood.

One thing *Casino Royale* reveals is how Bond-crazy the world was in 1966–67. Only the thought of the record-breaking houses for the other Bond films could have convinced Charles K. Feldman to create such a cinematic monstrosity. The entire film has the appearance of a wild party celebrating the James Bond cult; the trouble is we don't know any of these people and we are uncomfortable being there. The film should not be considered part of the James Bond series.

□ NEVER SAY NEVER AGAIN (1983)

Never Say Never Again, released in the fall of 1983, on the other hand, is very much a James Bond film, even though a rival production company, Taliafilm, is responsible for the picture. Producer Jack Schwartzman made it possible when he purchased a license to make one James Bond based on "The Film Scripts" and the THUNDERBALL film rights originally assigned to Kevin McClory from Paradise Film Productions III of Nassau, Bahamas. Schwartzman, with experience as a Hollywood lawyer, successfully overcame the tremendous legal obstacles plaguing the production of the film. After obtaining foreign distribution rights, Schwartzman received backing from Warner Brothers.

The producers promised a different sort of Bond film from the Eon series; hopefully, the new film would concentrate more on character development and would be played straight. The film's obvious draw was the return of Sean Connery to the role of agent 007. Connery took a big risk with the film. No matter how it was received, it would be looked at by the public and critics as "Sean Connery's New Bond Film"—its success rested on his shoulders. Therefore, Connery had much say in the production and approved the script as well as each shot. He reportedly worked very closely with director Irvin Kershner.

Shooting began in October 1982 in the south of France and continued in the Bahamas. The film was in the can by the spring of 1983 and a few pickup shots were filmed during the summer. Apogee Inc. in Los Angeles was responsible for the optical and visual effects.

Naturally, there were many things which the producers could not include in the film for legal reasons. There was no opening gun-barrel logo (the trademark is owned by United Artists/Eon), and no "James Bond Theme" music. Although perhaps a bit confusing to the uninformed viewer expecting a traditional Bond film, this had no detrimental effect at all on the picture.

The screenplay by Lorenzo Semple, Jr., based on the original story by Kevin McClory, Jack Whittingham, and Ian Fleming, incorporates the basic *Thunderball* plot with many deviations. (Reportedly, Sean Connery and Irvin Kershner had a hand in the script as well.) Most of the characters in the story are the same with slight variations in their names (for example, Largo is Maximillian Largo rather than Emilio Largo). Two atomic bombs are abducted by SPECTRE and are used to hold the world at ransom, but the methods employed by SPECTRE to steal the bombs are quite different. Here, Domino's brother, now named *Jack* Petachi, has been brainwashed by SPECTRE and has undergone surgery on his right eye. An exact replica of the retina of the right eye belonging to the President of the United States has been implanted in

Sean Connery with co-star Kim Basinger (as Domino) on the set of Never Say Never Again. *(Wide World Photo.)*

Petachi's head. This will allow Petachi to override a security code protecting the device which arms atomic weapons on NATO bases—supposedly, only the president should be able to look into a telescope-like contraption which makes a positive identification clearance. Once Petachi has broken the security, he arms the two atomic missiles and programs them to veer off course from a test flight so that they will land in the Bahamas. There is no Vulcan aircraft, and all the sabotaging is done on the base in England.

This entire sequence is a little confusing and quite fanciful; but it's really the only disconcerting section of the film. The visual effects here are also not quite up to snuff; the missiles are obviously superimposed over the sky background.

Semple has also made some changes in Bond's world. The British Secret Service is now headed by a new and younger M who disagrees with his predecessor's belief that the Double-O Section was valuable; he doesn't trust these specialized agents. At the beginning of the film, Bond fails a war-games test and is subsequently sent to Shrublands Health Spa to "clean out." Bond at this point is in his fifties (Connery's age) and is on the reserves list for the Service. Agent 007 is only called to the case after M has no other choice. Even the Armourer, now named Algernon, complains that since the abolishment of the Double-O Section, there is never any real excitement in Q Branch. Once Bond is back on the job, Algernon tells him, "It's good to have you back. Now I hope we'll at least have some gratuitous sex and violence for a change."

Once Bond arrives in Nassau, there are many deviations from the *Thunderball* plot concerning 007's investigation of Largo and his mistress, Domino. Bond meets Domino later in France by sneaking into an elegant health club and pretends to be her masseuse in a very amusing scene. There is no scene in which Bond sucks the poison from Domino's foot after she steps on a sea urchin spine. Instead, Bond gains Domino's trust on a dance floor in a casino as the couple execute a marvelous tango. It is during the dance that Bond informs Domino that Largo killed her brother.

The femme fatale of the story is Fatima Blush, and the first half of the film deals with Fatima's attempts to do away with Bond. All of these sequences are cleverly written and well executed, but most of the credit goes to the performances of Connery and Barbara Carrera. The encounters with Fatima are quite different from Bond's dalliances with Fiona Volpe, the villainess from *Thunderball,* aside from the obligatory seduction of

the agent for Fatima's own selfish pleasure. There is a terrific scene in which Fatima has cornered Bond at last. She aims a gun at him and orders him to spread his legs. "Before you die," she says, "you must say that making love to Fatima was the greatest sensual pleasure of your life." Bond hesitates, then says sardonically, "Well, there *was* this girl in Philadelphia . . ."

The latter part of the film differs from *Thunderball* as well. SPECTRE does not plan to obliterate Miami with Bomb no. 1; instead, they have somehow planted the bomb under the White House in Washington (how they did this is never explained), and the second bomb will be used in the Middle East to destroy oil fields. Therefore, the locale changes for the climax of the film to North Africa. Finally, there is no underwater battle between SPECTRE and NATO paratroopers; instead, Bond and Leiter lead a group of men into SPECTRE's hidden cave for a land attack. Only Bond chases Largo into the water for the final showdown. The battle is just between the two of them until Domino appears in the nick of time to put a harpoon through her ex-lover and tormentor.

Irvin Kershner's direction brings an extremely fast-paced, energetic tempo to the film. This was Kershner's first film since *The Empire Strikes Back;* it is not surprising that some of the same style and flavor of that film would appear in the new one. The fast pace moves the picture along in such a way that the holes in the plot are not bothersome; things happen so quickly that the audience barely has time to catch its breath before a new action sequence unfolds. There is quite a lot of stuntwork and many action sequences, and they are all exciting and well done. There is nothing that is too unbelievable or fantastic, and Kershner deserves the credit for keeping the picture within a realistic framework.

The strongest aspect of the picture is the casting and the performances. *Never Say Never Again* contains the best ensemble of actors since, perhaps, *From Russia With Love.* It is Sean Connery, of course, who holds the picture together with one of his finest performances as 007. Basically he plays the character as he has always portrayed Bond. In a recent interview, Connery stated that he always approached the Bond role "through the serious door" and exits "through the humorous door." Connery's Bond, although still equipped with witty one-liners, was and still is a flesh-and-blood human being. Despite playing the part at his own age (and with a hairpiece), Connery looks fitter than he did twelve years earlier in *Diamonds Are*

Sean Connery returns to the role of James Bond in the rival film Never Say Never Again, *twenty years after he first appeared as 007. (Wide World Photo.)*

THE FILMS □ 243

Forever! He brings a lot of energy to the role this time, and appears as if he enjoyed every minute of making the film.

Klaus Maria Brandauer, the actor who was so good in *Mephisto,* is excellent as Largo. He brings a dynamic personification of a Fleming villain to the role. Playing the part as if Largo was indeed a bit mad, Brandauer uses his smile and shining eyes to reveal the villain's deranged mind. At one point, Domino asks Largo what he would do if she ever left him. Largo smiles slightly, then quickly changes his expression to that of a demon and says, "I would slit your throat." He then smiles again broadly and maniacally—we know that this time the villain means business.

The show-stealer, however, is Barbara Carrera as Fatima Blush. Carrera brings to her role an energy and forcefulness hitherto unseen in any other similar character. The actress has incorporated dancelike movements in her walk and gives the villainess a classy manner which transcends the usual wanton antics of most femme fatales. The character she portrays is tough, intelligent, and resourceful, and Carrera pulls it off beautifully.

Swedish actor Max von Sydow portrays Ernst Stavro Blofeld in a couple of cameo appearances. This bit of casting is more successful than the choices made for the three Eon films in which Blofeld appears. Yet somehow, von Sydow is a bit too mannered and charming for Blofeld. One strange trait was held over from the Eon series—Blofeld is still petting that white cat.

The extremely lovely Kim Basinger portrays Domino. Although she doesn't seem Italian, she fits Fleming's description of the character from the original THUNDERBALL story—blond, beautiful, classy, and athletic. Basinger brings a vulnerability to the role which is immediately appealing, and the actress turns in a performance which is quite satisfactory. Bernie Casey, an American black actor, portrays Felix Leiter. Casey told *Starlog* magazine that it was Connery's idea to use a black Leiter simply because the character is never remembered—perhaps this change would make the American CIA agent more noticeable. The change in race alters nothing in the context of the story, but unfortunately, the part is underwritten. The Leiter role is still relatively thankless, and the character only serves as Bond's yes-man in the latter part of the film. Casey, however, at least has a screen presence which is interesting and engaging.

Edward Fox portrays the young M in stereotypical stuffy British upper-class tradition. Fox's M is a bit too hard on Bond, and their scenes together bear no resemblance to the Bond/M relationship set up by Fleming. This is one disappointing aspect of the film. Alec McCowan, on the other hand, is fine as Algernon the Armourer, and brings a good degree of humor to the role. Miss Moneypenny is portrayed by the attractive Pamela Salem, but her role is very minor. There isn't enough rapport between Moneypenny and 007 to adequately depict the years of mutual flirtation that has passed between the two characters.

The filmmakers have also included an Obligatory Sacrificial Lamb named Nicole—a French agent who briefly aids Bond. Nicole meets her doom at the hands of Fatima Blush. Also worth mentioning is Rowan Atkinson as a bumbling government official in Nassau named Small-Fawcett who tries desperately to get in the swing of the undercover business. Naturally, he fails miserably, much to Bond's and the audience's amusement. Luckily, the comic antics of the character stop short of slapstick.

The look of the film is impressive. Director of photography Douglas Slocombe brings the same polish to the production that he gave to *Raiders of the Lost Ark.* Production designers Philip Harrison and Stephen Grimes (also from the *Raiders* team) have used a Ken Adam–like decor for most of the interiors, except for the final scene in Largo's hidden cave. The cave is supposed to be part of an ancient temple, and here the scenery is reminiscent of scenery in *Raiders.* Film editor Robert Lawrence keeps the picture moving at breakneck speed, and the fight scenes are especially well cut. Stunt coordinators Glenn Randall and Vic Armstrong have done a splendid job on the picture's many action sequences. The fight between Bond and Fatima's super-strong henchman at Shrublands recalls the good old Oddjob days, while the chase involving the new Q Branch motorcycle recalls the Aston Martin chase in *Goldfinger.* The motorcycle is equipped with jet propulsion, which allows the bike to speed-jump over gaps in the road and even over other vehicles. Other gadgets, always obligatory in a Bond film, include a wristwatch containing a laser beam apparatus, and a fountain pen which fires explosive cartridges.

The most disappointing feature of the film is the score by Michel Legrand. The title song with lyrics by Alan and Marilyn Bergman and performed by Lani Hall is quite unmemorable, and the rest of the score seems to be a mixture of calypso rhythms with lush orchestral passages. Needless to say, it doesn't work.

Never Say Never Again actually recalls the flavor and style of the very early Eon Bond films, especially *Goldfinger.* Many of the same formulized ingredients have gone into the film; what distinguishes it is the de-emphasis on external humor and the concentration on character development. Even though the picture is not an official Bond, it certainly ranks with the best of the authorized series, and it is something which Ian Fleming probably would have liked.

1983, then, marked an important year in the history of Bondmania. Besides being the 30th anniversary of the publication of CASINO ROYALE, the year brought Bond fans *double* Double-O Sevens. The film industry may have considered *Octopussy* and *Never Say Never*

Again as competitors, but to most admirers of the Bond cult they are simply two new versions of the institution created by Ian Fleming over thirty years ago. James Bond will no doubt live on and become as timeless as Sherlock Holmes. Even now, Broccoli and company are in pre-production for the fourteenth film of their series, *A View to a Kill.* With the added prospect of new titles and stories being generated by John Gardner, it is highly likely that 007 will be with us for a while longer. Perhaps the phenomenon is rooted in a line delivered by Connery in *Never Say Never Again.* Asked if he is as good a loser as he is a winner, Connery, as Bond, replies with a twinkle in his eye, "I wouldn't know—I've never lost."

Agent 007 and his Nassau pick-up (Valerie Leon) are relieved that they decided to go to her room instead of his. A bomb had been planted beneath the bed in Bond's hotel suite. James Bond has always had an explosive effect on his bedside companions, but that would have been a bit much. From Never Say Never Again. (Wide World Photo.)

Glossary

NOTE: Many of the entries and their definitions are fictional

AWABI. Shells for which Kissy Suzuki dives in YOU ONLY LIVE TWICE.

BUREAU OF ALL-ASIAN FOLKWAYS. The cover name for the Japanese Secret Service.

CIA. Central Intelligence Agency. The American Secret Service which grew out of its predecessor, the OSS—Office of Strategic Services.

C.M.G. Companion to the Order of St. Michael and St. George.

"CRASH DIVE." Code term for an emergency.

DEUXIÈME BUREAU. The French Secret Service.

DOUBLE-O SECTION. The department in the British Secret Service to which James Bond belongs.

"EYES ONLY." Code term for top secret—the specific document is meant only for the agent to whom it is addressed. ("For your eyes only" is also used.)

F.I.R.C.O. The cover name for SPECTRE when the organization's headquarters was located on the Boulevard Haussmann in Paris. Supposedly F.I.R.C.O. was an organization which helped locate missing members of the French Resistance.

G.R.U. The Soviet Union's intelligence department of the General Staff of the Army.

GAIJIN. Japanese term for "foreigner."

K.G.B. The current name for the Soviet Secret Service. Formerly the M.G.B.

M.G.B. The former name for the Soviet Secret Service.

M.I. 5. Cover title given to British Security Service, responsible for counter-espionage. Works under Home Office.

M.I. 6. Cover title given to British Secret Intelligence Services (S.I.S.). Works under Foreign Office.

M.V.D. Forerunner of the M.G.B.

MAGIC 44. A secret ciphering method developed by the Japanese Secret Service.

NINJA. A Japanese guerilla trained in the art of stealth and invisibility.

R.N.V.R. Royal Naval Volunteer Reserve. James Bond was assigned to the Special Branch.

R.U.M.I.D. The Soviet Union's intelligence department of Ministry of Foreign Affairs.

SHAPE. Supreme Headquarters for Allied Powers in Europe. A branch of NATO.

"SHINER." A device used by cheaters when gambling at cards. Usually it is a metallic object with a reflective surface, such as a cigarette lighter, which allows the user to see the faces of cards as he deals them over the shiner.

SMERSH. The Soviet Secret Service's murder organization. SMERSH is a conjunction of two Russian words ("Smyert Shpionam") meaning roughly "Death to Spies." Its headquarters is No. 13 on the Sretenka Ulitsa in Moscow, and its leader, in 1957, was Colonel General Grubozaboyschikov, known in the building as "General G." SMERSH is divided into five departments:

Dept. I. Counterintelligence among Soviet organizations at home and abroad.

Dept. II. Operations, executions. (Also referred to as "the Department of Torture and Death.")

Dept. III. Administration and finance.

Dept. IV. Investigations and legal work; personnel.

Dept. V. Prosecutions and judgment.

SPECIAL OPERATIONS EXECUTIVE. Organization set up in WWII to plan and carry out irregular counterintelligence operations.

SPECTRE. The Special Executive for Counterintelligence, Terrorism, Revenge, and Extortion. Organization created by Ernst Stavro Blofeld consisting of international terrorists with no criminal record.

TRANSWORLD CONSORTIUM. The current cover name for the British Secret Service.

UNION CORSE. Controls most of the organized crime in France. It is older and more deadly than the Unione Siciliano, the Mafia.

UNIVERSAL EXPORT CO. The former cover name for the British Secret Service. Its headquarters is located in a "grey building" directly across the street from Regent's Park.

(With contributions by Iwan Hedman)

Appendix I

NOTABLE BOOKS RELATING TO JAMES BOND AND IAN FLEMING

☐ HISTORY AND BIOGRAPHY

Bryce, Ivar. *YOU ONLY LIVE ONCE—MEMORIES OF IAN FLEMING*. Weidenfeld & Nicolson, 1975. Interesting and revealing. Very difficult to find; book withdrawn shortly after its publication due to legal complications. Highly recommended.

Gant, Richard. *IAN FLEMING: THE MAN WITH THE GOLDEN PEN*. Mayflower-Dell Paperback, 1966. Lightweight but informative. Out of print.

Pearson, John. *THE LIFE OF IAN FLEMING*. Jonathan Cape, Ltd., 1966. (U.S.—McGraw-Hill). The definitive biography of Ian Fleming. Highly recommended. Out of print.

Plomer, William. *IAN FLEMING, 28th MAY, 1908–12th AUGUST, 1964*. Address given at the Memorial Service. Privately printed, 1964. Highly recommended. Very rare.

Zeiger, Henry A. *IAN FLEMING: THE SPY WHO CAME IN WITH THE GOLD*. Duell, Sloan & Pearce, New York, 1965. Lightweight but informative. Out of print.

☐ JAMES BOND AND THE NOVELS

Amis, Kingsley. *THE JAMES BOND DOSSIER*. Jonathan Cape, Ltd., 1965. (U.S.—New American Library). The definitive work on the novels. Very entertaining. Highly recommended. Out of print in the U.S.

del Buono, Oreste and Eco, Umberto. *THE BOND AFFAIR*. Macdonald, 1966. A series of essays first published in Italy. Informative. Out of print.

Lane, Sheldon, ed. *FOR BOND LOVERS ONLY*. Panther Books, Ltd., 1965. (U.S.—Dell). A series of articles compiled by Lane on different subjects—Sean Connery, Ian Fleming, etc. Out of print.

Pearson, John. *JAMES BOND—THE AUTHORIZED BIOGRAPHY OF 007*. Sidgwick & Jackson, 1973. (U.S.—William Morrow & Co.). Brilliant fictionalized biography of Bond based on the Fleming novels. Highly recommended. Out of print.

Snelling, O. F. *007 JAMES BOND: A REPORT*. Neville Spearman, Holland Press, 1964. (U.S.—Signet). The first study of the novels. Informative and readable. Out of print.

Tanner, Lt.-Col. William "Bill" (Pseudonym for Kingsley Amis). *THE BOOK OF BOND, OR EVERY MAN HIS OWN 007*. Jonathan Cape, Ltd., 1965. (U.S.—Viking Press). Amusing and informative trivia book. Out of print.

☐ JAMES BOND FILMS

Brosnan, John. *JAMES BOND IN THE CINEMA*. The Tantivy Press, 1972. (U.S.—1972 A. S. Barnes & Co., revised second edition published 1981). Highly entertaining and affectionate look at the series. Highly recommended.

Rubin, Steven Jay. *THE JAMES BOND FILMS*. Arlington House, 1981. Crown Publishers, 1983. An informed "behind-the-scenes" look at the films. Very enjoyable. Highly recommended.

☐ MISCELLANY

Bond, Mary Wickham. *HOW 007 GOT HIS NAME*. Collins, 1966. The story of the first meeting between Ian Fleming and ornithologist James Bond. Out of print.

Campbell, Iain. *IAN FLEMING: A CATALOGUE OF A COLLECTION*. Privately printed, 1977. A detailed listing of a very complete and extensive Fleming collection. Very handy as a reference book and bibliography. Highly recommended.

Fl*m*ng, I*n. *ALLIGATOR*. A Harvard Lampoon parody, 1962. Very funny. Hits its target on the bull's-eye. Highly recommended Out of print.

Appendix II

BESIDES THE FAMOUS BERETTA .25 USED IN THE FIRST FIVE NOVELS AND THE WALTHER PPK FROM THE REMAINING FLEMING NOVELS, THE FOLLOWING IS A LIST OF WEAPONS THAT JAMES BOND HAS BEEN KNOWN TO USE:

CASINO ROYALE:
.38 Colt Police Positive

LIVE AND LET DIE:
steel-capped shoes
Champion harpoon gun
limpet mine
Colt .38 Detective Special

MOONRAKER:
long-barreled .45 Colt Army Special
nuclear missile

DIAMONDS ARE FOREVER:
Bofors anti-aircraft gun

FROM RUSSIA, WITH LOVE:
Wilkinson throwing knives
.25 electric gun concealed in a copy of WAR AND PEACE
gun-metal cigarette lighter and an Eric Ambler novel (for defense)
an ordinary chair

DOCTOR NO:
.38 Smith & Wesson Centennial Airweight
steak knife
spear fashioned out of wire mesh
a crane with a load of bird guano

GOLDFINGER:
daggers concealed in soles of shoes
bazooka
his bare hands

"From a View to a Kill":
long-barreled .45 Colt

"For Your Eyes Only":
Savage 99F rifle

THUNDERBALL:
Turkish steam cabinet
knife
spears fashioned out of broom handles and knives

THE SPY WHO LOVED ME:
presumably standard issue gun (Walther PPK)

ON HER MAJESTY'S SECRET SERVICE:
ski poles
Rolex watch used as a knuckle-duster
plastique bombs

YOU ONLY LIVE TWICE:
quarter-staff
his bare hands

THE MAN WITH THE GOLDEN GUN:
cyanide gun

"The Living Daylights":
Winchester .308 target rifle

COLONEL SUN:
knife
Mills grenades

LICENSE RENEWED:
9mm Browning automatic
cigarette lighter containing "knock out" gas
antique dueling pistol
tear gas
Ruger Super Blackhawk .44 magnum
Colt Python .357 magnum
Crossbow
MBA Gyrojet rocket pistol

FOR SPECIAL SERVICES:
Sykes-Fairbairn throwing knives
Heckler & Koch VP70 automatic
blinding aircraft light concealed in Saab
gasoline bomb
Winchester pump gun
Armalite AR18 machine gun

ICEBREAKER:
Heckler & Koch P7 automatic
Lapp skinning knife
Ruger Redhawk .44 magnum revolver
L2A2 grenades

(contributed by George Almond)

Appendix III

HE'S A TOUGH GUY—A LIST OF THE INJURIES SUSTAINED BY BOND IN THE NOVELS:

CASINO ROYALE:
Minor shock from camera-bomb blast
Minor injuries from wrecking Bentley
Genitals mangled by carpet beater
Back of right hand lacerated by SMERSH agent

LIVE AND LET DIE:
Little finger of left hand is broken
Loss of a hunk of flesh when a barracuda bites his shoulder
Back and legs flayed on a coral reef

MOONRAKER:
Minor injuries from cliff-fall
Minor injuries from wrecking Bentley
Abrasions and contusions from a beating administered by Drax
Second degree burns from high-pressure steam hose

DIAMONDS ARE FOREVER:
Abrasions and contusions resulting from being kicked repeatedly by a pair of football-booted thugs
Hit in shoulder with thrown knife during final scuffle with Wint and Kidd

FROM RUSSIA, WITH LOVE:
Minor injuries from fight with Red Grant
Nerve poisoning from Rosa Klebb's knife-wielding shoe

DOCTOR NO:
Electric burn across palm of right hand
Superficial burns from heated area of the obstacle course
Superficial wounds on abdomen from tentacles of giant squid

GOLDFINGER:
Knocked out by Goldfinger's guards before buzz-saw torture
Minor abrasions and contusions from fight with Goldfinger

"Risico":
Knocked out by Colombo's men on the beach at Lido

THUNDERBALL:
Shock and surface abrasion of nerve-ends inflicted by sabotaged traction machine
Battle fatigue from underwater combat

ON HER MAJESTY'S SECRET SERVICE:
Fatigue from ski escape down Piz Gloria
Minor injuries from bobsled ordeal

YOU ONLY LIVE TWICE:
Severe depression brought on by the murder of his wife
Amnesia caused by head wound

THE MAN WITH THE GOLDEN GUN:
Bullet wound in shoulder
Nerve poisoning from bullet dipped in cobra venom

COLONEL SUN:
Drugged at Quarterdeck by M's captors
Knocked out on beach by Sun's men
Tortured with probing devices in the orifices of his head
Minor abrasions and contusions from fight with Von Richter

LICENSE RENEWED:
Tortured with sound waves
Minor abrasions and contusions from fights with Franco and Caber

FOR SPECIAL SERVICES:
Drugged and brainwashed by SPECTRE

ICEBREAKER:
Wounded in right shoulder by knife
Shock and frostbite from being immersed in freezing water
Two gunshot wounds in upper chest

(with contributions by George Almond)

For information on how to join The James Bond 007 Fan Club, send a self-addressed stamped envelope to:

The James Bond 007 Fan Club
PO Box 414
Bronxville, NY 10708
USA

For information on how to join The James Bond British Fan Club, send inquiries to:

The James Bond British
Fan Club
19 Preston Waye
Harrow, Middlesex HA3
0QG
U.K.

The James Bond British
Fan Club
5210 Broadway
Bronx, NY 10463
USA

Index

ABOUT THE AUTHOR

RAYMOND BENSON comes from West Texas and received a BFA in Directing from the University of Texas at Austin. Primarily a theatre person, Raymond has directed several productions off-off-Broadway and elsewhere. Also a composer, he has collaborated with many playwrights on original musicals, which have been seen around the country. *The James Bond Bedside Companion* is his first book.

(Photo by Paul Dantuono)